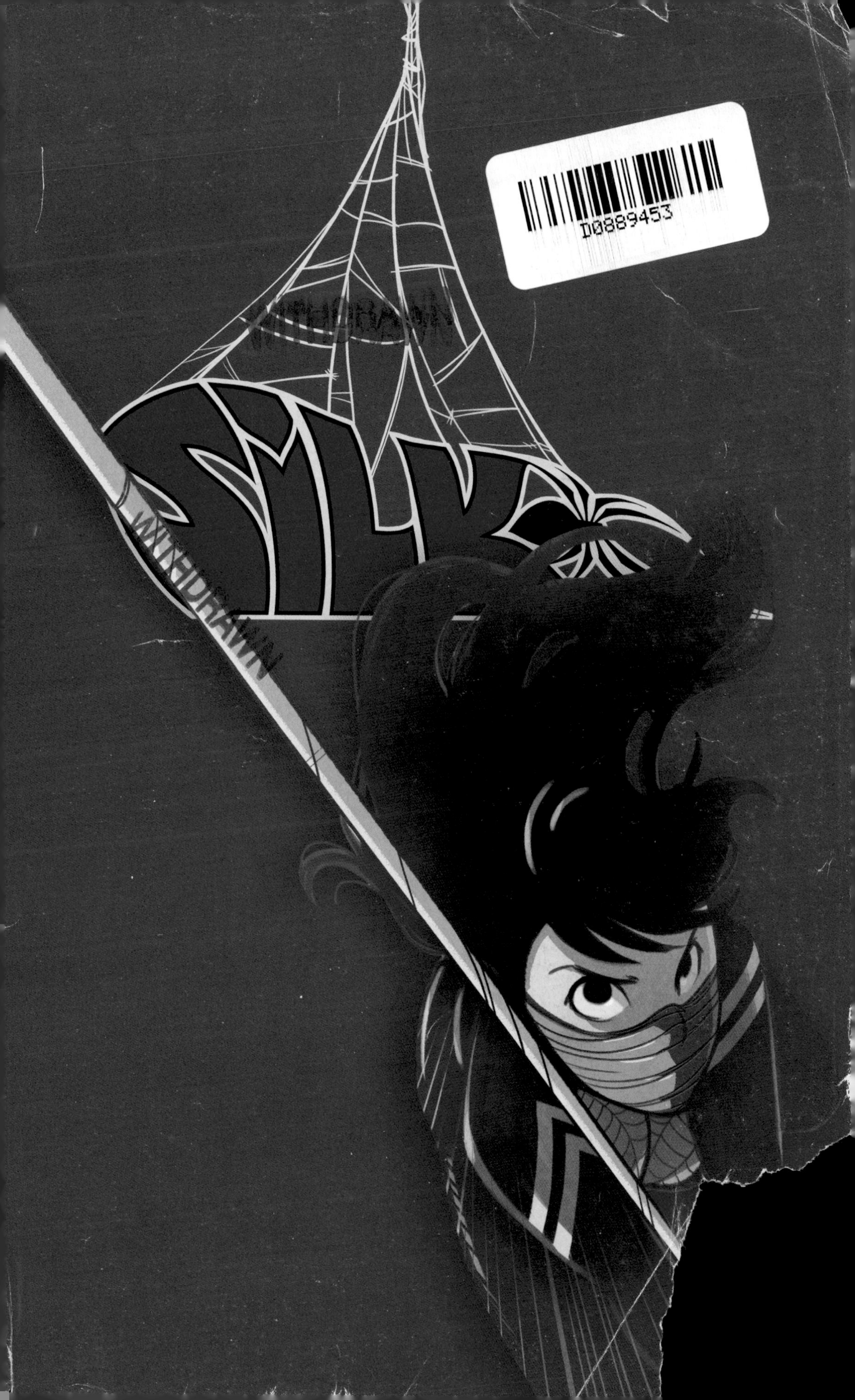
SILK

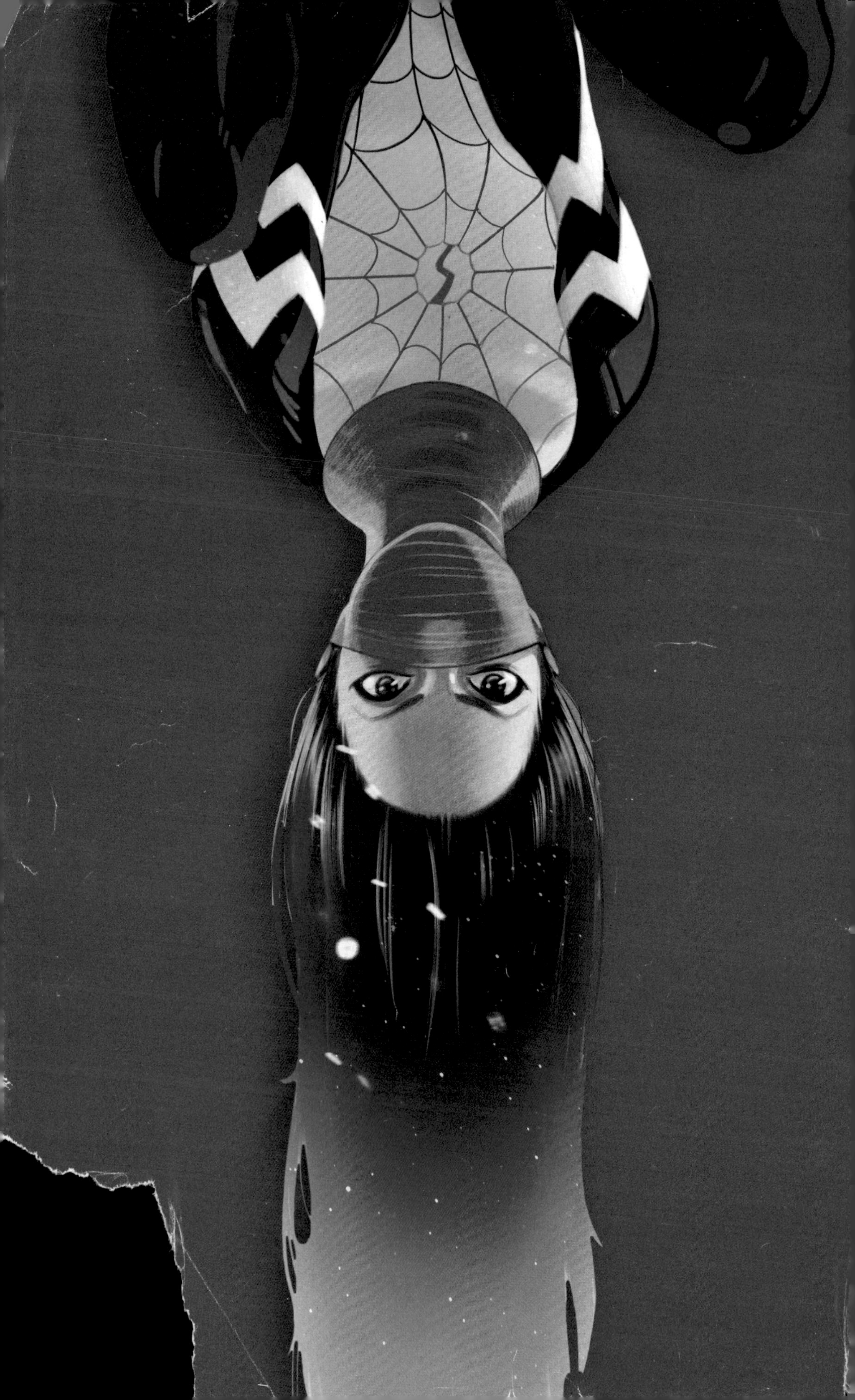

THE LIFE AND TIMES OF CINDY MOON

Writer **Robbie Thompson**

Artists **Stacey Lee** (#1–3 & #5–6),
Annapaola Martello (#4) &
Tana Ford (#7)

Color Artist **Ian Herring**
Letterer **VC's Travis Lanham**

Cover Artist **Dave Johnson**

Assistant Editor **Devin Lewis**
Editors **Nick Lowe** & **Ellie Pyle**

Collection Editor **Jennifer Grünwald**
Assistant Editor **Sarah Branstad**
Associate Managing Editor **Alex Starbuck**
Editor, Special Projects **Mark D. Beazley**
Senior Editor, Special Projects **Jeff Youngquist**
SVP Print, Sales & Marketing **David Gabriel**

Editor in Chief **Axel Alonso**
Chief Creative Officer **Joe Quesada**
Publisher **Dan Buckley**
Executive Producer **Alan Fine**

SILK VOL. 0: THE LIFE AND TIMES OF CINDY MOON. Contains material originally published in magazine form as SILK #1-7. First printing 2015. ISBN# 978-0-7851-9704-1. Published by MARVEL WORLDWIDE, INC., a subsidiary of MARVEL ENTERTAINMENT, LLC. OFFICE OF PUBLICATION: 135 West 50th Street, New York, NY 10020. Copyright © 2015 MARVEL No similarity between any of the names, characters, persons, and/or institutions in this magazine with those of any living or dead person or institution is intended, and any such similarity which may exist is purely coincidental. **Printed in the U.S.A.** ALAN FINE, President, Marvel Entertainment; DAN BUCKLEY, President, TV, Publishing and Brand Management; JOE QUESADA, Chief Creative Officer; TOM BREVOORT, SVP of Publishing; DAVID BOGART, SVP of Operations & Procurement, Publishing; C.B. CEBULSKI, VP of International Development & Brand Management; DAVID GABRIEL, SVP Print, Sales & Marketing; JIM O'KEEFE, VP of Operations & Logistics; DAN CARR, Executive Director of Publishing Technology; SUSAN CRESPI, Editorial Operations Manager; ALEX MORALES, Publishing Operations Manager; STAN LEE, Chairman Emeritus. For information regarding advertising in Marvel Comics or on Marvel.com, please contact Jonathan Rheingold, VP of Custom Solutions & Ad Sales, at jrheingold@marvel.com. For Marvel subscription inquiries, please call 800-217-9158. **Manufactured between 9/4/2015 and 10/12/2015** by R.R. DONNELLEY, INC., SALEM, VA, USA.
10 9 8 7 6 5 4 3 2 1

AS A TEENAGER, CINDY MOON WAS BITTEN BY THE SAME SPIDER
THAT BIT PETER PARKER, GIVING HER POWERS SIMILAR TO
THOSE OF THE AMAZING SPIDER-MAN: POWERS OF ADHESION,
A UNIQUE PRECOGNITIVE AWARENESS OF DANGER AND THE
ABILITY TO WEAVE SPIDERWEBS FROM HER FINGERTIPS. SHE
NOW SWINGS THROUGH THE SKIES OF NEW YORK CITY AS...

TO PROTECT EARTH FROM A DEADLY FAMILY OF SPIDER-HUNTERS AND MURDERERS
CALLED THE INHERITORS, CINDY MOON WAS LOCKED IN A BUNKER THAT PREVENTED
THEM FROM SENSING HER PRESENCE. SPIDER-MAN UNWITTINGLY OPENED THE
BUNKER, UNAWARE OF THE DANGER THAT REVEALING CINDY'S EXISTENCE COULD
CAUSE, AND SET THE EVENTS OF SPIDER-VERSE IN MOTION. AFTER FIGHTING
SIDE-BY-SIDE WITH COUNTLESS OTHER SPIDERS AGAINST THE INHERITORS AND
SAVING THE WORLD, CINDY IS NOW BACK IN NEW YORK, FIGHTING CRIME AND
TRYING TO FIND HER PLACE IN A WORLD SHE HASN'T LIVED IN FOR YEARS.

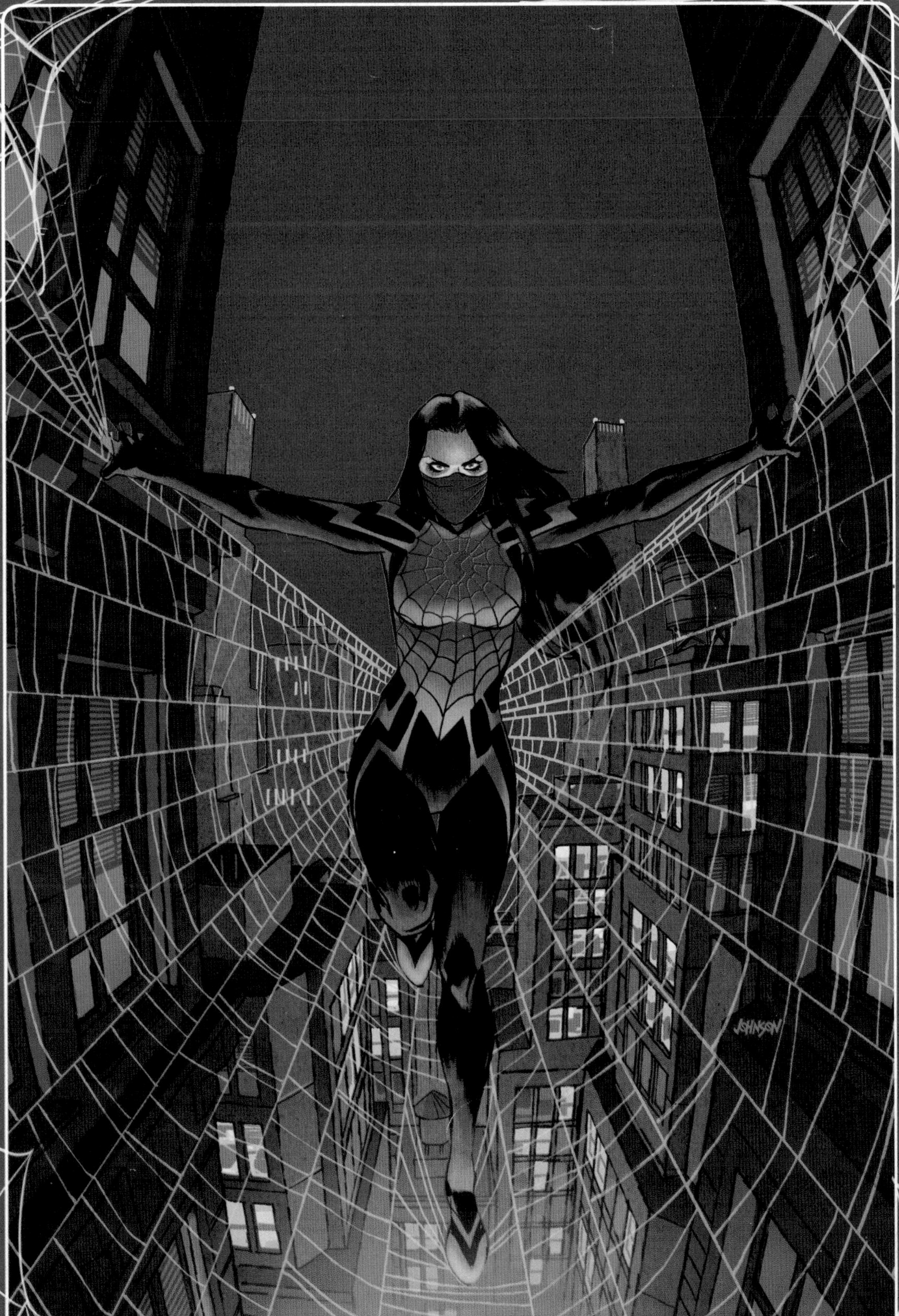
JOHNSON

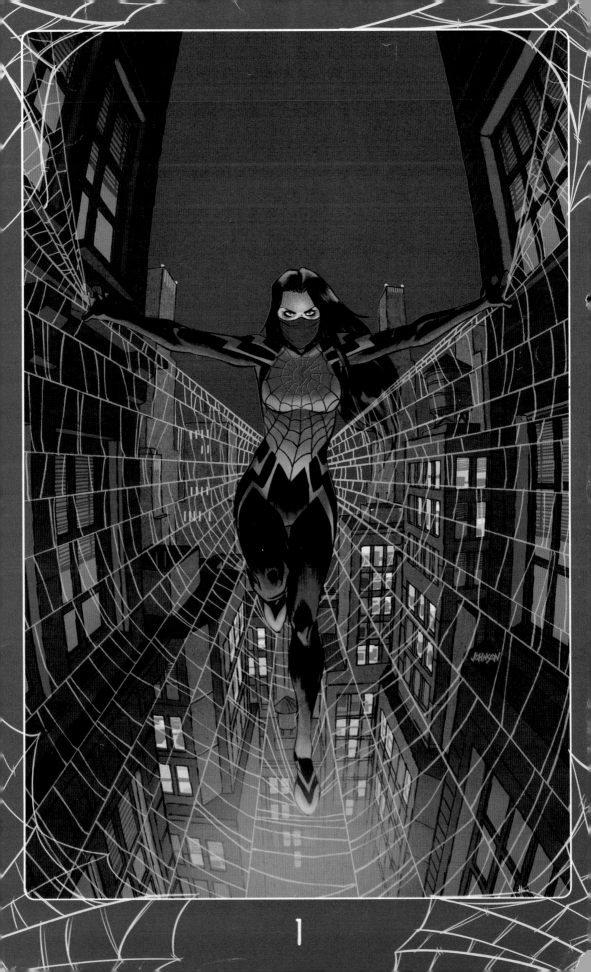

1

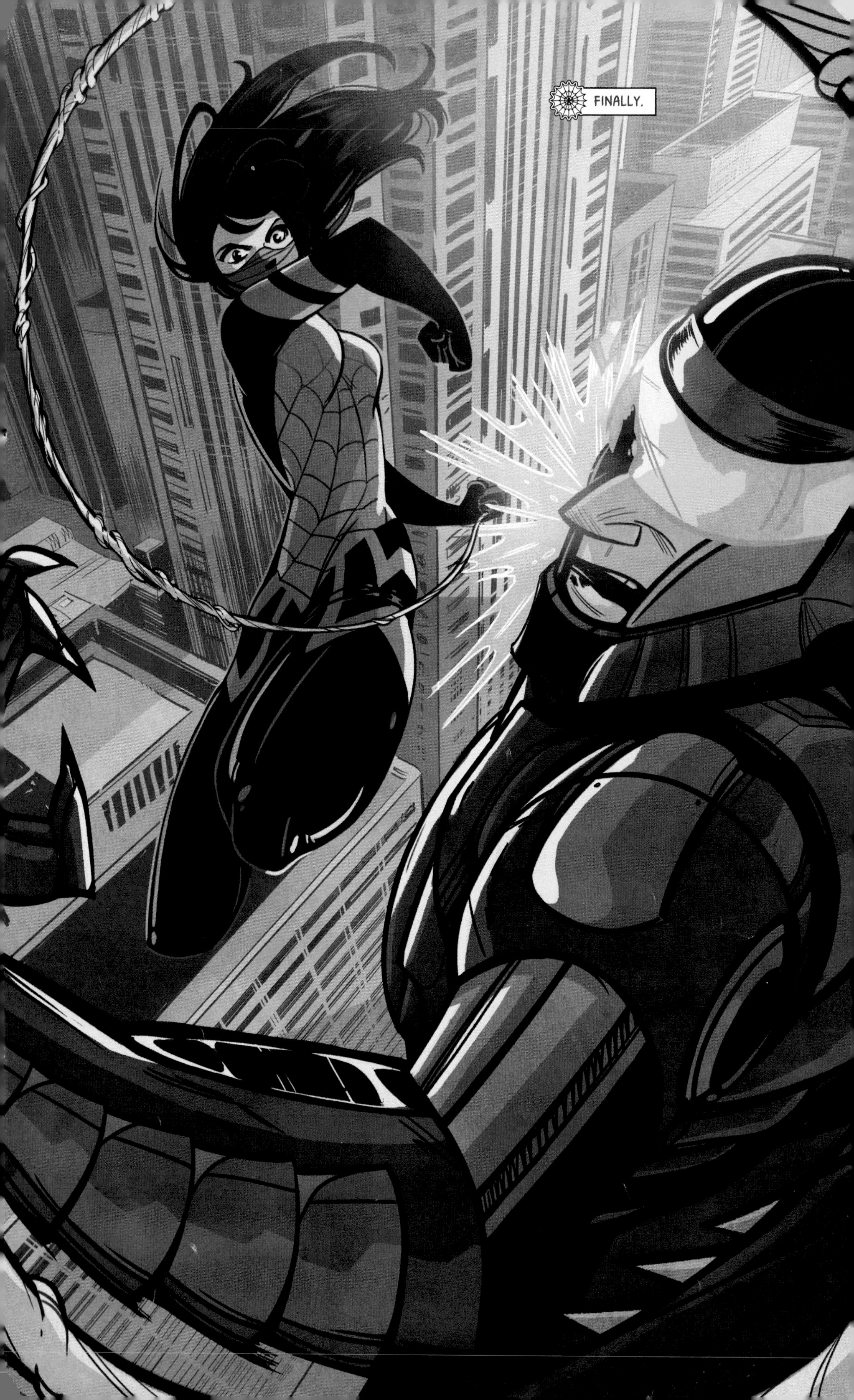
FINALLY.

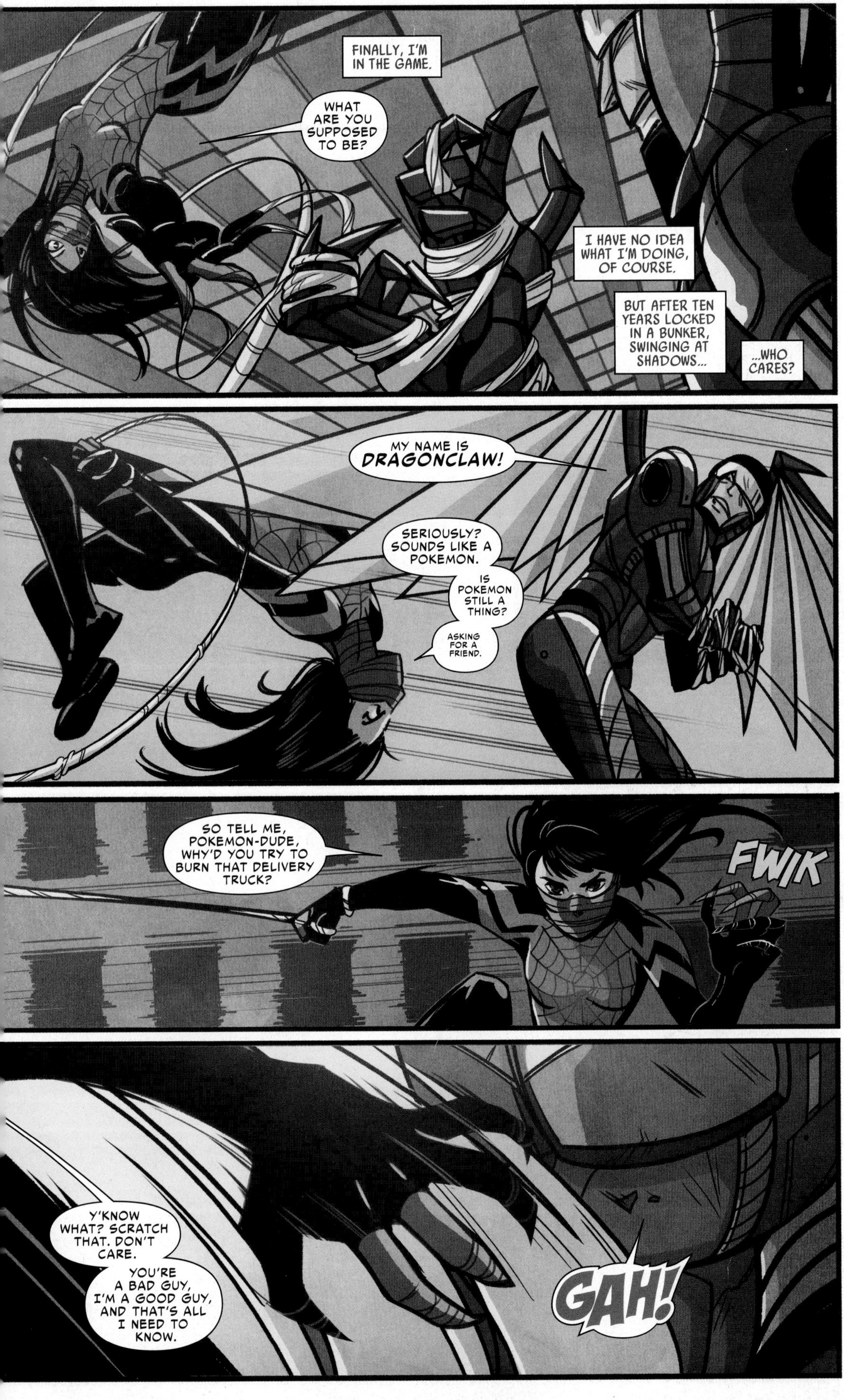

FINALLY, I'M IN THE GAME.
WHAT ARE YOU SUPPOSED TO BE?
I HAVE NO IDEA WHAT I'M DOING, OF COURSE.
BUT AFTER TEN YEARS LOCKED IN A BUNKER, SWINGING AT SHADOWS...
...WHO CARES?
MY NAME IS DRAGONCLAW!
SERIOUSLY? SOUNDS LIKE A POKEMON.
IS POKEMON STILL A THING?
ASKING FOR A FRIEND.
SO TELL ME, POKEMON-DUDE, WHY'D YOU TRY TO BURN THAT DELIVERY TRUCK?
FWIK
Y'KNOW WHAT? SCRATCH THAT. DON'T CARE.
YOU'RE A BAD GUY, I'M A GOOD GUY, AND THAT'S ALL I NEED TO KNOW.
GAH!

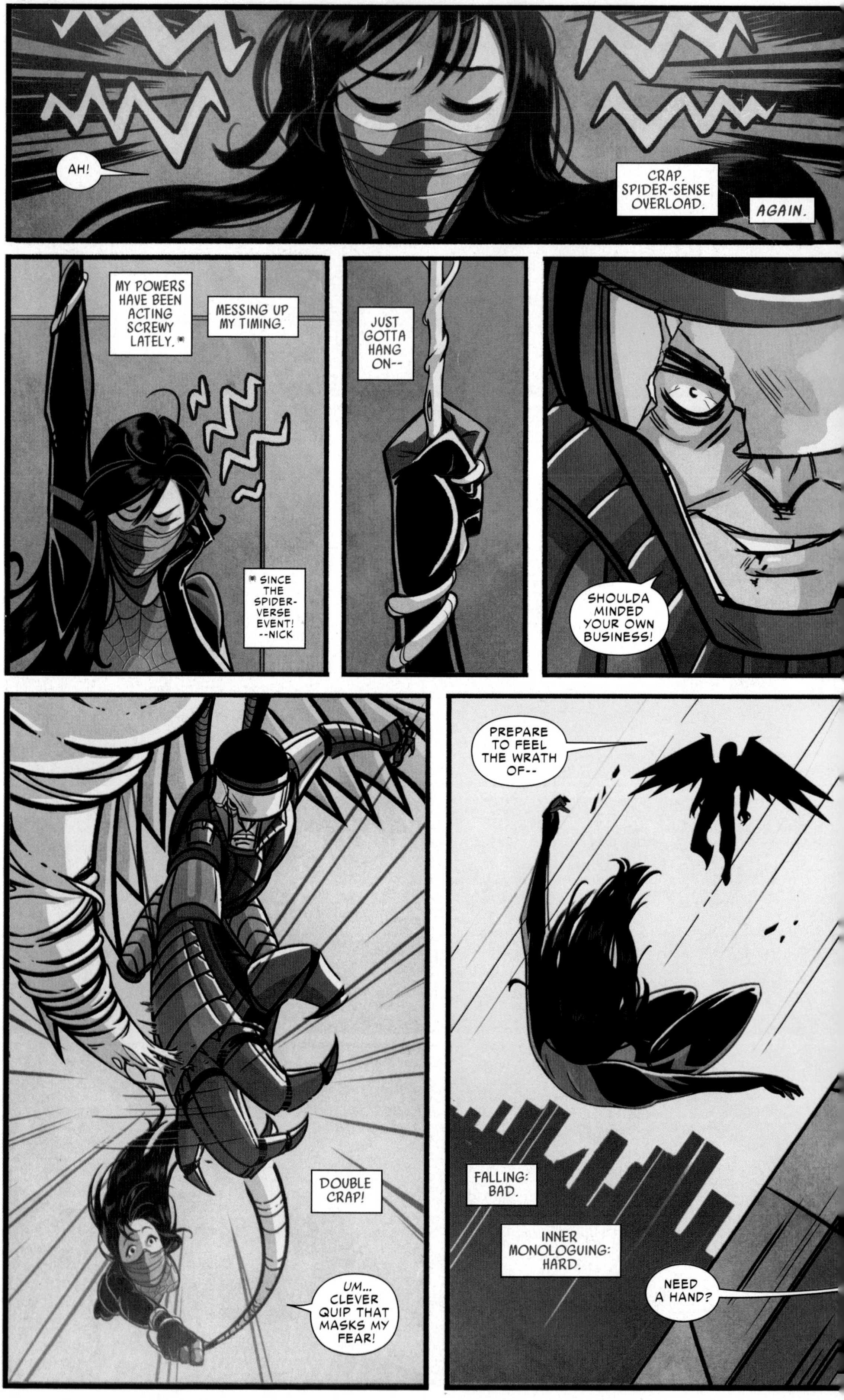
AH!
CRAP. SPIDER-SENSE OVERLOAD.
AGAIN.
MY POWERS HAVE BEEN ACTING SCREWY LATELY.
MESSING UP MY TIMING.
SINCE THE SPIDER-VERSE EVENT! --NICK
JUST GOTTA HANG ON--
SHOULDA MINDED YOUR OWN BUSINESS!
DOUBLE CRAP!
UM... CLEVER QUIP THAT MASKS MY FEAR!
PREPARE TO FEEL THE WRATH OF--
FALLING: BAD.
INNER MONOLOGUING: HARD.
NEED A HAND?

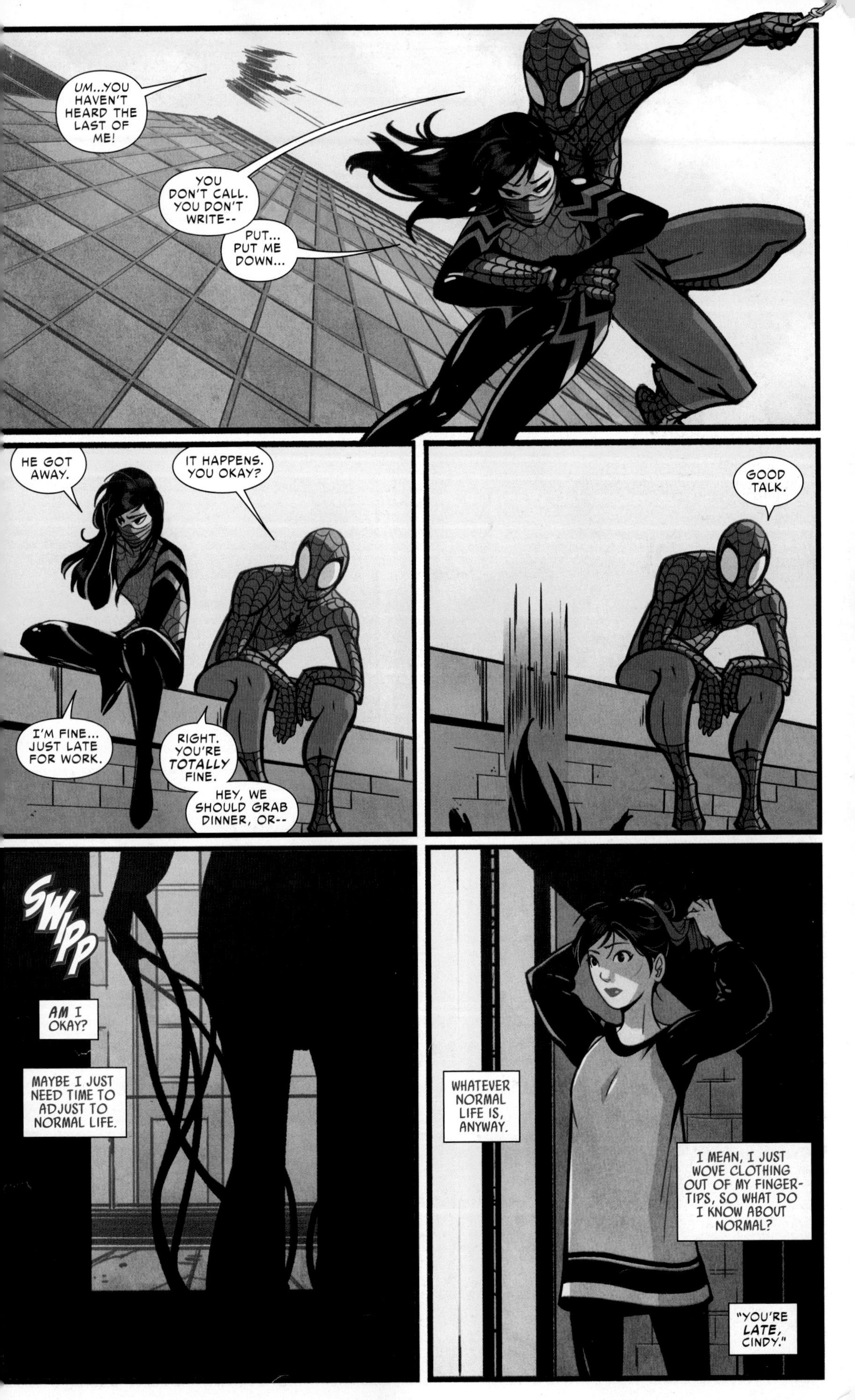
UM...YOU HAVEN'T HEARD THE LAST OF ME!
YOU DON'T CALL. YOU DON'T WRITE--
PUT... PUT ME DOWN...
HE GOT AWAY.
IT HAPPENS. YOU OKAY?
I'M FINE... JUST LATE FOR WORK.
RIGHT. YOU'RE *TOTALLY* FINE.
HEY, WE SHOULD GRAB DINNER, OR--
GOOD TALK.
SWIPP
AM I OKAY?
MAYBE I JUST NEED TIME TO ADJUST TO NORMAL LIFE.
WHATEVER NORMAL LIFE IS, ANYWAY.
I MEAN, I JUST WOVE CLOTHING OUT OF MY FINGER-TIPS, SO WHAT DO I KNOW ABOUT NORMAL?
"YOU'RE *LATE*, CINDY."

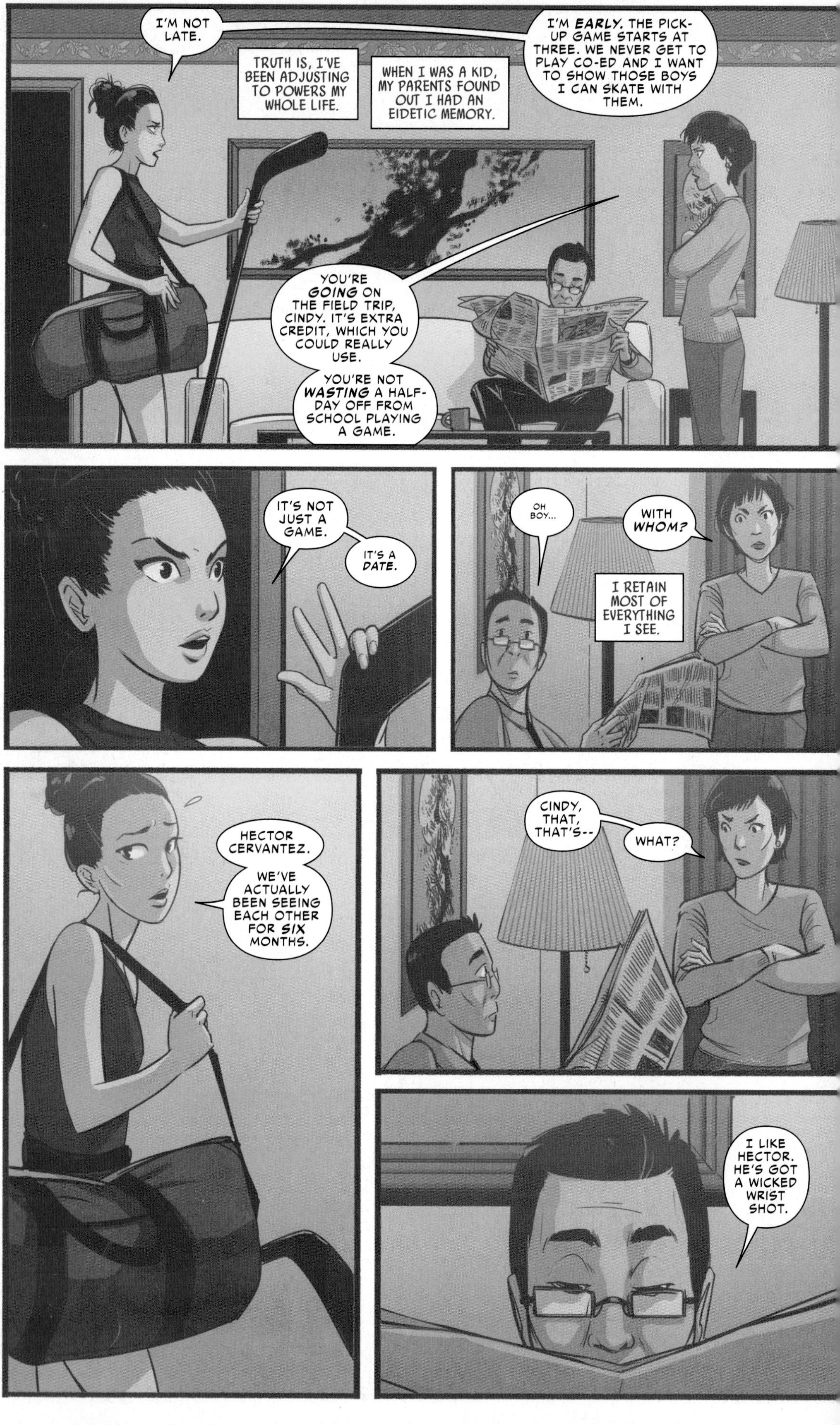

I'M NOT LATE.
TRUTH IS, I'VE BEEN ADJUSTING TO POWERS MY WHOLE LIFE.
WHEN I WAS A KID, MY PARENTS FOUND OUT I HAD AN EIDETIC MEMORY.
I'M EARLY. THE PICK-UP GAME STARTS AT THREE. WE NEVER GET TO PLAY CO-ED AND I WANT TO SHOW THOSE BOYS I CAN SKATE WITH THEM.
YOU'RE GOING ON THE FIELD TRIP, CINDY. IT'S EXTRA CREDIT, WHICH YOU COULD REALLY USE.
YOU'RE NOT WASTING A HALF-DAY OFF FROM SCHOOL PLAYING A GAME.
IT'S NOT JUST A GAME.
IT'S A DATE.
OH BOY...
WITH WHOM?
I RETAIN MOST OF EVERYTHING I SEE.
HECTOR CERVANTEZ.
WE'VE ACTUALLY BEEN SEEING EACH OTHER FOR SIX MONTHS.
CINDY, THAT, THAT'S--
WHAT?
I LIKE HECTOR. HE'S GOT A WICKED WRIST SHOT.

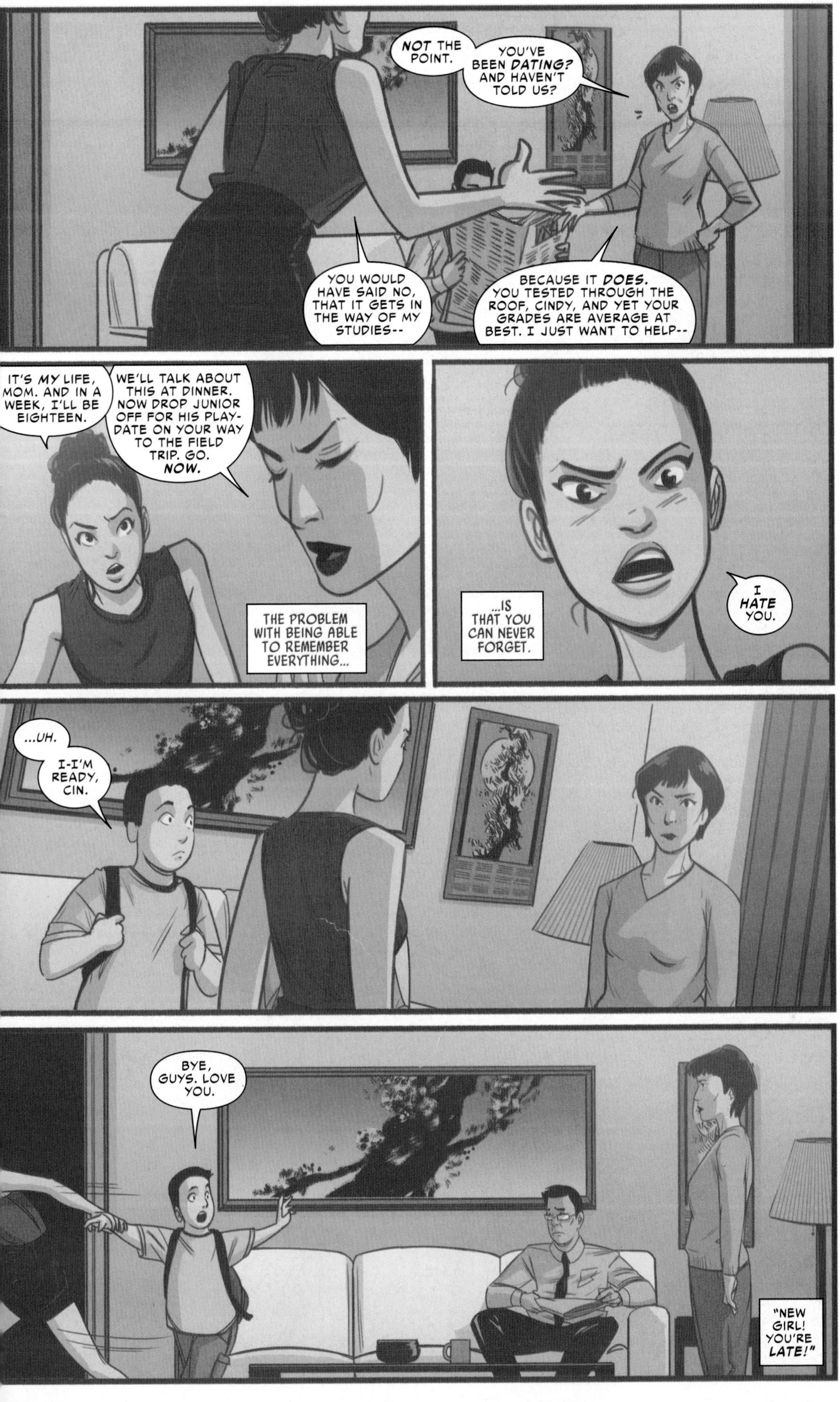

YOU'VE BEEN DATING? AND HAVEN'T TOLD US?
NOT THE POINT.
YOU WOULD HAVE SAID NO, THAT IT GETS IN THE WAY OF MY STUDIES--
BECAUSE IT DOES. YOU TESTED THROUGH THE ROOF, CINDY, AND YET YOUR GRADES ARE AVERAGE AT BEST. I JUST WANT TO HELP--
IT'S MY LIFE, MOM. AND IN A WEEK, I'LL BE EIGHTEEN.
WE'LL TALK ABOUT THIS AT DINNER. NOW DROP JUNIOR OFF FOR HIS PLAY-DATE ON YOUR WAY TO THE FIELD TRIP. GO. NOW.
THE PROBLEM WITH BEING ABLE TO REMEMBER EVERYTHING...
...IS THAT YOU CAN NEVER FORGET.
I HATE YOU.
...UH.
I-I'M READY, CIN.
BYE, GUYS. LOVE YOU.
"NEW GIRL! YOU'RE LATE!"

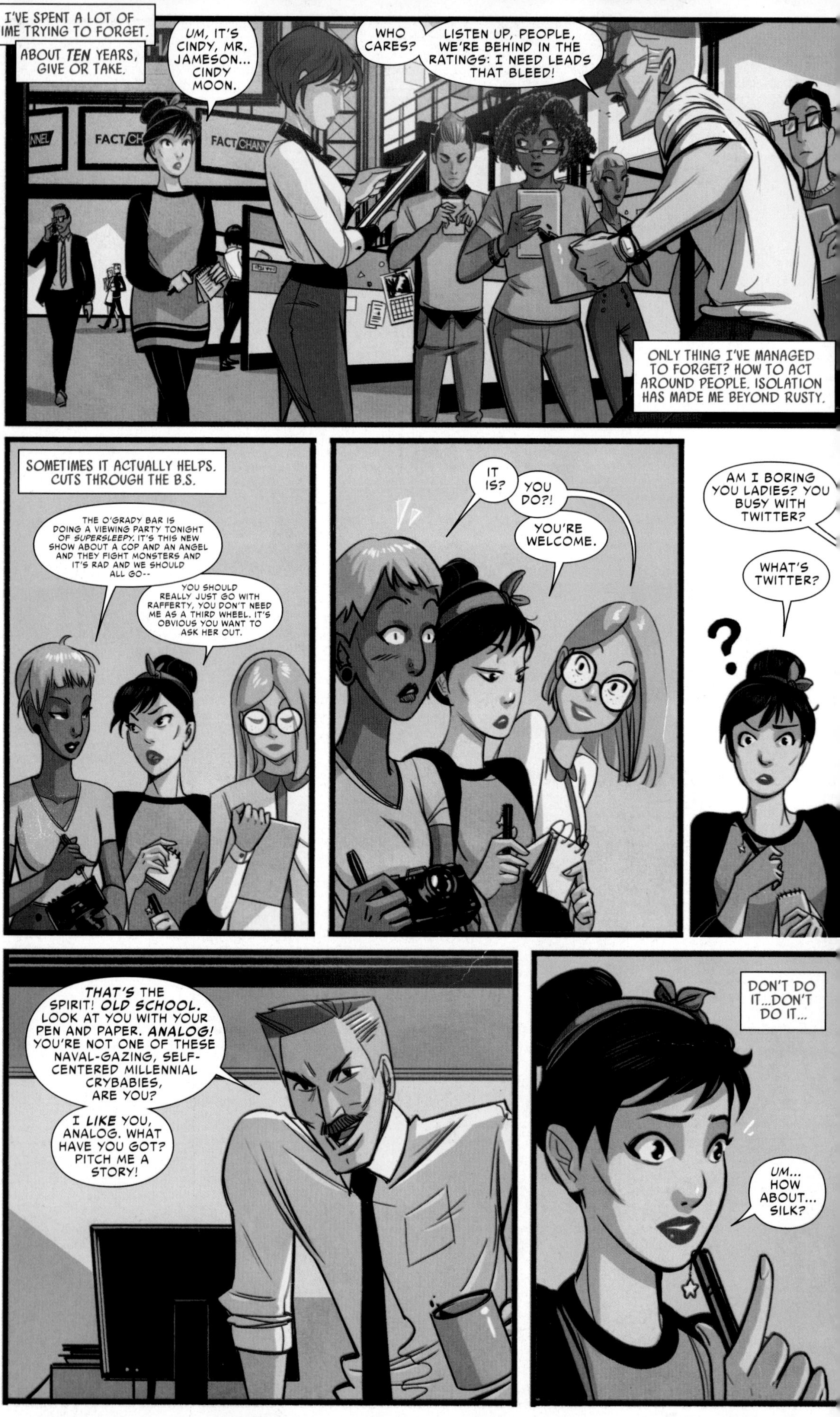
I'VE SPENT A LOT OF TIME TRYING TO FORGET.
ABOUT TEN YEARS, GIVE OR TAKE.
UM, IT'S CINDY, MR. JAMESON... CINDY MOON.
WHO CARES?
LISTEN UP, PEOPLE, WE'RE BEHIND IN THE RATINGS: I NEED LEADS THAT BLEED!
FACT CH
FACT CHANN
ONLY THING I'VE MANAGED TO FORGET? HOW TO ACT AROUND PEOPLE. ISOLATION HAS MADE ME BEYOND RUSTY.
SOMETIMES IT ACTUALLY HELPS. CUTS THROUGH THE B.S.
THE O'GRADY BAR IS DOING A VIEWING PARTY TONIGHT OF SUPERSLEEPY. IT'S THIS NEW SHOW ABOUT A COP AND AN ANGEL AND THEY FIGHT MONSTERS AND IT'S RAD AND WE SHOULD ALL GO--
YOU SHOULD REALLY JUST GO WITH RAFFERTY, YOU DON'T NEED ME AS A THIRD WHEEL. IT'S OBVIOUS YOU WANT TO ASK HER OUT.
IT IS?
YOU DO?!
YOU'RE WELCOME.
AM I BORING YOU LADIES? YOU BUSY WITH TWITTER?
WHAT'S TWITTER?
?
THAT'S THE SPIRIT! OLD SCHOOL. LOOK AT YOU WITH YOUR PEN AND PAPER. ANALOG! YOU'RE NOT ONE OF THESE NAVAL-GAZING, SELF-CENTERED MILLENNIAL CRYBABIES, ARE YOU?
I LIKE YOU, ANALOG. WHAT HAVE YOU GOT? PITCH ME A STORY!
DON'T DO IT...DON'T DO IT...
UM... HOW ABOUT... SILK?

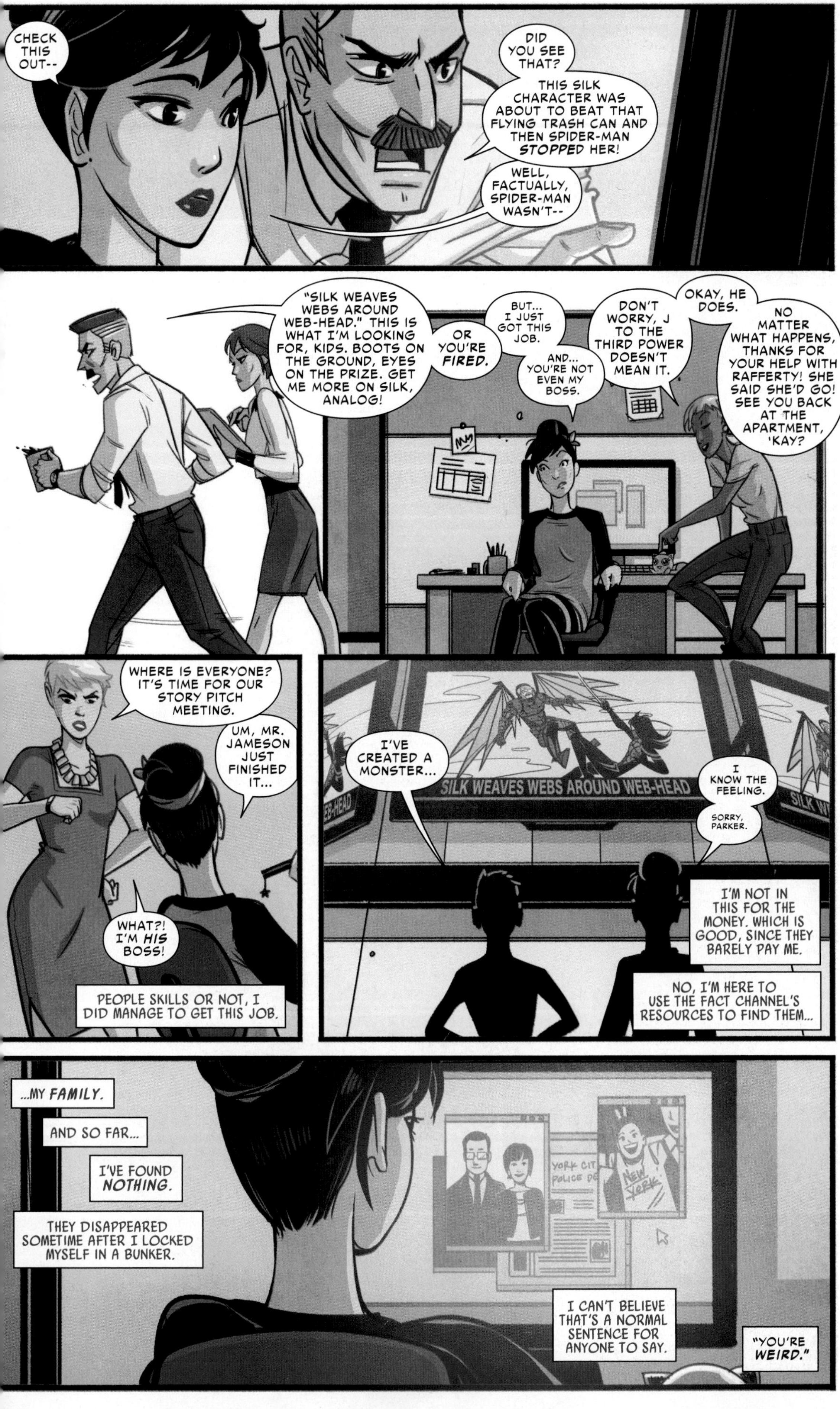
CHECK THIS OUT--
DID YOU SEE THAT?
THIS SILK CHARACTER WAS ABOUT TO BEAT THAT FLYING TRASH CAN AND THEN SPIDER-MAN STOPPED HER!
WELL, FACTUALLY, SPIDER-MAN WASN'T--
"SILK WEAVES WEBS AROUND WEB-HEAD." THIS IS WHAT I'M LOOKING FOR, KIDS. BOOTS ON THE GROUND, EYES ON THE PRIZE. GET ME MORE ON SILK, ANALOG!
OR YOU'RE FIRED.
BUT... I JUST GOT THIS JOB.
AND... YOU'RE NOT EVEN MY BOSS.
DON'T WORRY, J TO THE THIRD POWER DOESN'T MEAN IT.
OKAY, HE DOES.
NO MATTER WHAT HAPPENS, THANKS FOR YOUR HELP WITH RAFFERTY! SHE SAID SHE'D GO! SEE YOU BACK AT THE APARTMENT, 'KAY?
WHERE IS EVERYONE? IT'S TIME FOR OUR STORY PITCH MEETING.
UM, MR. JAMESON JUST FINISHED IT...
WHAT?! I'M HIS BOSS!
PEOPLE SKILLS OR NOT, I DID MANAGE TO GET THIS JOB.
SILK WEAVES WEBS AROUND WEB-HEAD
I'VE CREATED A MONSTER...
I KNOW THE FEELING.
SORRY, PARKER.
I'M NOT IN THIS FOR THE MONEY. WHICH IS GOOD, SINCE THEY BARELY PAY ME.
NO, I'M HERE TO USE THE FACT CHANNEL'S RESOURCES TO FIND THEM...
...MY FAMILY.
AND SO FAR...
I'VE FOUND NOTHING.
THEY DISAPPEARED SOMETIME AFTER I LOCKED MYSELF IN A BUNKER.
I CAN'T BELIEVE THAT'S A NORMAL SENTENCE FOR ANYONE TO SAY.
"YOU'RE WEIRD."

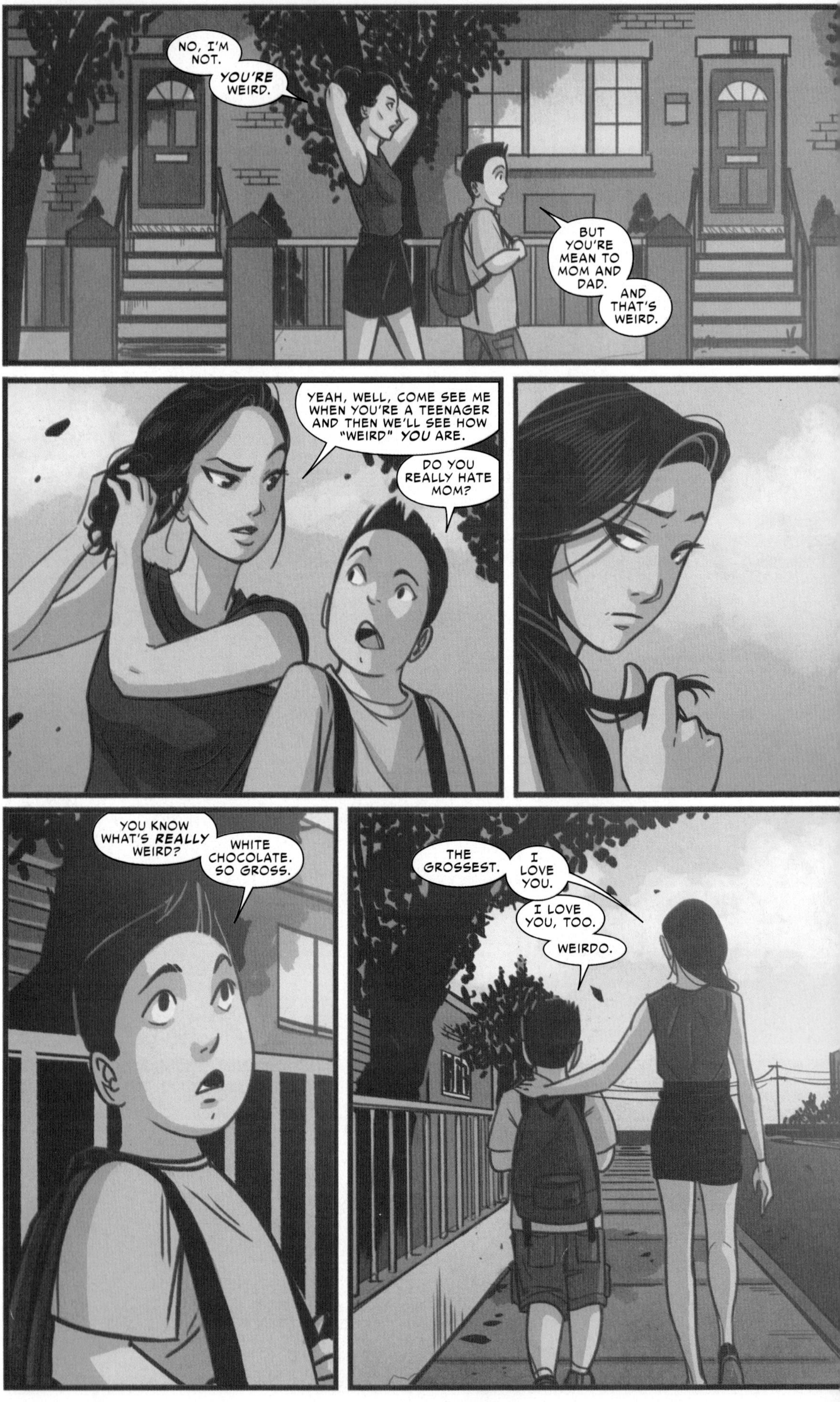
NO, I'M NOT. YOU'RE WEIRD.
BUT YOU'RE MEAN TO MOM AND DAD.
AND THAT'S WEIRD.
YEAH, WELL, COME SEE ME WHEN YOU'RE A TEENAGER AND THEN WE'LL SEE HOW "WEIRD" YOU ARE.
DO YOU REALLY HATE MOM?
YOU KNOW WHAT'S REALLY WEIRD?
WHITE CHOCOLATE. SO GROSS.
THE GROSSEST.
I LOVE YOU.
I LOVE YOU, TOO.
WEIRDO.

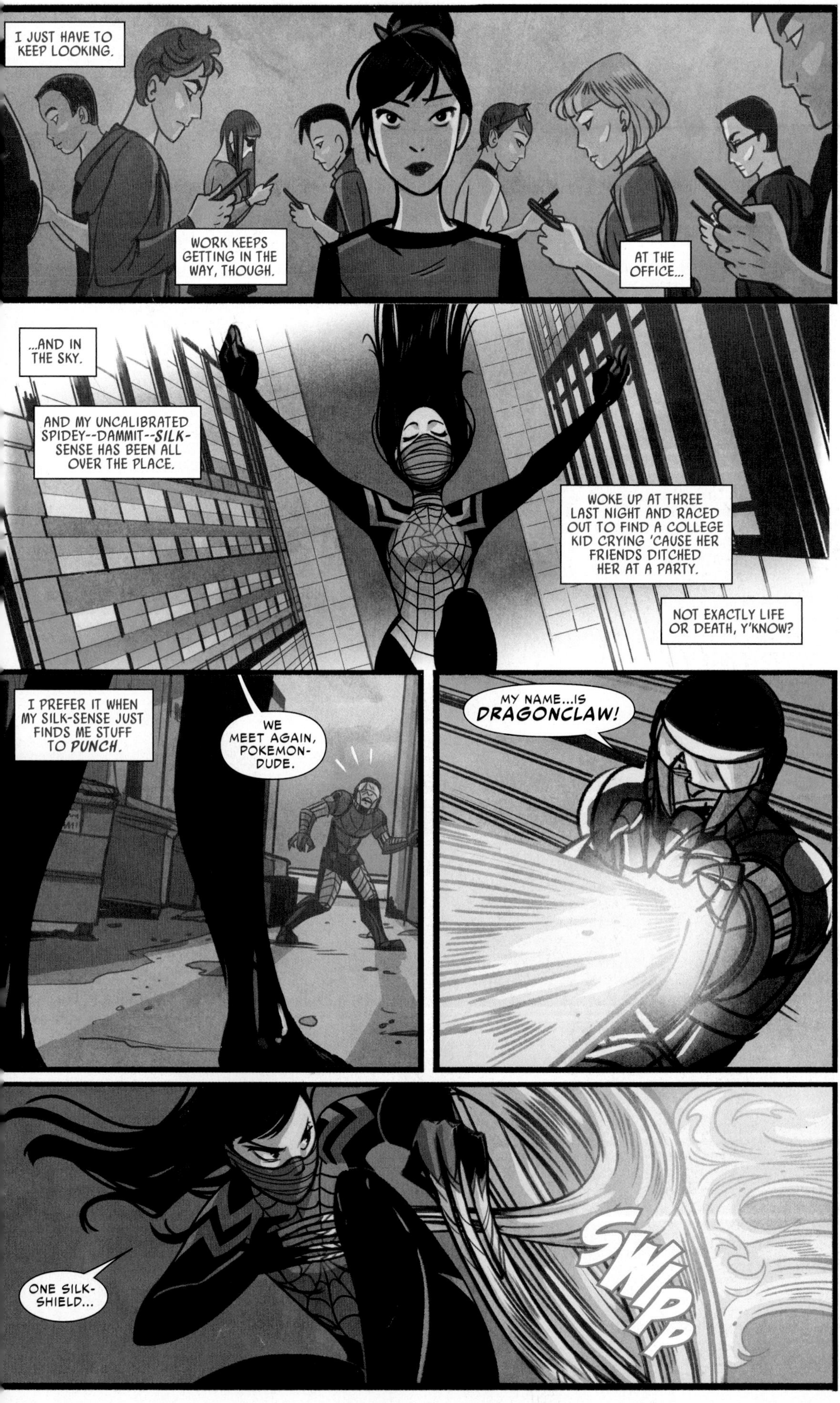

I JUST HAVE TO KEEP LOOKING.
WORK KEEPS GETTING IN THE WAY, THOUGH.
AT THE OFFICE...
...AND IN THE SKY.
AND MY UNCALIBRATED SPIDEY--DAMMIT--SILK-SENSE HAS BEEN ALL OVER THE PLACE.
WOKE UP AT THREE LAST NIGHT AND RACED OUT TO FIND A COLLEGE KID CRYING 'CAUSE HER FRIENDS DITCHED HER AT A PARTY.
NOT EXACTLY LIFE OR DEATH, Y'KNOW?
I PREFER IT WHEN MY SILK-SENSE JUST FINDS ME STUFF TO PUNCH.
WE MEET AGAIN, POKEMON-DUDE.
MY NAME...IS DRAGONCLAW!
ONE SILK-SHIELD...
SWIPP

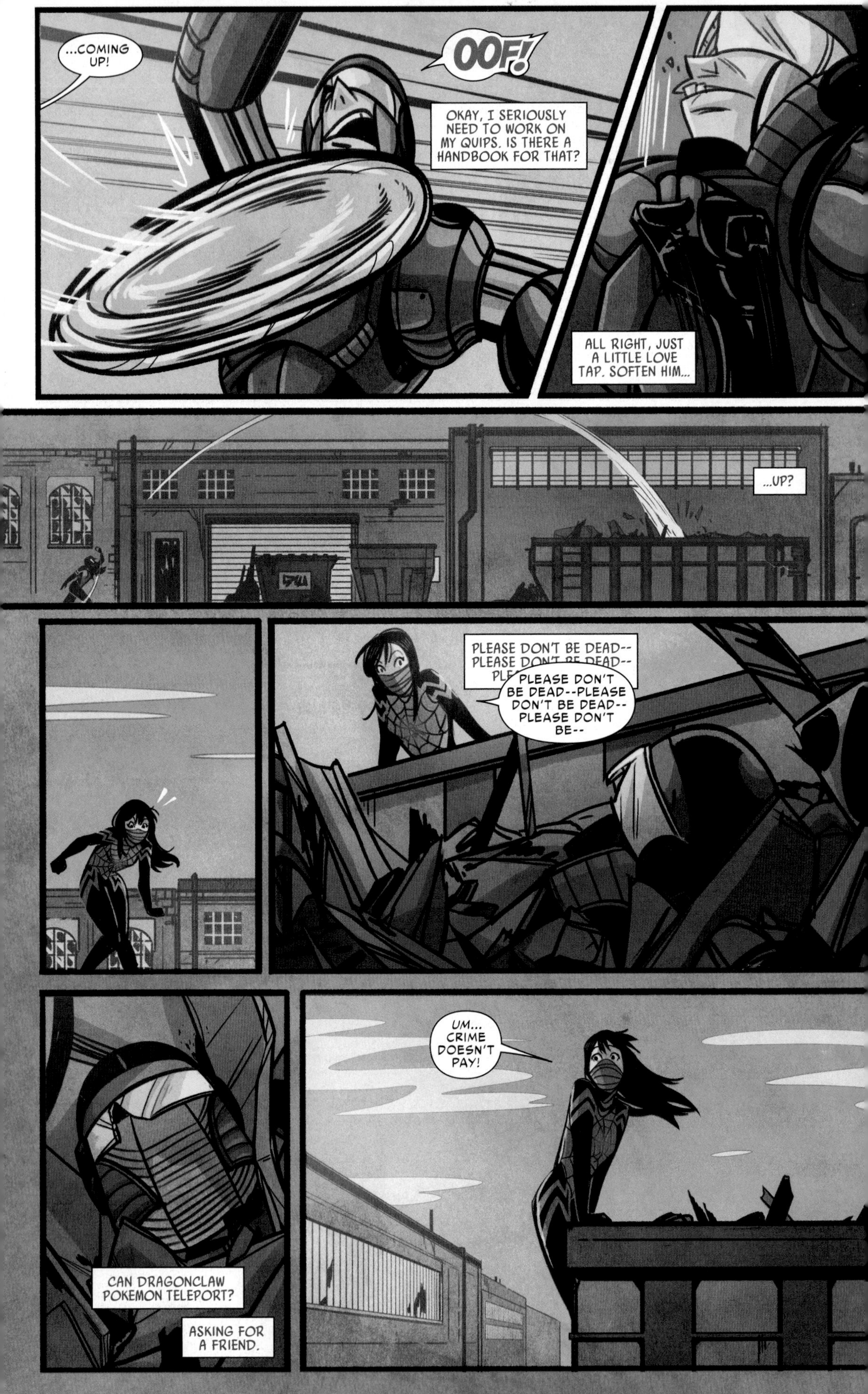
...COMING UP!
OOF!
OKAY, I SERIOUSLY NEED TO WORK ON MY QUIPS. IS THERE A HANDBOOK FOR THAT?
ALL RIGHT, JUST A LITTLE LOVE TAP. SOFTEN HIM...
...UP?
PLEASE DON'T BE DEAD--PLEASE DON'T BE DEAD--
PLEASE DON'T BE DEAD--PLEASE DON'T BE DEAD--PLEASE DON'T BE--
UM... CRIME DOESN'T PAY!
CAN DRAGONCLAW POKEMON TELEPORT?
ASKING FOR A FRIEND.

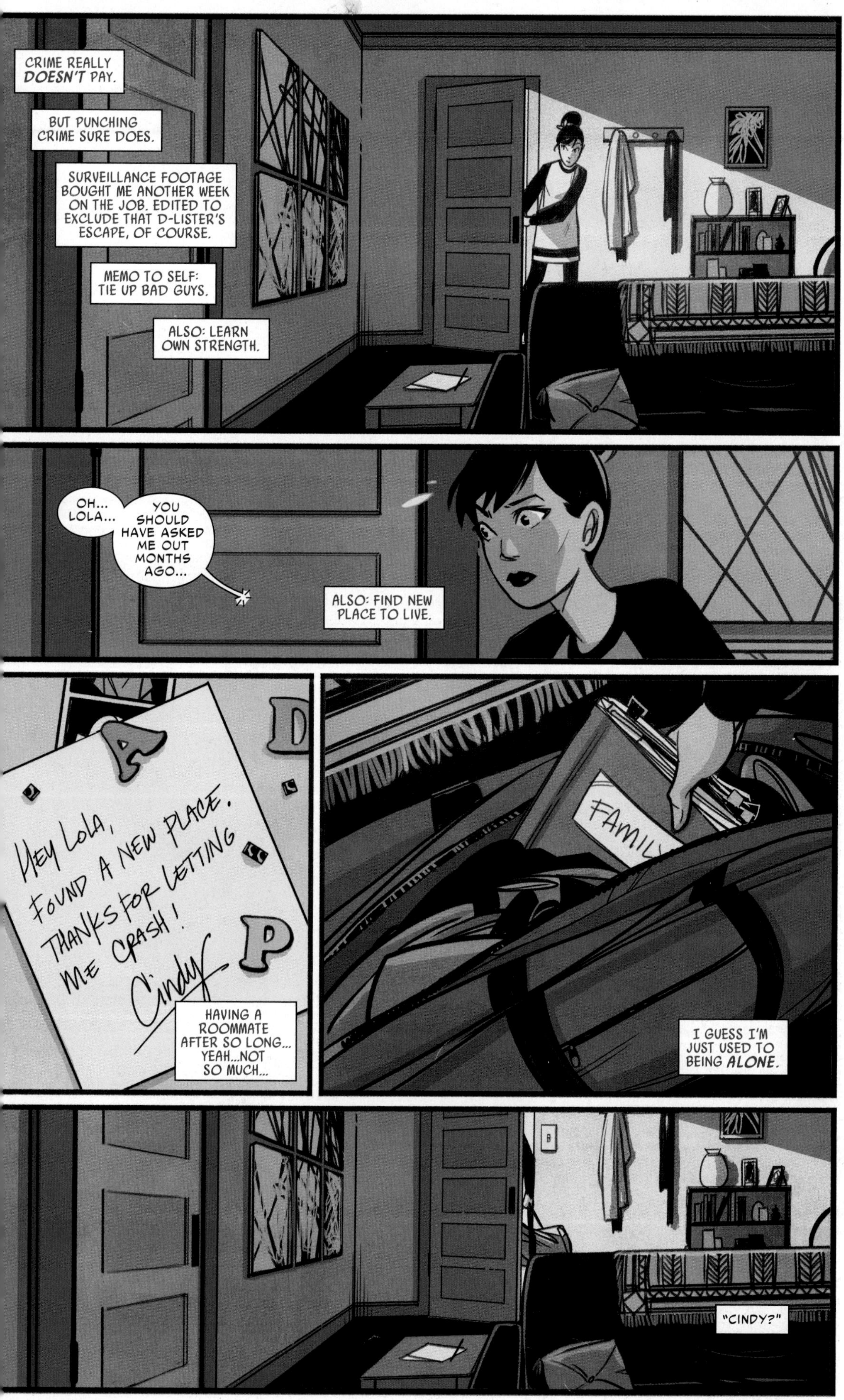
CRIME REALLY DOESN'T PAY.
BUT PUNCHING CRIME SURE DOES.
SURVEILLANCE FOOTAGE BOUGHT ME ANOTHER WEEK ON THE JOB. EDITED TO EXCLUDE THAT D-LISTER'S ESCAPE, OF COURSE.
MEMO TO SELF: TIE UP BAD GUYS.
ALSO: LEARN OWN STRENGTH.
OH... LOLA...
YOU SHOULD HAVE ASKED ME OUT MONTHS AGO...
ALSO: FIND NEW PLACE TO LIVE.
Hey Lola, Found a new place. Thanks for letting me crash! Cindy
HAVING A ROOMMATE AFTER SO LONG... YEAH...NOT SO MUCH...
FAMIL
I GUESS I'M JUST USED TO BEING ALONE.
"CINDY?"

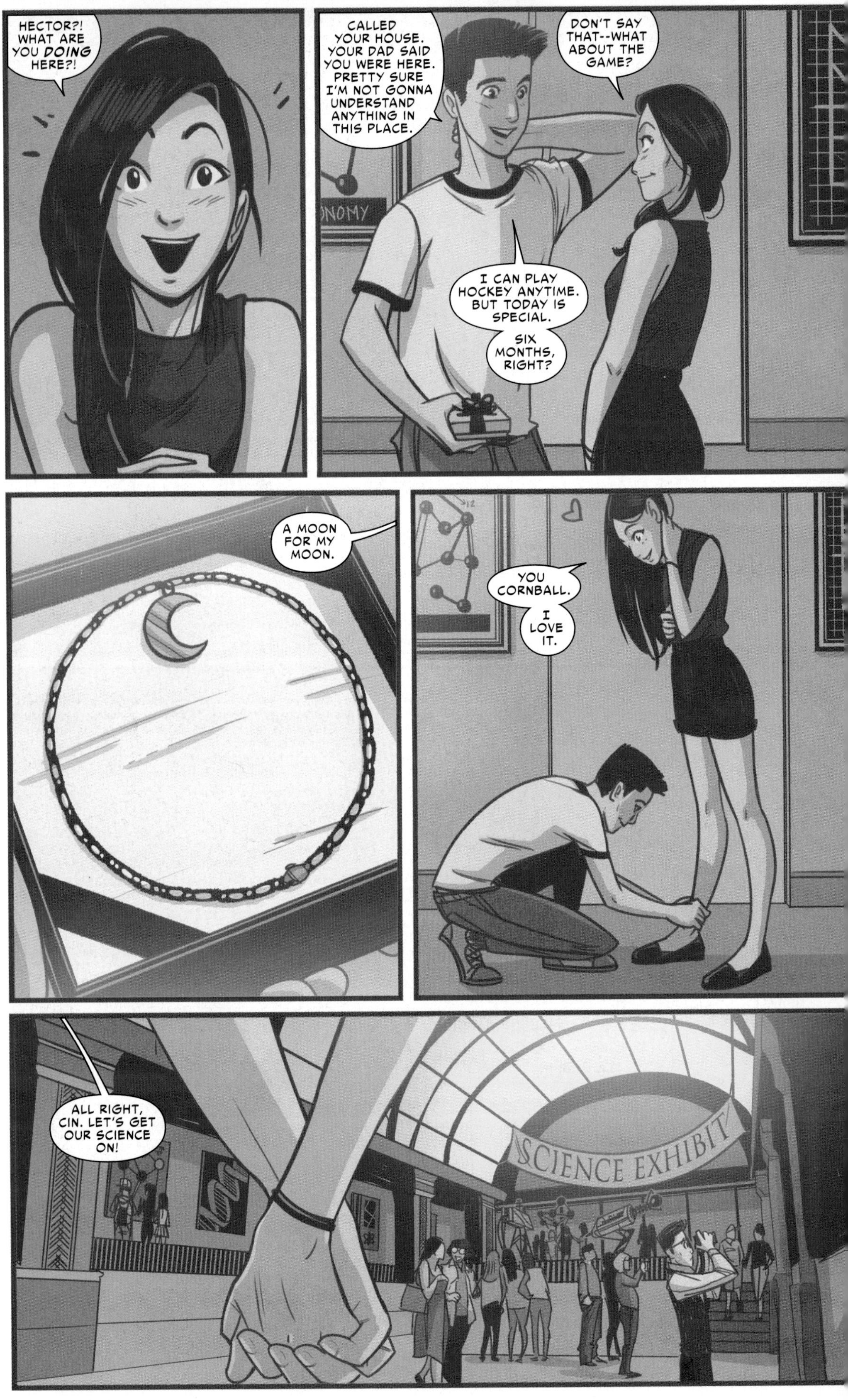
HECTOR?! WHAT ARE YOU *DOING* HERE?!
CALLED YOUR HOUSE. YOUR DAD SAID YOU WERE HERE. PRETTY SURE I'M NOT GONNA UNDERSTAND ANYTHING IN THIS PLACE.
DON'T SAY THAT--WHAT ABOUT THE GAME?
I CAN PLAY HOCKEY ANYTIME. BUT TODAY IS SPECIAL.
SIX MONTHS, RIGHT?
A MOON FOR MY MOON.
YOU CORNBALL.
I LOVE IT.
ALL RIGHT, CIN. LET'S GET OUR SCIENCE ON!
SCIENCE EXHIBIT

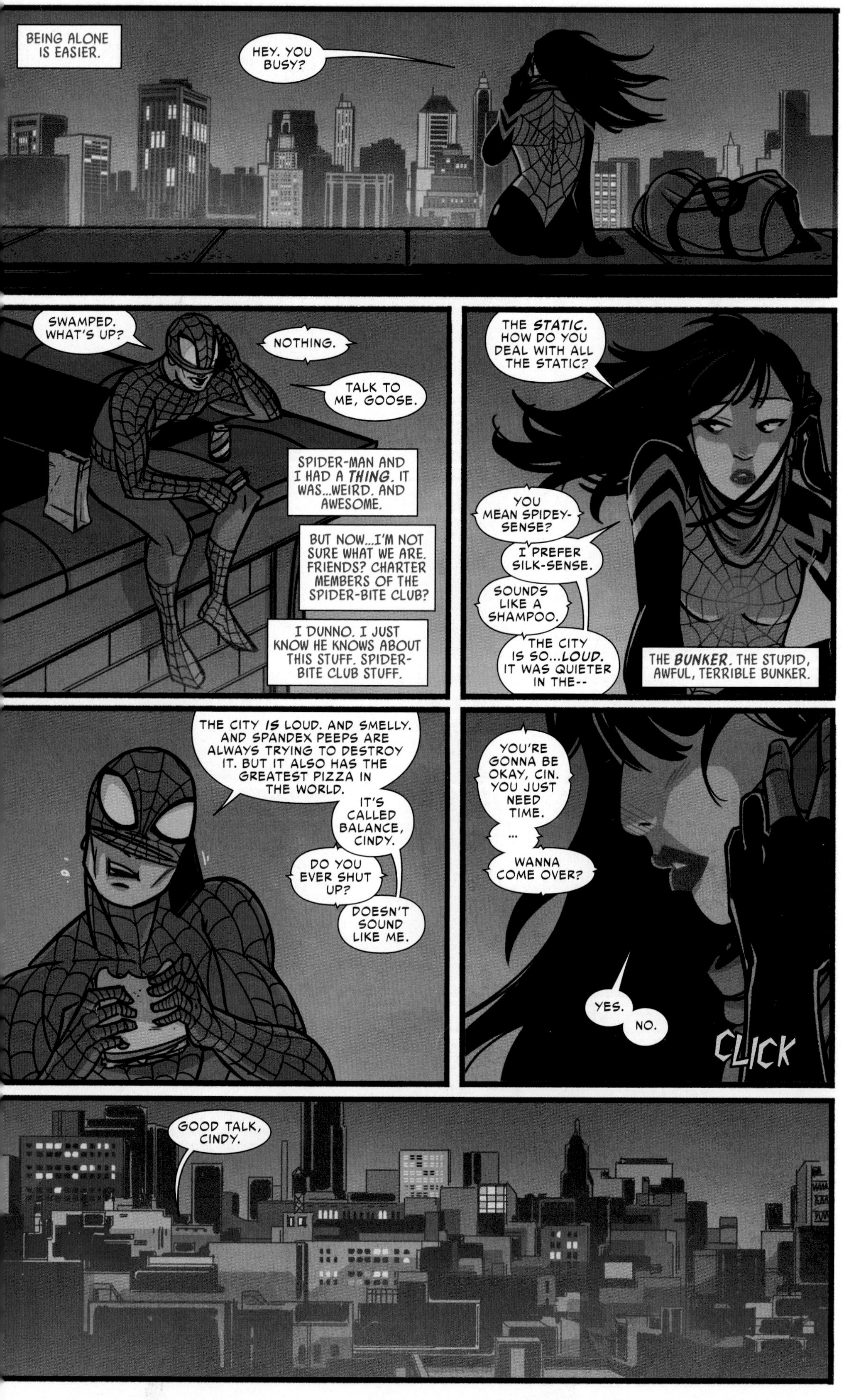

BEING ALONE IS EASIER.
HEY. YOU BUSY?
SWAMPED. WHAT'S UP?
NOTHING.
TALK TO ME, GOOSE.
SPIDER-MAN AND I HAD A *THING*. IT WAS...WEIRD. AND AWESOME.
BUT NOW...I'M NOT SURE WHAT WE ARE. FRIENDS? CHARTER MEMBERS OF THE SPIDER-BITE CLUB?
I DUNNO. I JUST KNOW HE KNOWS ABOUT THIS STUFF. SPIDER-BITE CLUB STUFF.
THE *STATIC*. HOW DO YOU DEAL WITH ALL THE STATIC?
YOU MEAN SPIDEY-SENSE?
I PREFER SILK-SENSE.
SOUNDS LIKE A SHAMPOO.
THE CITY IS SO...*LOUD*. IT WAS QUIETER IN THE--
THE *BUNKER*. THE STUPID, AWFUL, TERRIBLE BUNKER.
THE CITY *IS* LOUD. AND SMELLY. AND SPANDEX PEEPS ARE ALWAYS TRYING TO DESTROY IT. BUT IT ALSO HAS THE GREATEST PIZZA IN THE WORLD.
IT'S CALLED BALANCE, CINDY.
DO YOU EVER SHUT UP?
DOESN'T SOUND LIKE ME.
YOU'RE GONNA BE OKAY, CIN. YOU JUST NEED TIME.
...
WANNA COME OVER?
YES.
NO.
CLICK
GOOD TALK, CINDY.

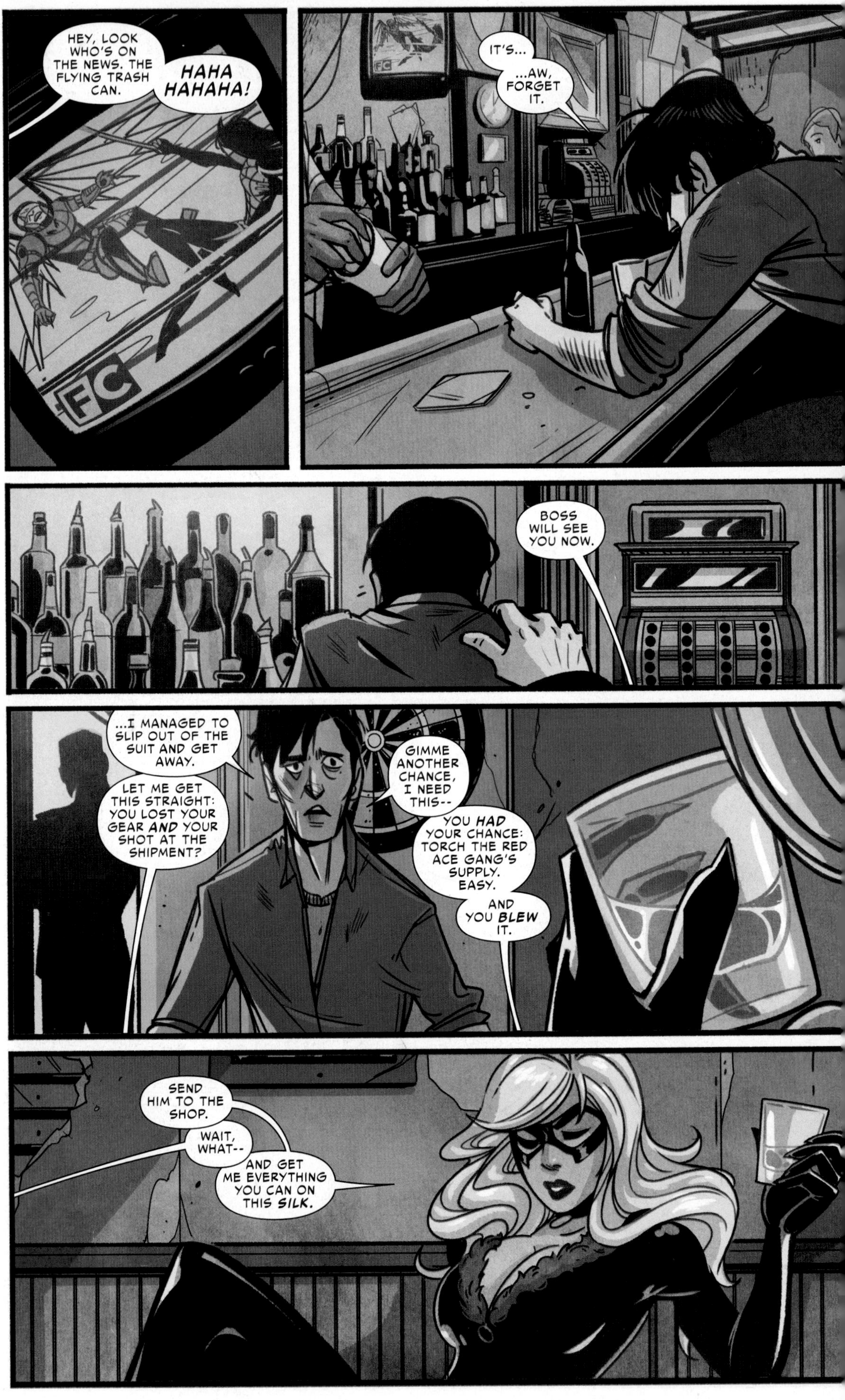
HEY, LOOK WHO'S ON THE NEWS. THE FLYING TRASH CAN.
HAHA HAHAHA!
FC
IT'S...
...AW, FORGET IT.
BOSS WILL SEE YOU NOW.
...I MANAGED TO SLIP OUT OF THE SUIT AND GET AWAY.
LET ME GET THIS STRAIGHT: YOU LOST YOUR GEAR AND YOUR SHOT AT THE SHIPMENT?
GIMME ANOTHER CHANCE, I NEED THIS--
YOU HAD YOUR CHANCE: TORCH THE RED ACE GANG'S SUPPLY. EASY.
AND YOU BLEW IT.
SEND HIM TO THE SHOP.
WAIT, WHAT--
AND GET ME EVERYTHING YOU CAN ON THIS SILK.

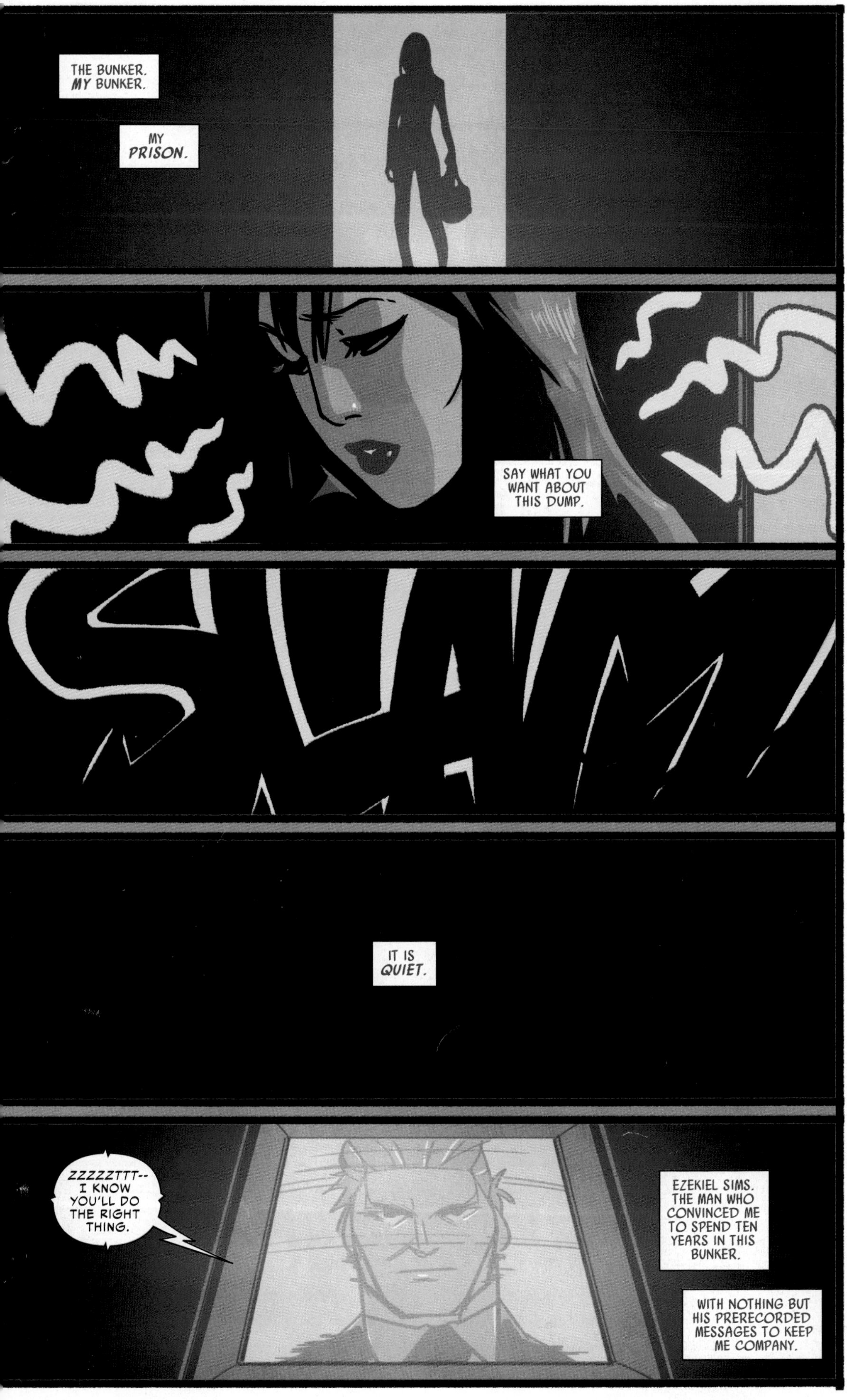
THE BUNKER. MY BUNKER.
MY PRISON.
SAY WHAT YOU WANT ABOUT THIS DUMP.
IT IS QUIET.
ZZZZZTTT-- I KNOW YOU'LL DO THE RIGHT THING.
EZEKIEL SIMS. THE MAN WHO CONVINCED ME TO SPEND TEN YEARS IN THIS BUNKER.
WITH NOTHING BUT HIS PRERECORDED MESSAGES TO KEEP ME COMPANY.

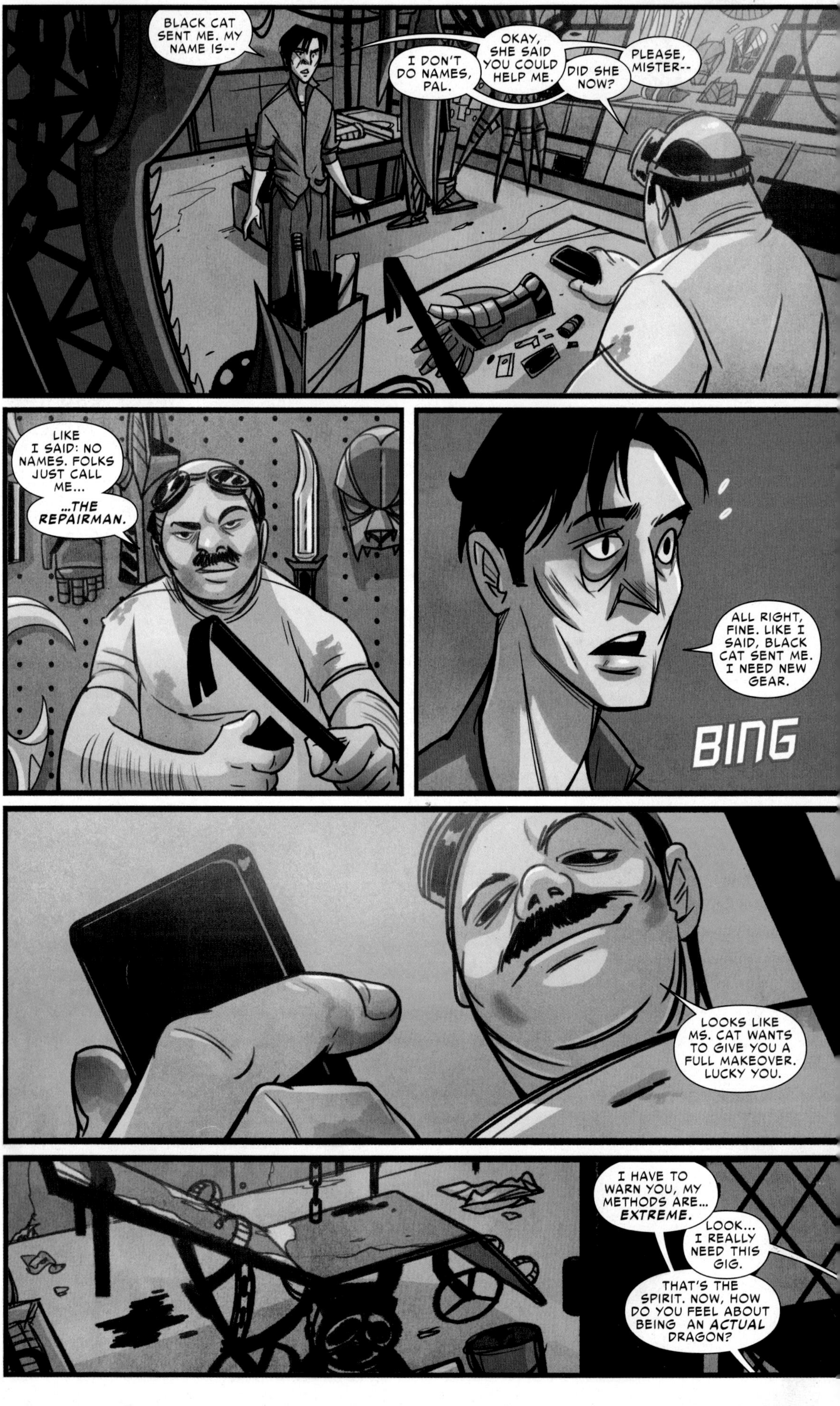
BLACK CAT SENT ME. MY NAME IS--
I DON'T DO NAMES, PAL.
OKAY, SHE SAID YOU COULD HELP ME.
DID SHE NOW?
PLEASE, MISTER--
LIKE I SAID: NO NAMES. FOLKS JUST CALL ME...
...THE REPAIRMAN.
ALL RIGHT, FINE. LIKE I SAID, BLACK CAT SENT ME. I NEED NEW GEAR.
BING
LOOKS LIKE MS. CAT WANTS TO GIVE YOU A FULL MAKEOVER. LUCKY YOU.
I HAVE TO WARN YOU, MY METHODS ARE... EXTREME.
LOOK... I REALLY NEED THIS GIG.
THAT'S THE SPIRIT. NOW, HOW DO YOU FEEL ABOUT BEING AN ACTUAL DRAGON?

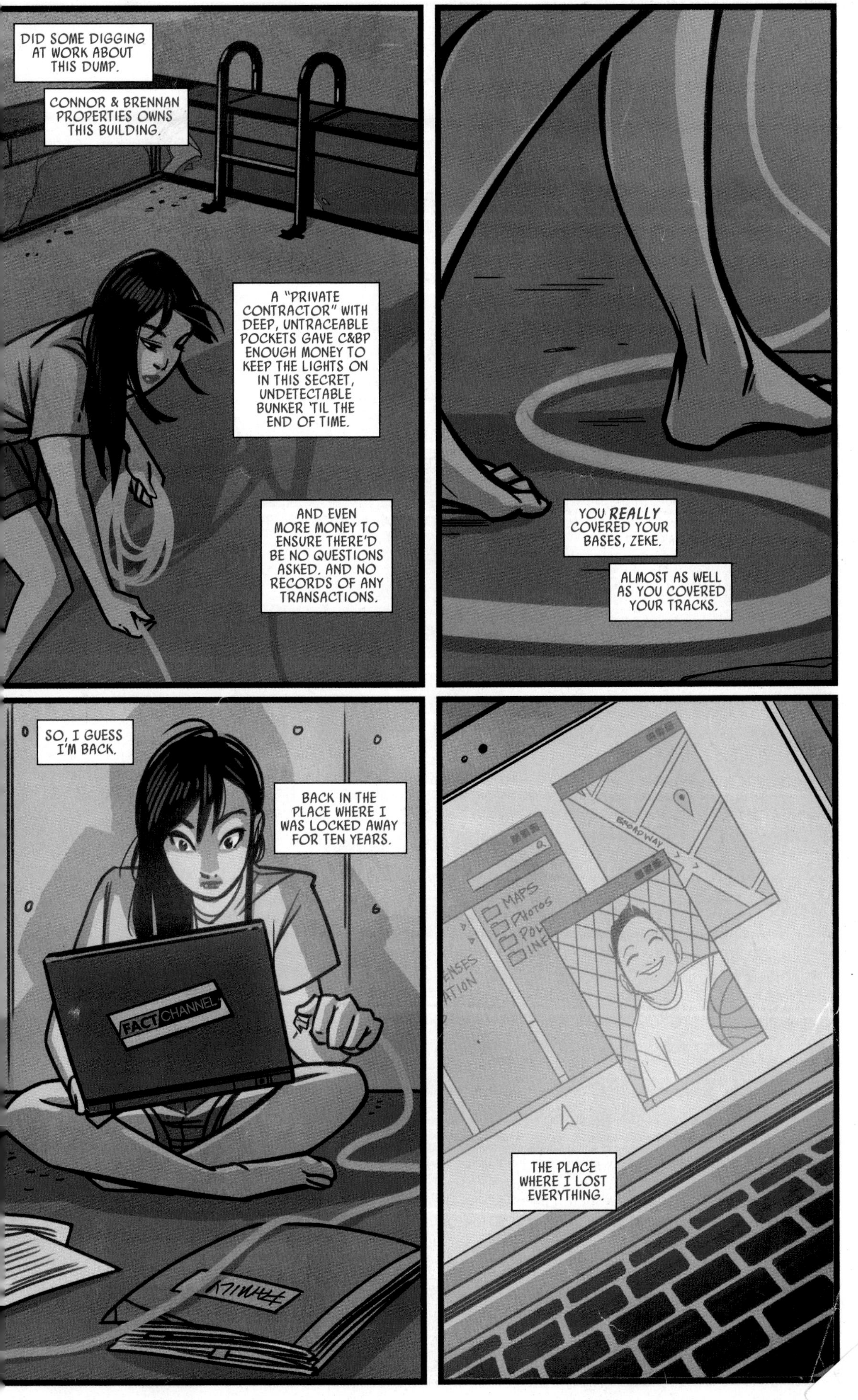
DID SOME DIGGING AT WORK ABOUT THIS DUMP.
CONNOR & BRENNAN PROPERTIES OWNS THIS BUILDING.
A "PRIVATE CONTRACTOR" WITH DEEP, UNTRACEABLE POCKETS GAVE C&BP ENOUGH MONEY TO KEEP THE LIGHTS ON IN THIS SECRET, UNDETECTABLE BUNKER 'TIL THE END OF TIME.
AND EVEN MORE MONEY TO ENSURE THERE'D BE NO QUESTIONS ASKED. AND NO RECORDS OF ANY TRANSACTIONS.
YOU *REALLY* COVERED YOUR BASES, ZEKE.
ALMOST AS WELL AS YOU COVERED YOUR TRACKS.
SO, I GUESS I'M BACK.
BACK IN THE PLACE WHERE I WAS LOCKED AWAY FOR TEN YEARS.
FACT CHANNEL
BROADWAY
MAPS
PHOTOS
THE PLACE WHERE I LOST EVERYTHING.

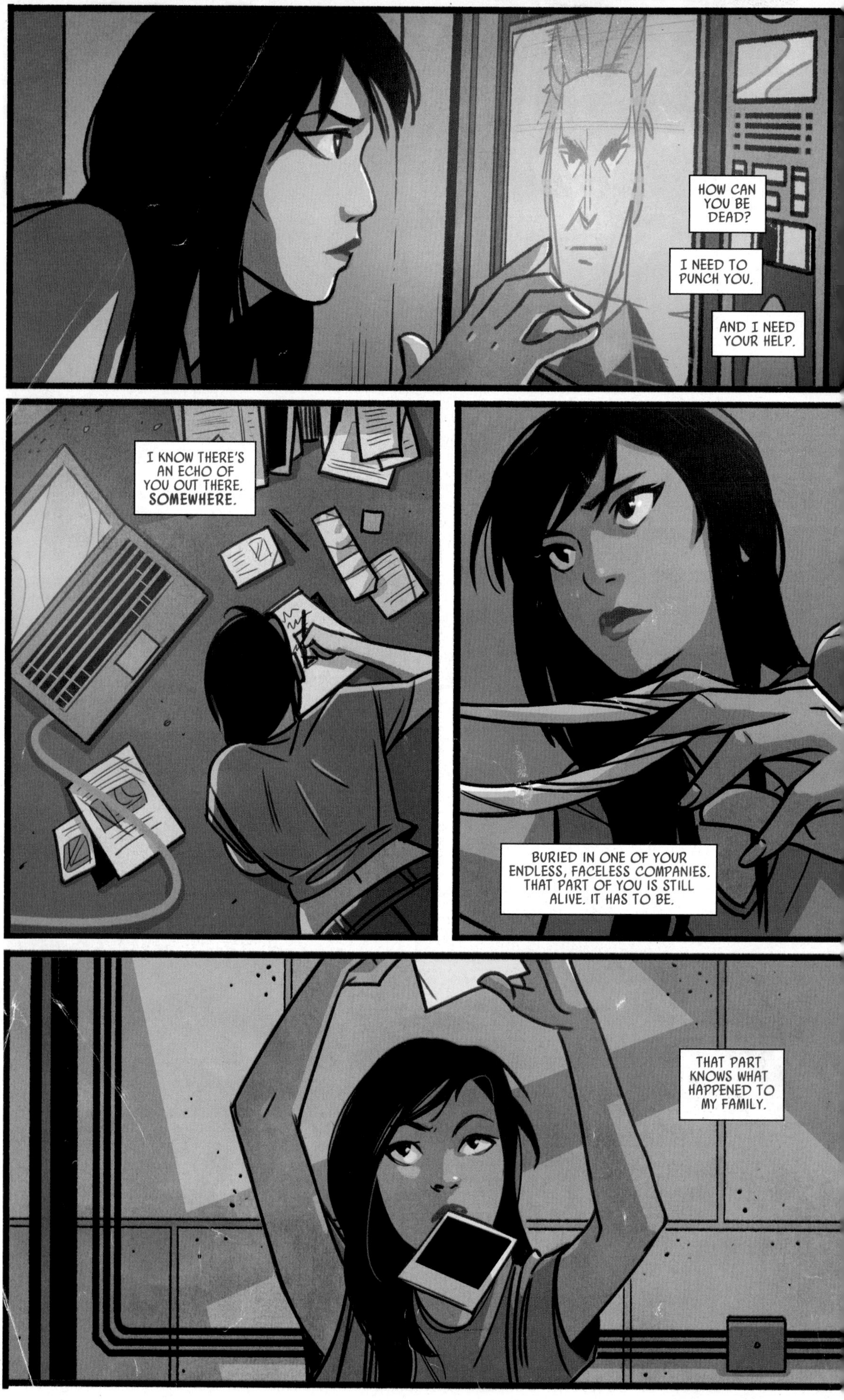
HOW CAN YOU BE DEAD?
I NEED TO PUNCH YOU.
AND I NEED YOUR HELP.
I KNOW THERE'S AN ECHO OF YOU OUT THERE. **SOMEWHERE.**
BURIED IN ONE OF YOUR ENDLESS, FACELESS COMPANIES. THAT PART OF YOU IS STILL ALIVE. IT HAS TO BE.
THAT PART KNOWS WHAT HAPPENED TO MY FAMILY.

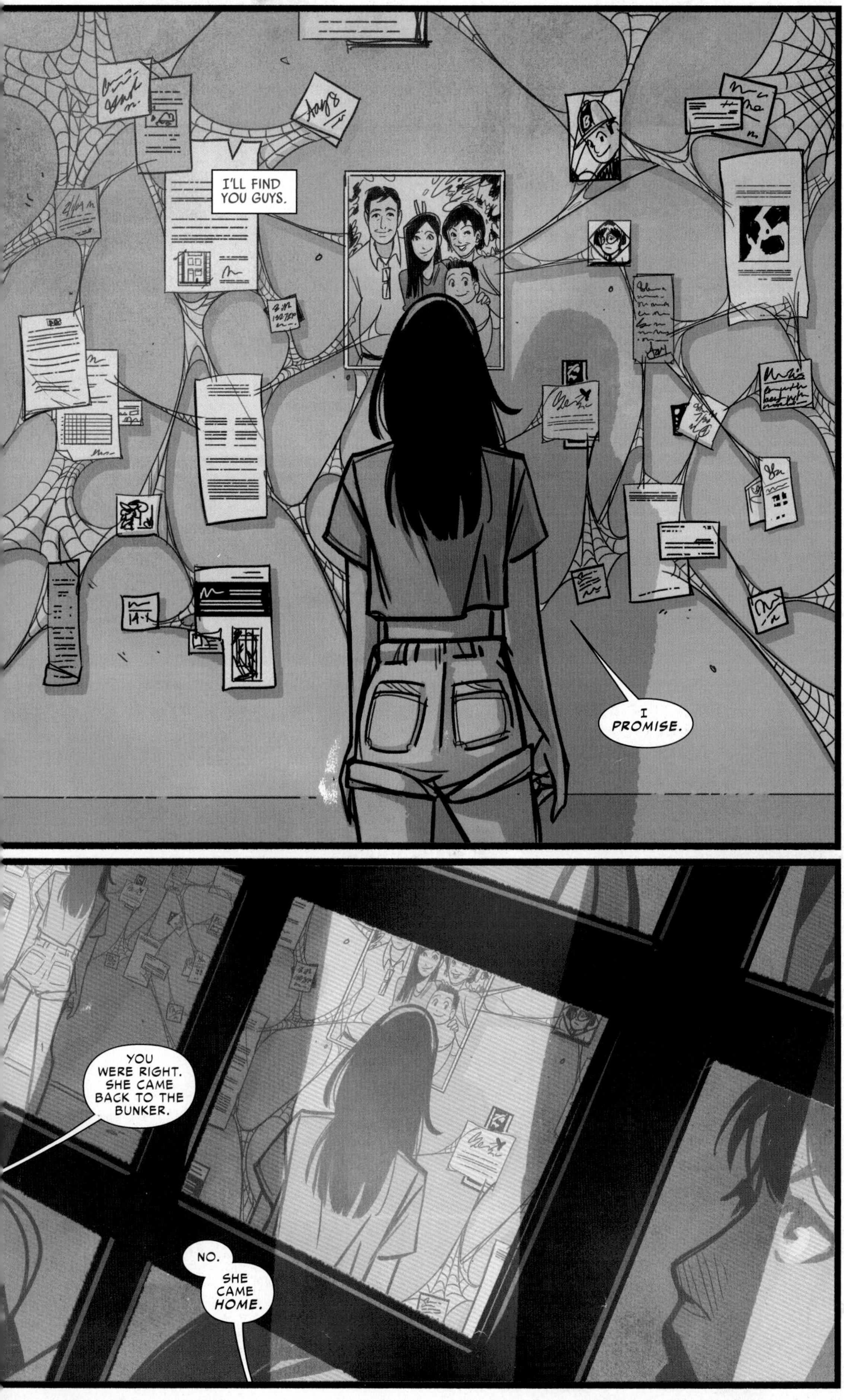
I'LL FIND YOU GUYS.
I PROMISE.
YOU WERE RIGHT. SHE CAME BACK TO THE BUNKER.
NO.
SHE CAME HOME.

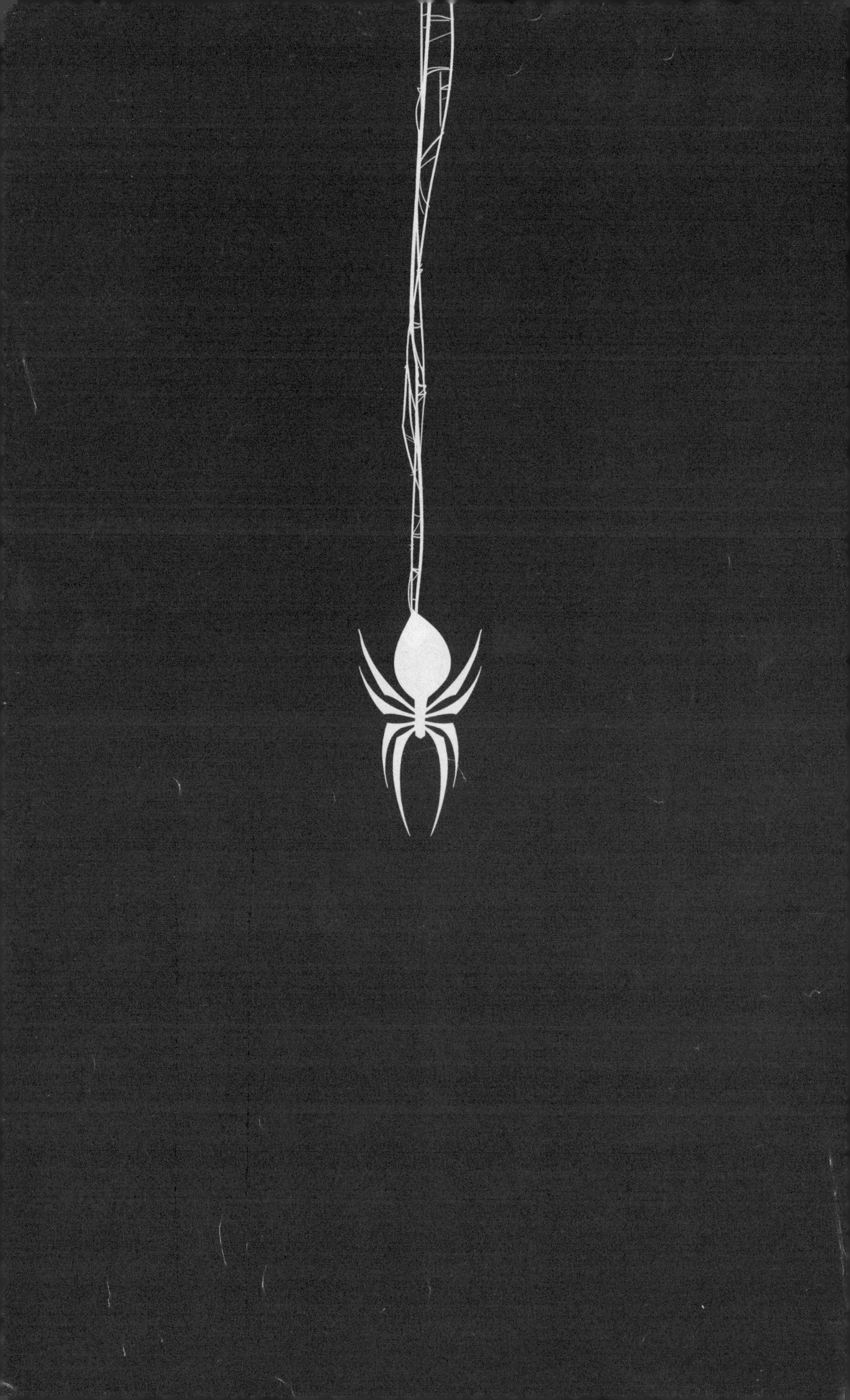

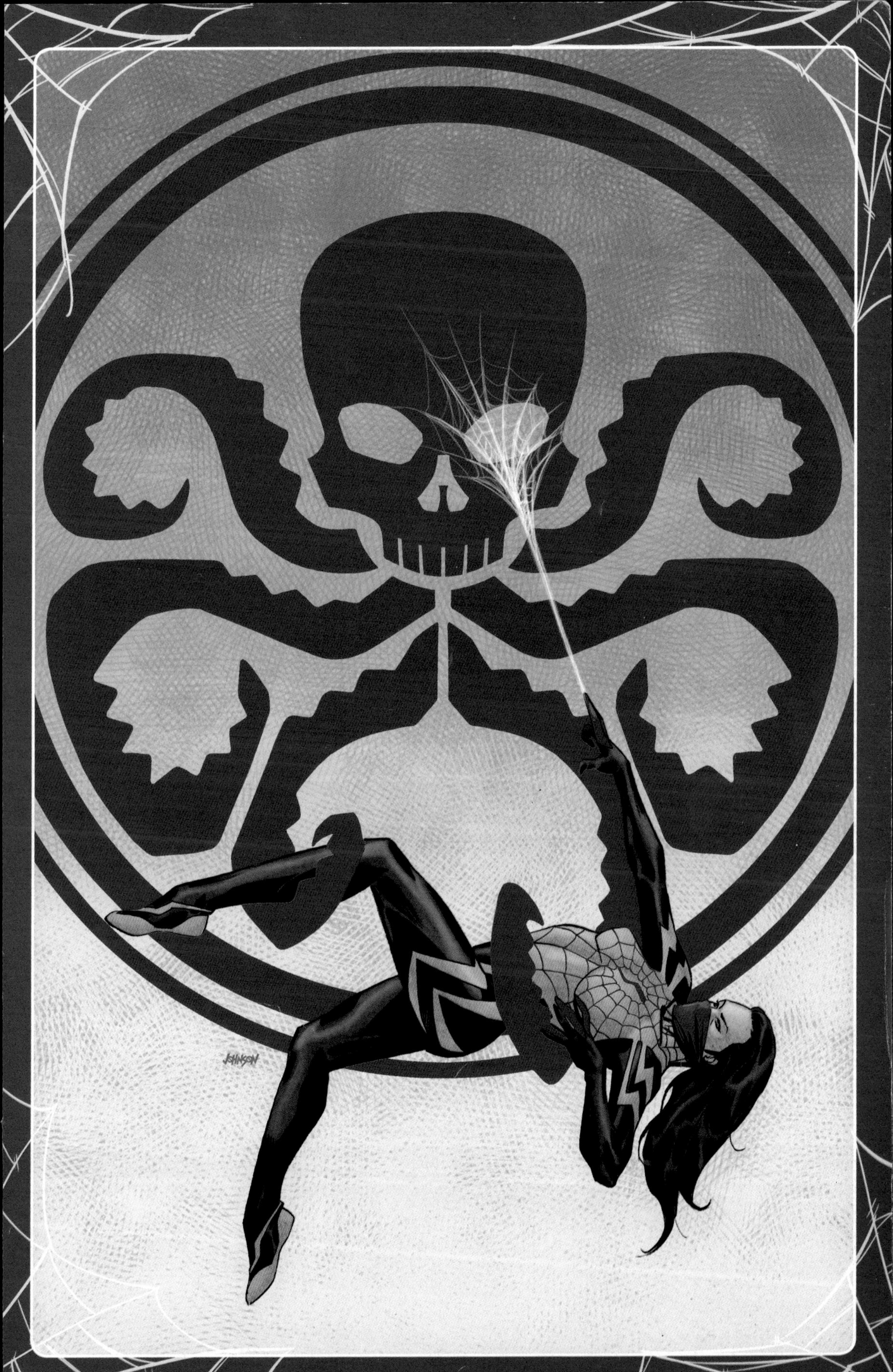
JOHNSON

2

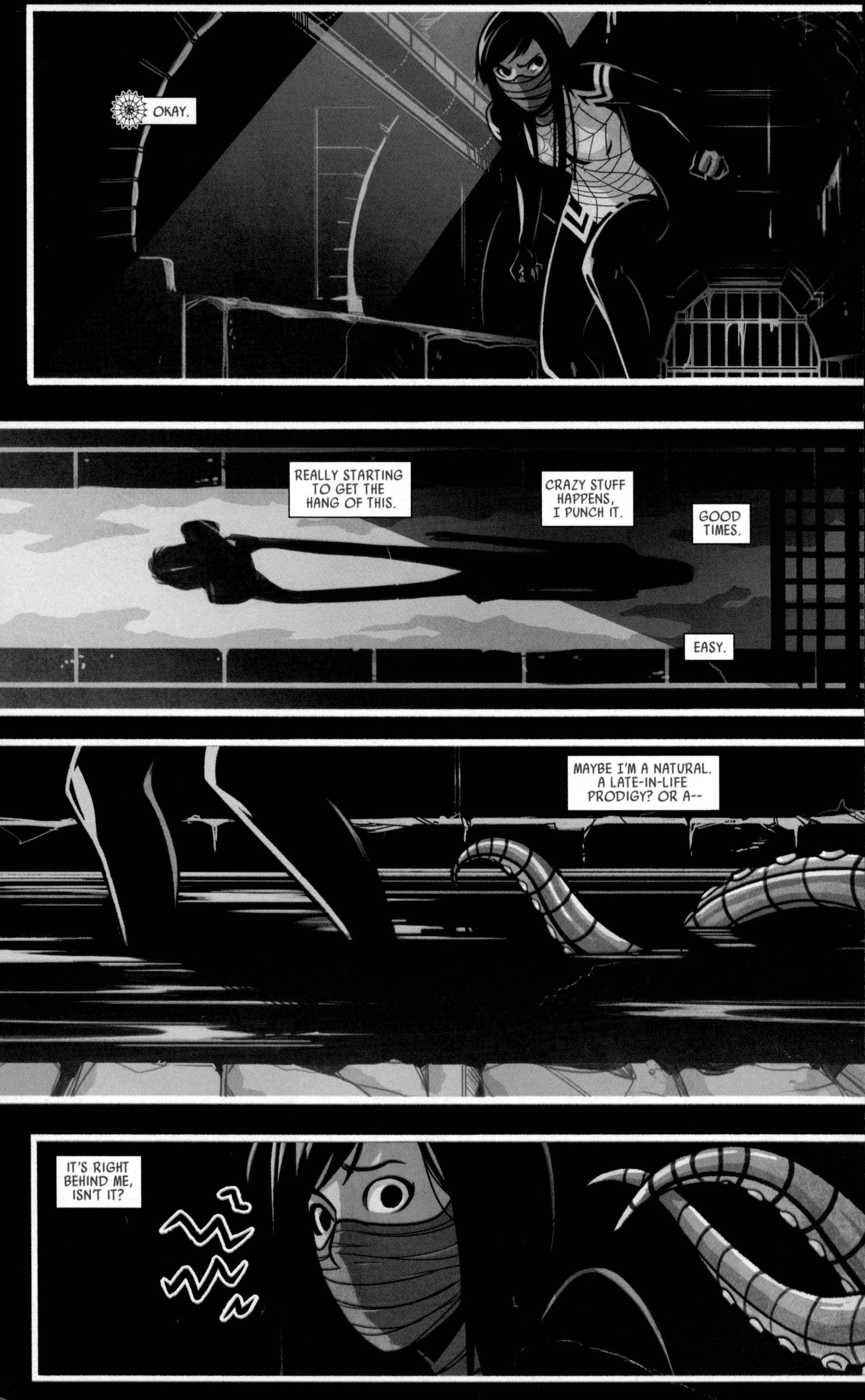
OKAY.
REALLY STARTING TO GET THE HANG OF THIS.
CRAZY STUFF HAPPENS, I PUNCH IT.
GOOD TIMES.
EASY.
MAYBE I'M A NATURAL. A LATE-IN-LIFE PRODIGY? OR A--
IT'S RIGHT BEHIND ME, ISN'T IT?

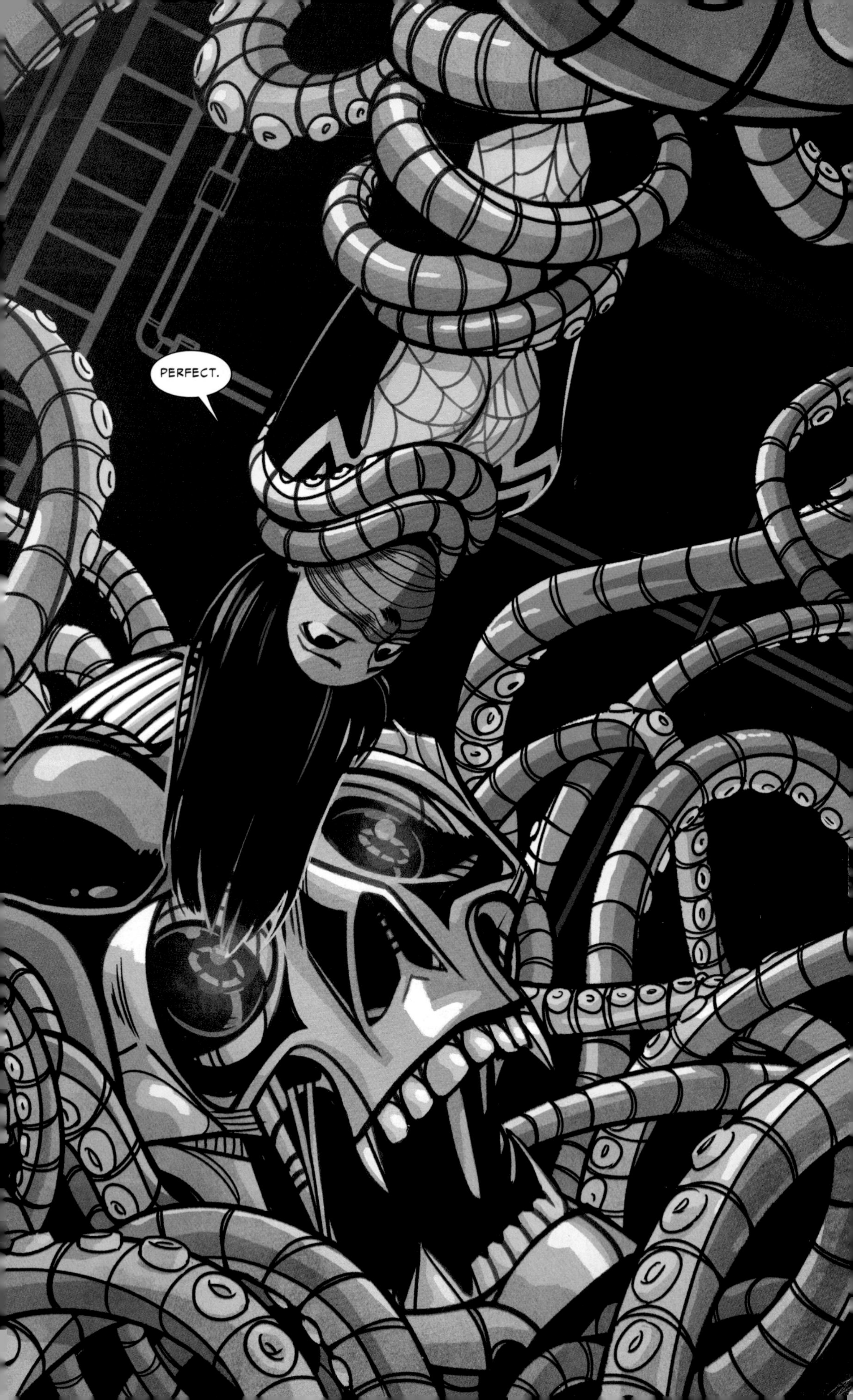
PERFECT.

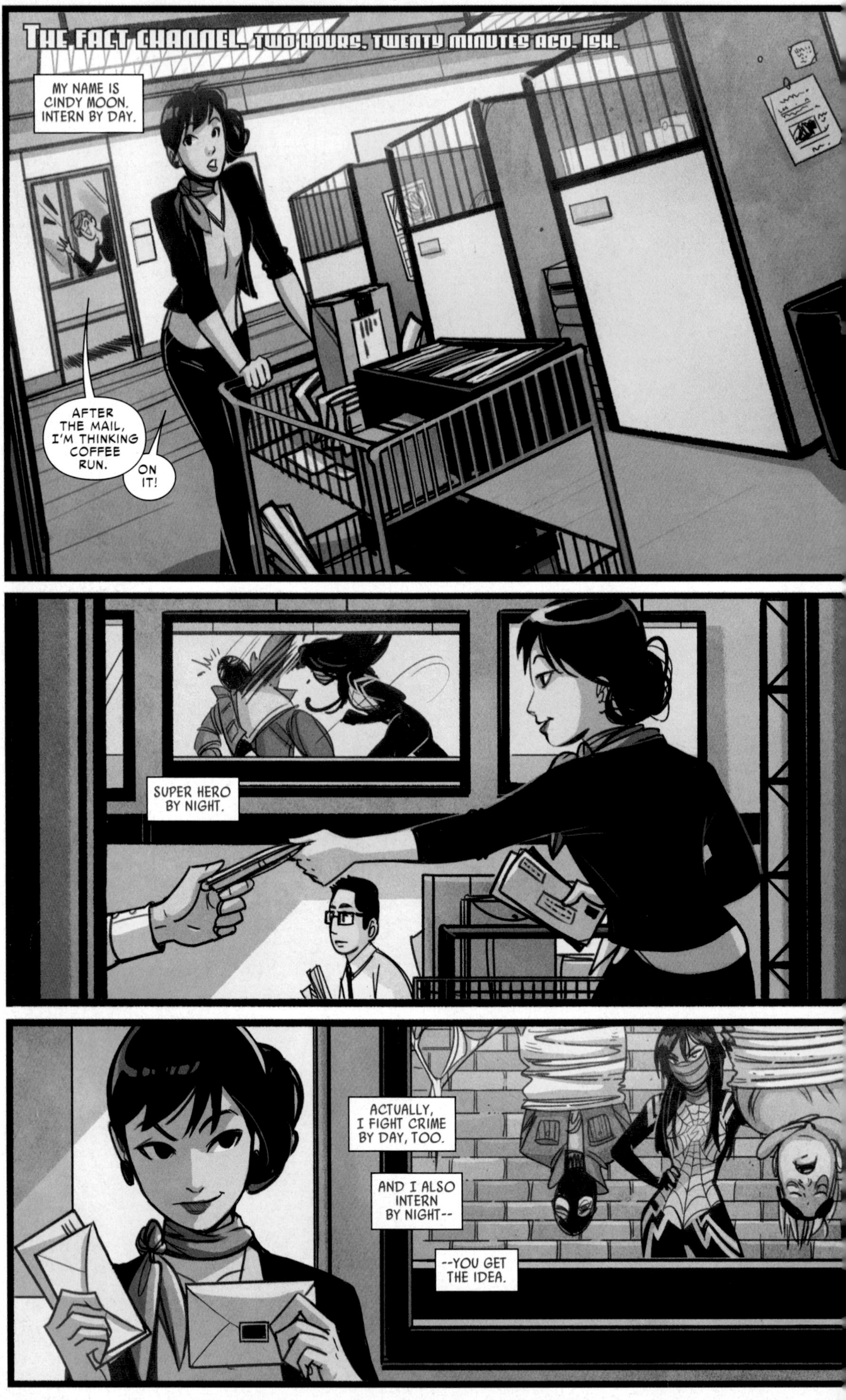

THE FACT CHANNEL. TWO HOURS, TWENTY MINUTES AGO. ISH.
MY NAME IS CINDY MOON. INTERN BY DAY.
AFTER THE MAIL, I'M THINKING COFFEE RUN.
ON IT!
SUPER HERO BY NIGHT.
ACTUALLY, I FIGHT CRIME BY DAY, TOO.
AND I ALSO INTERN BY NIGHT--
--YOU GET THE IDEA.

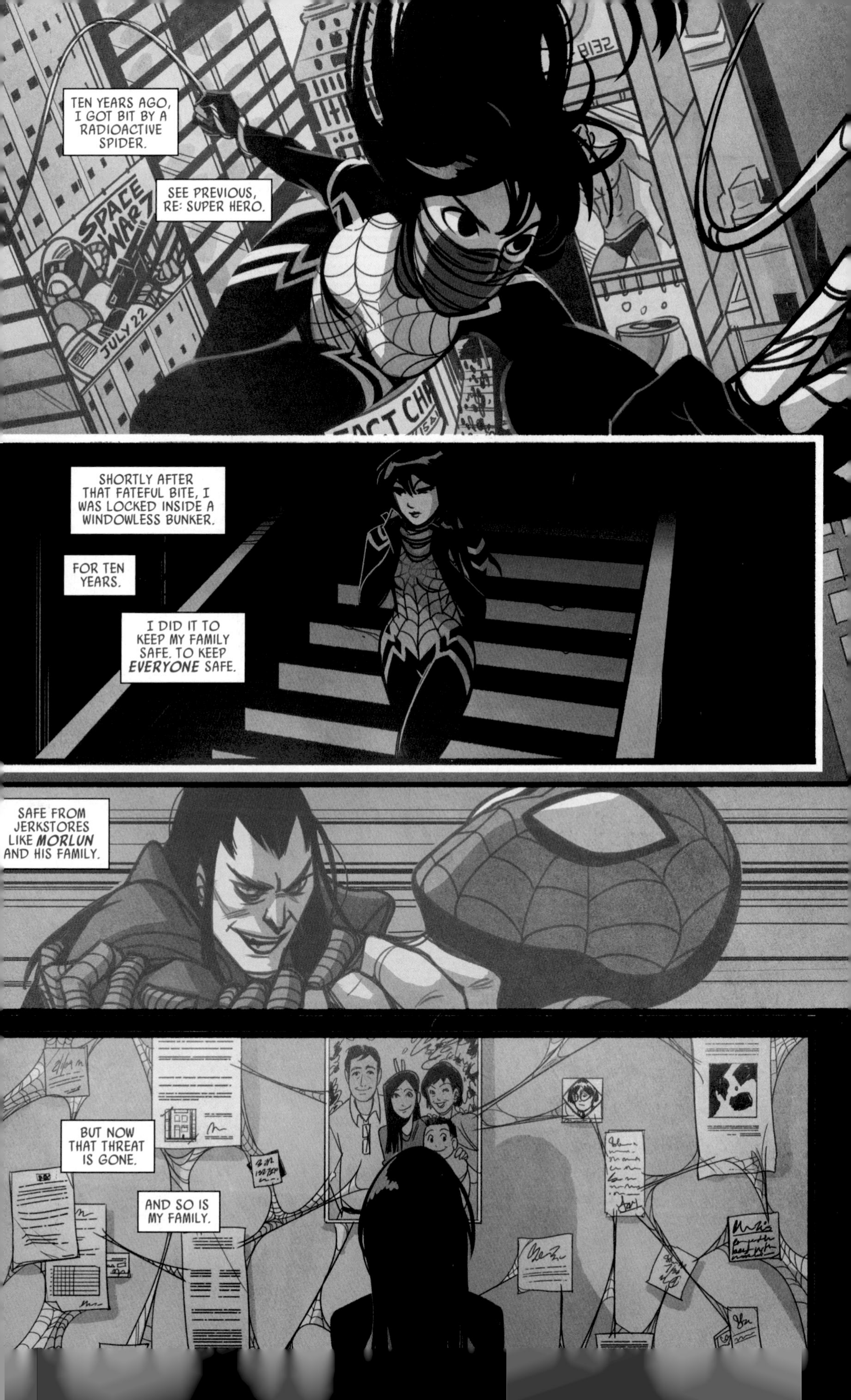

TEN YEARS AGO, I GOT BIT BY A RADIOACTIVE SPIDER.
SEE PREVIOUS, RE: SUPER HERO.
SPACE WAR 7
JULY 22
SHORTLY AFTER THAT FATEFUL BITE, I WAS LOCKED INSIDE A WINDOWLESS BUNKER.
FOR TEN YEARS.
I DID IT TO KEEP MY FAMILY SAFE. TO KEEP *EVERYONE* SAFE.
SAFE FROM JERKSTORES LIKE *MORLUN* AND HIS FAMILY.
BUT NOW THAT THREAT IS GONE.
AND SO IS MY FAMILY.

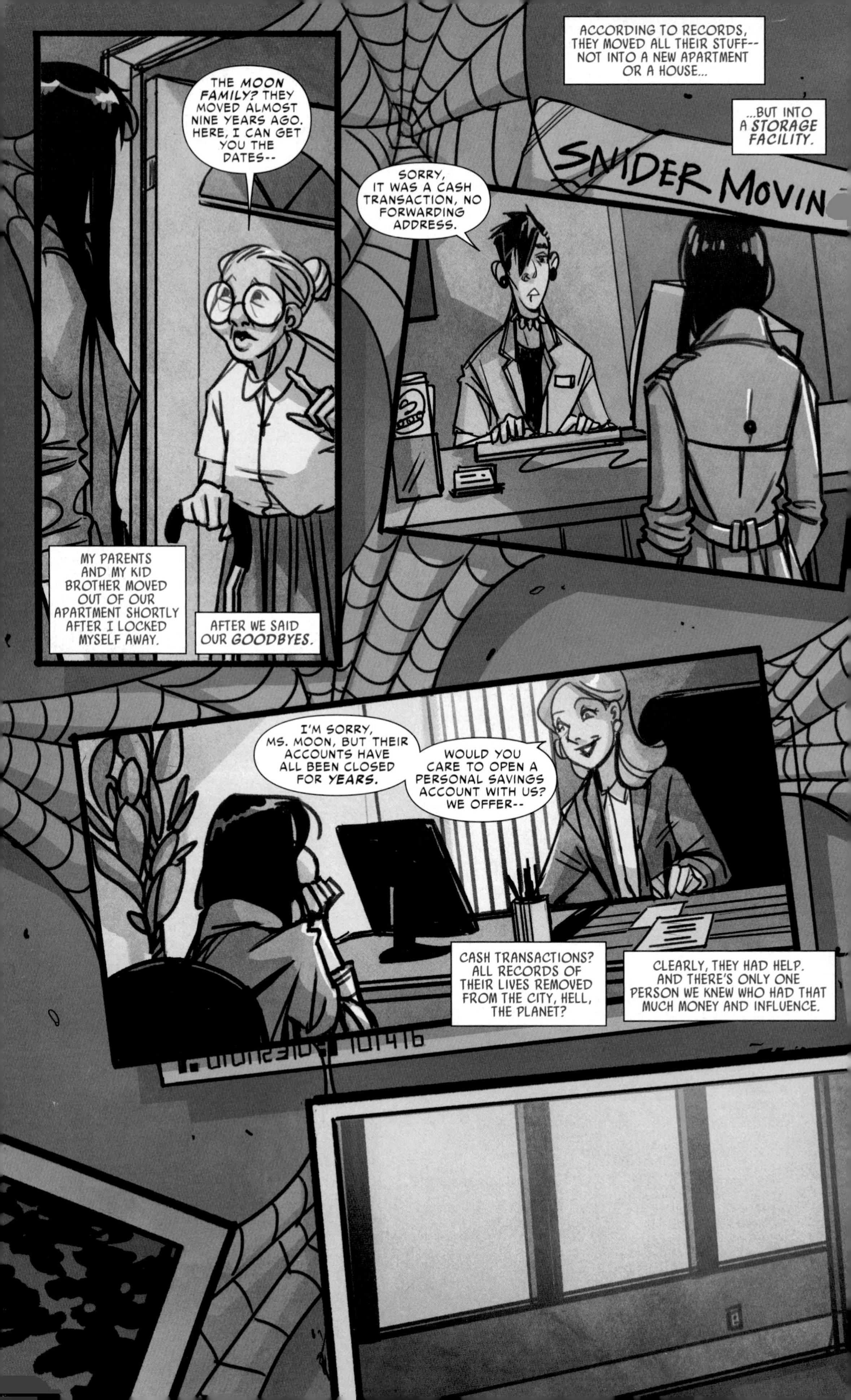

THE MOON FAMILY? THEY MOVED ALMOST NINE YEARS AGO. HERE, I CAN GET YOU THE DATES--
MY PARENTS AND MY KID BROTHER MOVED OUT OF OUR APARTMENT SHORTLY AFTER I LOCKED MYSELF AWAY.
AFTER WE SAID OUR GOODBYES.
ACCORDING TO RECORDS, THEY MOVED ALL THEIR STUFF-- NOT INTO A NEW APARTMENT OR A HOUSE...
...BUT INTO A STORAGE FACILITY.
SNIDER MOVIN
SORRY, IT WAS A CASH TRANSACTION, NO FORWARDING ADDRESS.
I'M SORRY, MS. MOON, BUT THEIR ACCOUNTS HAVE ALL BEEN CLOSED FOR YEARS.
WOULD YOU CARE TO OPEN A PERSONAL SAVINGS ACCOUNT WITH US? WE OFFER--
CASH TRANSACTIONS? ALL RECORDS OF THEIR LIVES REMOVED FROM THE CITY, HELL, THE PLANET?
CLEARLY, THEY HAD HELP. AND THERE'S ONLY ONE PERSON WE KNEW WHO HAD THAT MUCH MONEY AND INFLUENCE.

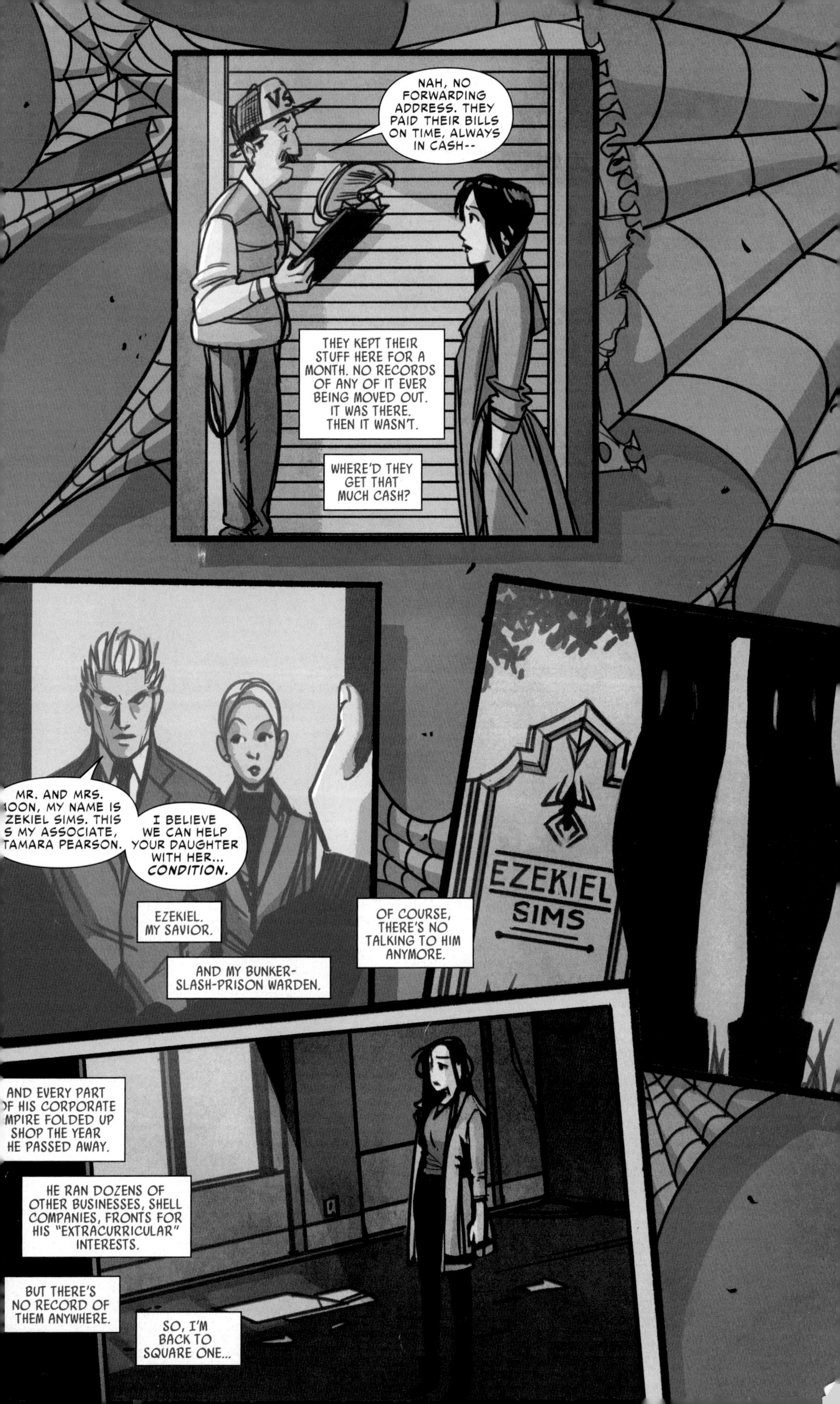

NAH, NO FORWARDING ADDRESS. THEY PAID THEIR BILLS ON TIME, ALWAYS IN CASH--
THEY KEPT THEIR STUFF HERE FOR A MONTH. NO RECORDS OF ANY OF IT EVER BEING MOVED OUT. IT WAS THERE. THEN IT WASN'T.
WHERE'D THEY GET THAT MUCH CASH?
MR. AND MRS. [cut off]OON, MY NAME IS [cut off]ZEKIEL SIMS. THIS [cut off]S MY ASSOCIATE, TAMARA PEARSON.
I BELIEVE WE CAN HELP YOUR DAUGHTER WITH HER... CONDITION.
EZEKIEL. MY SAVIOR.
AND MY BUNKER-SLASH-PRISON WARDEN.
OF COURSE, THERE'S NO TALKING TO HIM ANYMORE.
EZEKIEL SIMS
AND EVERY PART [cut off]F HIS CORPORATE [cut off]MPIRE FOLDED UP SHOP THE YEAR HE PASSED AWAY.
HE RAN DOZENS OF OTHER BUSINESSES, SHELL COMPANIES, FRONTS FOR HIS "EXTRACURRICULAR" INTERESTS.
BUT THERE'S NO RECORD OF THEM ANYWHERE.
SO, I'M BACK TO SQUARE ONE...

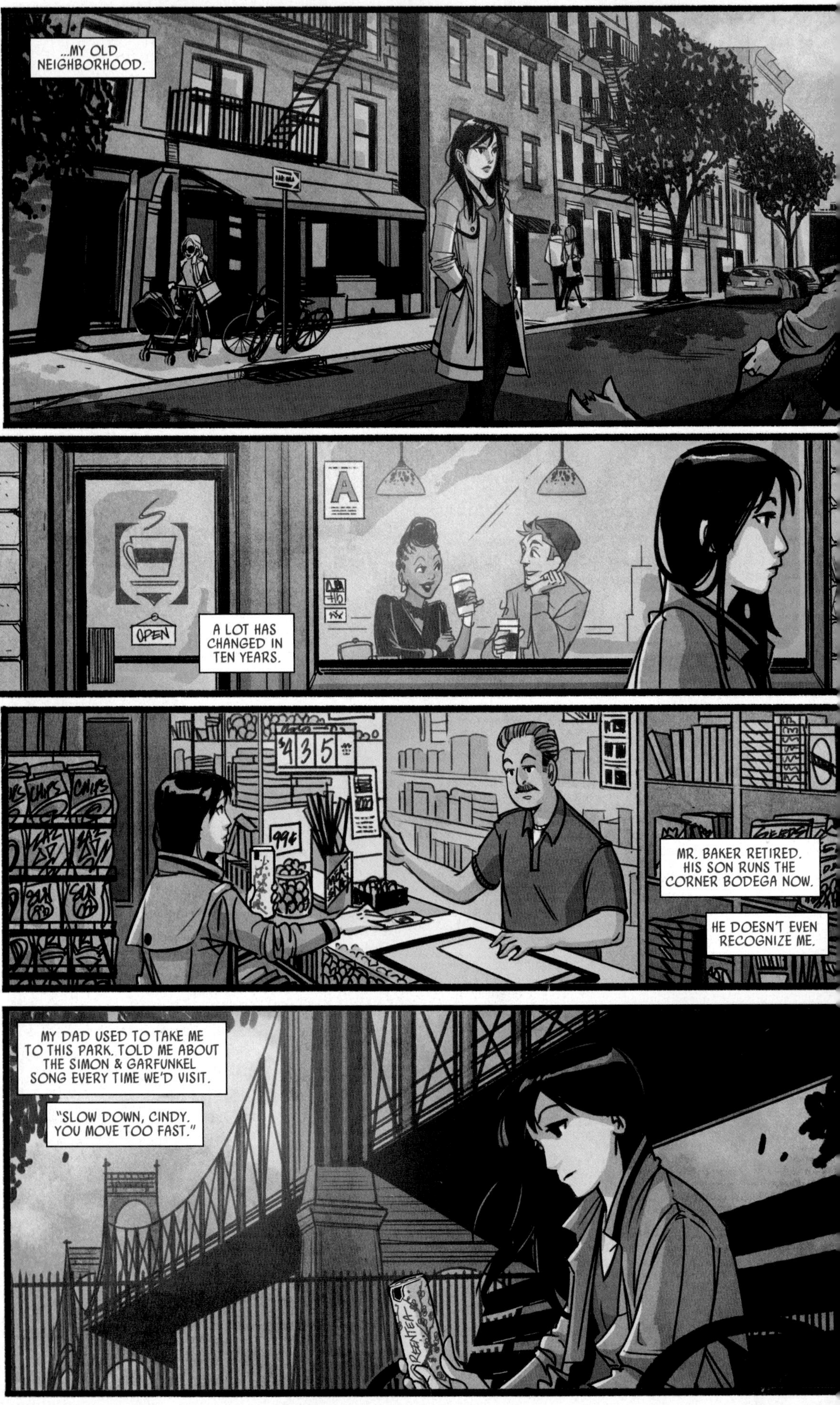

...MY OLD NEIGHBORHOOD.
OPEN
A LOT HAS CHANGED IN TEN YEARS.
MR. BAKER RETIRED. HIS SON RUNS THE CORNER BODEGA NOW.
HE DOESN'T EVEN RECOGNIZE ME.
MY DAD USED TO TAKE ME TO THIS PARK. TOLD ME ABOUT THE SIMON & GARFUNKEL SONG EVERY TIME WE'D VISIT.
"SLOW DOWN, CINDY. YOU MOVE TOO FAST."

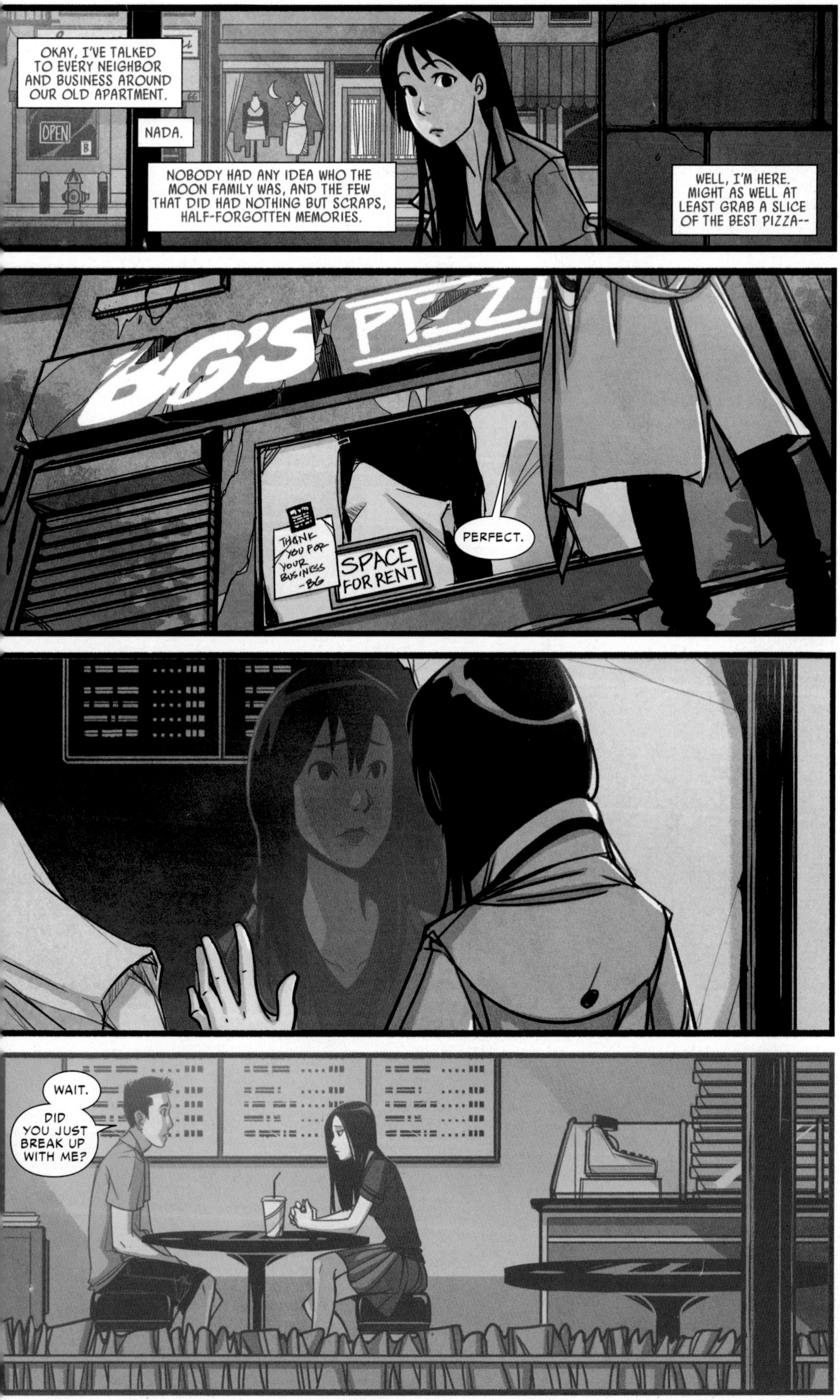
OKAY, I'VE TALKED TO EVERY NEIGHBOR AND BUSINESS AROUND OUR OLD APARTMENT.
OPEN
NADA.
NOBODY HAD ANY IDEA WHO THE MOON FAMILY WAS, AND THE FEW THAT DID HAD NOTHING BUT SCRAPS, HALF-FORGOTTEN MEMORIES.
WELL, I'M HERE. MIGHT AS WELL AT LEAST GRAB A SLICE OF THE BEST PIZZA--
BG'S PIZZ
THANK YOU FOR YOUR BUSINESS -BG
SPACE FOR RENT
PERFECT.
WAIT.
DID YOU JUST BREAK UP WITH ME?

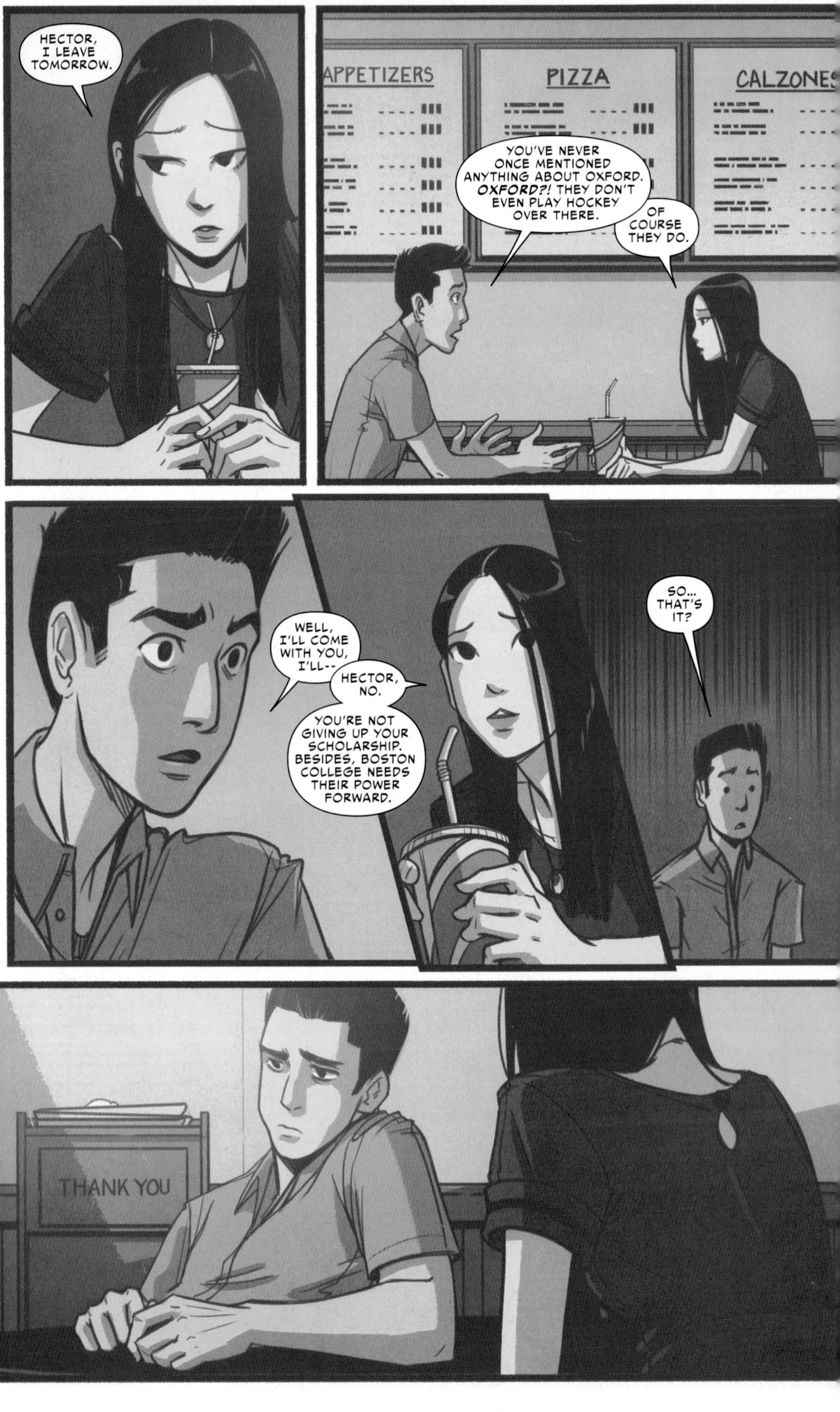
HECTOR, I LEAVE TOMORROW.
APPETIZERS
PIZZA
CALZONES
YOU'VE NEVER ONCE MENTIONED ANYTHING ABOUT OXFORD. OXFORD?! THEY DON'T EVEN PLAY HOCKEY OVER THERE.
OF COURSE THEY DO.
WELL, I'LL COME WITH YOU, I'LL--
HECTOR, NO.
YOU'RE NOT GIVING UP YOUR SCHOLARSHIP. BESIDES, BOSTON COLLEGE NEEDS THEIR POWER FORWARD.
SO... THAT'S IT?
THANK YOU

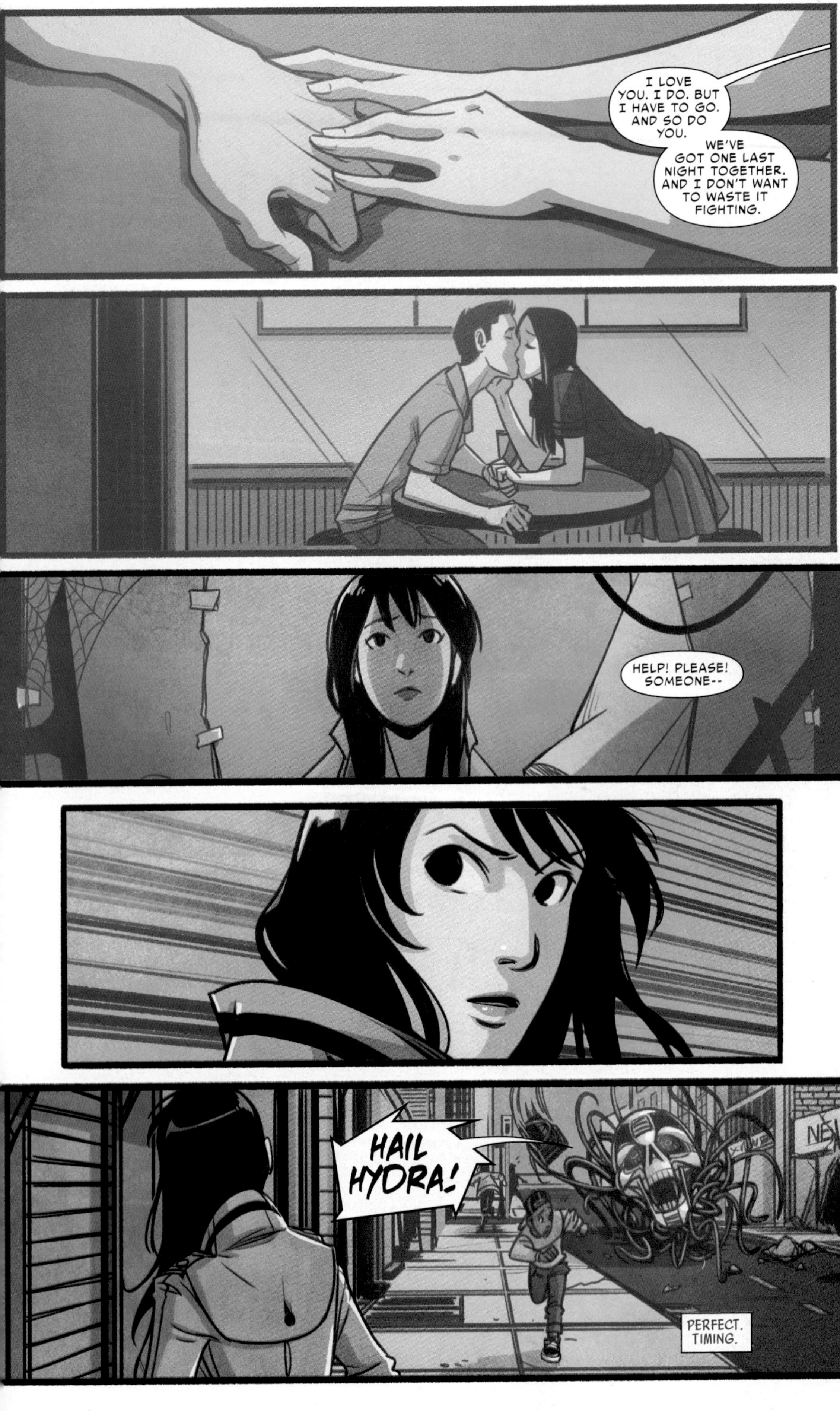
I LOVE YOU. I DO. BUT I HAVE TO GO. AND SO DO YOU.
WE'VE GOT ONE LAST NIGHT TOGETHER. AND I DON'T WANT TO WASTE IT FIGHTING.
HELP! PLEASE! SOMEONE--
HAIL HYDRA!
PERFECT. TIMING.

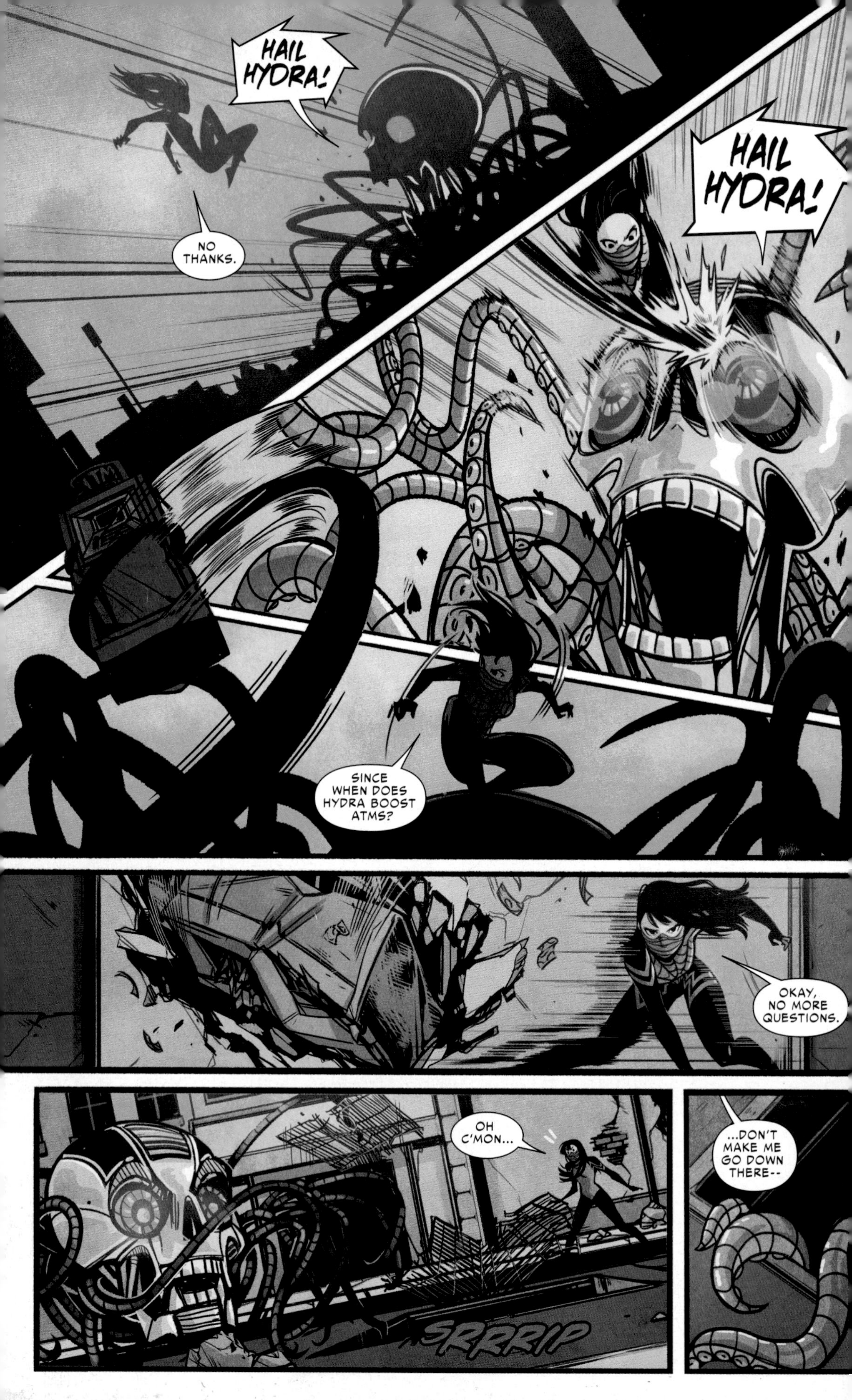
HAIL HYDRA!
NO THANKS.
HAIL HYDRA!
SINCE WHEN DOES HYDRA BOOST ATMS?
ATM
OKAY, NO MORE QUESTIONS.
OH C'MON...
...DON'T MAKE ME GO DOWN THERE--
SRRRIP

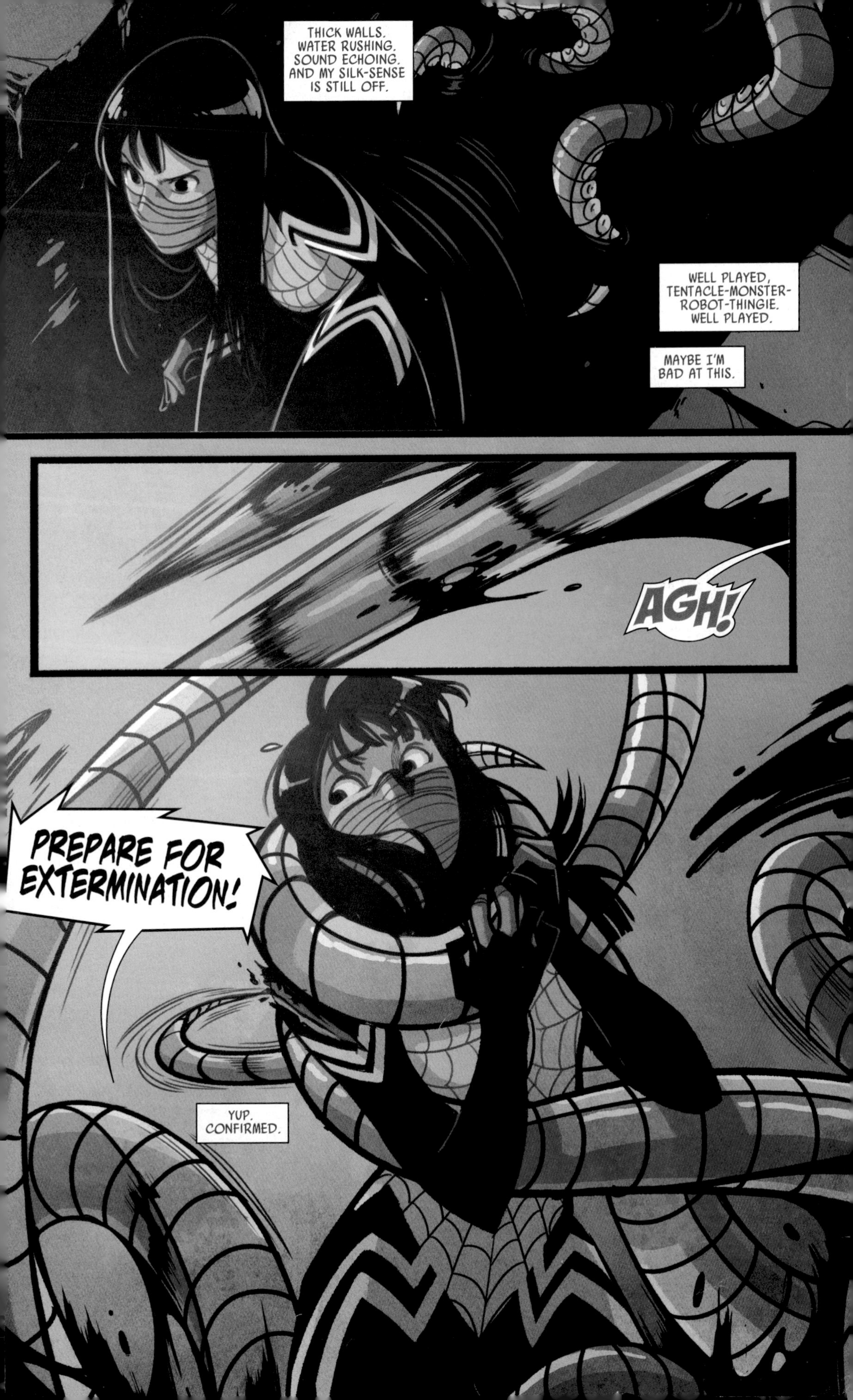
THICK WALLS. WATER RUSHING. SOUND ECHOING. AND MY SILK-SENSE IS STILL OFF.
WELL PLAYED, TENTACLE-MONSTER-ROBOT-THINGIE. WELL PLAYED.
MAYBE I'M BAD AT THIS.
AGH!
PREPARE FOR EXTERMINATION!
YUP. CONFIRMED.

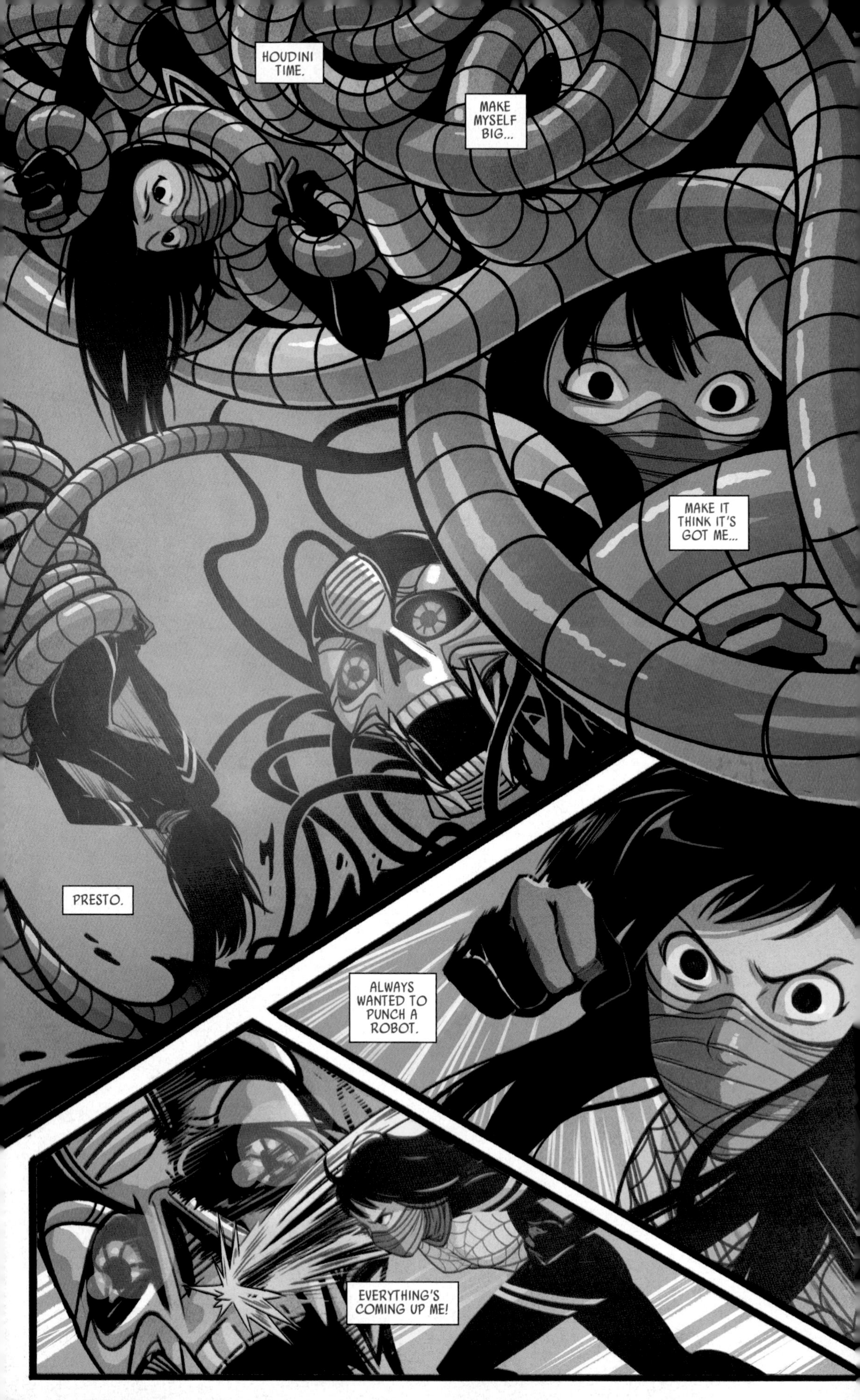

HOUDINI TIME.
MAKE MYSELF BIG...
MAKE IT THINK IT'S GOT ME...
PRESTO.
ALWAYS WANTED TO PUNCH A ROBOT.
EVERYTHING'S COMING UP ME!

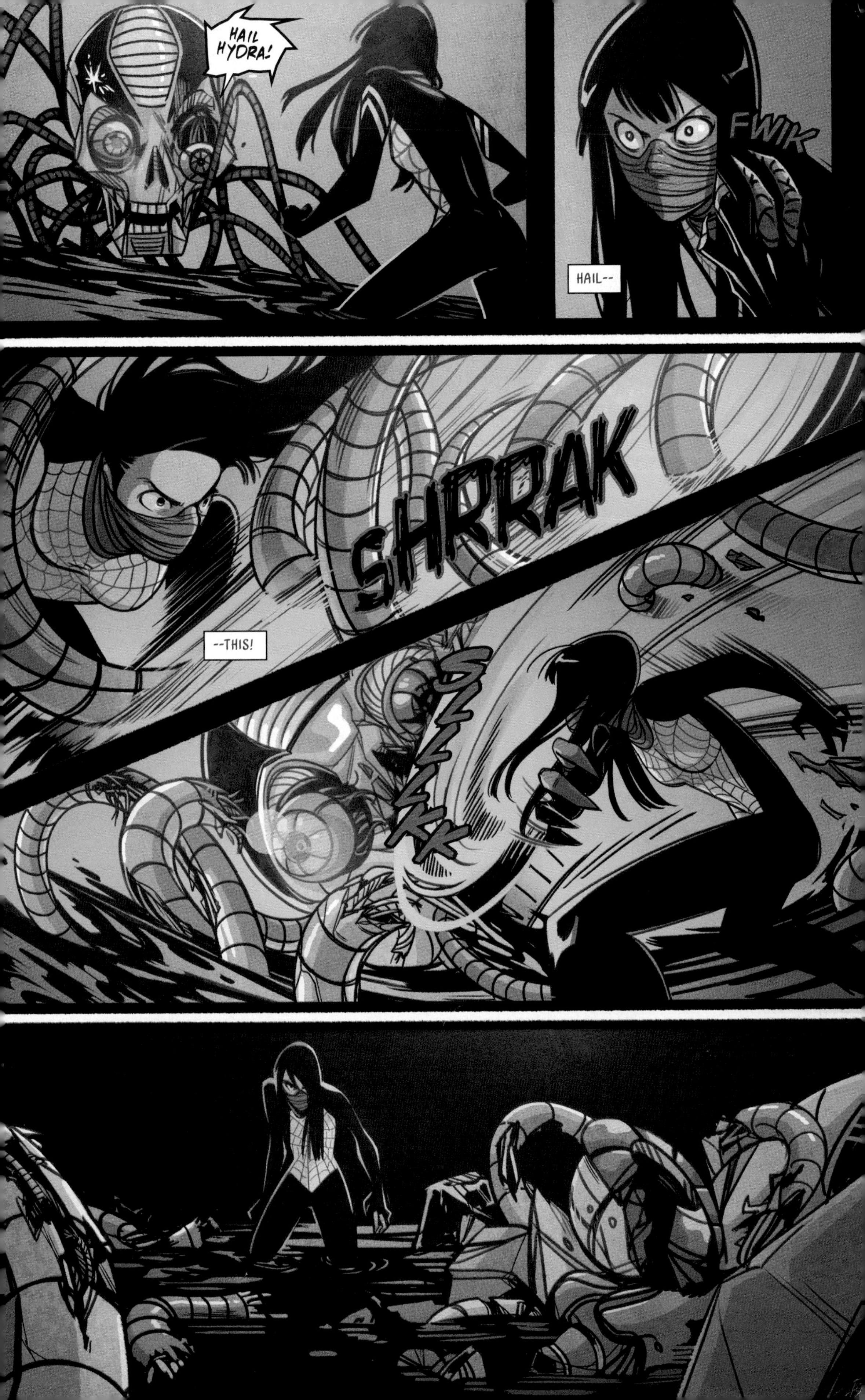
HAIL HYDRA!
HAIL--
FWIK
SHRRAK
--THIS!
SHLUKK

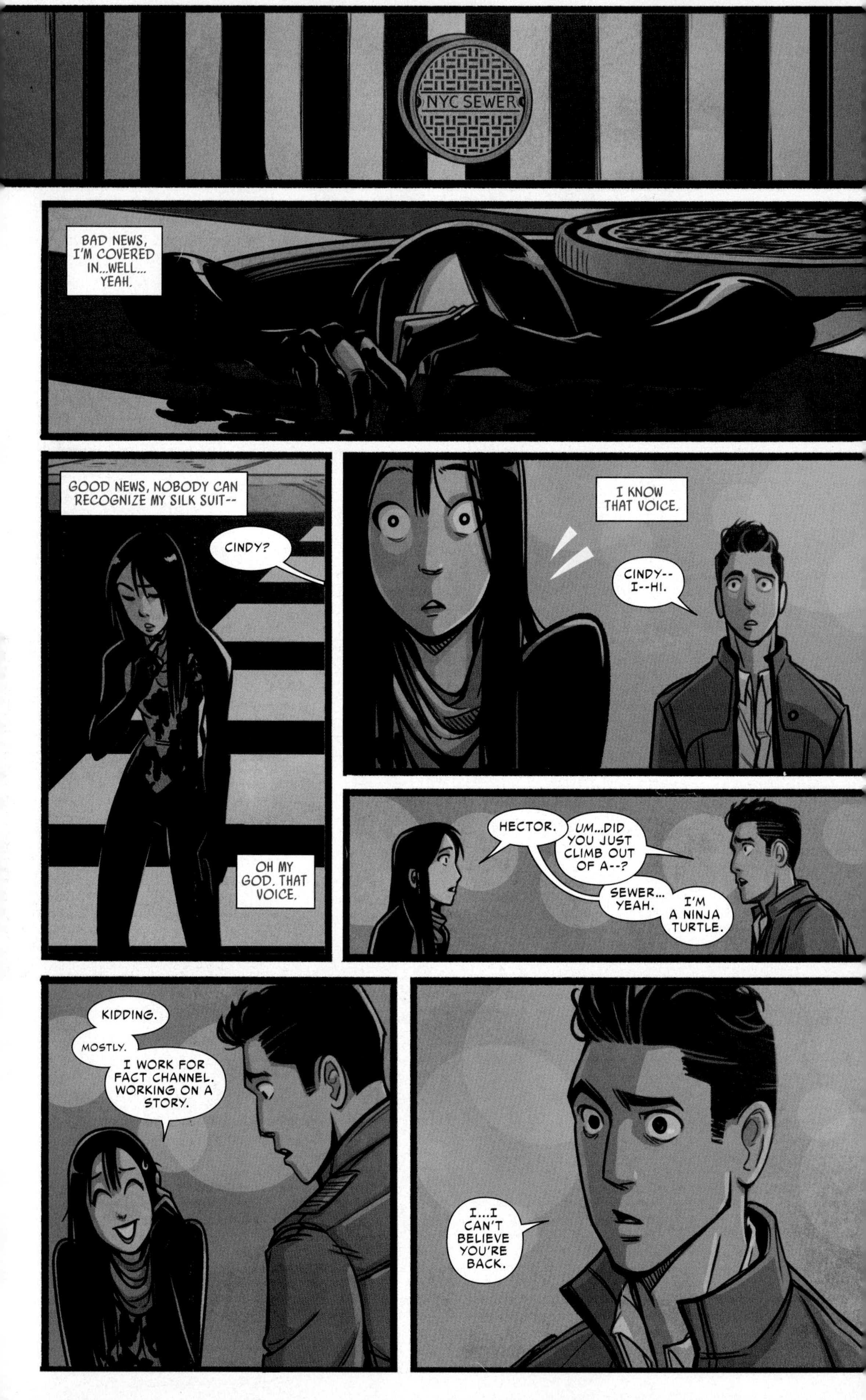
NYC SEWER
BAD NEWS, I'M COVERED IN...WELL... YEAH.
GOOD NEWS, NOBODY CAN RECOGNIZE MY SILK SUIT--
CINDY?
OH MY GOD. THAT VOICE.
I KNOW THAT VOICE.
CINDY-- I--HI.
HECTOR.
UM...DID YOU JUST CLIMB OUT OF A--?
SEWER... YEAH.
I'M A NINJA TURTLE.
KIDDING.
MOSTLY.
I WORK FOR FACT CHANNEL. WORKING ON A STORY.
I...I CAN'T BELIEVE YOU'RE BACK.

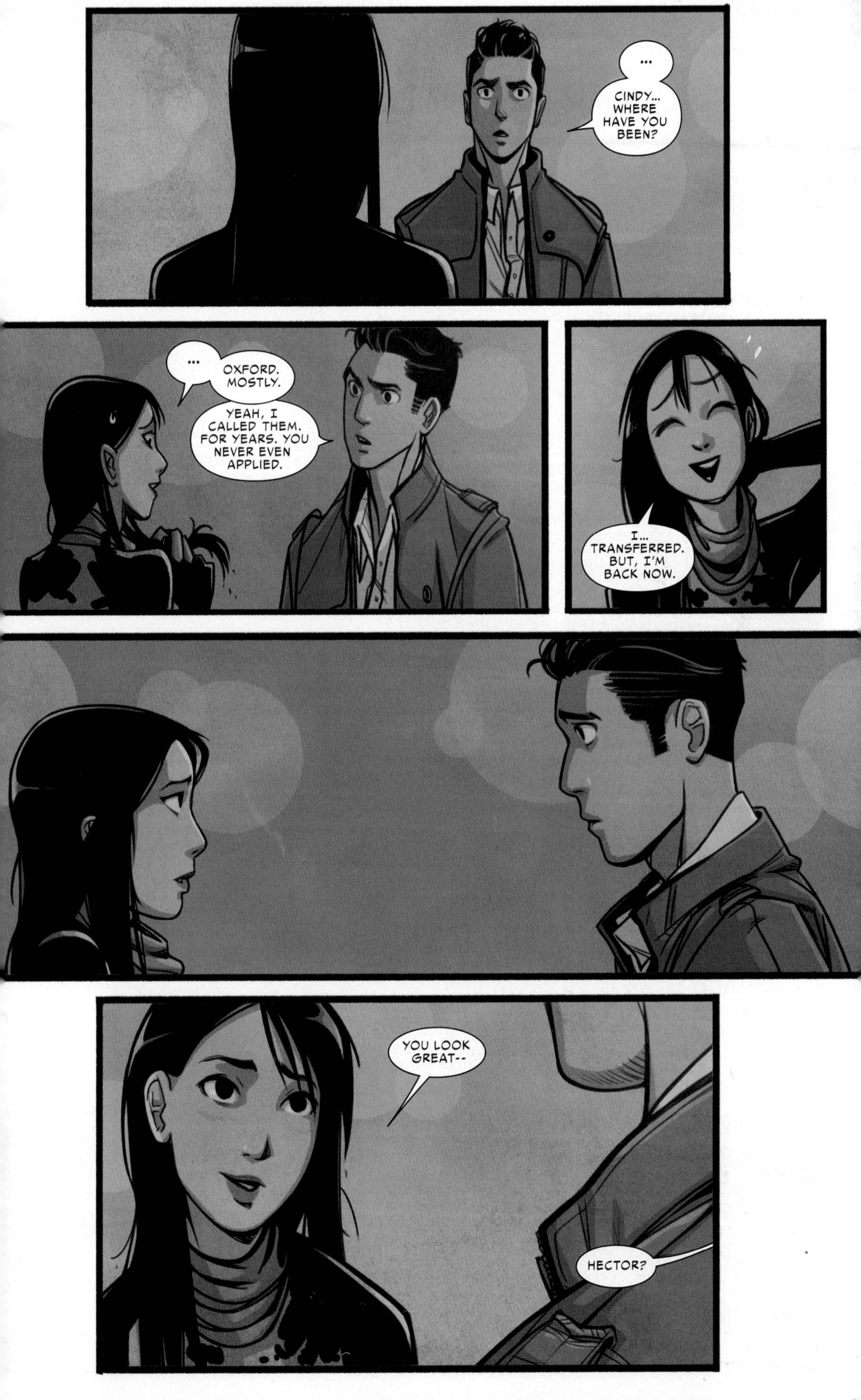
...
CINDY... WHERE HAVE YOU BEEN?
...
OXFORD. MOSTLY.
YEAH, I CALLED THEM. FOR YEARS. YOU NEVER EVEN APPLIED.
I... TRANSFERRED. BUT, I'M BACK NOW.
YOU LOOK GREAT--
HECTOR?

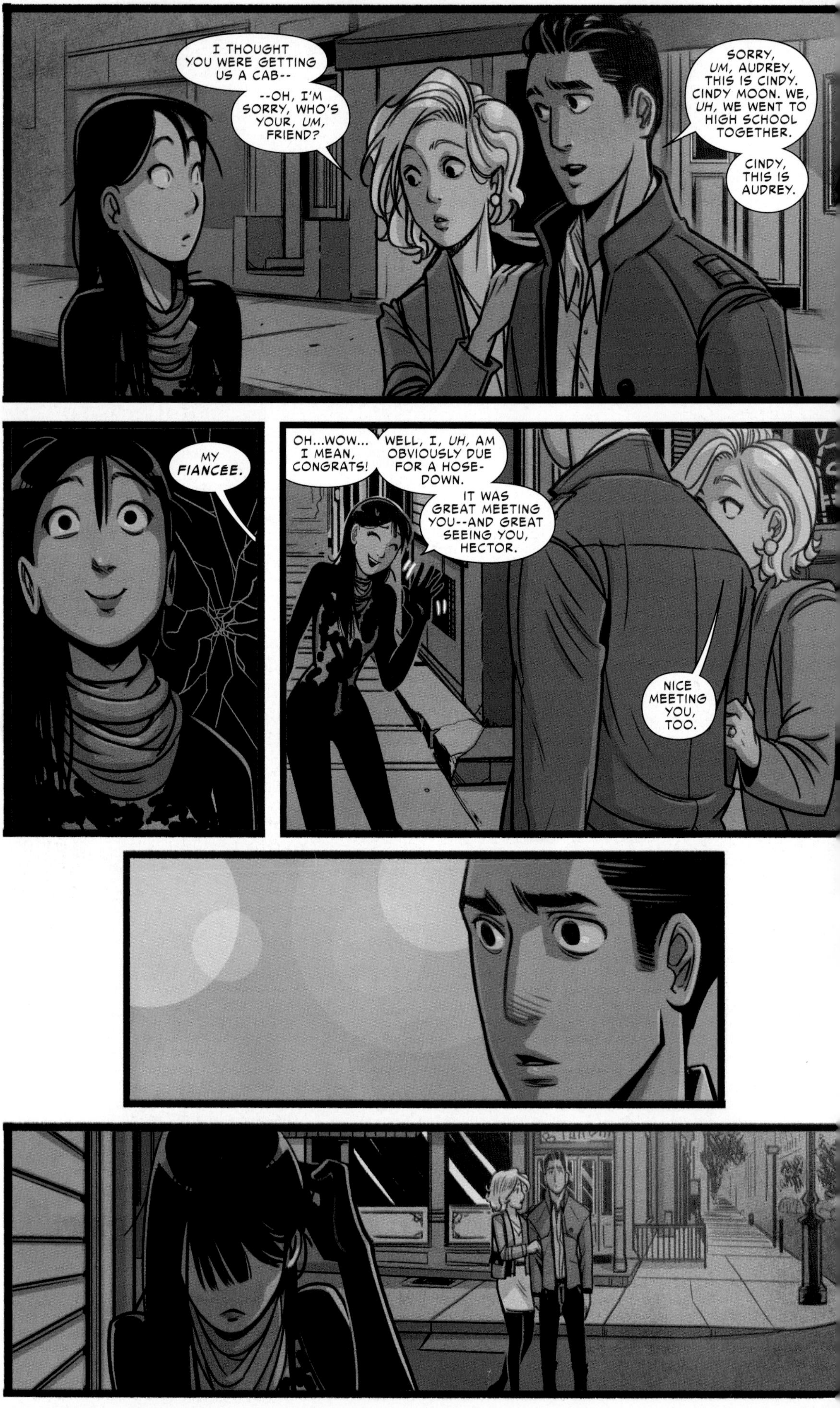
I THOUGHT YOU WERE GETTING US A CAB--
--OH, I'M SORRY, WHO'S YOUR, UM, FRIEND?
SORRY, UM, AUDREY, THIS IS CINDY. CINDY MOON. WE, UH, WE WENT TO HIGH SCHOOL TOGETHER.
CINDY, THIS IS AUDREY.
MY FIANCEE.
OH...WOW... I MEAN, CONGRATS!
WELL, I, UH, AM OBVIOUSLY DUE FOR A HOSE-DOWN.
IT WAS GREAT MEETING YOU--AND GREAT SEEING YOU, HECTOR.
NICE MEETING YOU, TOO.

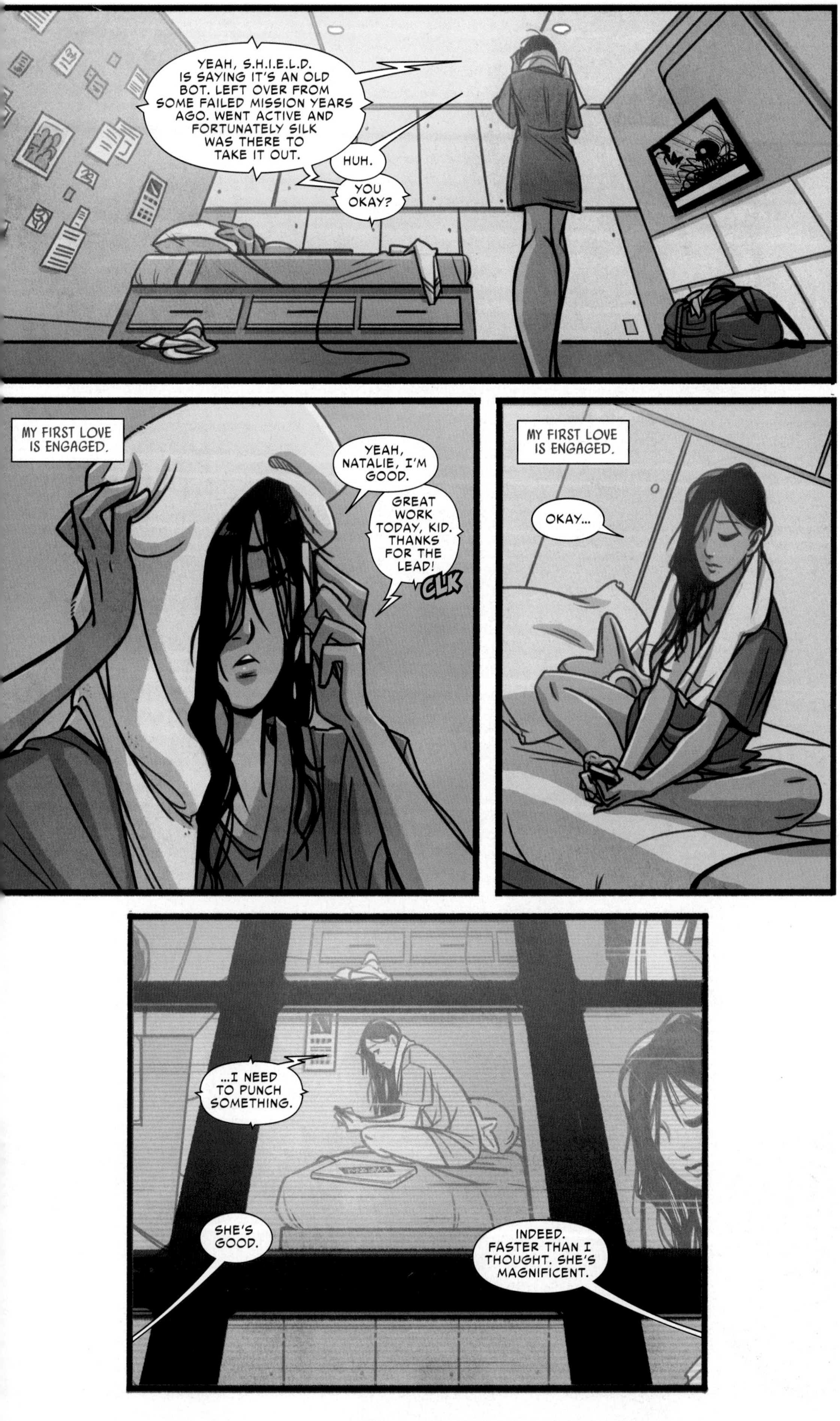
YEAH, S.H.I.E.L.D. IS SAYING IT'S AN OLD BOT. LEFT OVER FROM SOME FAILED MISSION YEARS AGO. WENT ACTIVE AND FORTUNATELY SILK WAS THERE TO TAKE IT OUT.
HUH.
YOU OKAY?
MY FIRST LOVE IS ENGAGED.
YEAH, NATALIE, I'M GOOD.
GREAT WORK TODAY, KID. THANKS FOR THE LEAD!
CLK
MY FIRST LOVE IS ENGAGED.
OKAY...
...I NEED TO PUNCH SOMETHING.
SHE'S GOOD.
INDEED. FASTER THAN I THOUGHT. SHE'S MAGNIFICENT.

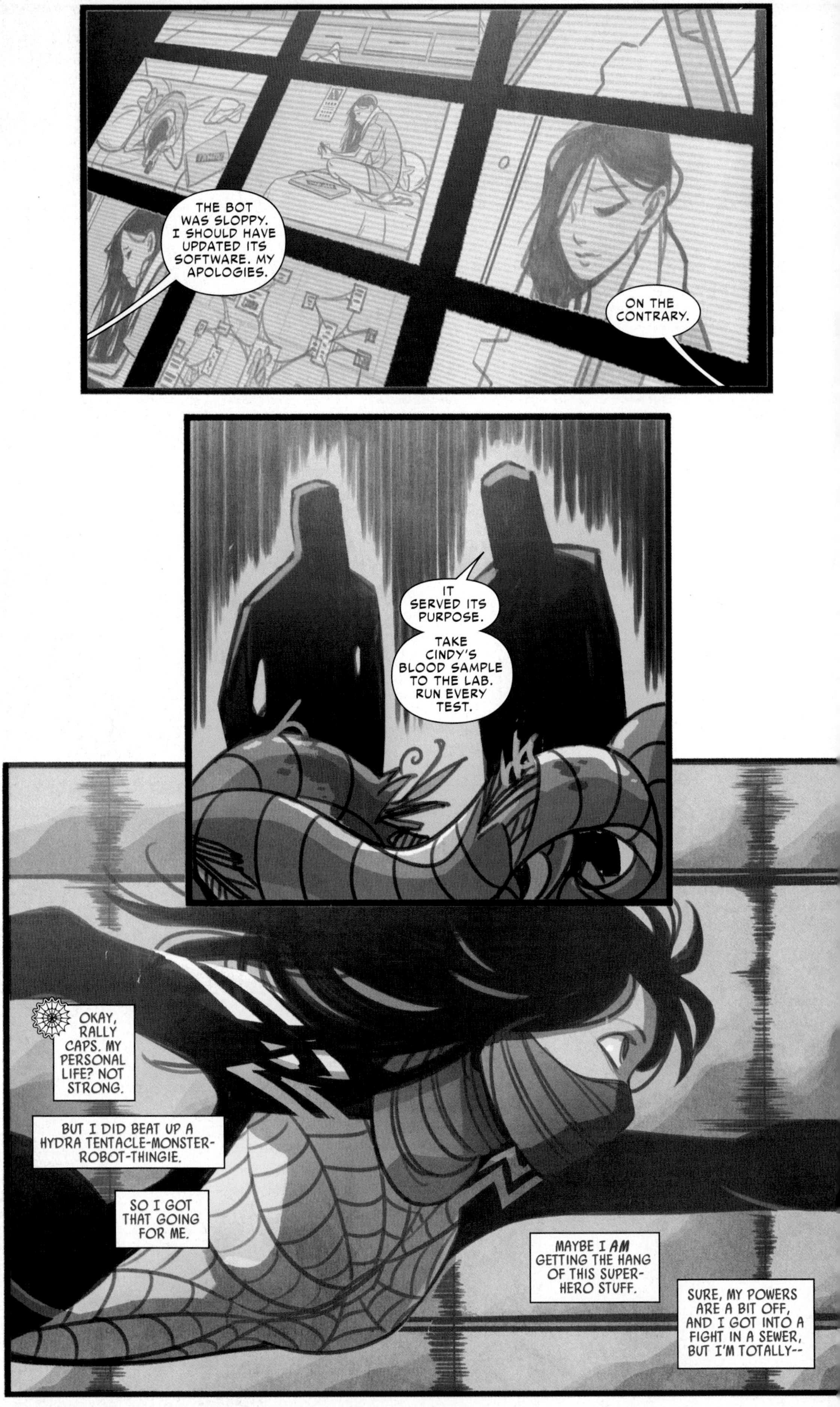

THE BOT WAS SLOPPY. I SHOULD HAVE UPDATED ITS SOFTWARE. MY APOLOGIES.
ON THE CONTRARY.
IT SERVED ITS PURPOSE.
TAKE CINDY'S BLOOD SAMPLE TO THE LAB. RUN EVERY TEST.
OKAY, RALLY CAPS. MY PERSONAL LIFE? NOT STRONG.
BUT I DID BEAT UP A HYDRA TENTACLE-MONSTER-ROBOT-THINGIE.
SO I GOT THAT GOING FOR ME.
MAYBE I AM GETTING THE HANG OF THIS SUPER-HERO STUFF.
SURE, MY POWERS ARE A BIT OFF, AND I GOT INTO A FIGHT IN A SEWER, BUT I'M TOTALLY--

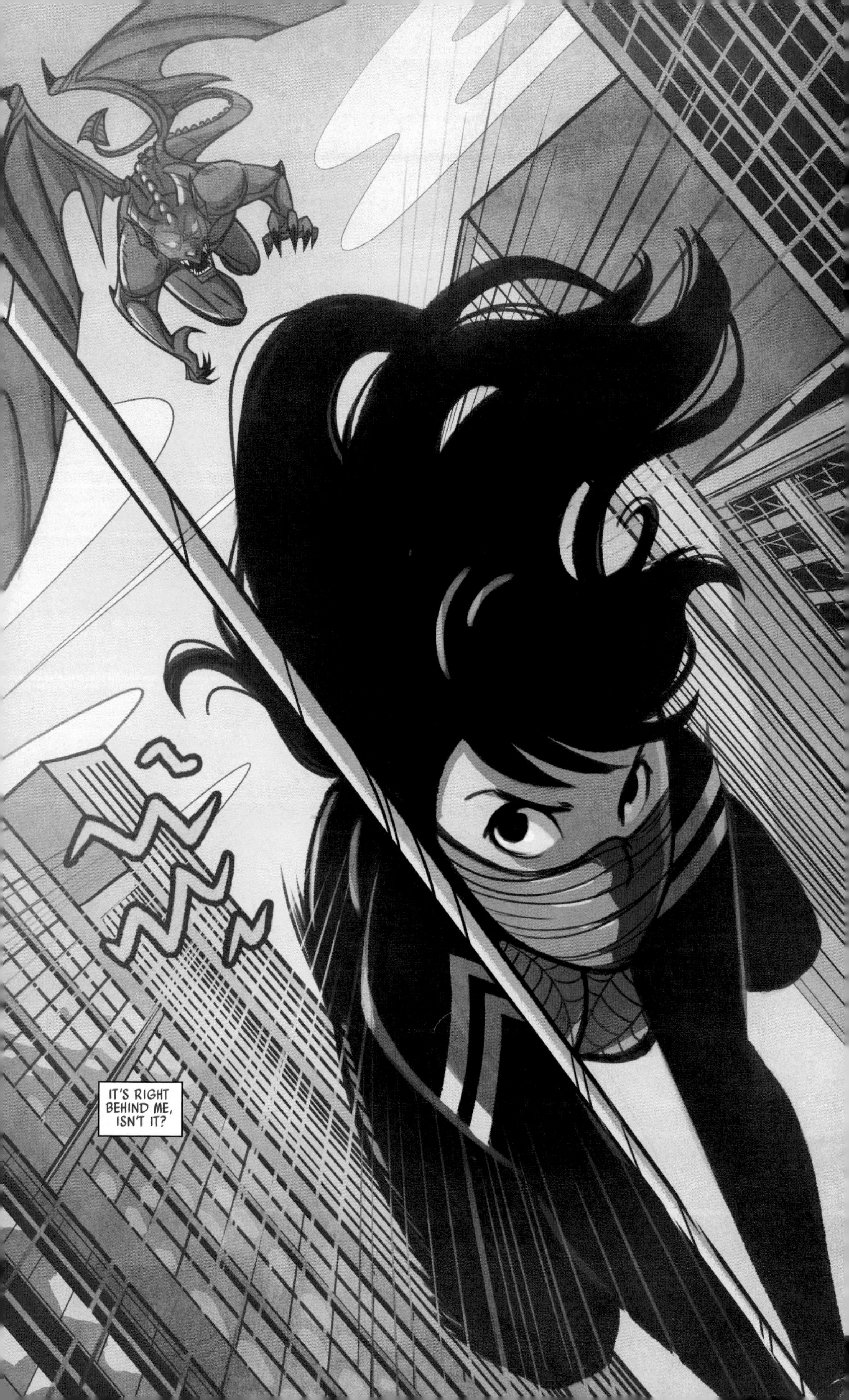
IT'S RIGHT BEHIND ME, ISN'T IT?

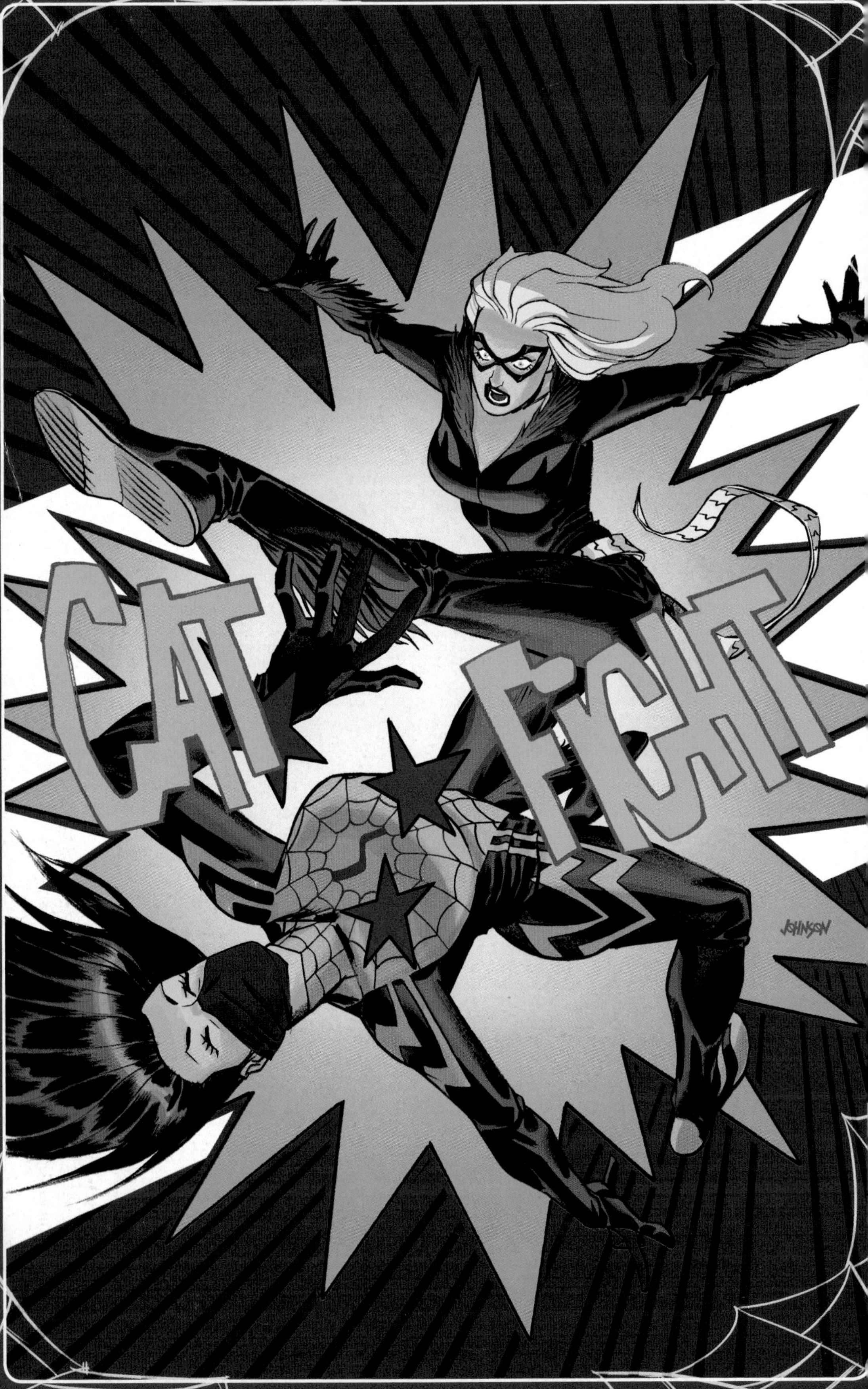
CAT FIGHT
JOHNSON

3

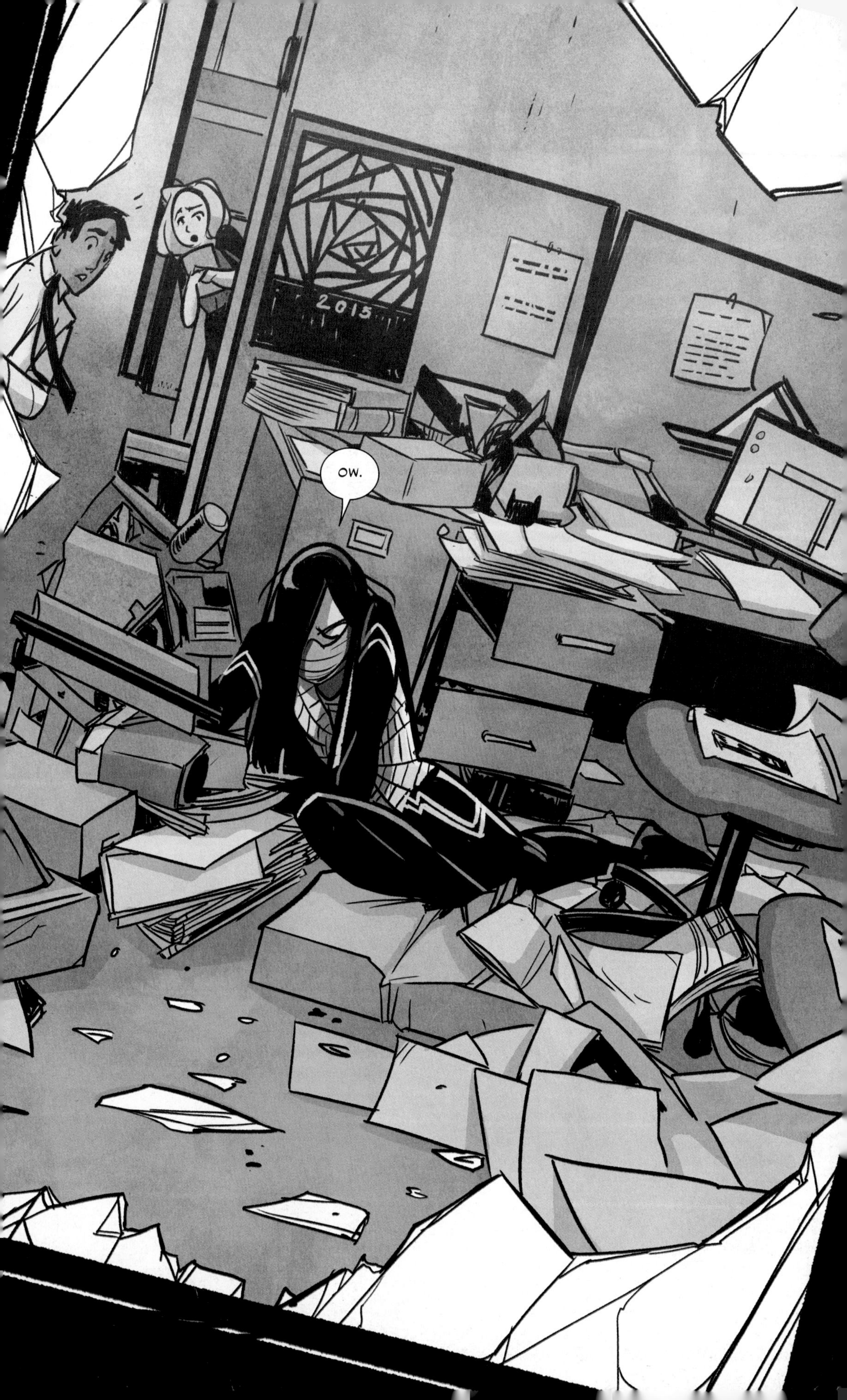
2015
OW.

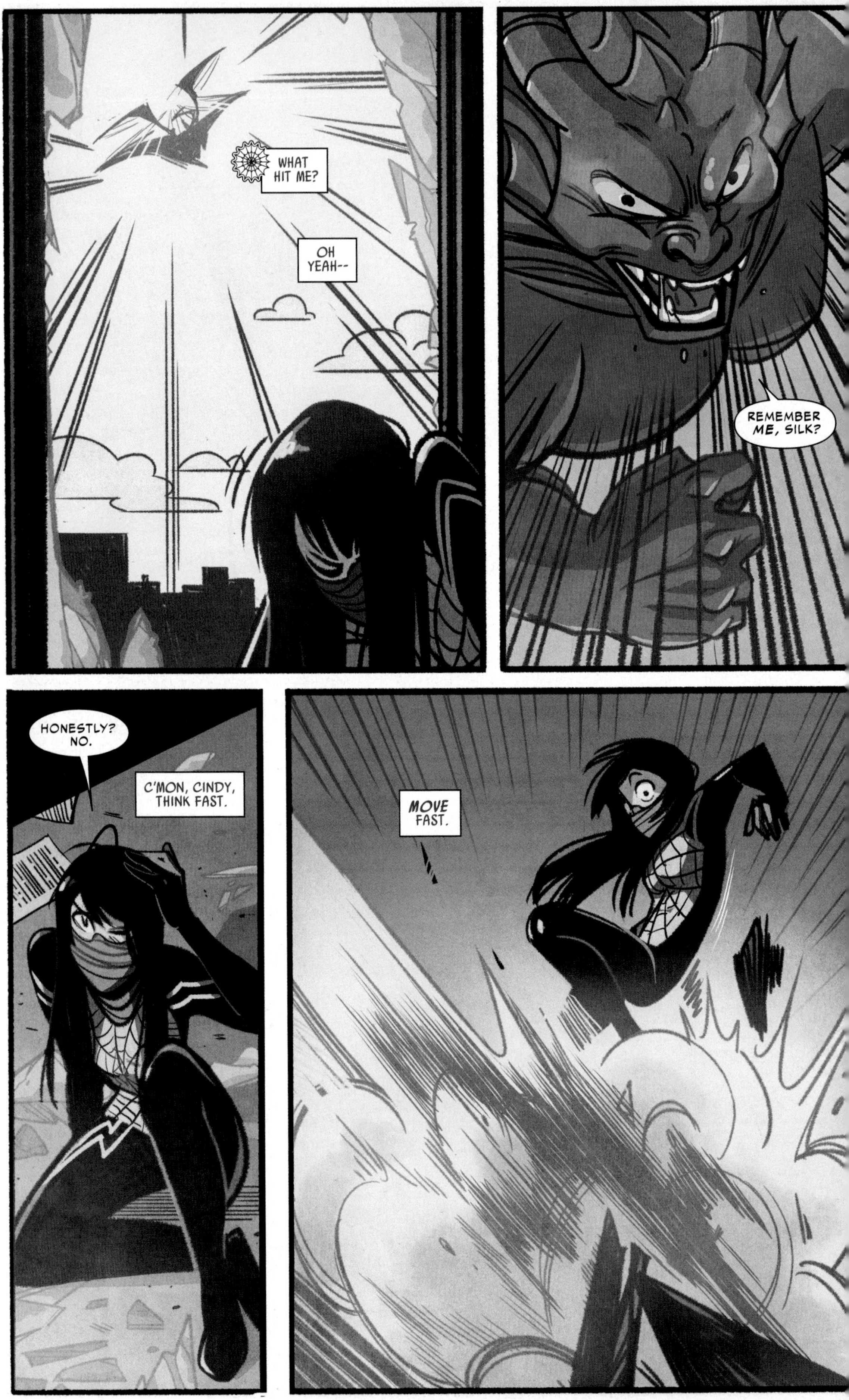
WHAT HIT ME?
OH YEAH--
REMEMBER ME, SILK?
HONESTLY? NO.
C'MON, CINDY, THINK FAST.
MOVE FAST.

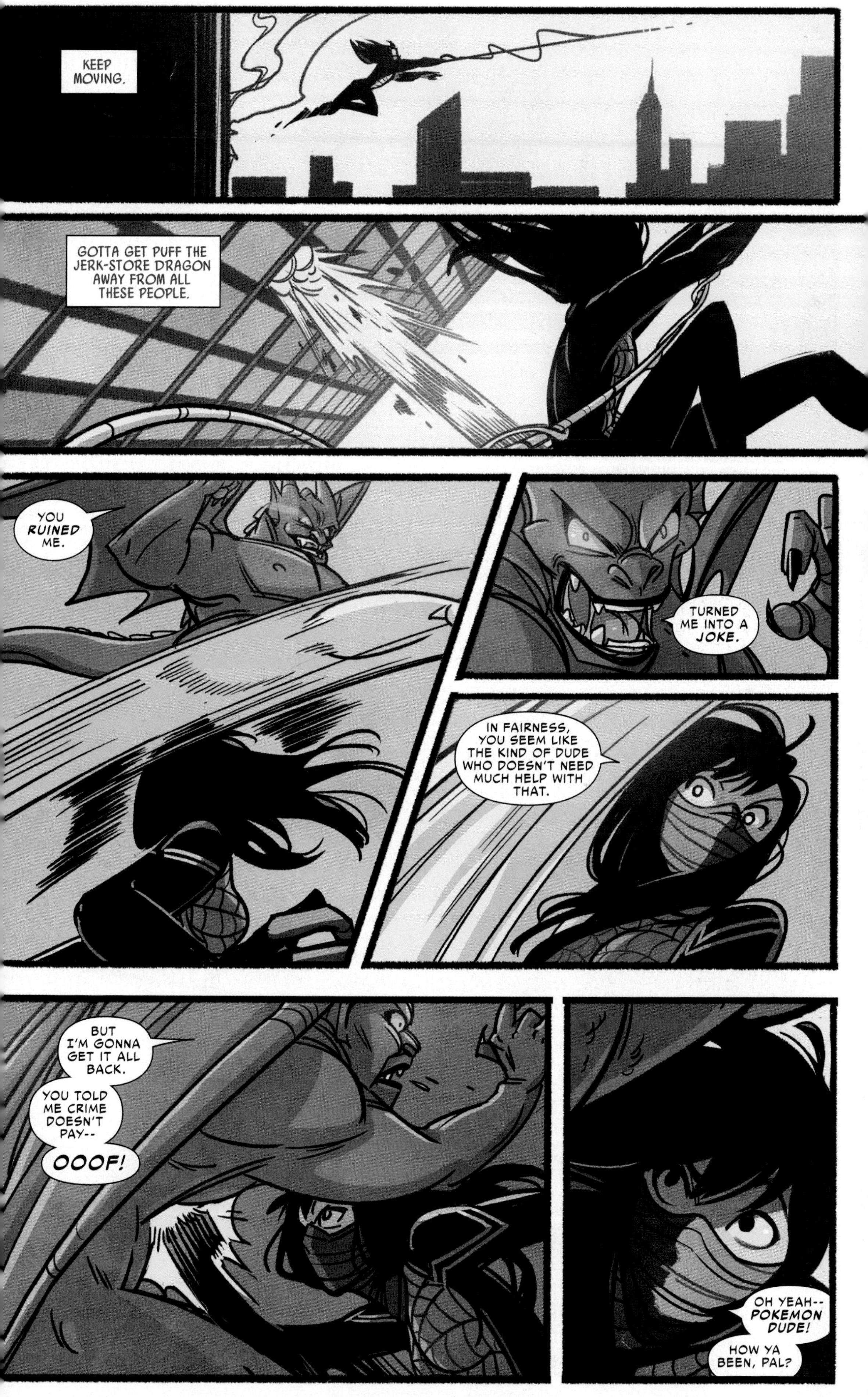
KEEP MOVING.
GOTTA GET PUFF THE JERK-STORE DRAGON AWAY FROM ALL THESE PEOPLE.
YOU RUINED ME.
TURNED ME INTO A JOKE.
IN FAIRNESS, YOU SEEM LIKE THE KIND OF DUDE WHO DOESN'T NEED MUCH HELP WITH THAT.
BUT I'M GONNA GET IT ALL BACK.
YOU TOLD ME CRIME DOESN'T PAY--
OOOF!
OH YEAH-- POKEMON DUDE!
HOW YA BEEN, PAL?

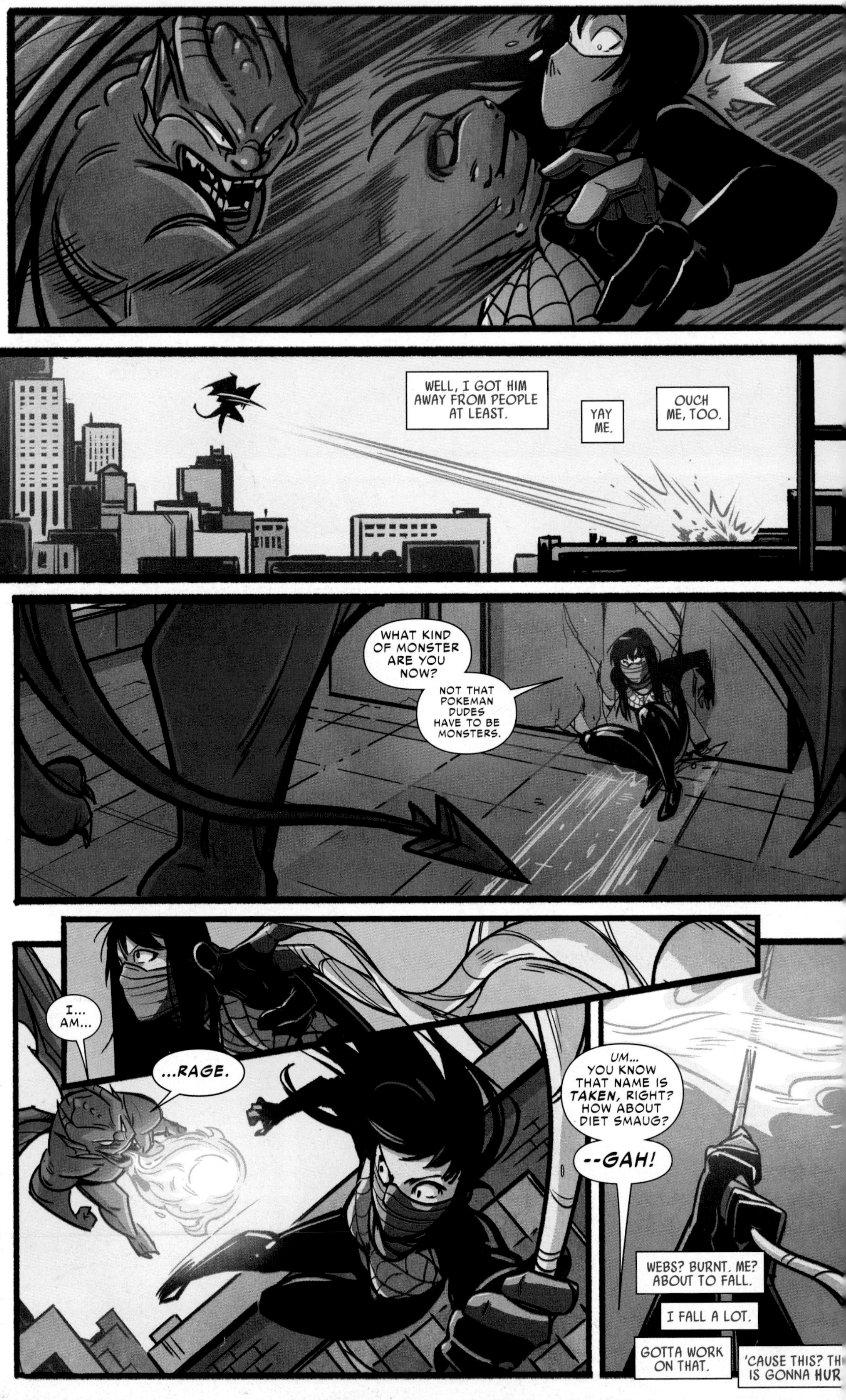
WELL, I GOT HIM AWAY FROM PEOPLE AT LEAST.
YAY ME.
OUCH ME, TOO.
WHAT KIND OF MONSTER ARE YOU NOW?
NOT THAT POKEMAN DUDES HAVE TO BE MONSTERS.
I... AM...
...RAGE.
UM... YOU KNOW THAT NAME IS TAKEN, RIGHT? HOW ABOUT DIET SMAUG?
--GAH!
WEBS? BURNT. ME? ABOUT TO FALL.
I FALL A LOT.
GOTTA WORK ON THAT.
'CAUSE THIS? TH
IS GONNA HUR

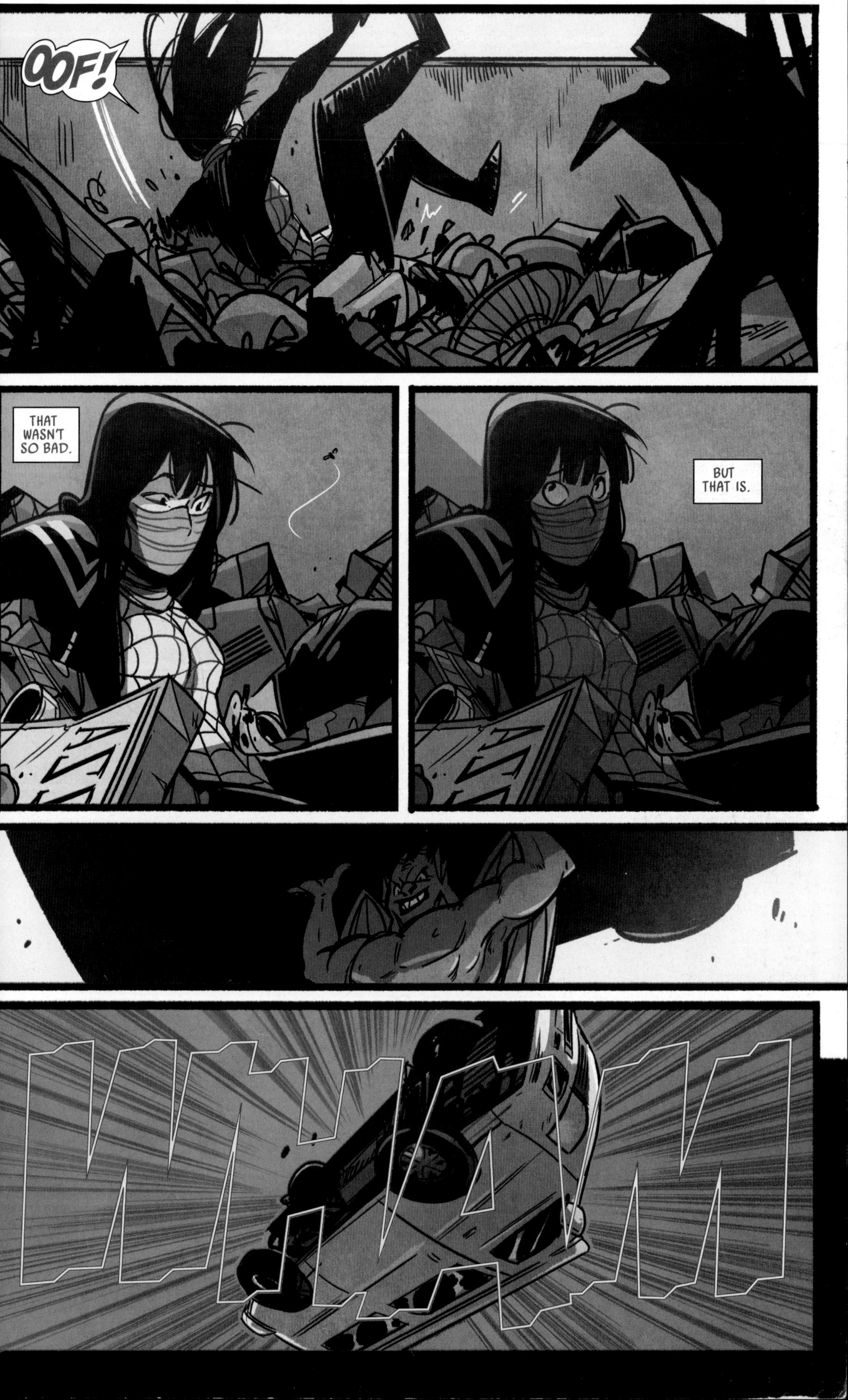
OOF!
THAT WASN'T SO BAD.
BUT THAT IS.
WHAM

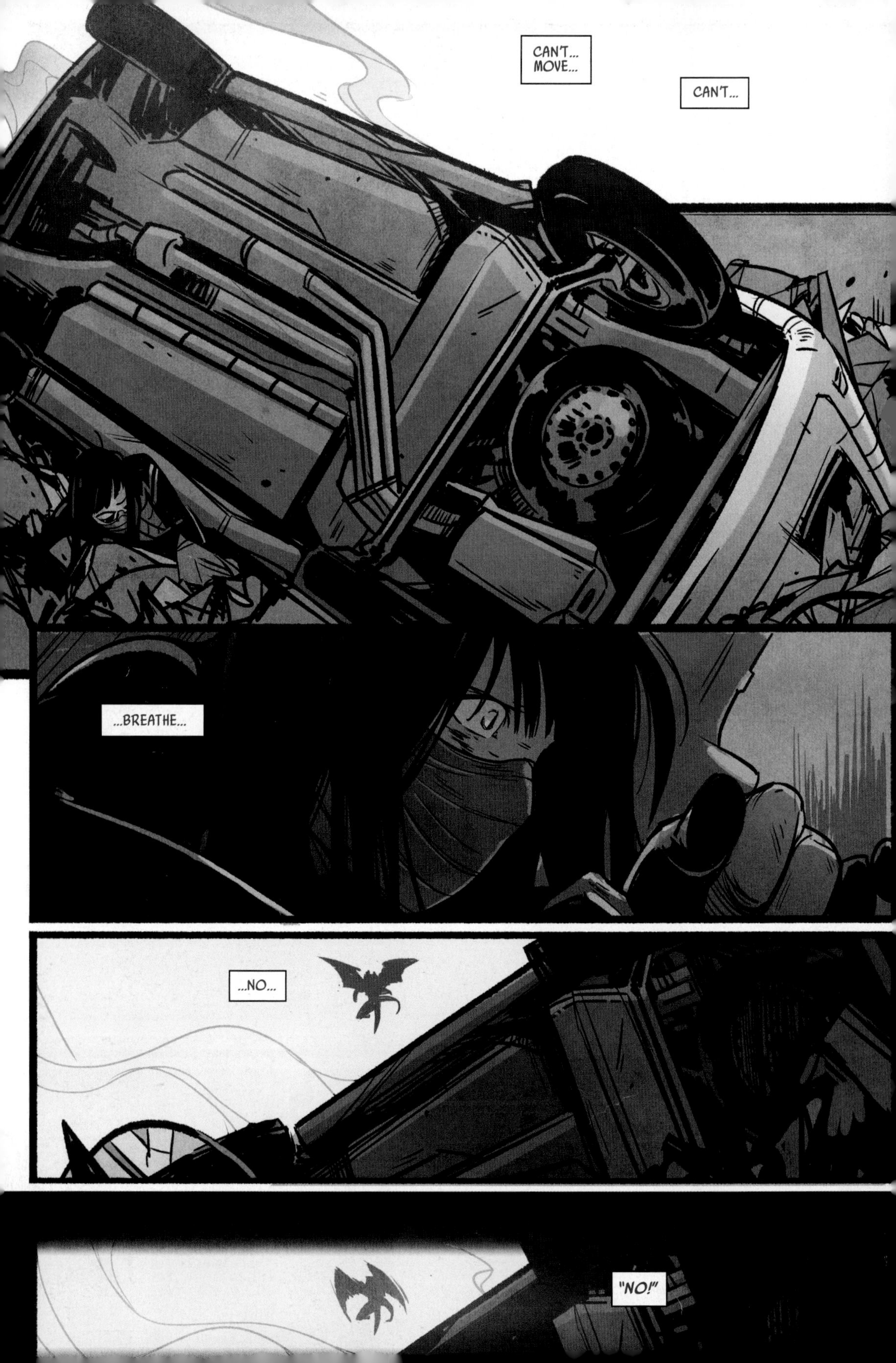
CAN'T... MOVE...
CAN'T...
...BREATHE...
...NO...
"NO!"

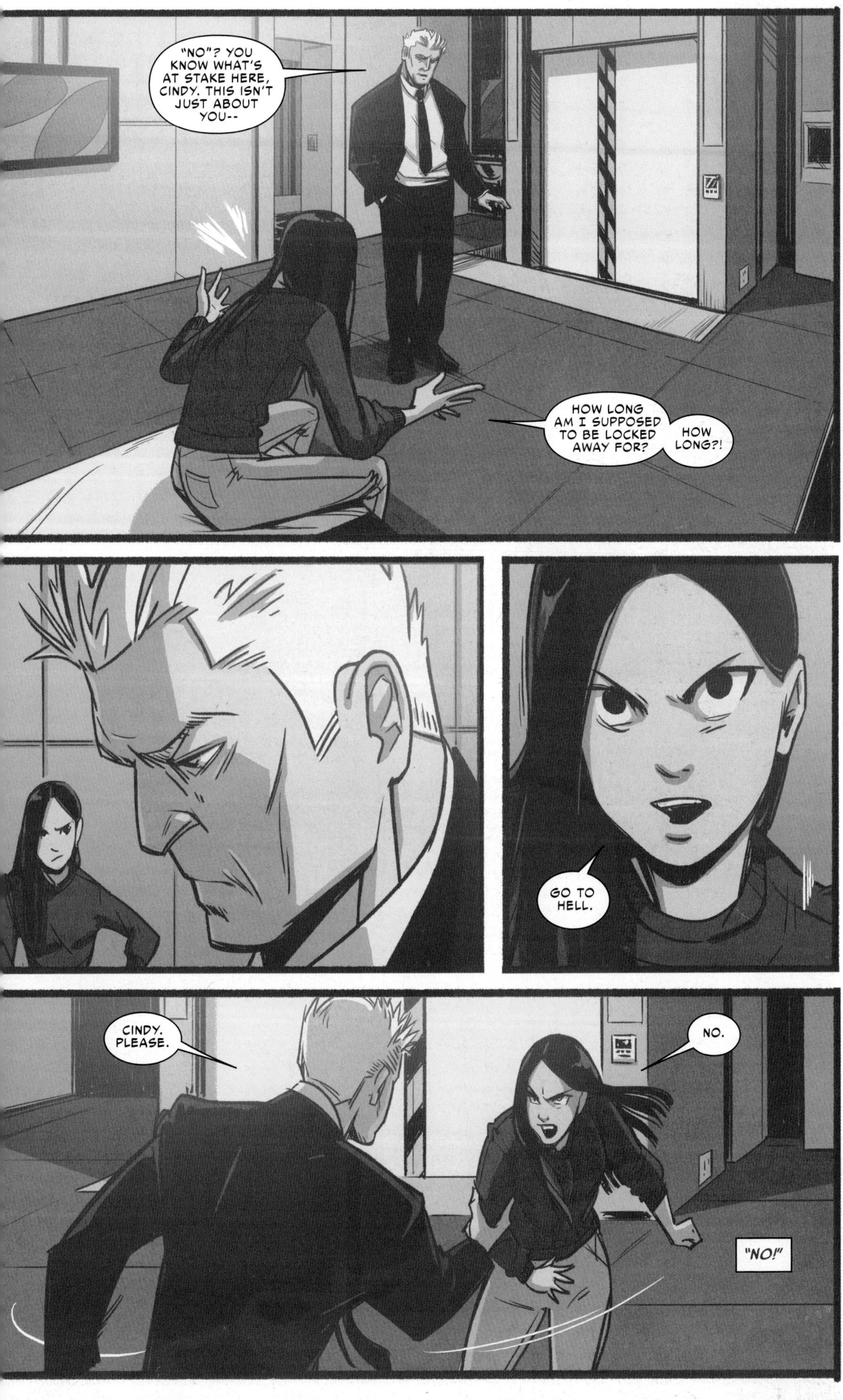
"NO"? YOU KNOW WHAT'S AT STAKE HERE, CINDY. THIS ISN'T JUST ABOUT YOU--
HOW LONG AM I SUPPOSED TO BE LOCKED AWAY FOR?
HOW LONG?!
GO TO HELL.
CINDY. PLEASE.
NO.
"NO!"

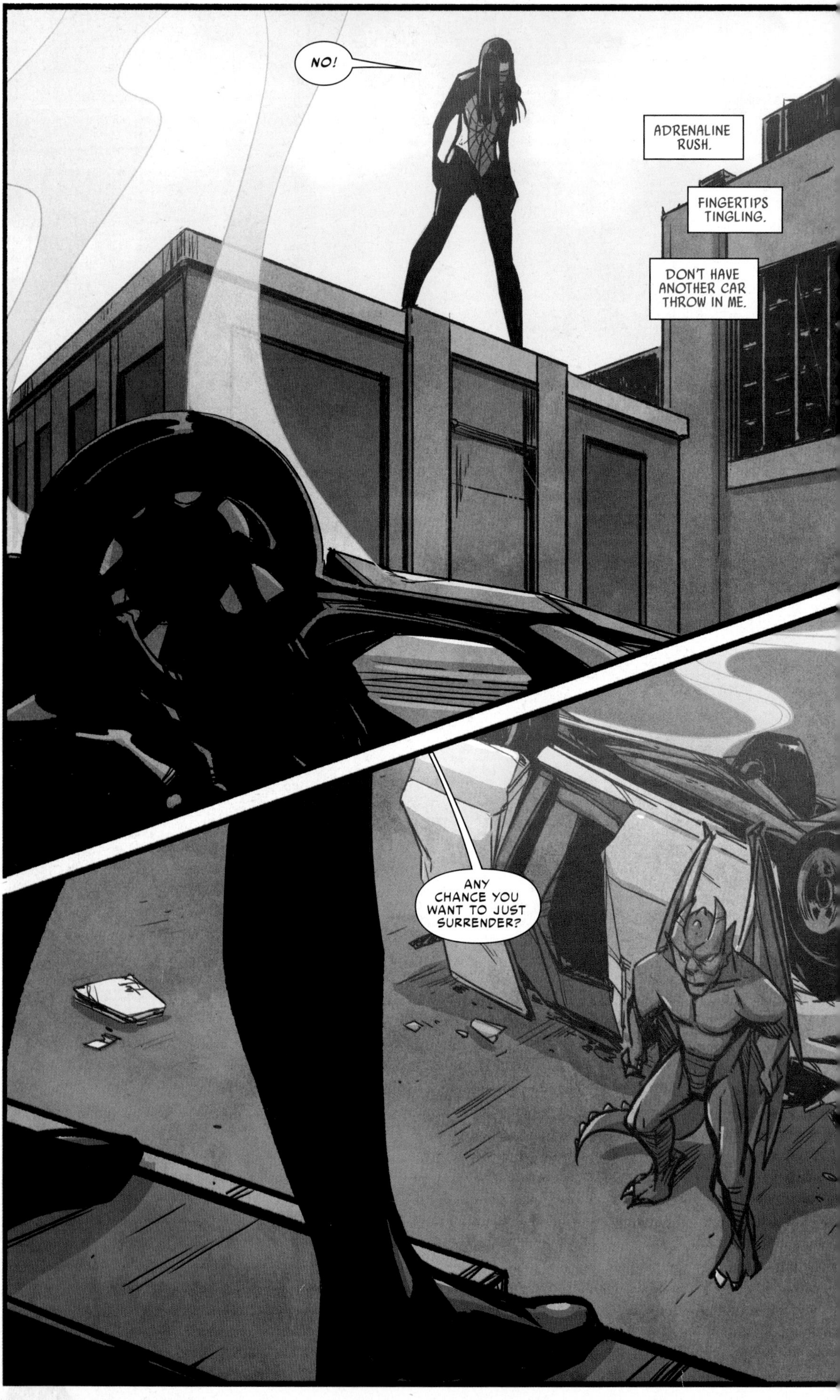
NO!
ADRENALINE RUSH.
FINGERTIPS TINGLING.
DON'T HAVE ANOTHER CAR THROW IN ME.
ANY CHANCE YOU WANT TO JUST SURRENDER?

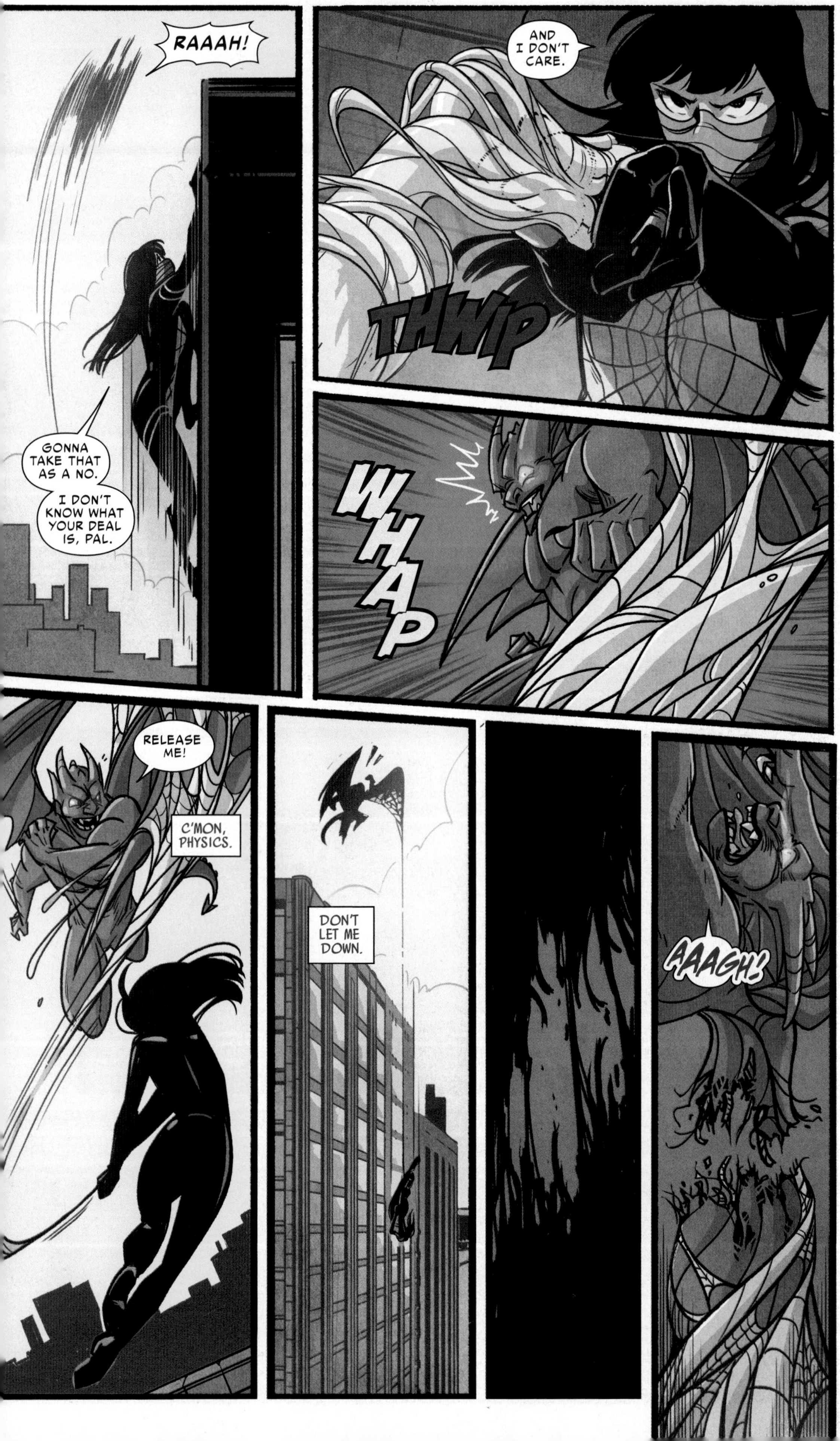
RAAAH!
GONNA TAKE THAT AS A NO.
I DON'T KNOW WHAT YOUR DEAL IS, PAL.
AND I DON'T CARE.
THWIP
WHAP
RELEASE ME!
C'MON, PHYSICS.
DON'T LET ME DOWN.
AAAGH!

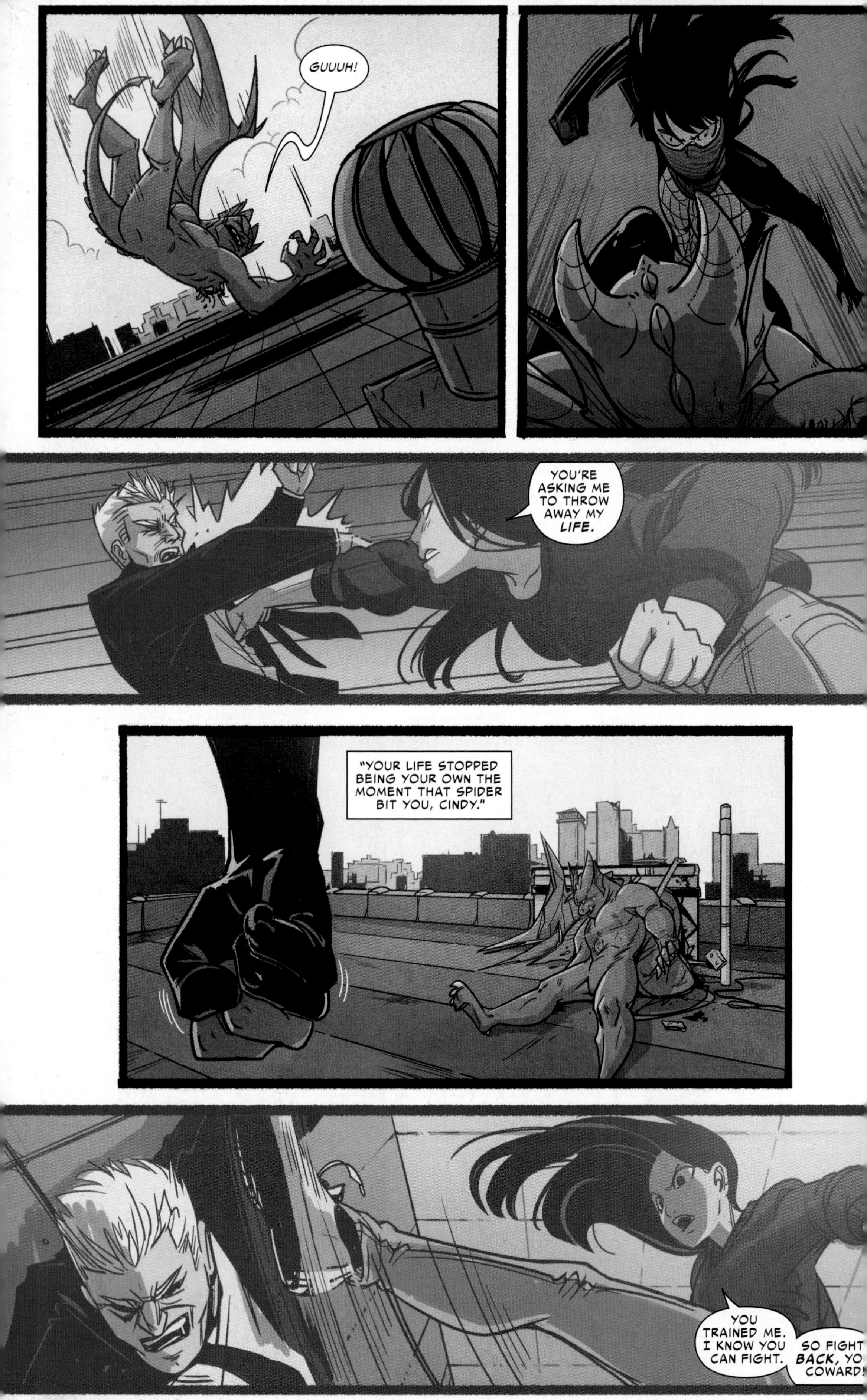
GUUUH!
YOU'RE ASKING ME TO THROW AWAY MY LIFE.
"YOUR LIFE STOPPED BEING YOUR OWN THE MOMENT THAT SPIDER BIT YOU, CINDY."
YOU TRAINED ME. I KNOW YOU CAN FIGHT.
SO FIGHT BACK, YO COWARD!

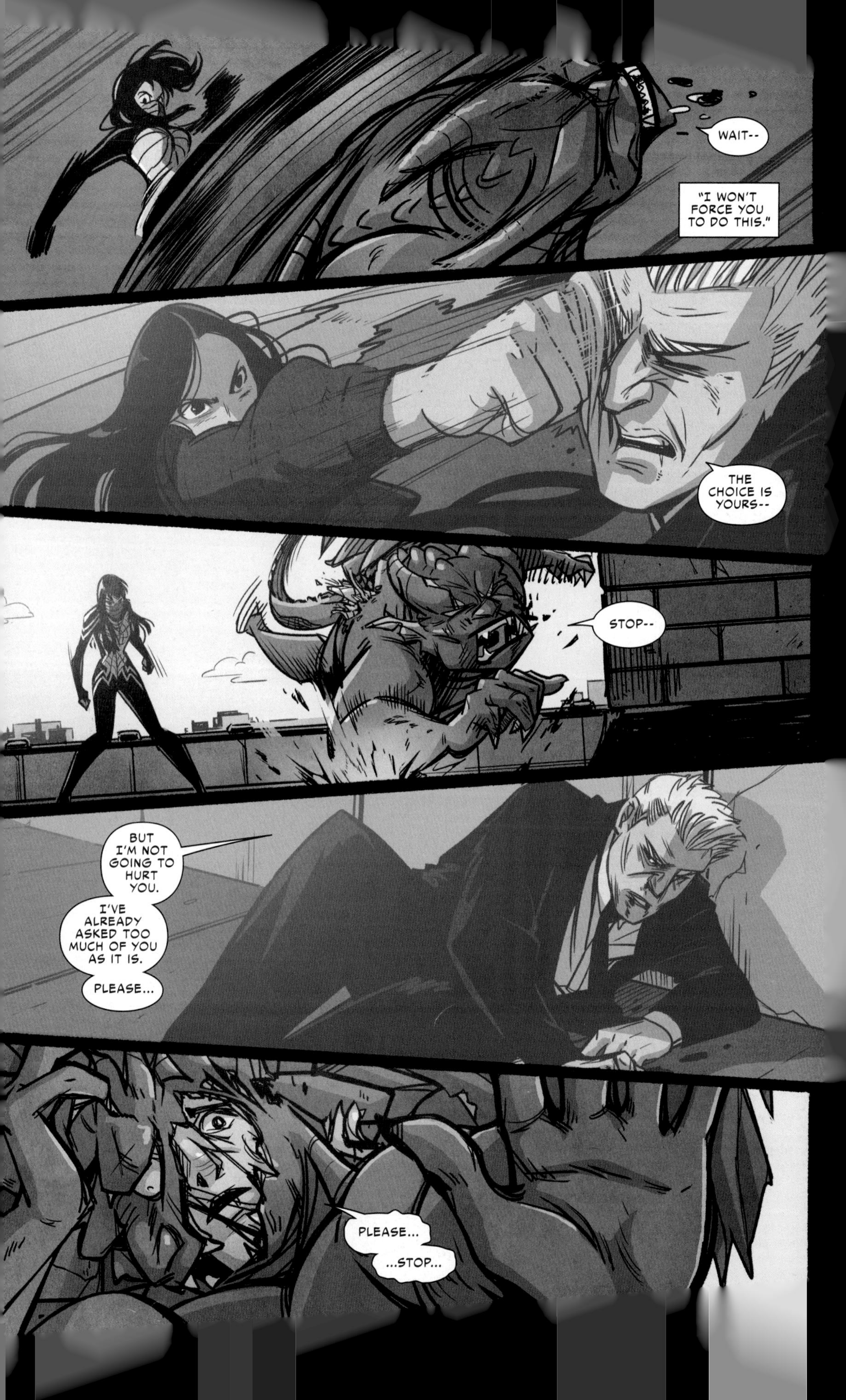
WAIT--
"I WON'T FORCE YOU TO DO THIS."
THE CHOICE IS YOURS--
STOP--
BUT I'M NOT GOING TO HURT YOU.
I'VE ALREADY ASKED TOO MUCH OF YOU AS IT IS.
PLEASE...
PLEASE...
...STOP...

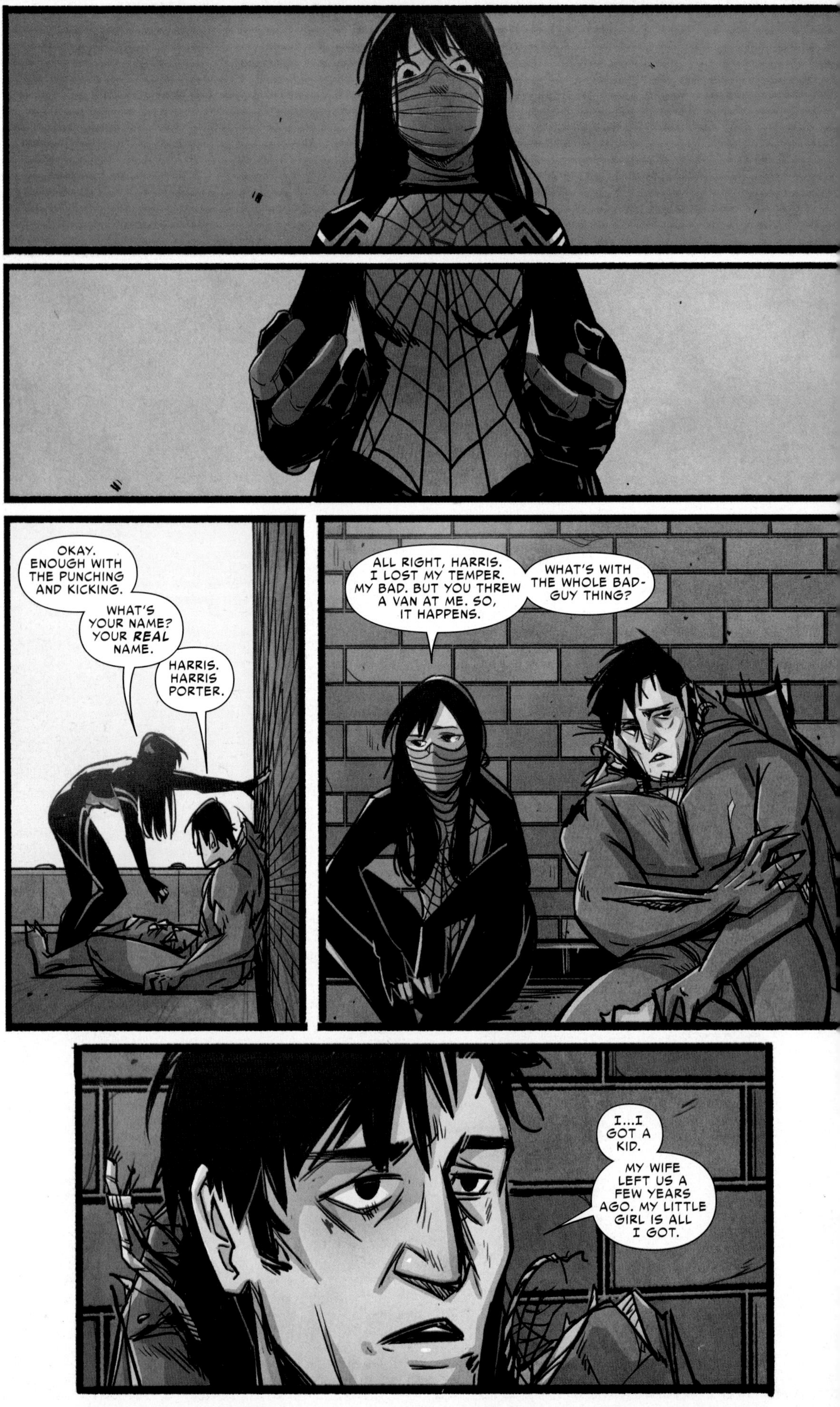
OKAY. ENOUGH WITH THE PUNCHING AND KICKING.
WHAT'S YOUR NAME? YOUR REAL NAME.
HARRIS. HARRIS PORTER.
ALL RIGHT, HARRIS. I LOST MY TEMPER. MY BAD. BUT YOU THREW A VAN AT ME. SO, IT HAPPENS.
WHAT'S WITH THE WHOLE BAD-GUY THING?
I...I GOT A KID.
MY WIFE LEFT US A FEW YEARS AGO. MY LITTLE GIRL IS ALL I GOT.

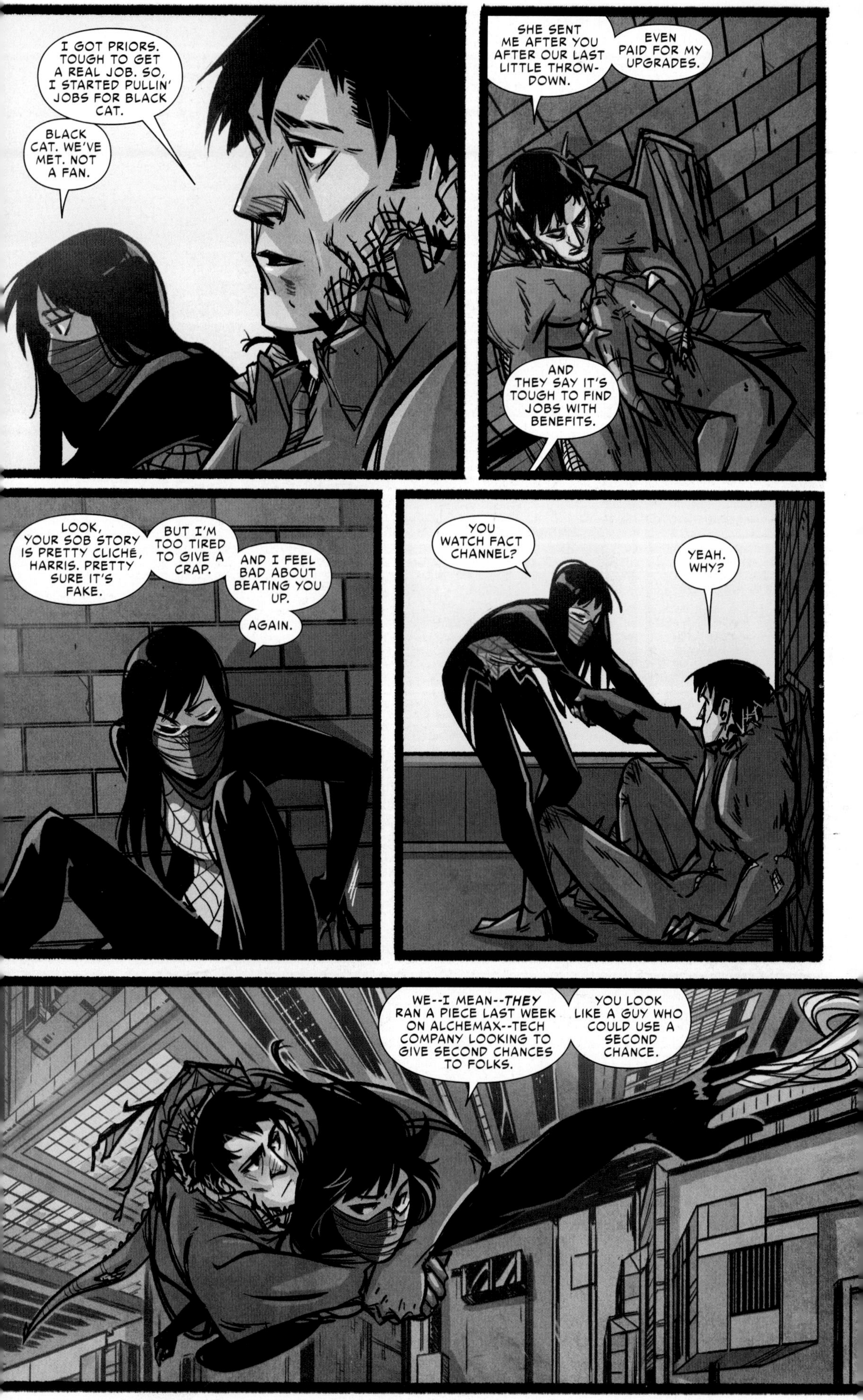
I GOT PRIORS. TOUGH TO GET A REAL JOB. SO, I STARTED PULLIN' JOBS FOR BLACK CAT.
BLACK CAT. WE'VE MET. NOT A FAN.
SHE SENT ME AFTER YOU AFTER OUR LAST LITTLE THROW-DOWN.
EVEN PAID FOR MY UPGRADES.
AND THEY SAY IT'S TOUGH TO FIND JOBS WITH BENEFITS.
LOOK, YOUR SOB STORY IS PRETTY CLICHÉ, HARRIS. PRETTY SURE IT'S FAKE.
BUT I'M TOO TIRED TO GIVE A CRAP.
AND I FEEL BAD ABOUT BEATING YOU UP.
AGAIN.
YOU WATCH FACT CHANNEL?
YEAH. WHY?
WE--I MEAN--*THEY* RAN A PIECE LAST WEEK ON ALCHEMAX--TECH COMPANY LOOKING TO GIVE SECOND CHANCES TO FOLKS.
YOU LOOK LIKE A GUY WHO COULD USE A SECOND CHANCE.

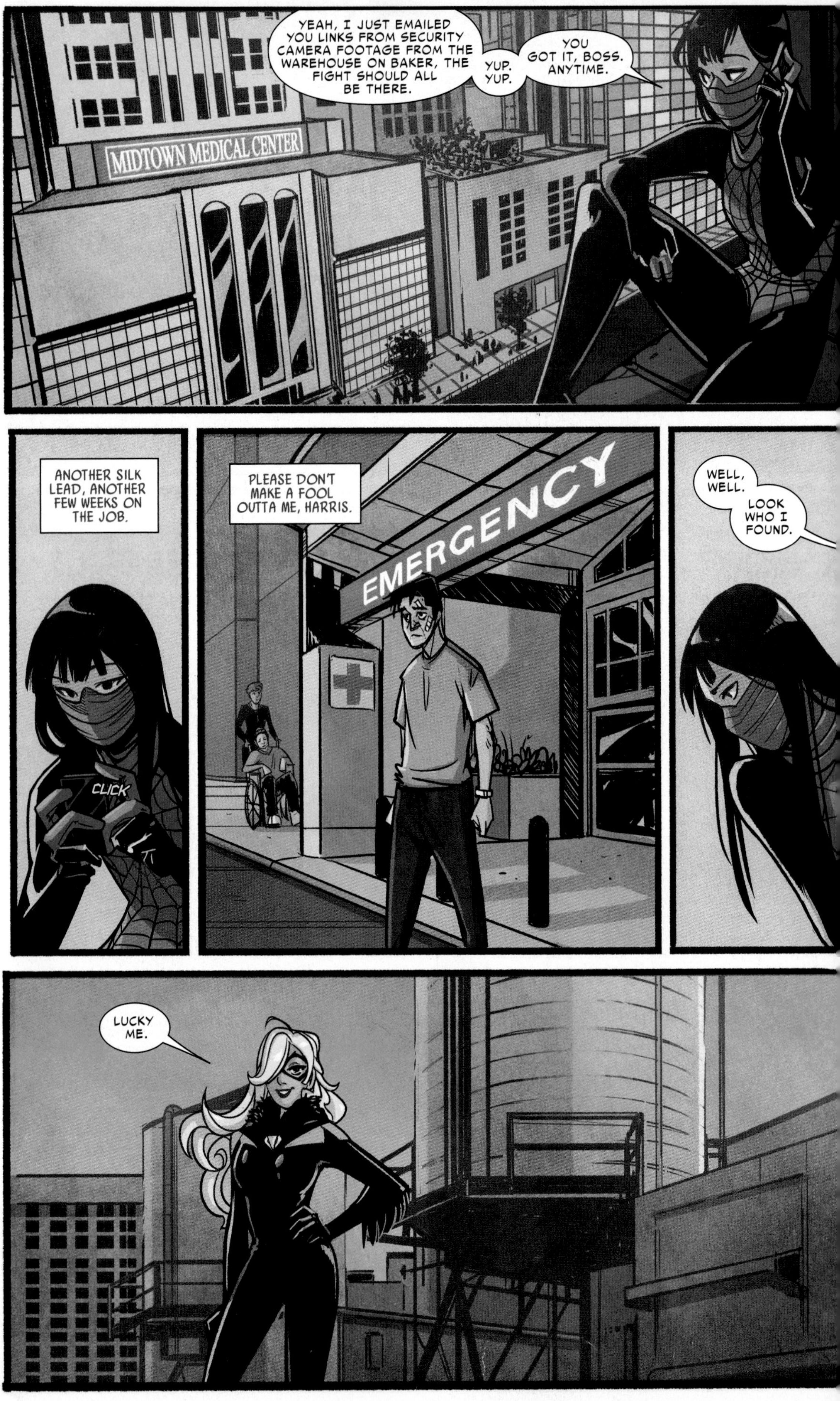
YEAH, I JUST EMAILED YOU LINKS FROM SECURITY CAMERA FOOTAGE FROM THE WAREHOUSE ON BAKER, THE FIGHT SHOULD ALL BE THERE.
YUP. YUP.
YOU GOT IT, BOSS. ANYTIME.
MIDTOWN MEDICAL CENTER
ANOTHER SILK LEAD, ANOTHER FEW WEEKS ON THE JOB.
CLICK
PLEASE DON'T MAKE A FOOL OUTTA ME, HARRIS.
EMERGENCY
WELL, WELL.
LOOK WHO I FOUND.
LUCKY ME.

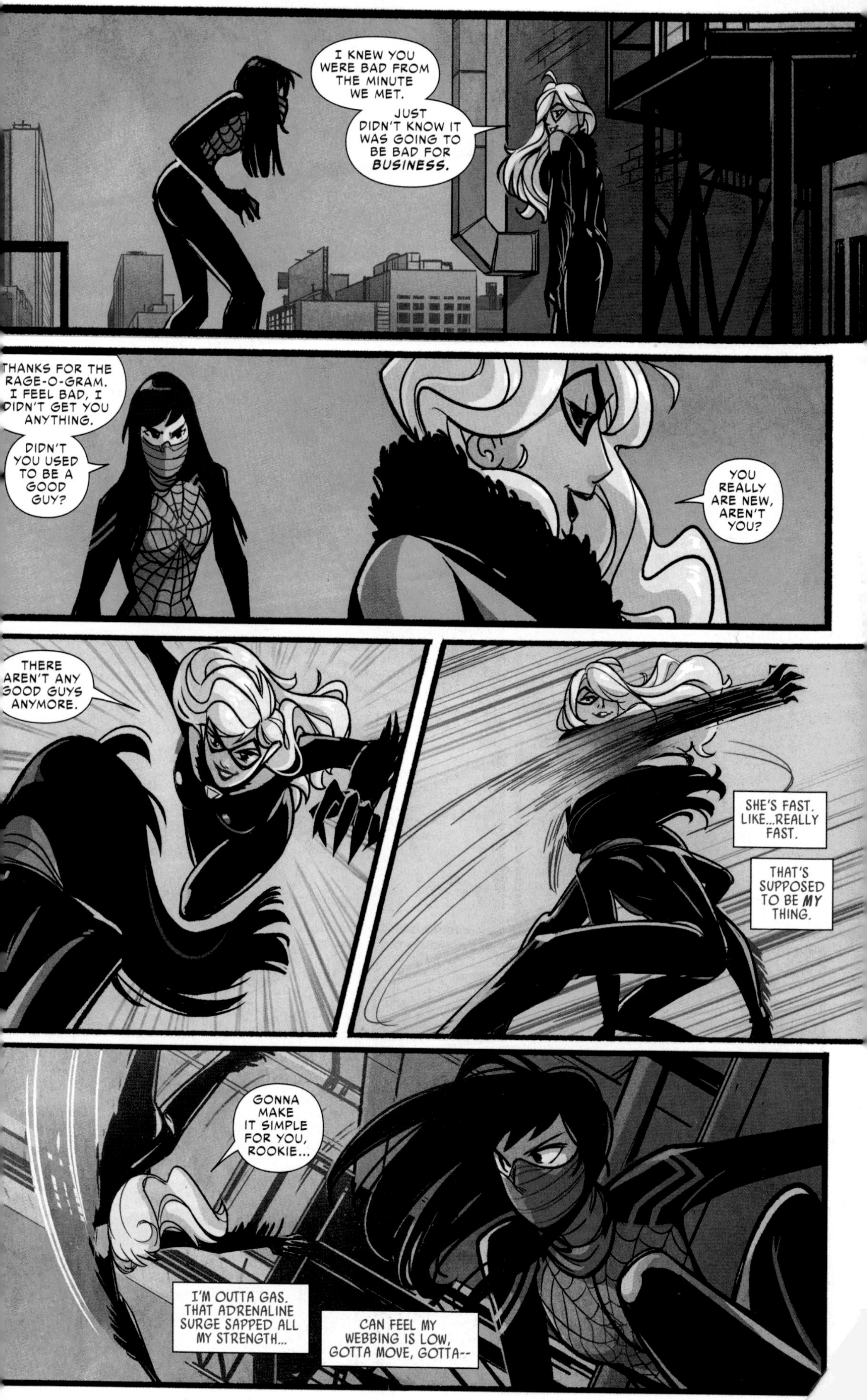
I KNEW YOU WERE BAD FROM THE MINUTE WE MET.
JUST DIDN'T KNOW IT WAS GOING TO BE BAD FOR *BUSINESS.*
THANKS FOR THE RAGE-O-GRAM. I FEEL BAD, I DIDN'T GET YOU ANYTHING.
DIDN'T YOU USED TO BE A GOOD GUY?
YOU REALLY ARE NEW, AREN'T YOU?
THERE AREN'T ANY GOOD GUYS ANYMORE.
SHE'S FAST. LIKE...REALLY FAST.
THAT'S SUPPOSED TO BE *MY* THING.
GONNA MAKE IT SIMPLE FOR YOU, ROOKIE...
I'M OUTTA GAS. THAT ADRENALINE SURGE SAPPED ALL MY STRENGTH...
CAN FEEL MY WEBBING IS LOW, GOTTA MOVE, GOTTA--

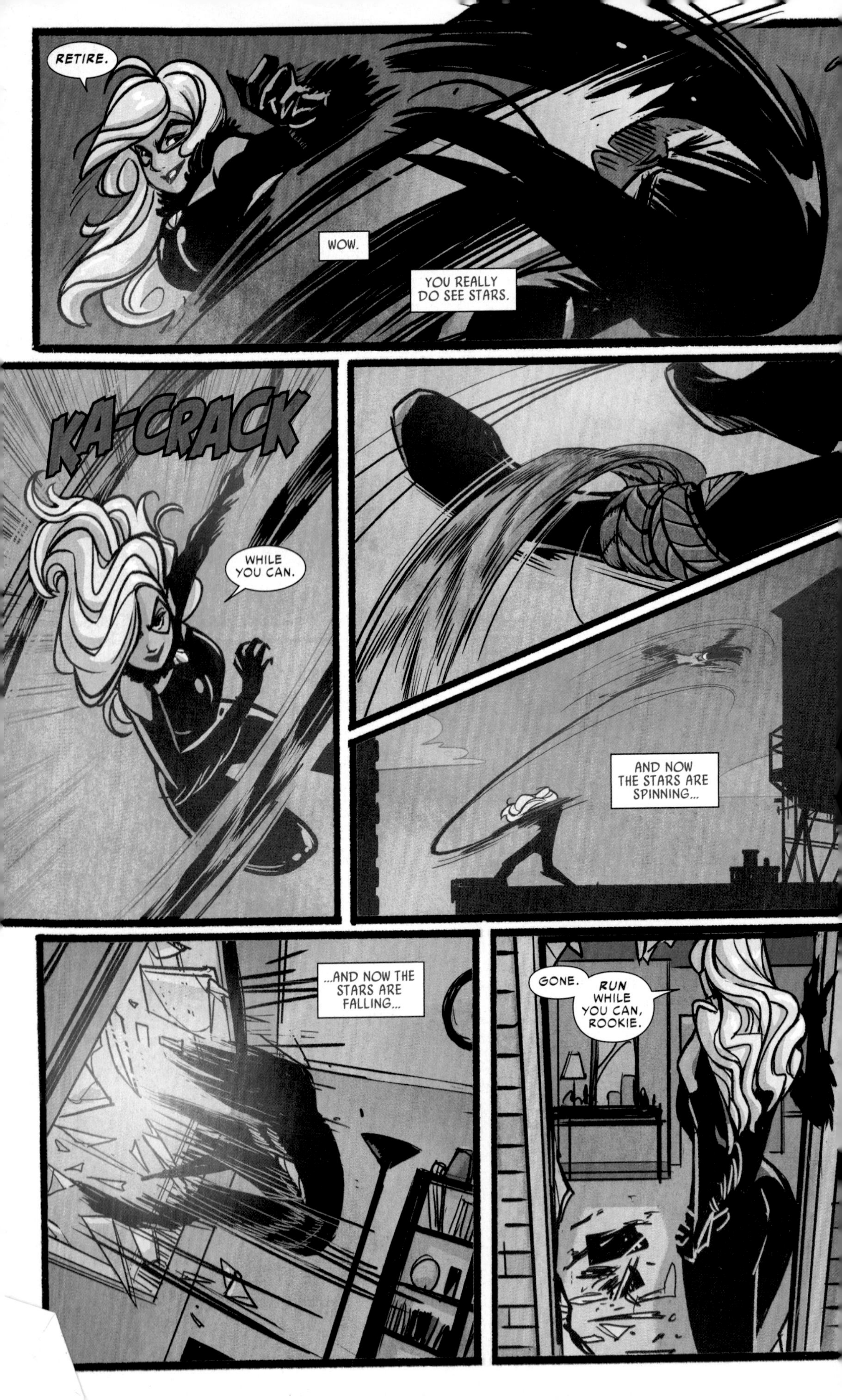
RETIRE.
WOW.
YOU REALLY DO SEE STARS.
KA-CRACK
WHILE YOU CAN.
AND NOW THE STARS ARE SPINNING...
...AND NOW THE STARS ARE FALLING...
GONE.
RUN WHILE YOU CAN, ROOKIE.

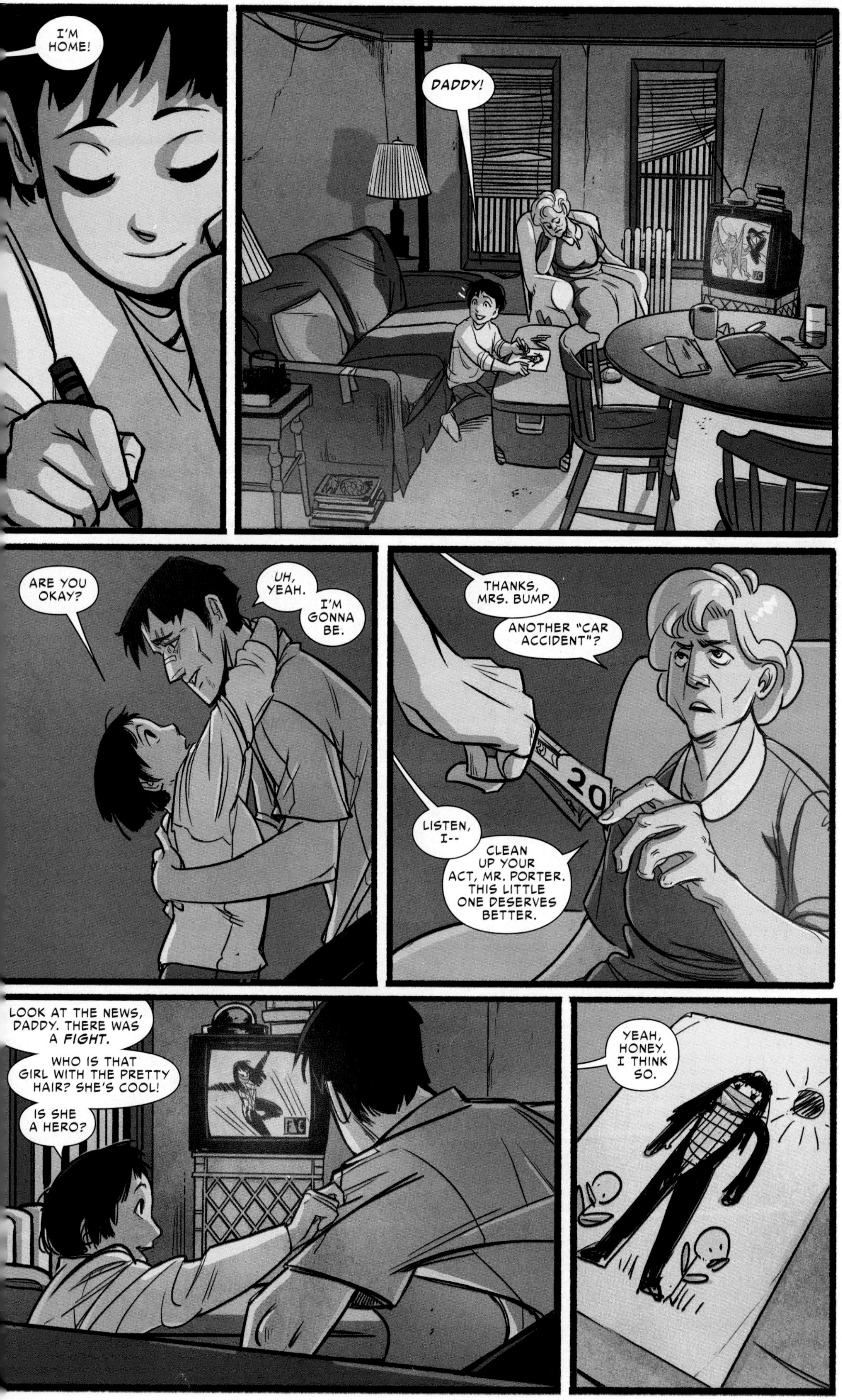
I'M HOME!
DADDY!
ARE YOU OKAY?
UH, YEAH.
I'M GONNA BE.
THANKS, MRS. BUMP.
ANOTHER "CAR ACCIDENT"?
LISTEN, I--
CLEAN UP YOUR ACT, MR. PORTER. THIS LITTLE ONE DESERVES BETTER.
20
LOOK AT THE NEWS, DADDY. THERE WAS A *FIGHT.*
WHO IS THAT GIRL WITH THE PRETTY HAIR? SHE'S COOL!
IS SHE A HERO?
YEAH, HONEY. I THINK SO.

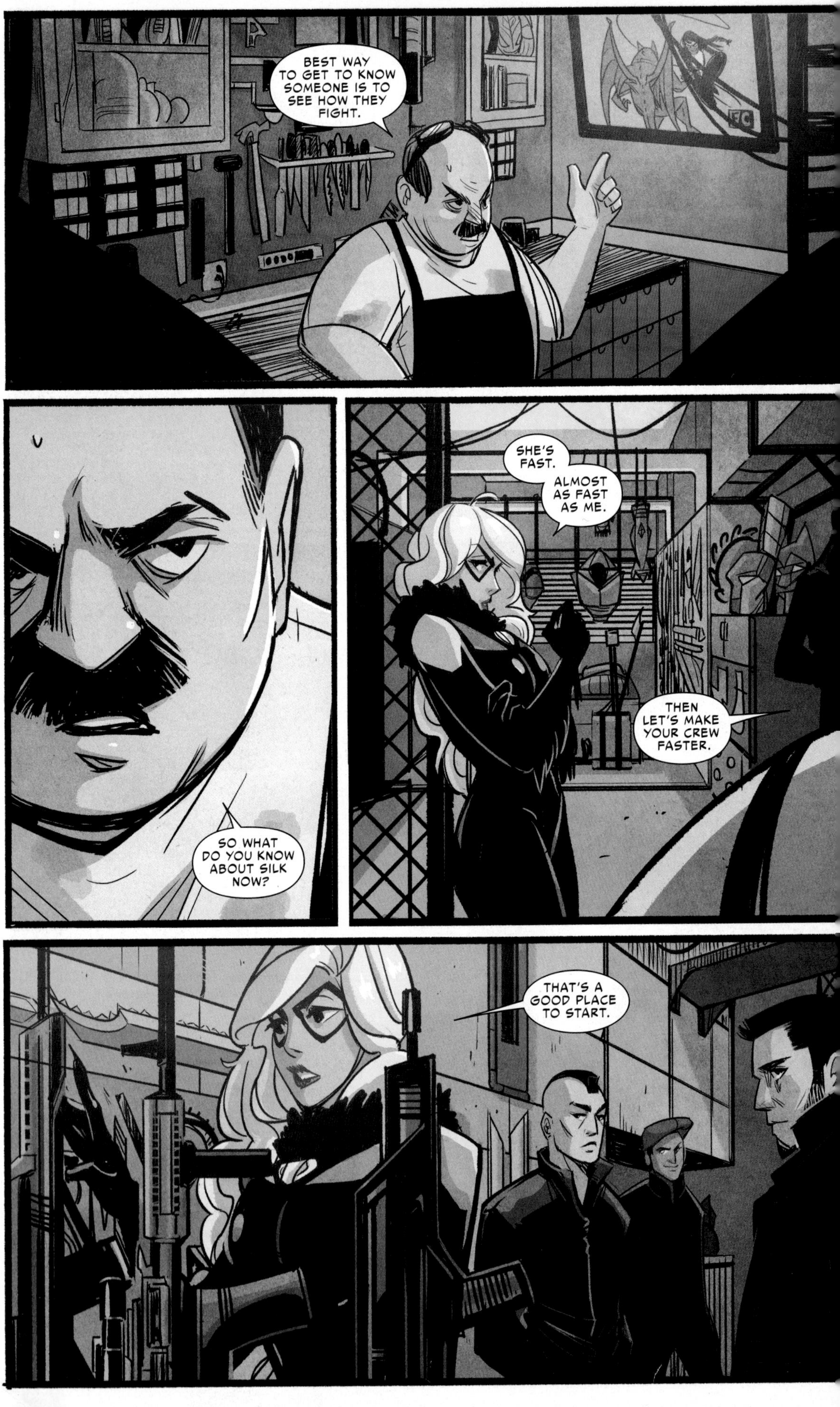
BEST WAY TO GET TO KNOW SOMEONE IS TO SEE HOW THEY FIGHT.
SO WHAT DO YOU KNOW ABOUT SILK NOW?
SHE'S FAST.
ALMOST AS FAST AS ME.
THEN LET'S MAKE YOUR CREW FASTER.
THAT'S A GOOD PLACE TO START.

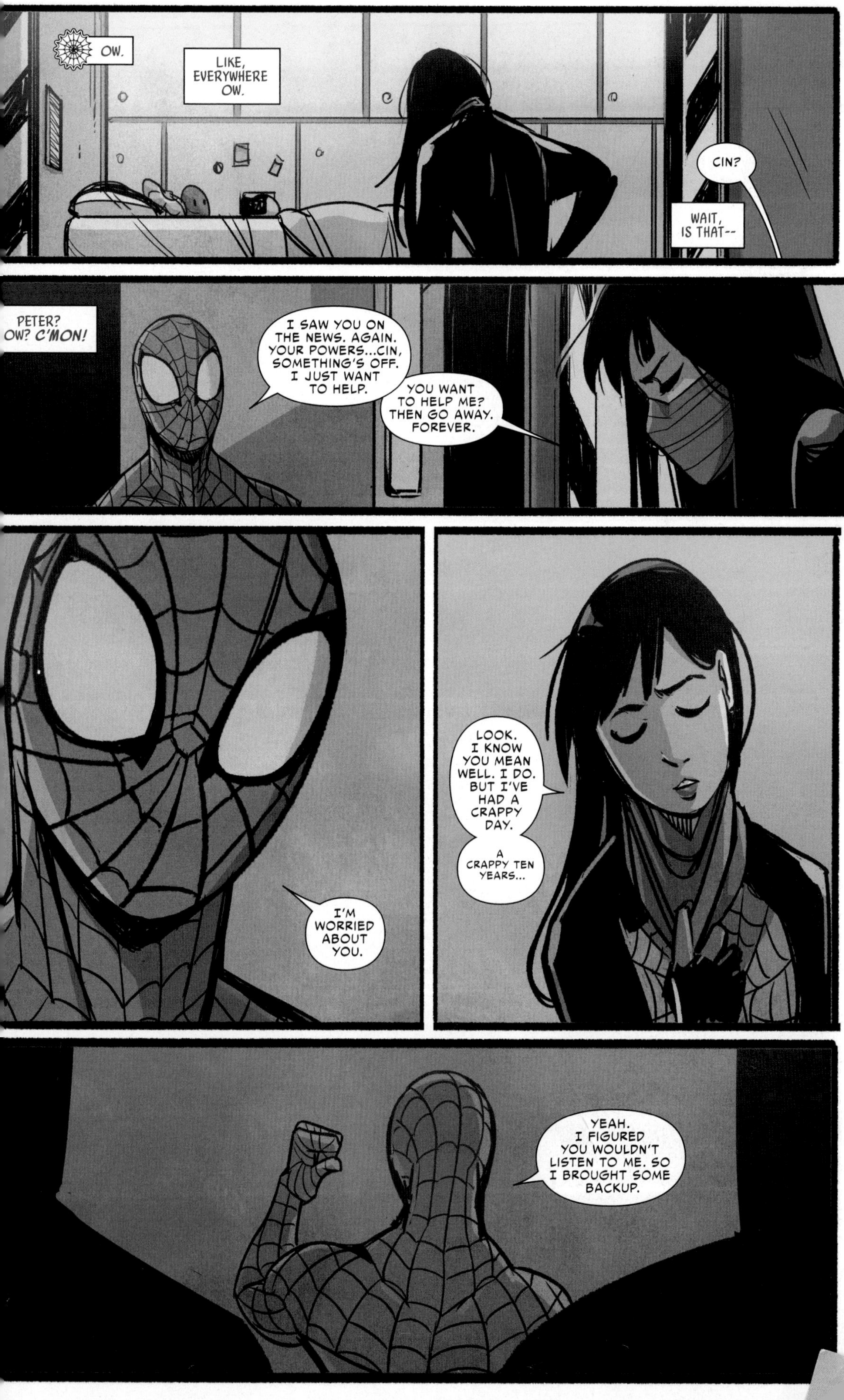
OW.
LIKE, EVERYWHERE OW.
CIN?
WAIT, IS THAT--
PETER? OW? C'MON!
I SAW YOU ON THE NEWS. AGAIN. YOUR POWERS...CIN, SOMETHING'S OFF. I JUST WANT TO HELP.
YOU WANT TO HELP ME? THEN GO AWAY. FOREVER.
I'M WORRIED ABOUT YOU.
LOOK. I KNOW YOU MEAN WELL. I DO. BUT I'VE HAD A CRAPPY DAY.
A CRAPPY TEN YEARS...
YEAH. I FIGURED YOU WOULDN'T LISTEN TO ME. SO I BROUGHT SOME BACKUP.

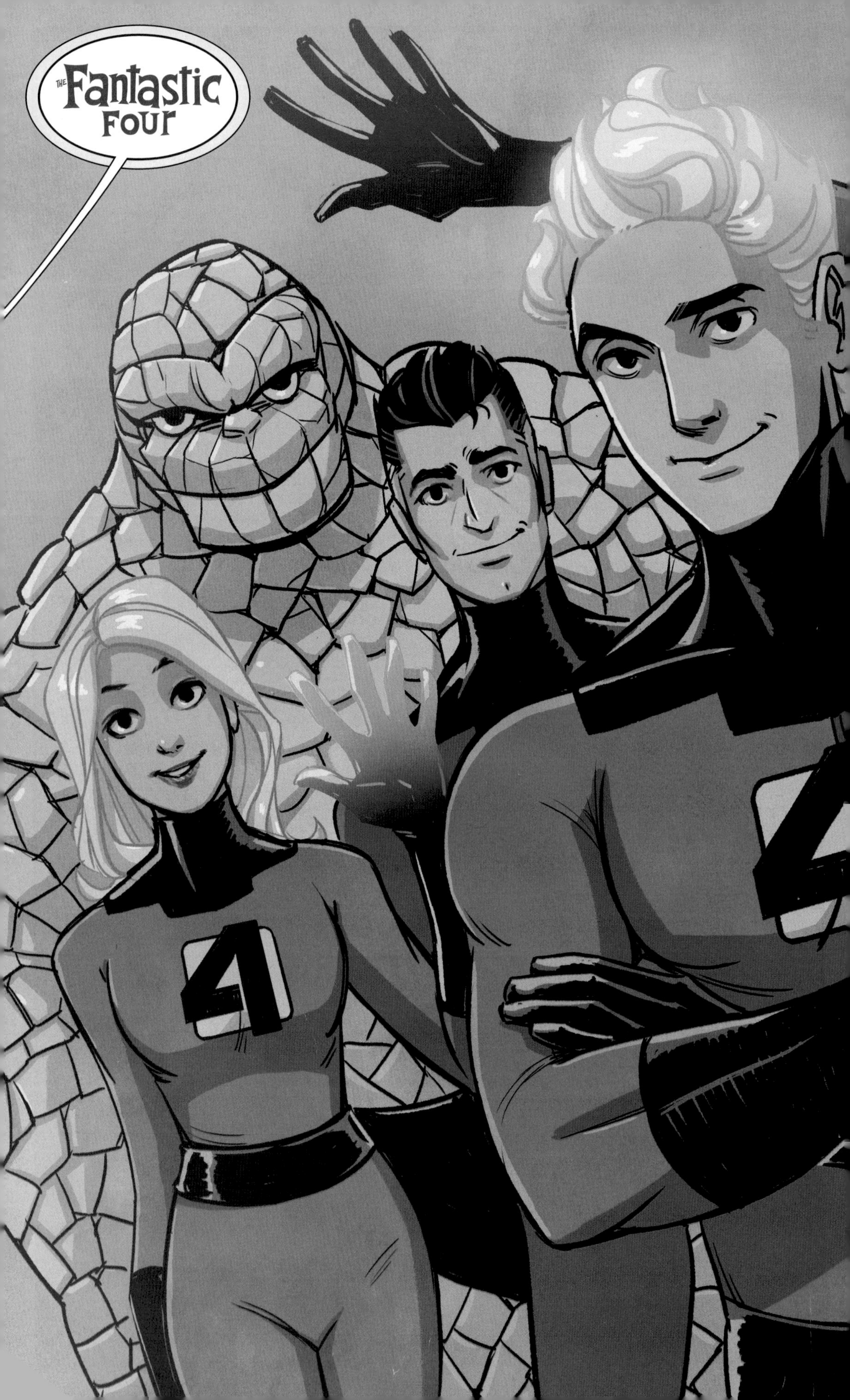
THE Fantastic Four

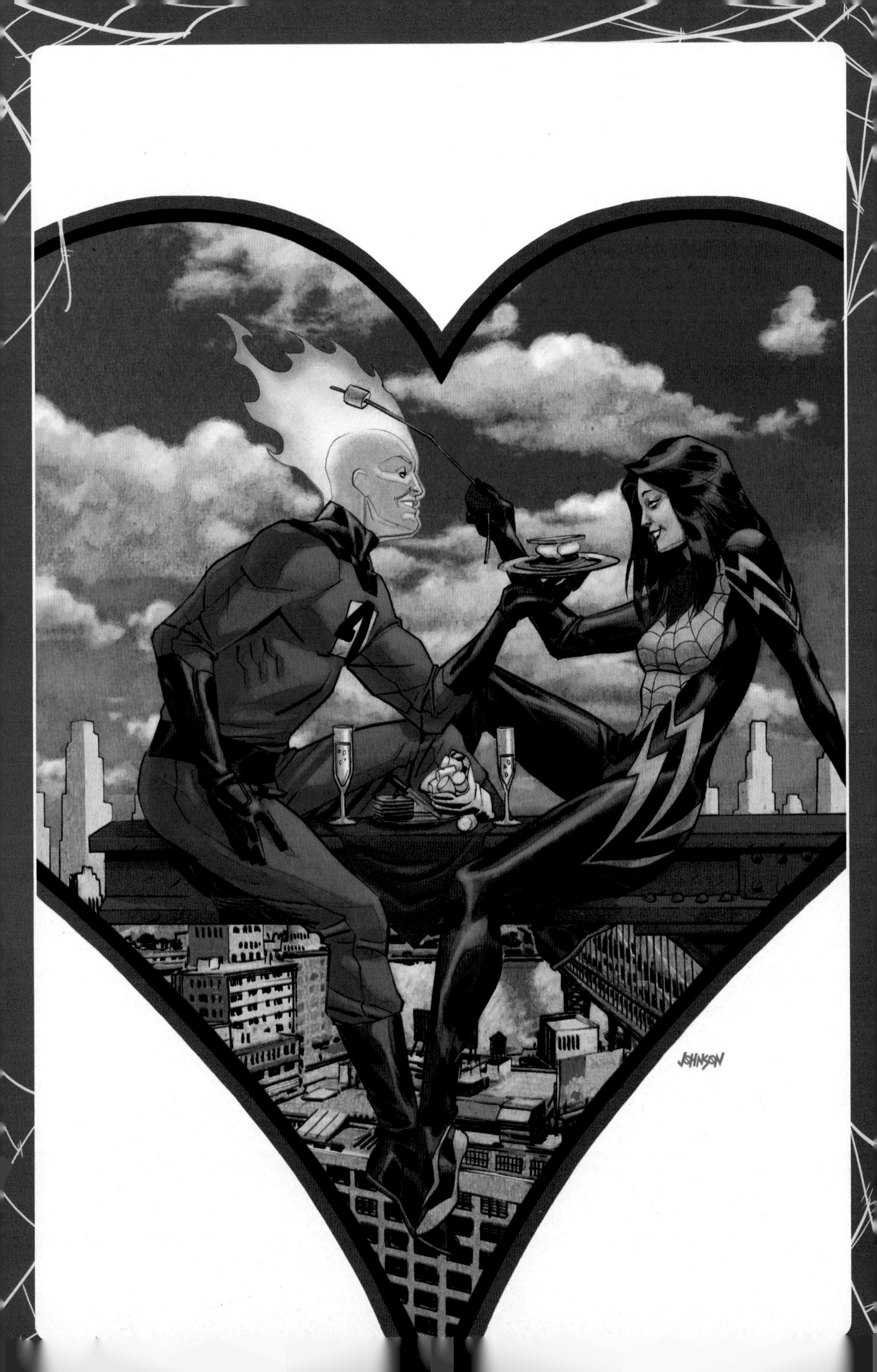
JOHNSON

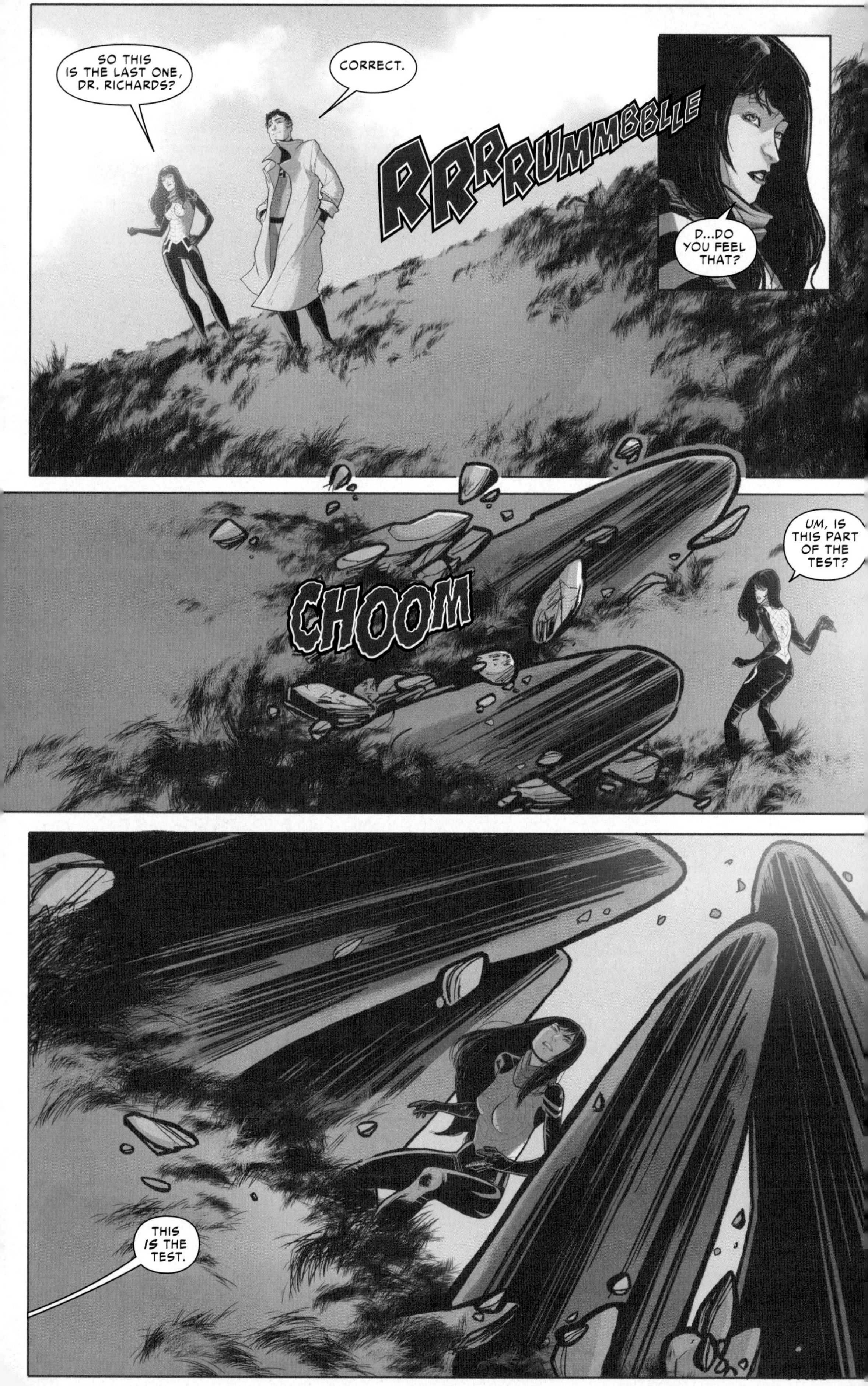
SO THIS IS THE LAST ONE, DR. RICHARDS?
CORRECT.
RRRRUMMBBLLE
D...DO YOU FEEL THAT?
CHOOM
UM, IS THIS PART OF THE TEST?
THIS IS THE TEST.

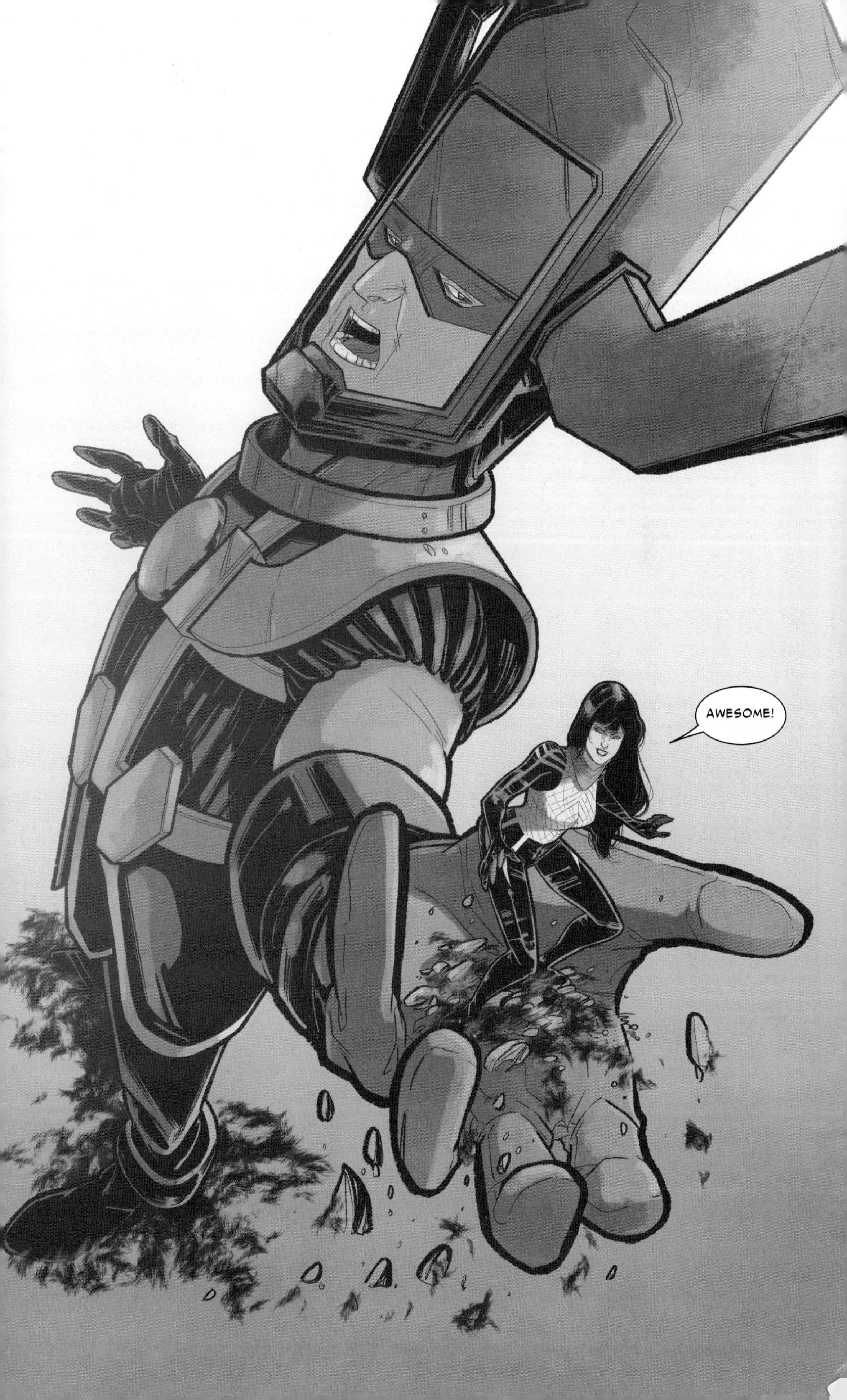
AWESOME!

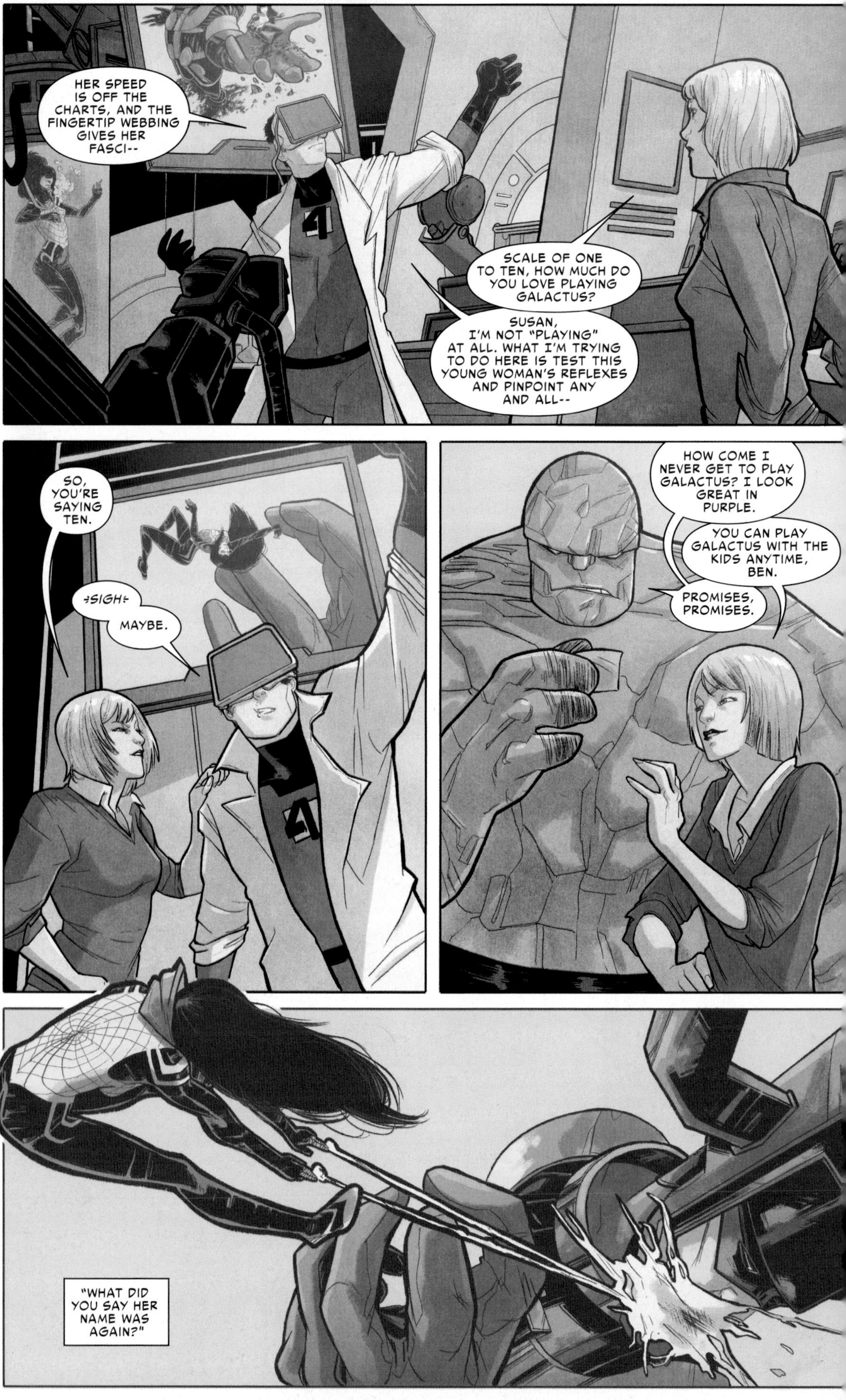
HER SPEED IS OFF THE CHARTS, AND THE FINGERTIP WEBBING GIVES HER FASCI--
SCALE OF ONE TO TEN, HOW MUCH DO YOU LOVE PLAYING GALACTUS?
SUSAN, I'M NOT "PLAYING" AT ALL. WHAT I'M TRYING TO DO HERE IS TEST THIS YOUNG WOMAN'S REFLEXES AND PINPOINT ANY AND ALL--
SO, YOU'RE SAYING TEN.
-SIGH-
MAYBE.
HOW COME I NEVER GET TO PLAY GALACTUS? I LOOK GREAT IN PURPLE.
YOU CAN PLAY GALACTUS WITH THE KIDS ANYTIME, BEN.
PROMISES, PROMISES.
"WHAT DID YOU SAY HER NAME WAS AGAIN?"

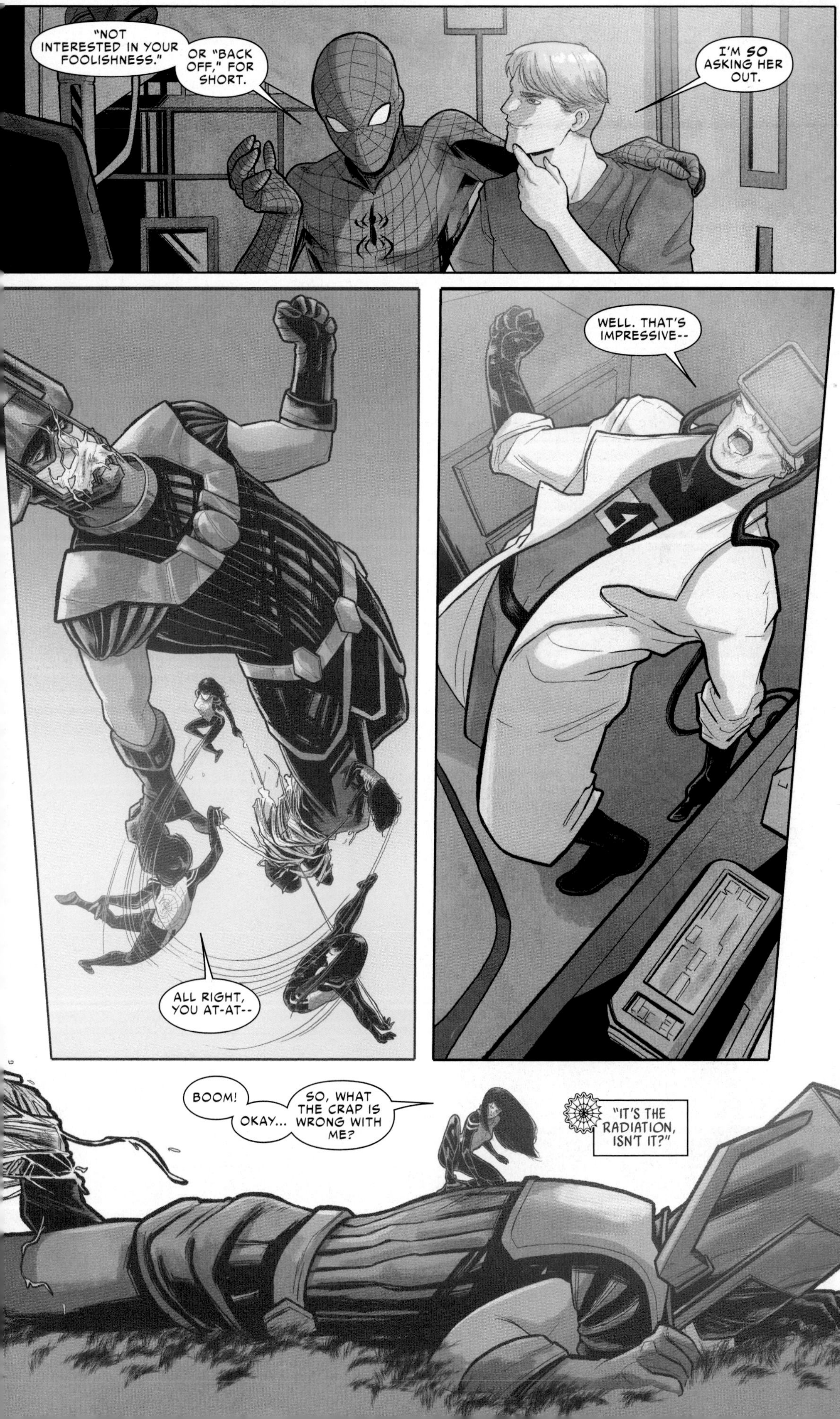
"NOT INTERESTED IN YOUR FOOLISHNESS."
OR "BACK OFF," FOR SHORT.
I'M SO ASKING HER OUT.
ALL RIGHT, YOU AT-AT--
WELL. THAT'S IMPRESSIVE--
BOOM!
OKAY...
SO, WHAT THE CRAP IS WRONG WITH ME?
"IT'S THE RADIATION, ISN'T IT?"

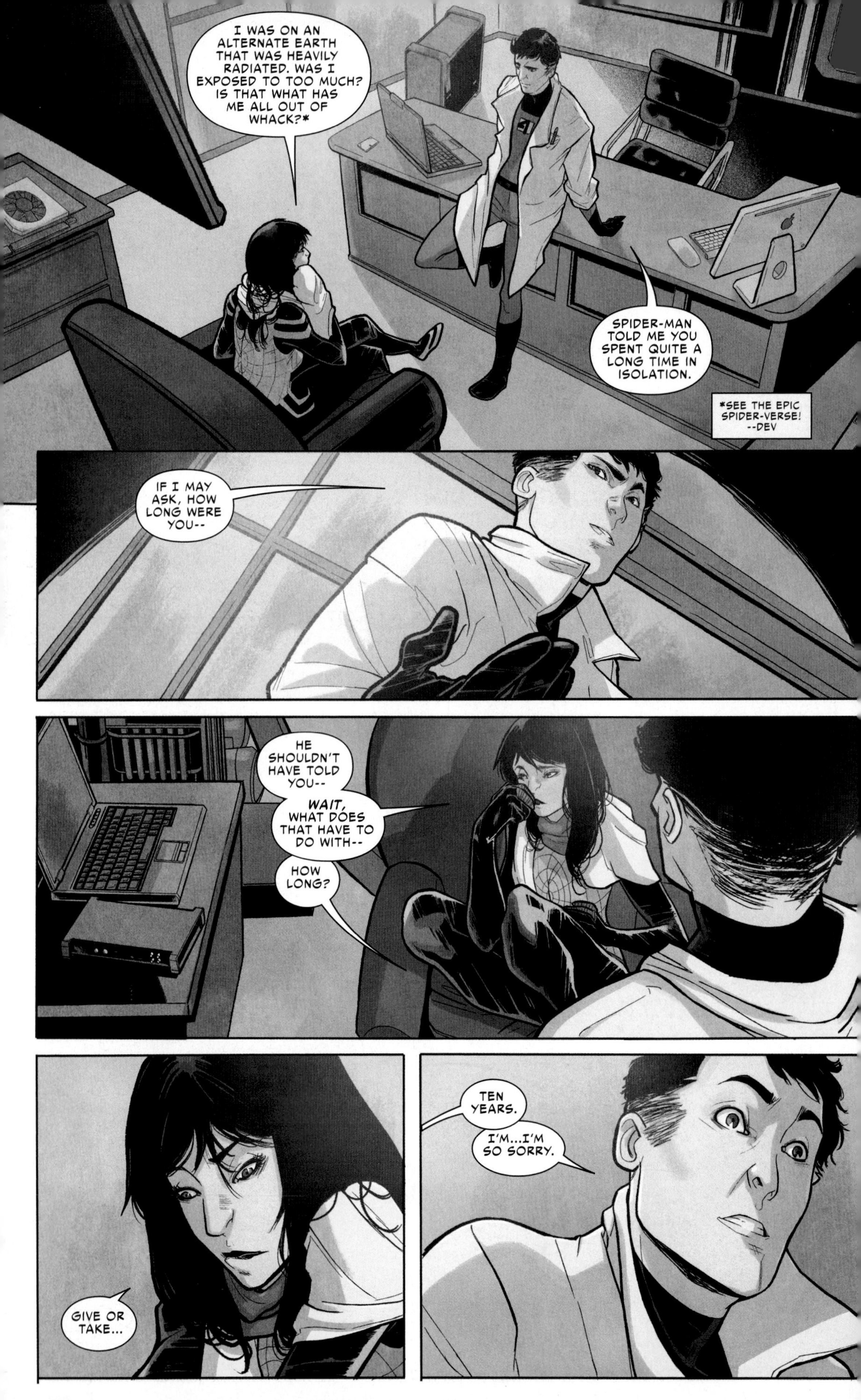
I WAS ON AN ALTERNATE EARTH THAT WAS HEAVILY RADIATED. WAS I EXPOSED TO TOO MUCH? IS THAT WHAT HAS ME ALL OUT OF WHACK?*
SPIDER-MAN TOLD ME YOU SPENT QUITE A LONG TIME IN ISOLATION.
*SEE THE EPIC SPIDER-VERSE! --DEV
IF I MAY ASK, HOW LONG WERE YOU--
HE SHOULDN'T HAVE TOLD YOU--
WAIT, WHAT DOES THAT HAVE TO DO WITH--
HOW LONG?
GIVE OR TAKE...
TEN YEARS.
I'M...I'M SO SORRY.

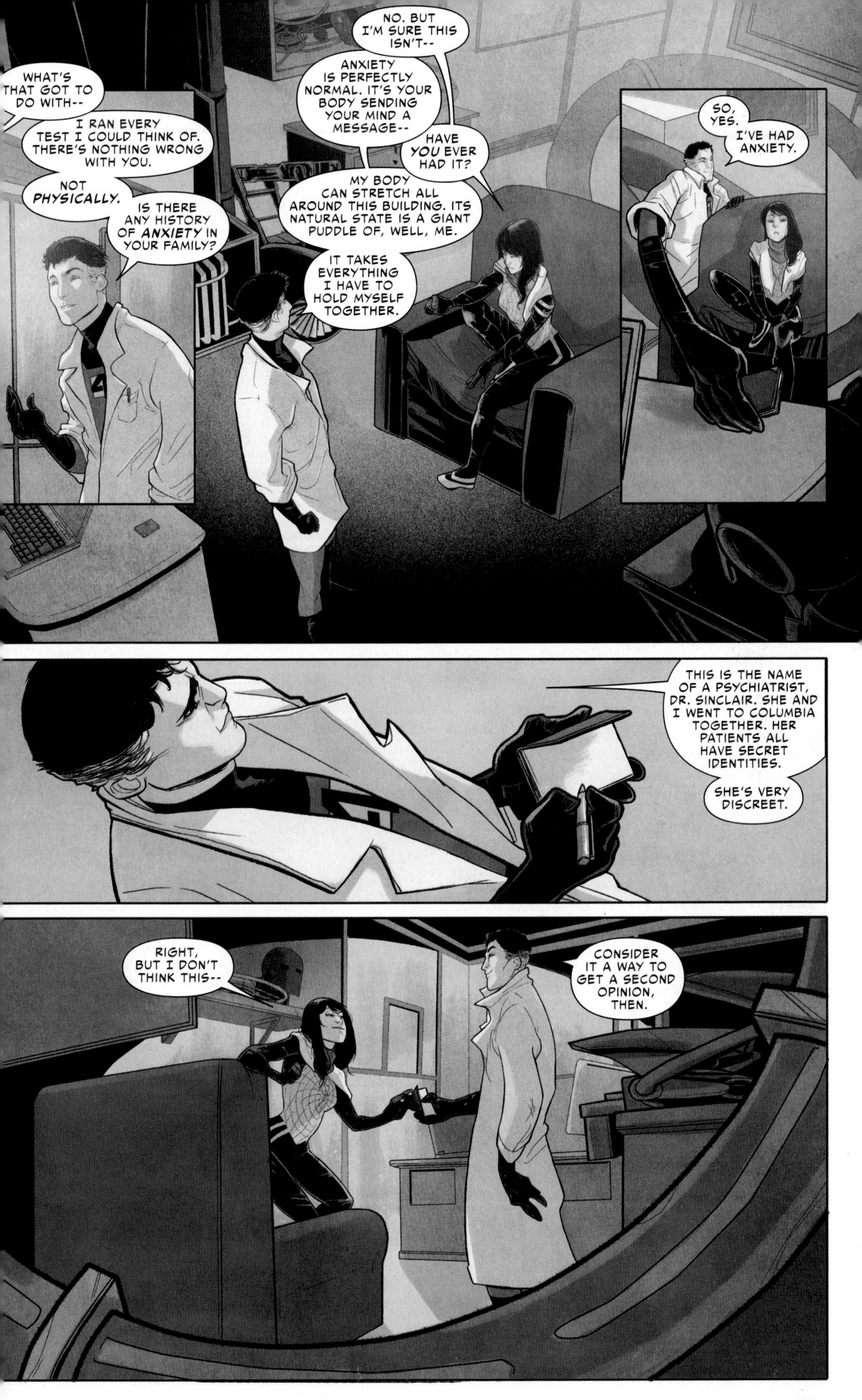
WHAT'S THAT GOT TO DO WITH--
I RAN EVERY TEST I COULD THINK OF. THERE'S NOTHING WRONG WITH YOU.
NOT *PHYSICALLY.*
IS THERE ANY HISTORY OF *ANXIETY* IN YOUR FAMILY?
NO. BUT I'M SURE THIS ISN'T--
ANXIETY IS PERFECTLY NORMAL. IT'S YOUR BODY SENDING YOUR MIND A MESSAGE--
HAVE *YOU* EVER HAD IT?
MY BODY CAN STRETCH ALL AROUND THIS BUILDING. ITS NATURAL STATE IS A GIANT PUDDLE OF, WELL, ME.
IT TAKES EVERYTHING I HAVE TO HOLD MYSELF TOGETHER.
SO, YES.
I'VE HAD ANXIETY.
THIS IS THE NAME OF A PSYCHIATRIST, DR. SINCLAIR. SHE AND I WENT TO COLUMBIA TOGETHER. HER PATIENTS ALL HAVE SECRET IDENTITIES.
SHE'S VERY DISCREET.
RIGHT, BUT I DON'T THINK THIS--
CONSIDER IT A WAY TO GET A SECOND OPINION, THEN.

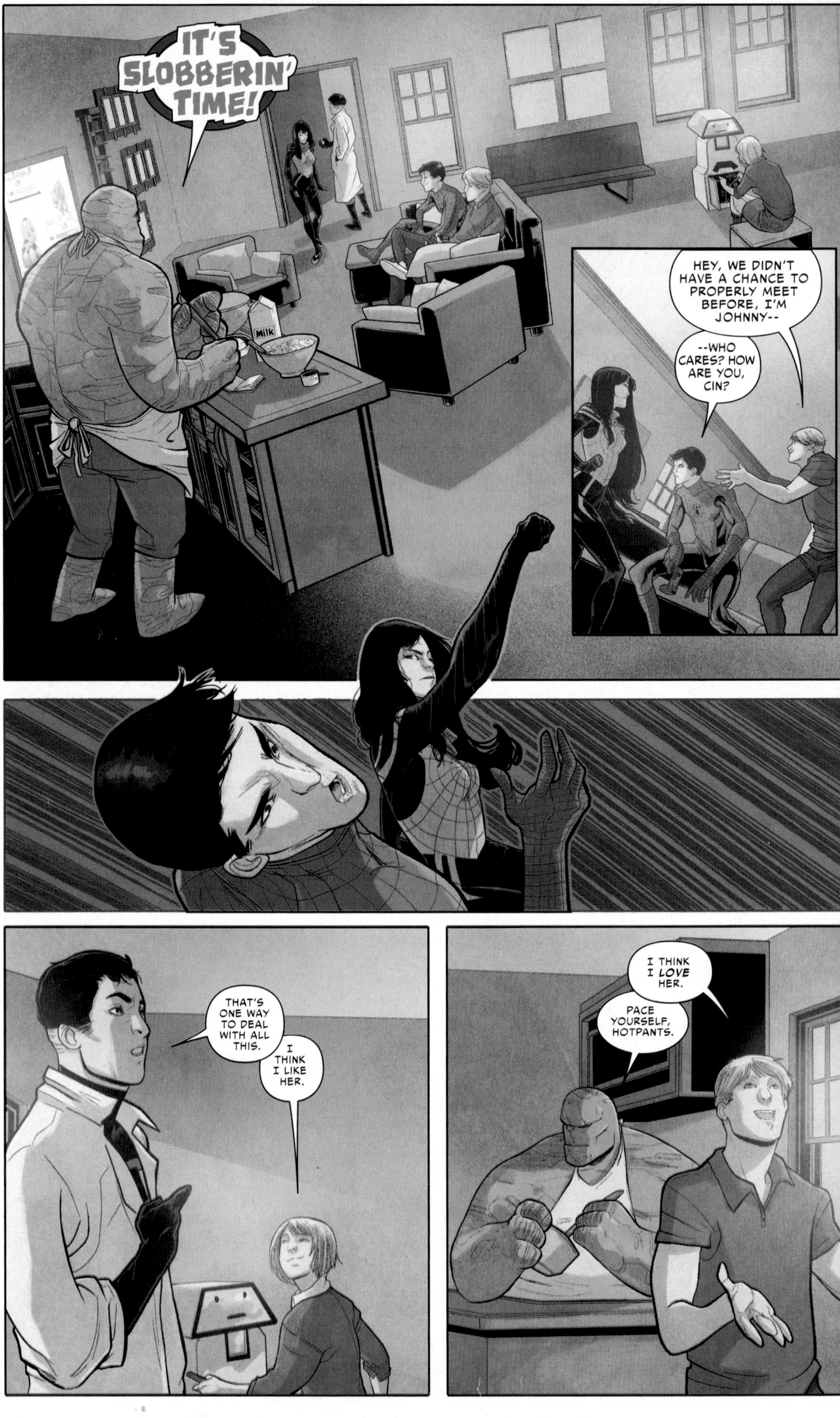
IT'S SLOBBERIN' TIME!
Milk
HEY, WE DIDN'T HAVE A CHANCE TO PROPERLY MEET BEFORE, I'M JOHNNY--
--WHO CARES? HOW ARE YOU, CIN?
THAT'S ONE WAY TO DEAL WITH ALL THIS.
I THINK I LIKE HER.
I THINK I *LOVE* HER.
PACE YOURSELF, HOTPANTS.

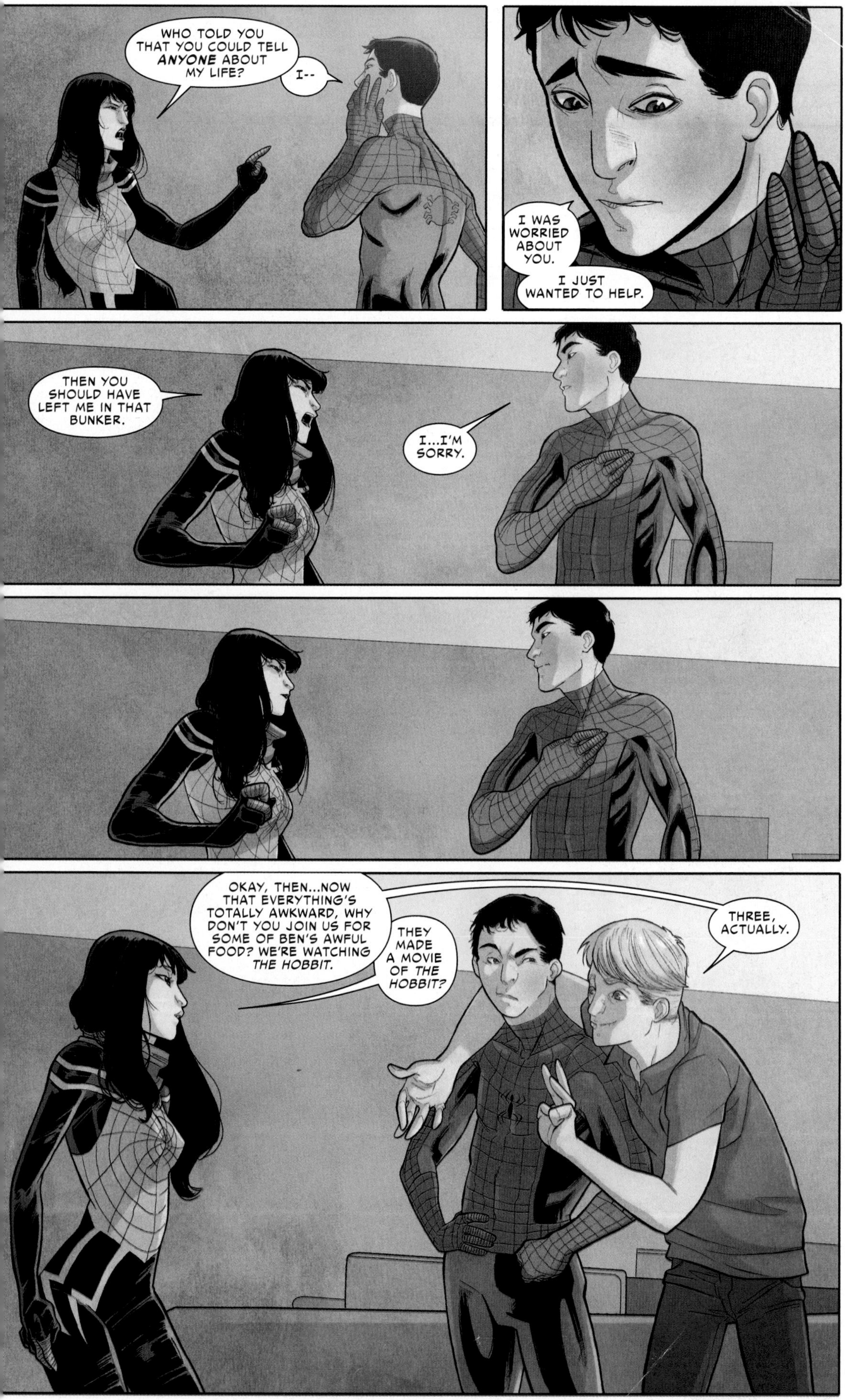
WHO TOLD YOU THAT YOU COULD TELL *ANYONE* ABOUT MY LIFE?
I--
I WAS WORRIED ABOUT YOU.
I JUST WANTED TO HELP.
THEN YOU SHOULD HAVE LEFT ME IN THAT BUNKER.
I...I'M SORRY.
OKAY, THEN...NOW THAT EVERYTHING'S TOTALLY AWKWARD, WHY DON'T YOU JOIN US FOR SOME OF BEN'S AWFUL FOOD? WE'RE WATCHING *THE HOBBIT*.
THEY MADE A MOVIE OF *THE HOBBIT*?
THREE, ACTUALLY.

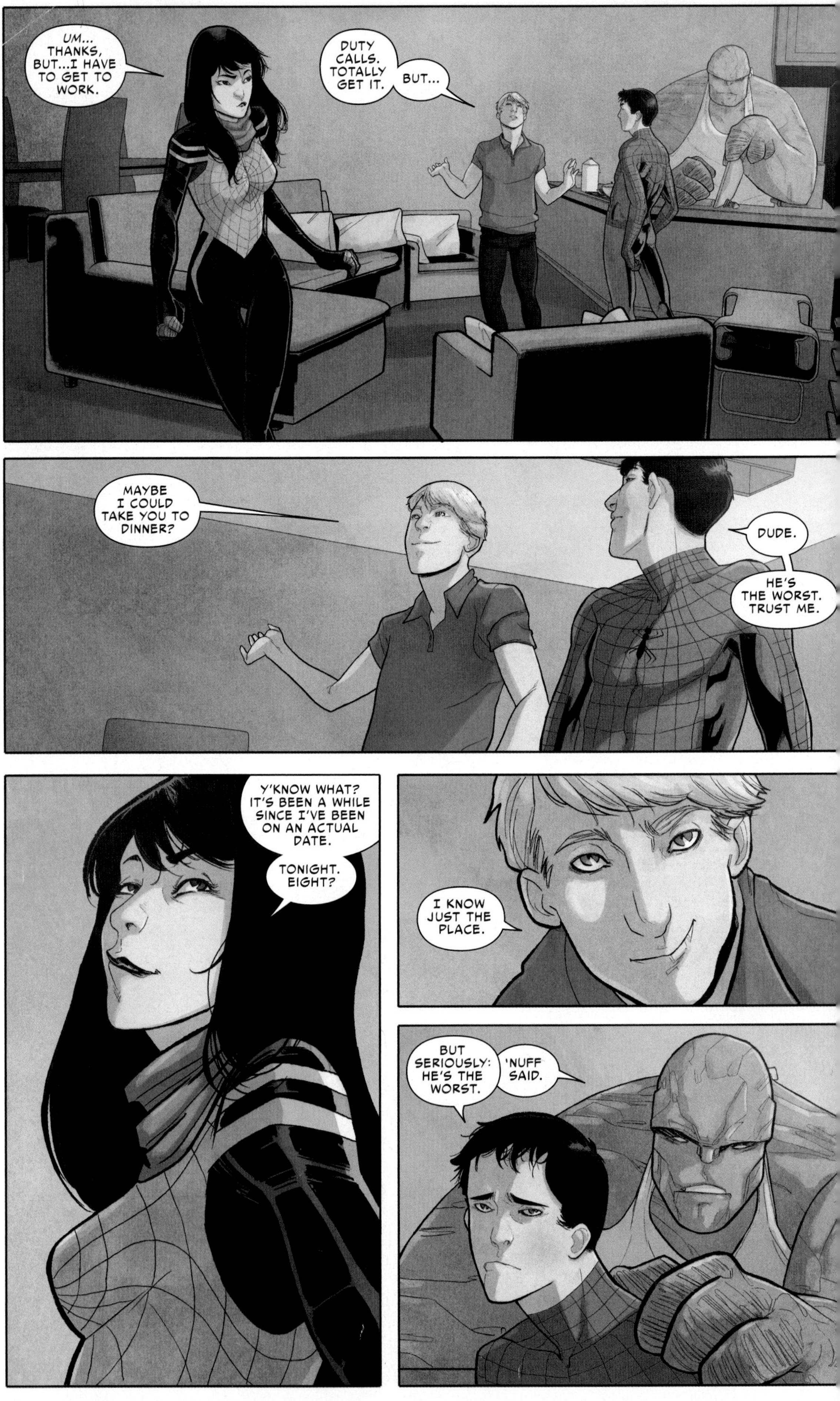
UM... THANKS, BUT...I HAVE TO GET TO WORK.
DUTY CALLS. TOTALLY GET IT.
BUT...
MAYBE I COULD TAKE YOU TO DINNER?
DUDE.
HE'S THE WORST. TRUST ME.
Y'KNOW WHAT? IT'S BEEN A WHILE SINCE I'VE BEEN ON AN ACTUAL DATE.
TONIGHT. EIGHT?
I KNOW JUST THE PLACE.
BUT SERIOUSLY: HE'S THE WORST.
'NUFF SAID.

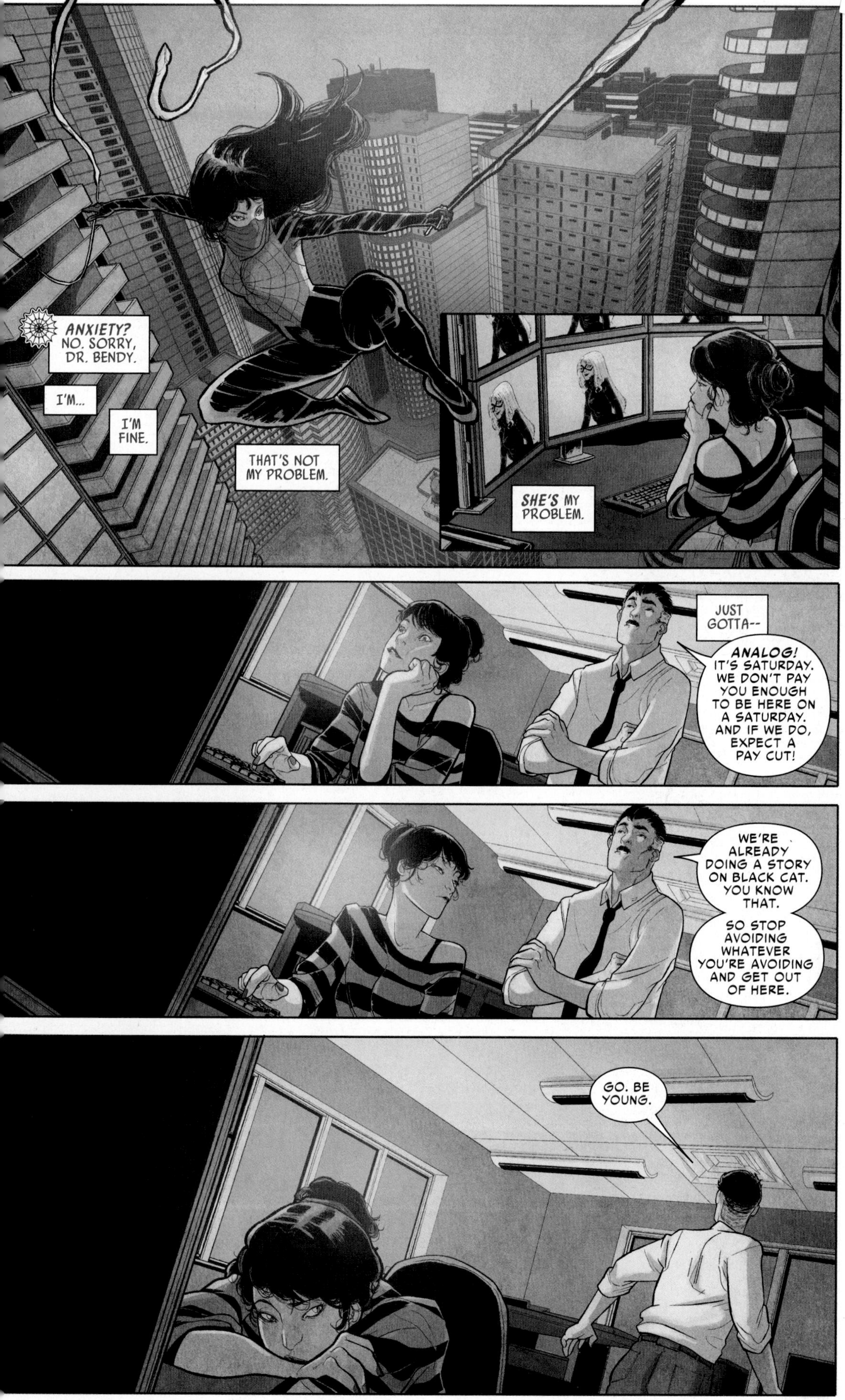
ANXIETY? NO. SORRY, DR. BENDY.
I'M...
I'M FINE.
THAT'S NOT MY PROBLEM.
SHE'S MY PROBLEM.
JUST GOTTA--
ANALOG! IT'S SATURDAY. WE DON'T PAY YOU ENOUGH TO BE HERE ON A SATURDAY. AND IF WE DO, EXPECT A PAY CUT!
WE'RE ALREADY DOING A STORY ON BLACK CAT. YOU KNOW THAT.
SO STOP AVOIDING WHATEVER YOU'RE AVOIDING AND GET OUT OF HERE.
GO. BE YOUNG.

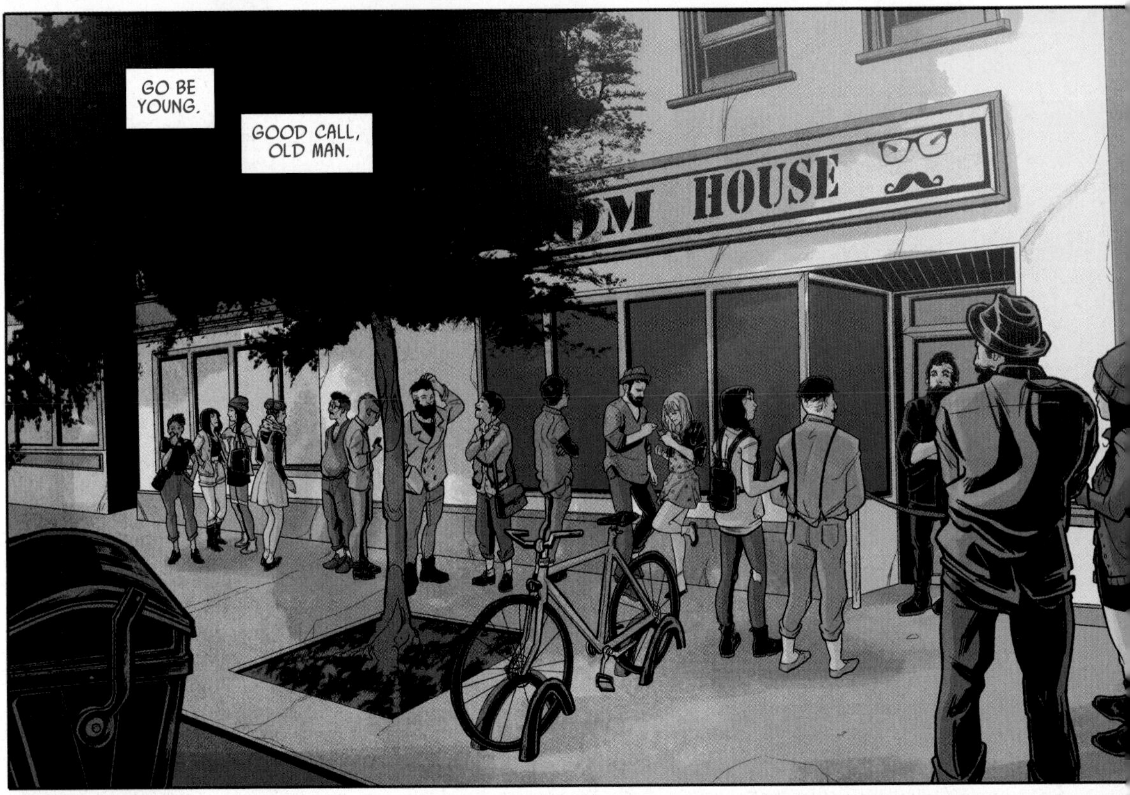
GO BE YOUNG.
GOOD CALL, OLD MAN.
OM HOUSE

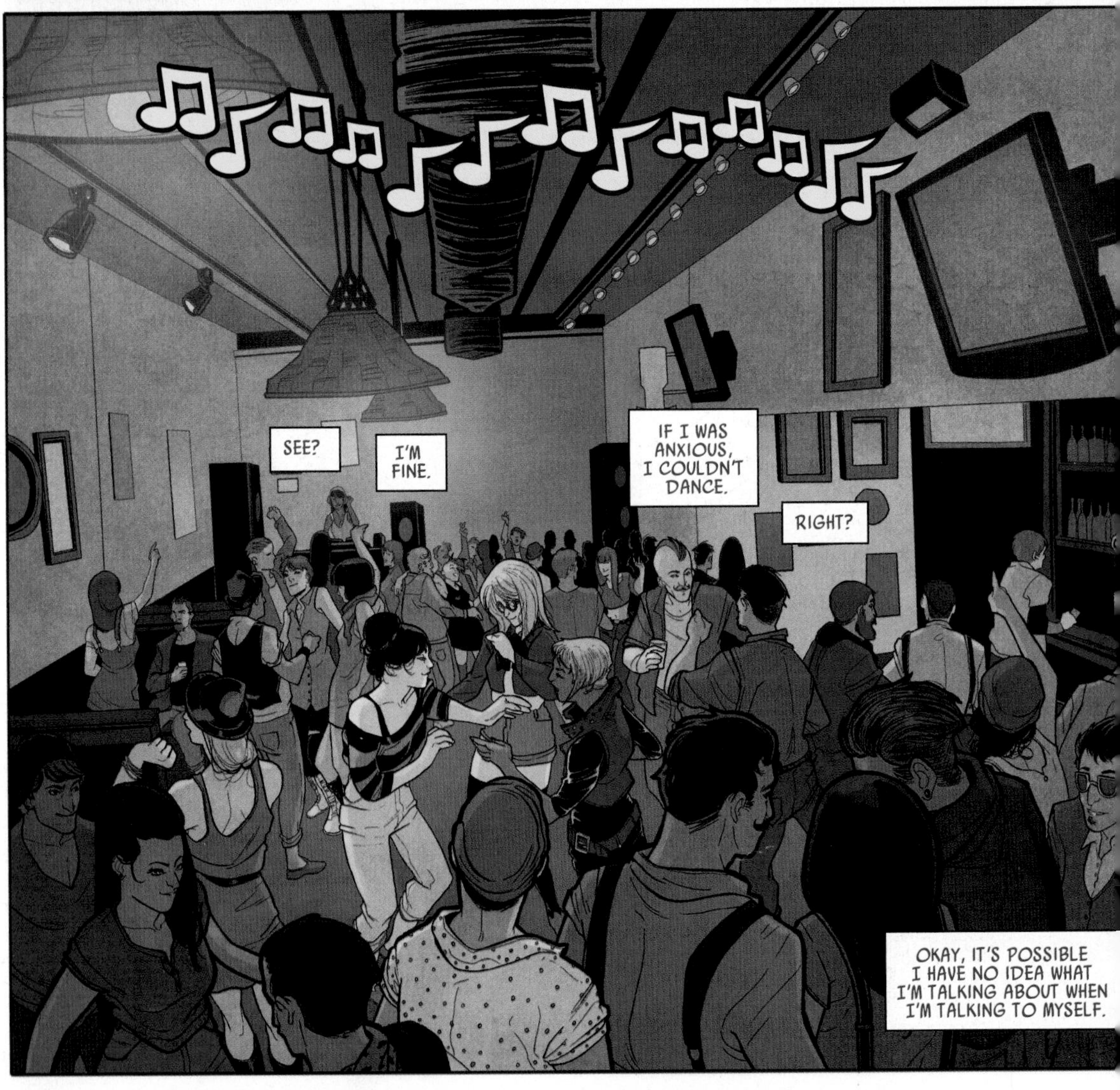
SEE?
I'M FINE.
IF I WAS ANXIOUS, I COULDN'T DANCE.
RIGHT?
OKAY, IT'S POSSIBLE I HAVE NO IDEA WHAT I'M TALKING ABOUT WHEN I'M TALKING TO MYSELF.

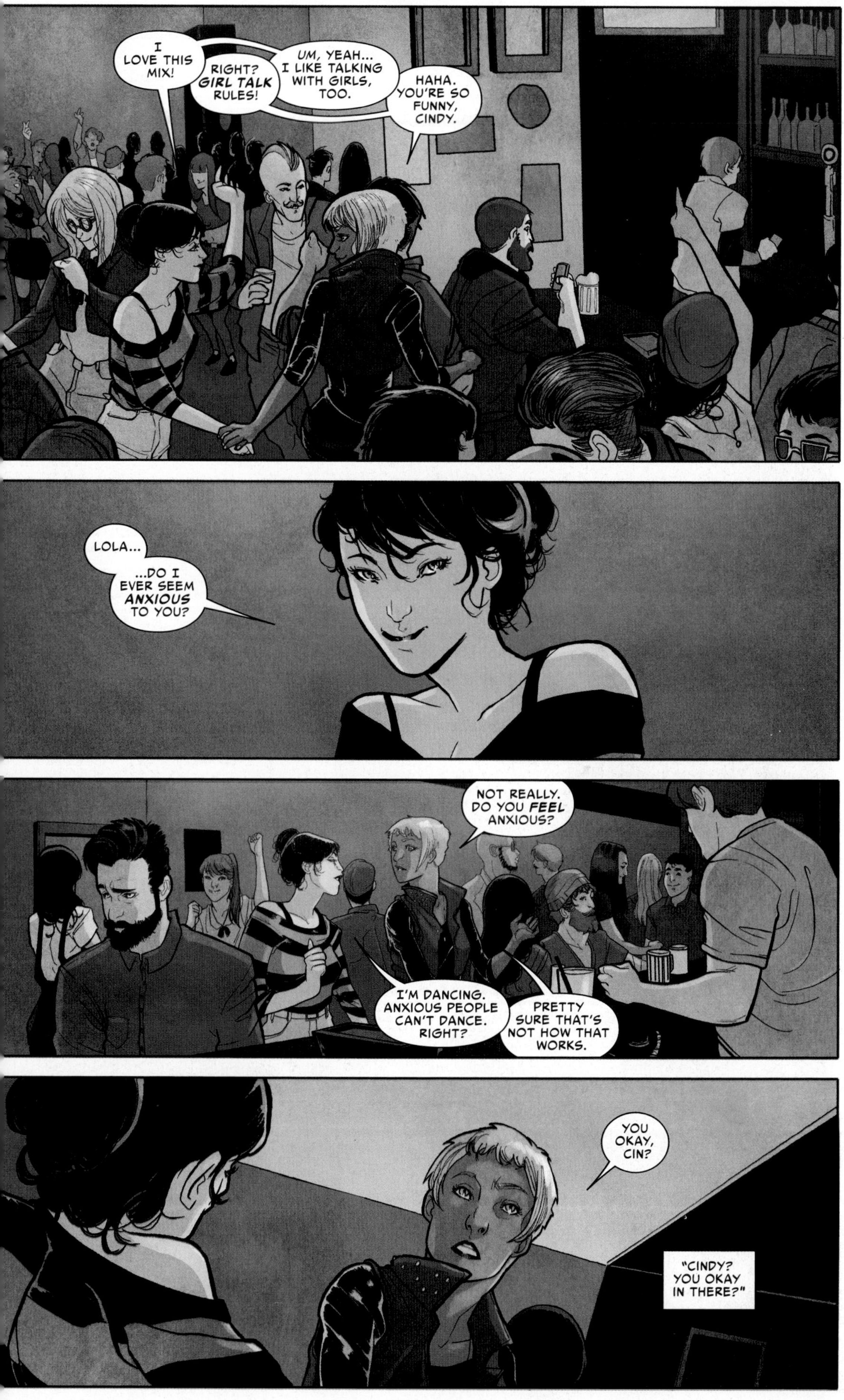
I LOVE THIS MIX!
RIGHT? GIRL TALK RULES!
UM, YEAH... I LIKE TALKING WITH GIRLS, TOO.
HAHA. YOU'RE SO FUNNY, CINDY.
LOLA...
...DO I EVER SEEM ANXIOUS TO YOU?
NOT REALLY. DO YOU FEEL ANXIOUS?
I'M DANCING. ANXIOUS PEOPLE CAN'T DANCE. RIGHT?
PRETTY SURE THAT'S NOT HOW THAT WORKS.
YOU OKAY, CIN?
"CINDY? YOU OKAY IN THERE?"

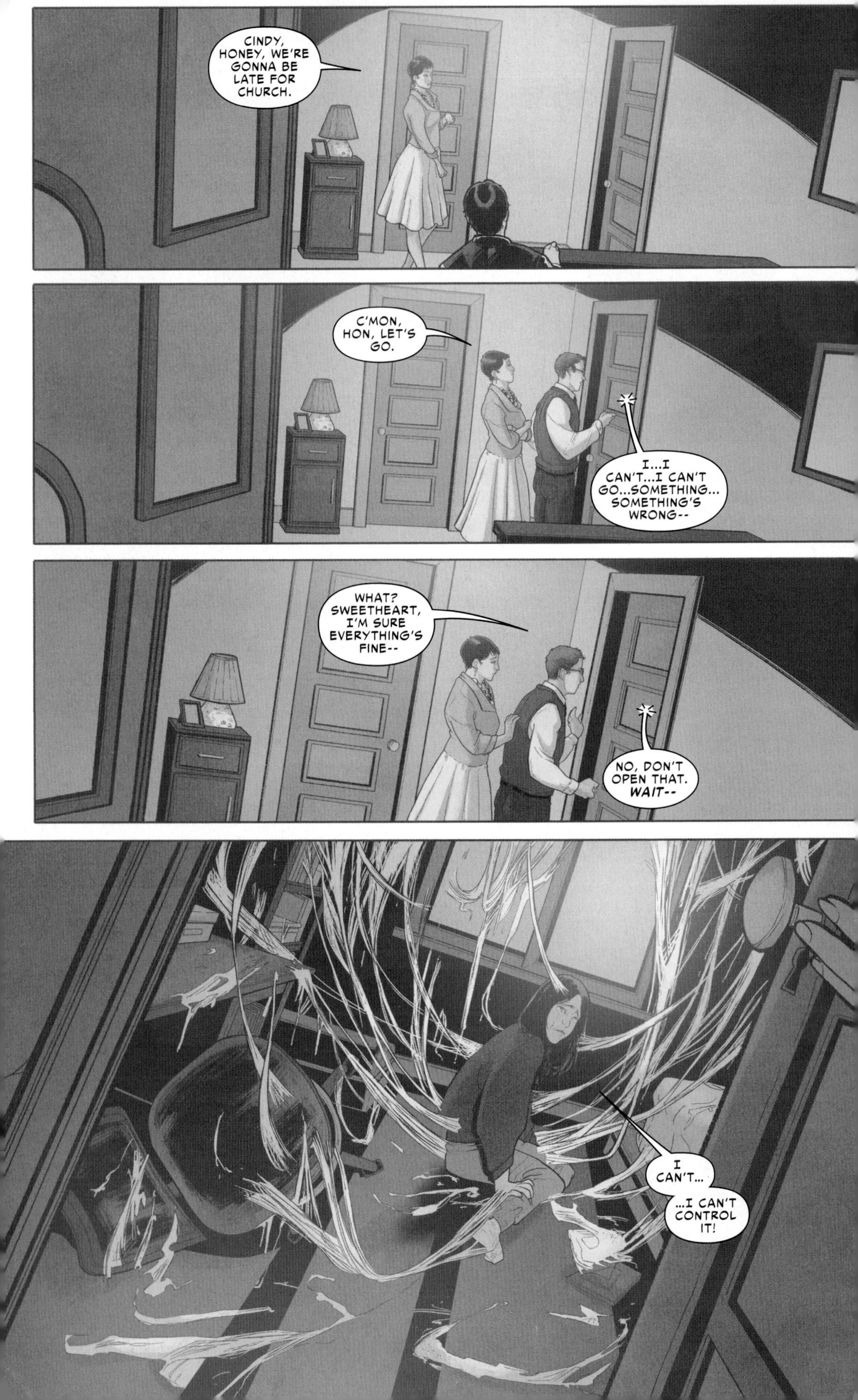
CINDY, HONEY, WE'RE GONNA BE LATE FOR CHURCH.
C'MON, HON, LET'S GO.
I...I CAN'T...I CAN'T GO...SOMETHING... SOMETHING'S WRONG--
WHAT? SWEETHEART, I'M SURE EVERYTHING'S FINE--
NO, DON'T OPEN THAT. WAIT--
I CAN'T...
...I CAN'T CONTROL IT!

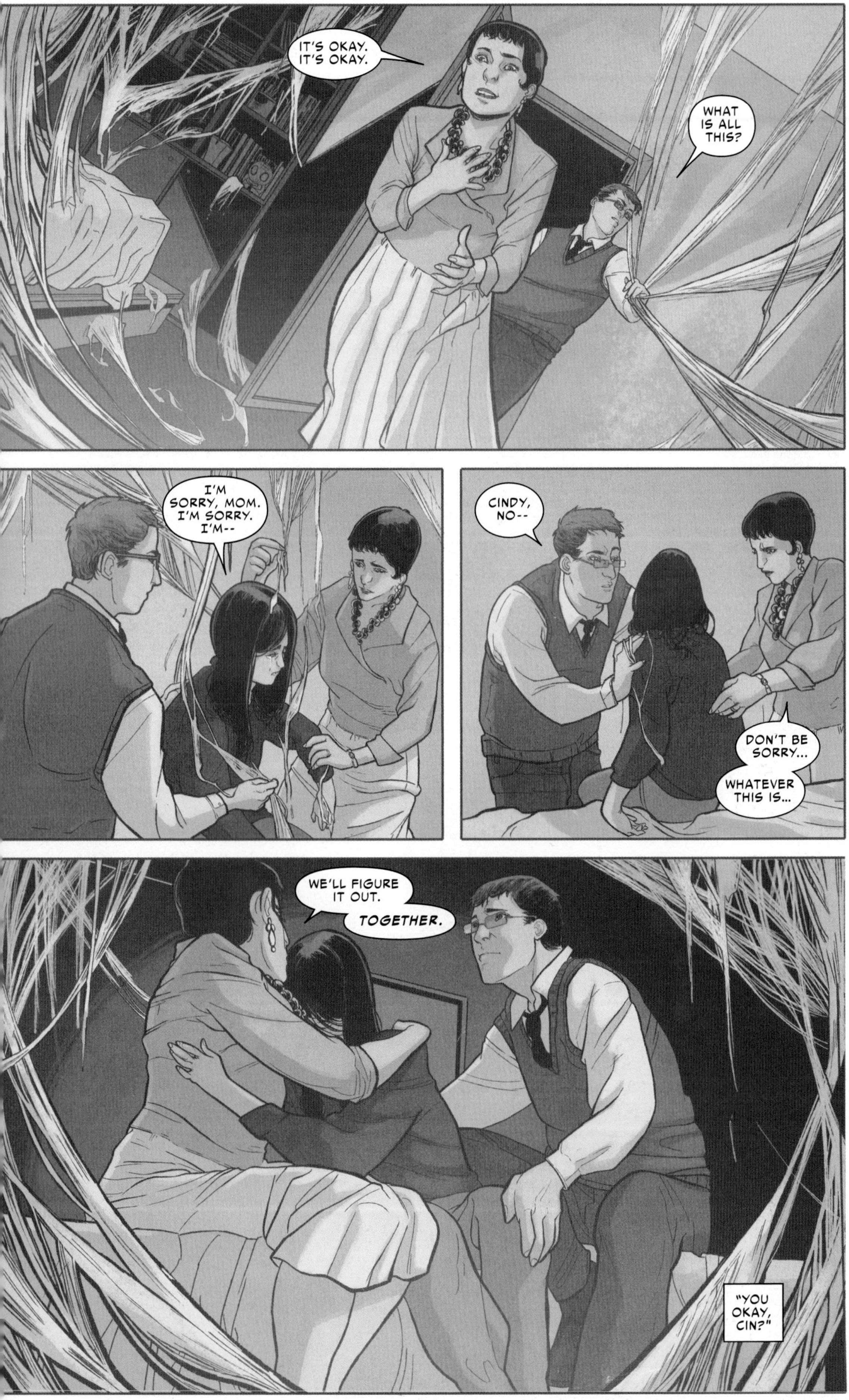
IT'S OKAY. IT'S OKAY.
WHAT IS ALL THIS?
I'M SORRY, MOM. I'M SORRY. I'M--
CINDY, NO--
DON'T BE SORRY...
WHATEVER THIS IS...
WE'LL FIGURE IT OUT.
TOGETHER.
"YOU OKAY, CIN?"

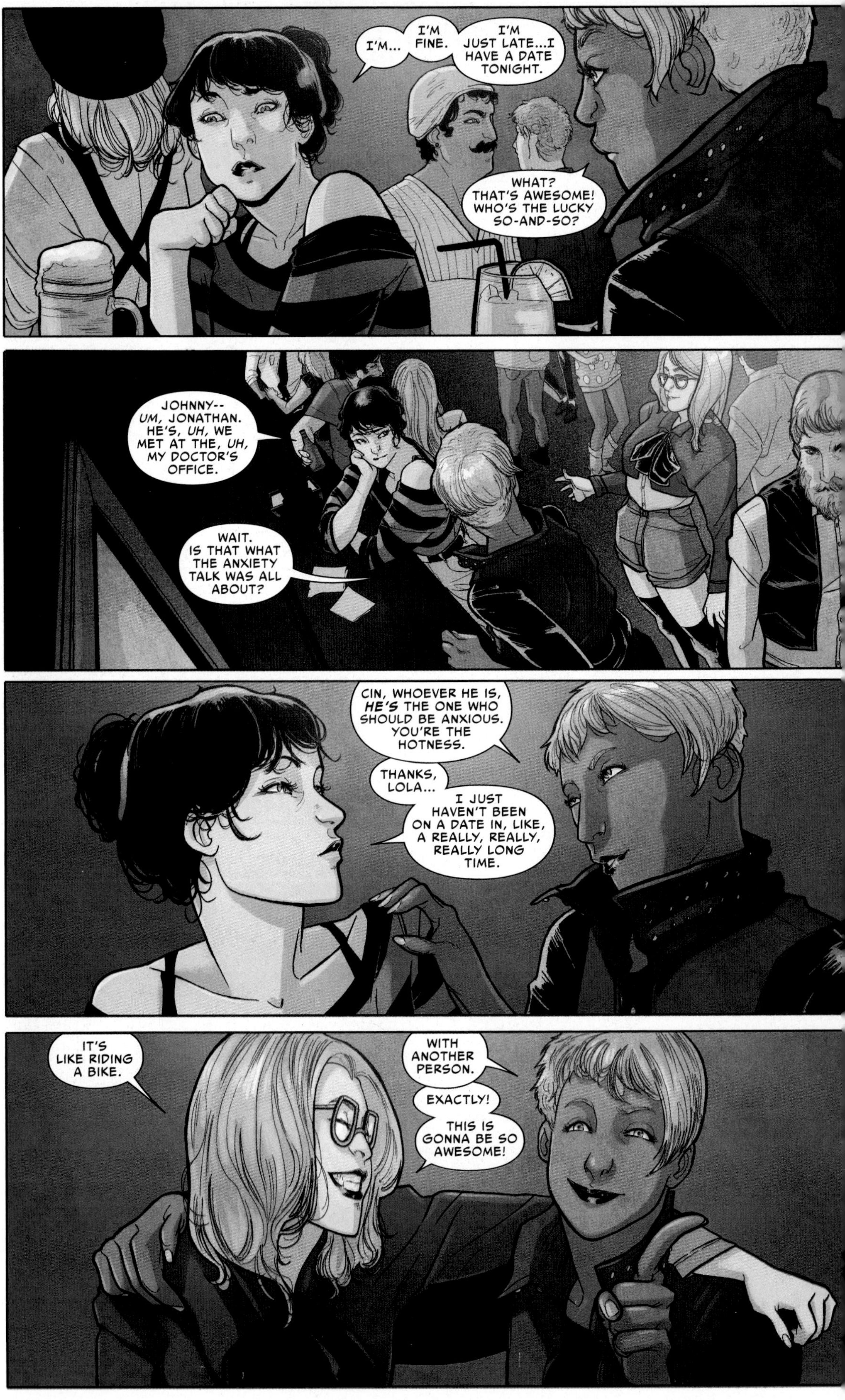
I'M...
I'M FINE.
I'M JUST LATE...I HAVE A DATE TONIGHT.
WHAT? THAT'S AWESOME! WHO'S THE LUCKY SO-AND-SO?
JOHNNY-- *UM,* JONATHAN. HE'S, *UH,* WE MET AT THE, *UH,* MY DOCTOR'S OFFICE.
WAIT. IS THAT WHAT THE ANXIETY TALK WAS ALL ABOUT?
CIN, WHOEVER HE IS, ***HE'S*** THE ONE WHO SHOULD BE ANXIOUS. YOU'RE THE HOTNESS.
THANKS, LOLA...
I JUST HAVEN'T BEEN ON A DATE IN, LIKE, A REALLY, REALLY, REALLY LONG TIME.
IT'S LIKE RIDING A BIKE.
WITH ANOTHER PERSON.
EXACTLY!
THIS IS GONNA BE SO AWESOME!

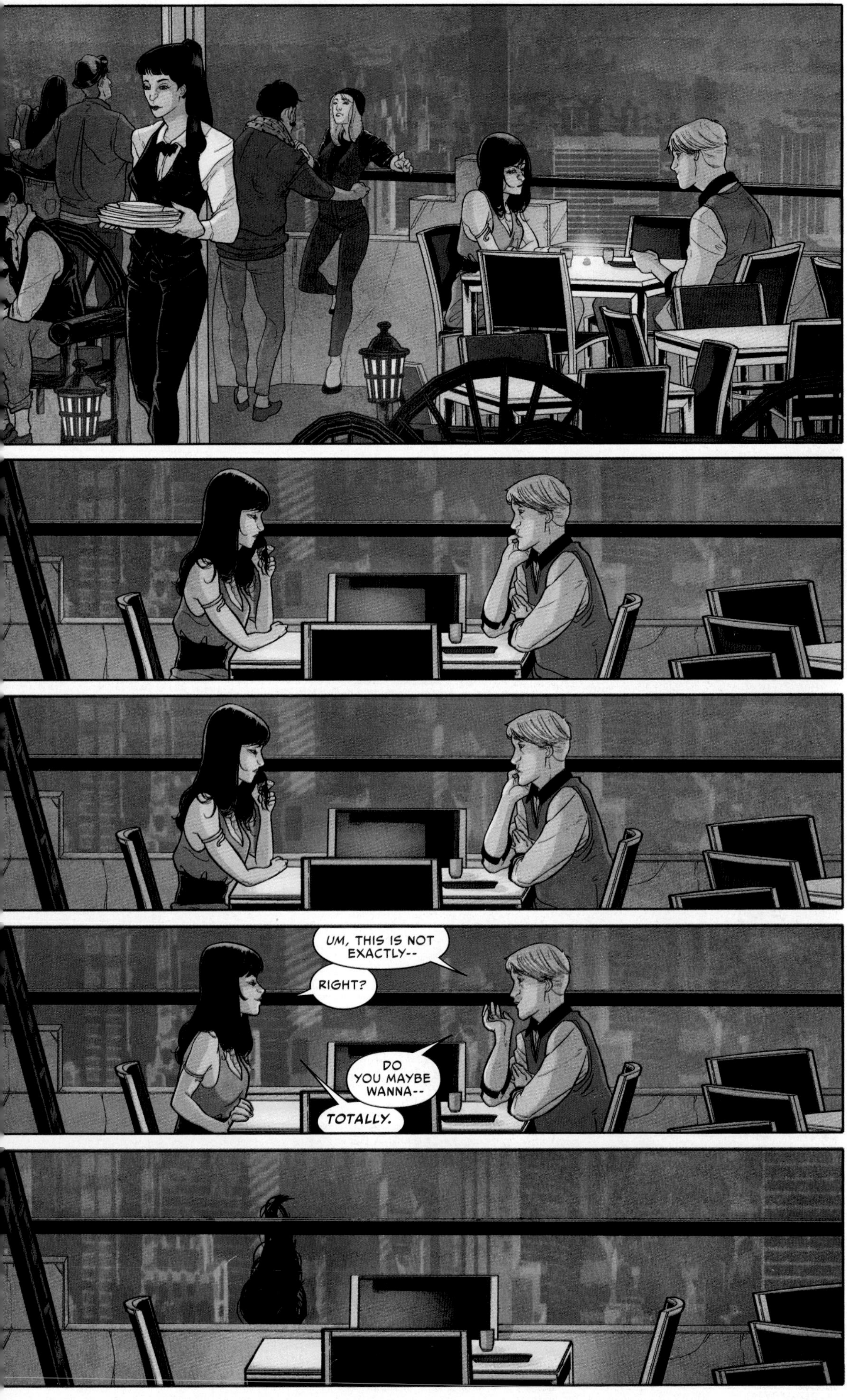
UM, THIS IS NOT EXACTLY--
RIGHT?
DO YOU MAYBE WANNA--
TOTALLY.

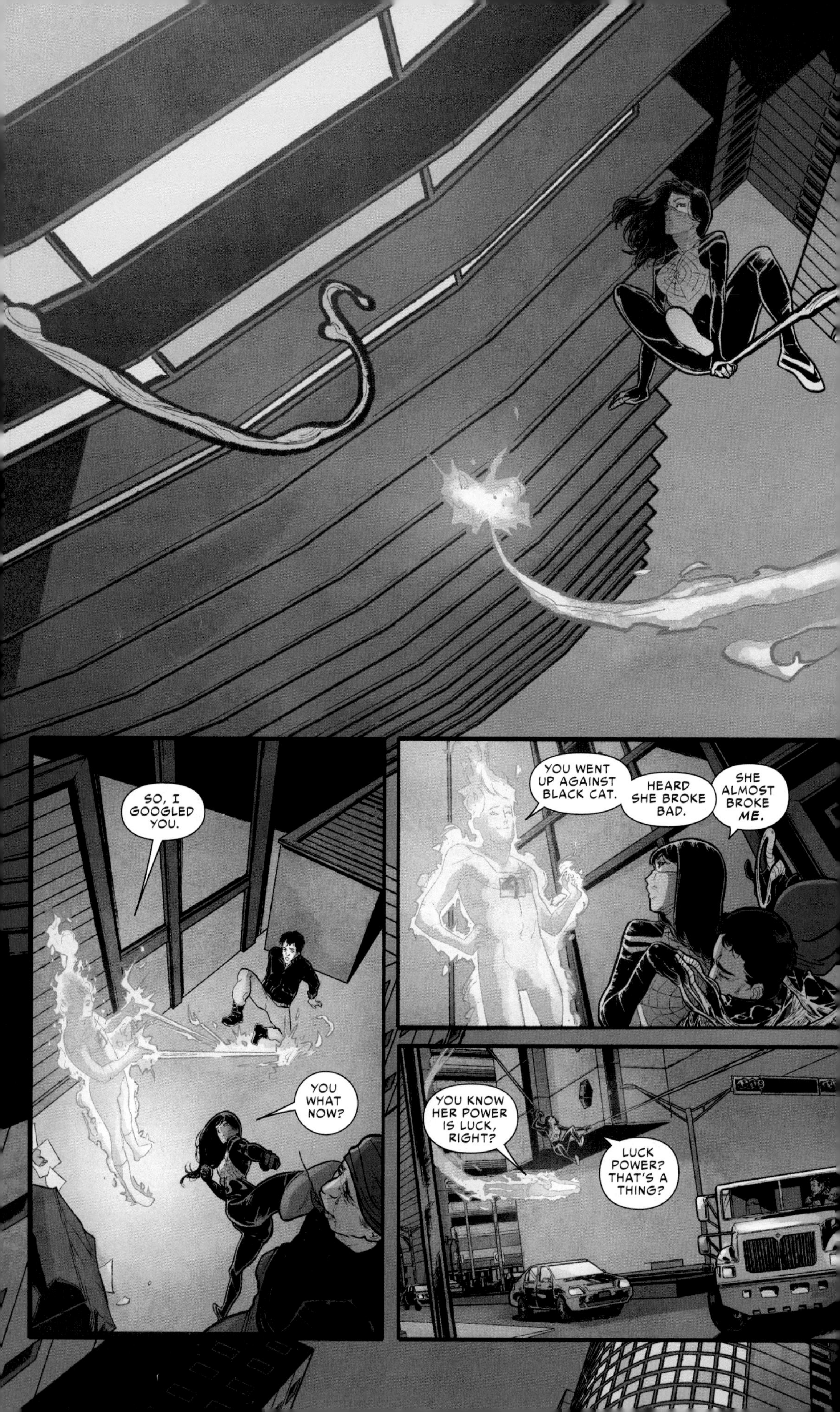
SO, I GOOGLED YOU.
YOU WHAT NOW?
YOU WENT UP AGAINST BLACK CAT.
HEARD SHE BROKE BAD.
SHE ALMOST BROKE *ME.*
YOU KNOW HER POWER IS LUCK, RIGHT?
LUCK POWER? THAT'S A THING?

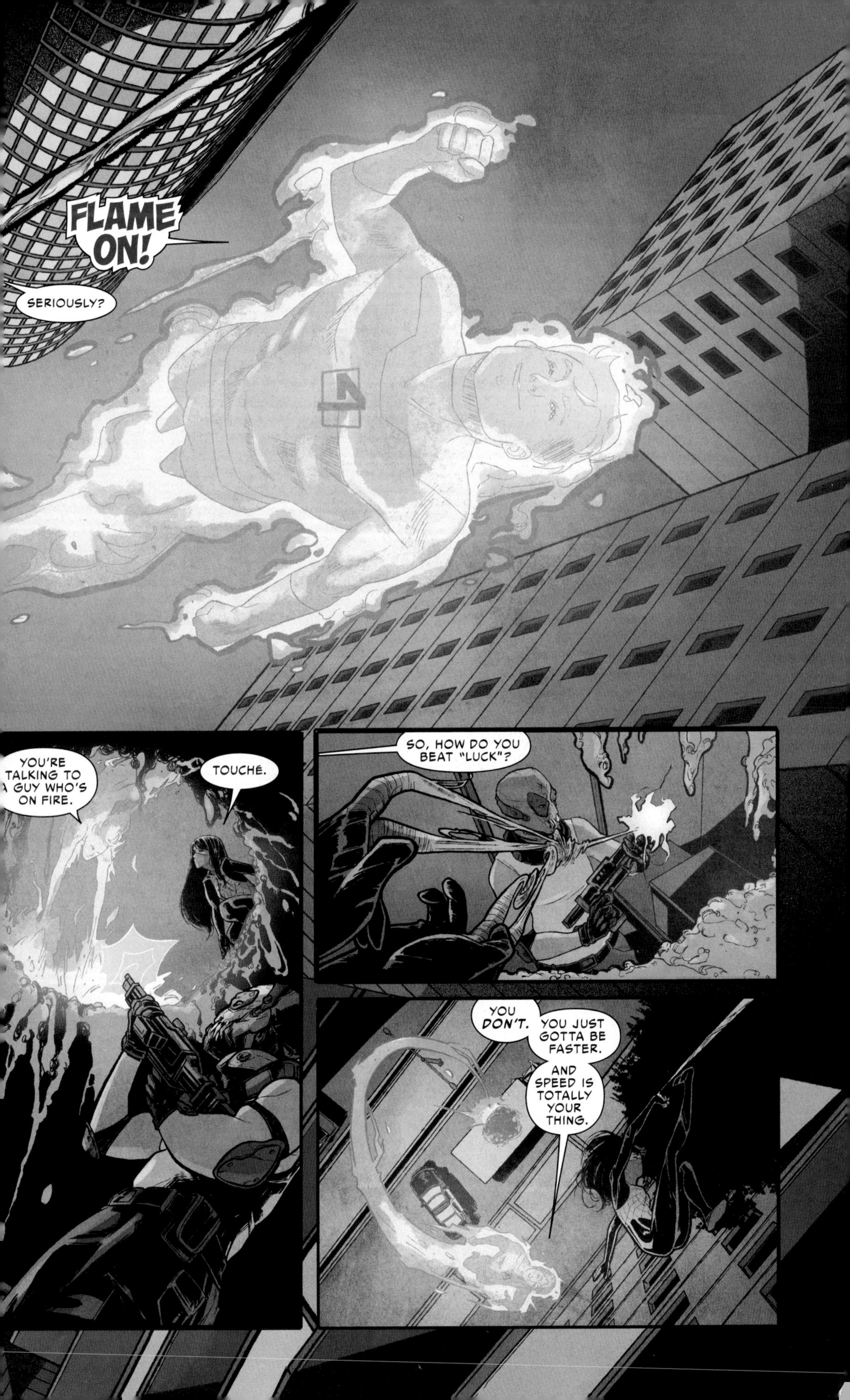
FLAME ON!
SERIOUSLY?
YOU'RE TALKING TO A GUY WHO'S ON FIRE.
TOUCHÉ.
SO, HOW DO YOU BEAT "LUCK"?
YOU DON'T.
YOU JUST GOTTA BE FASTER.
AND SPEED IS TOTALLY YOUR THING.

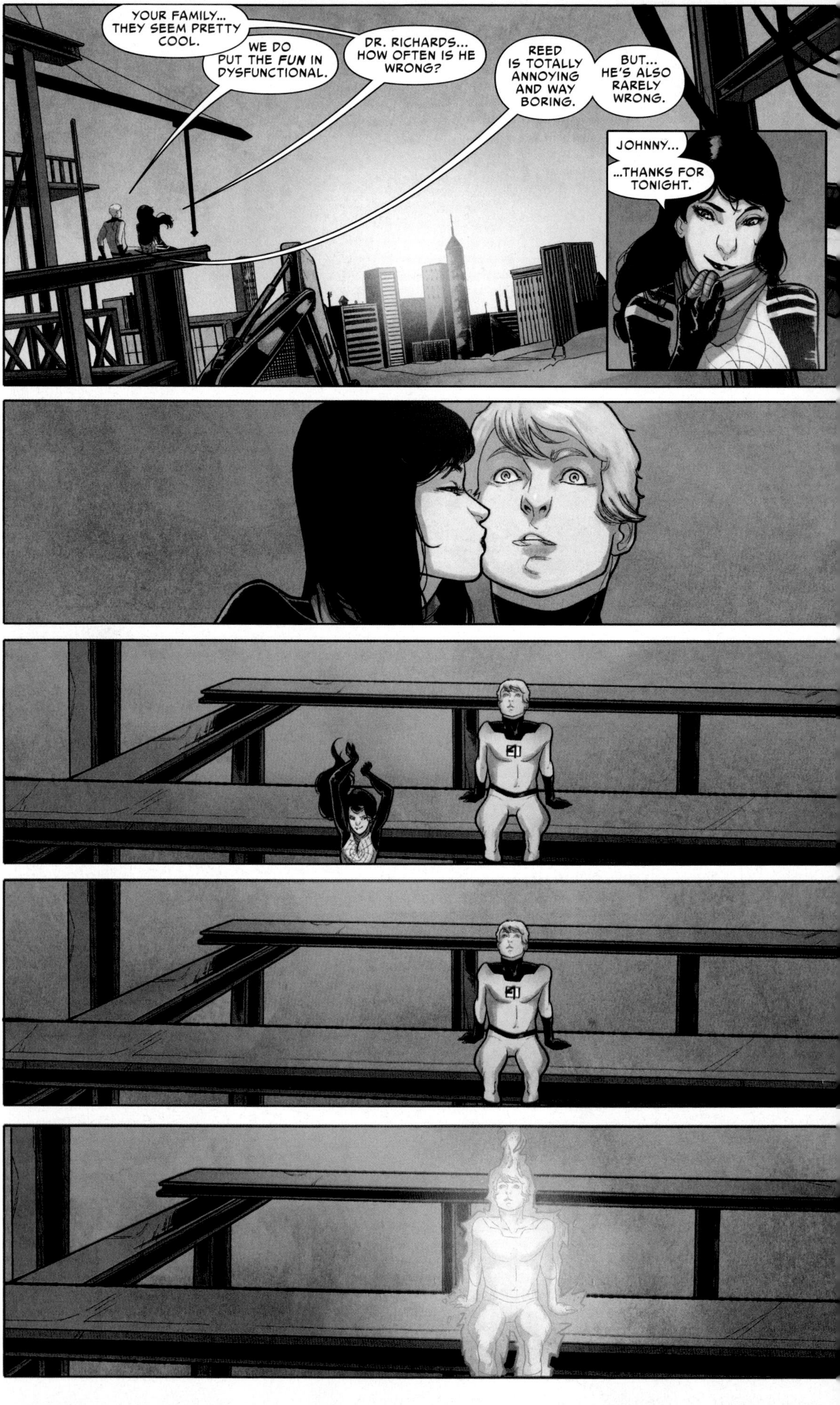
YOUR FAMILY... THEY SEEM PRETTY COOL.
WE DO PUT THE *FUN* IN DYSFUNCTIONAL.
DR. RICHARDS... HOW OFTEN IS HE WRONG?
REED IS TOTALLY ANNOYING AND WAY BORING.
BUT... HE'S ALSO RARELY WRONG.
JOHNNY...
...THANKS FOR TONIGHT.

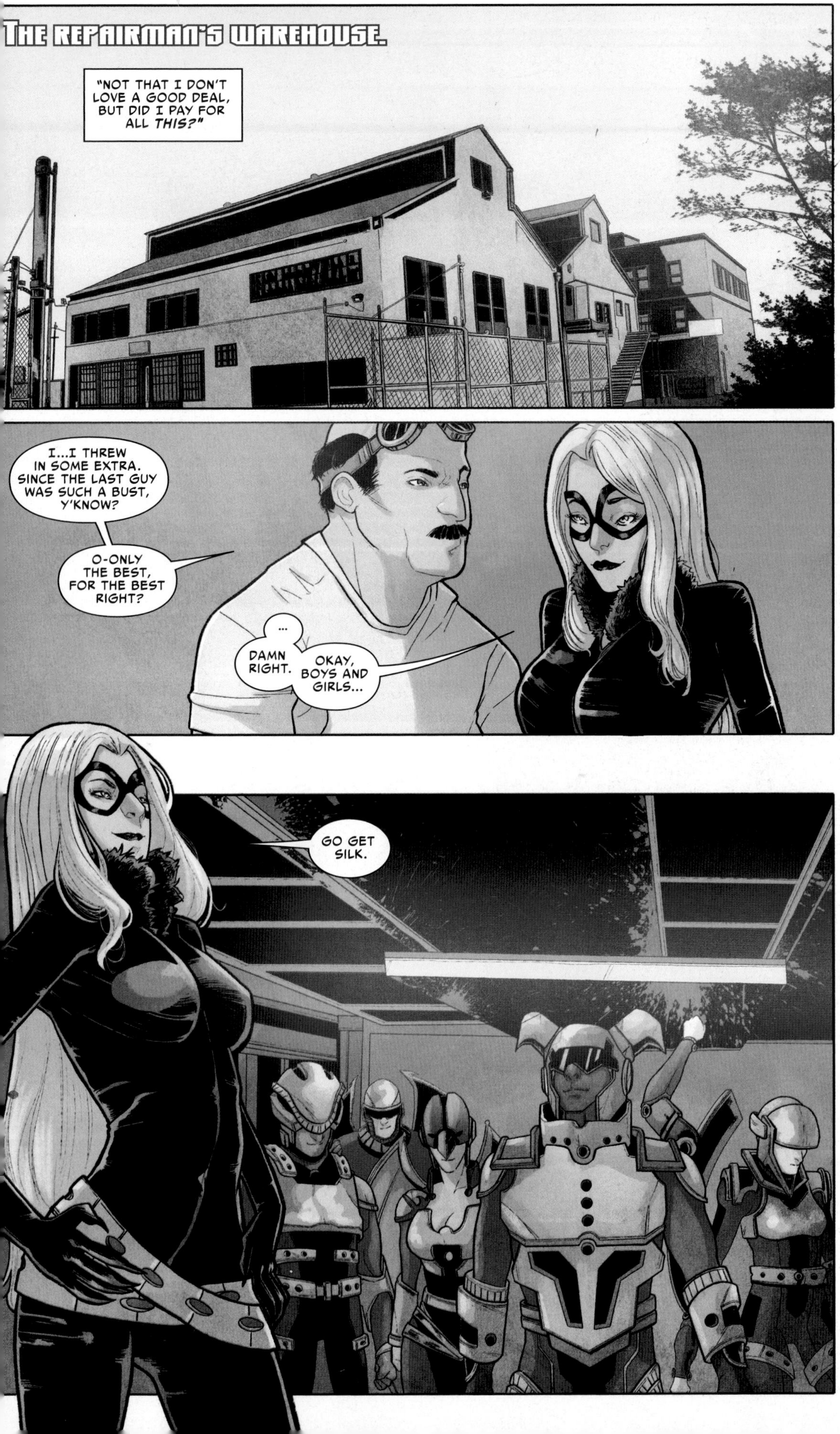
THE REPAIRMAN'S WAREHOUSE.
"NOT THAT I DON'T LOVE A GOOD DEAL, BUT DID I PAY FOR ALL THIS?"
I...I THREW IN SOME EXTRA. SINCE THE LAST GUY WAS SUCH A BUST, Y'KNOW?
O-ONLY THE BEST, FOR THE BEST RIGHT?
...
DAMN RIGHT.
OKAY, BOYS AND GIRLS...
GO GET SILK.

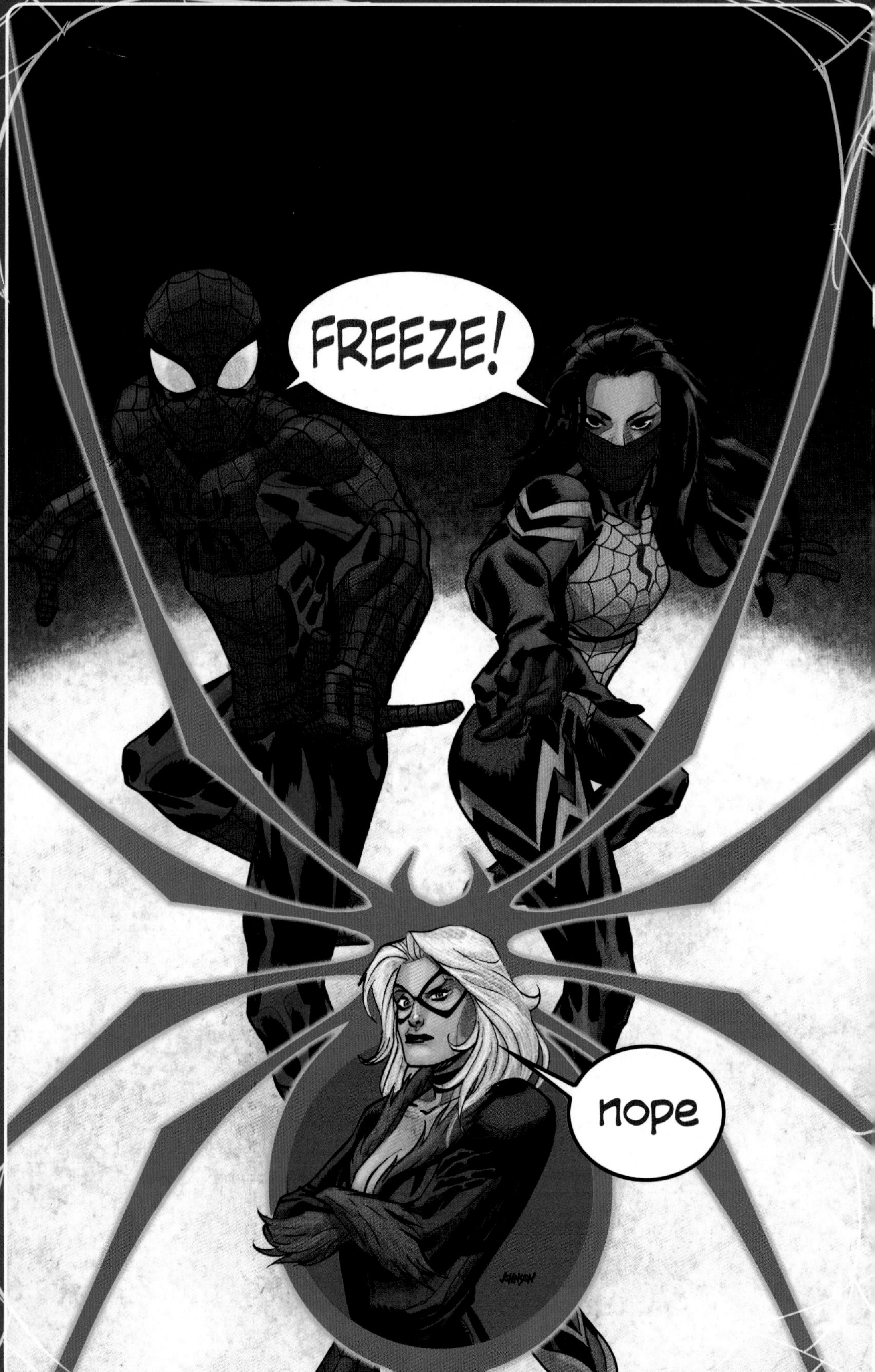
FREEZE!
nope
JOHNSON

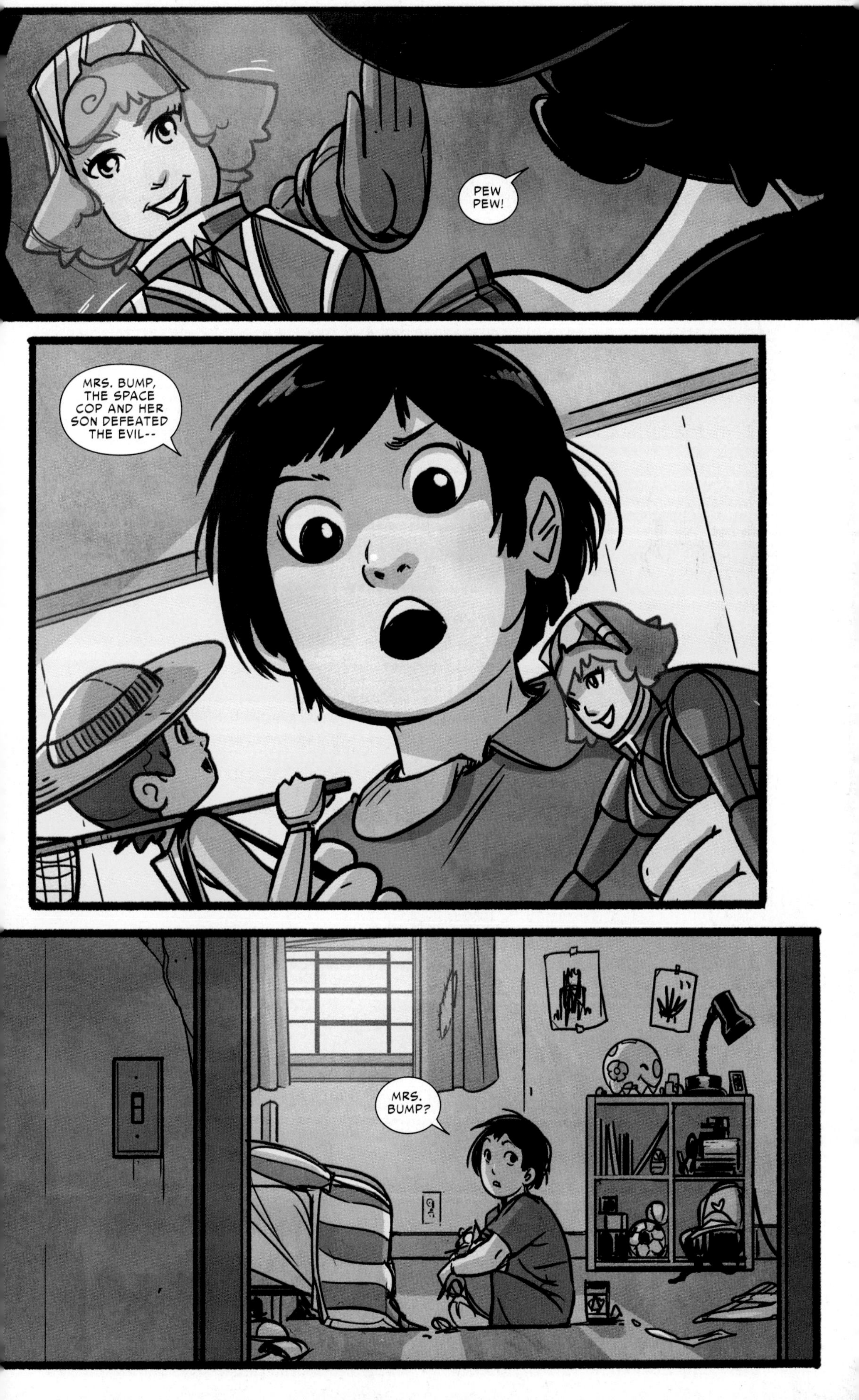
PEW PEW!
MRS. BUMP, THE SPACE COP AND HER SON DEFEATED THE EVIL--
MRS. BUMP?

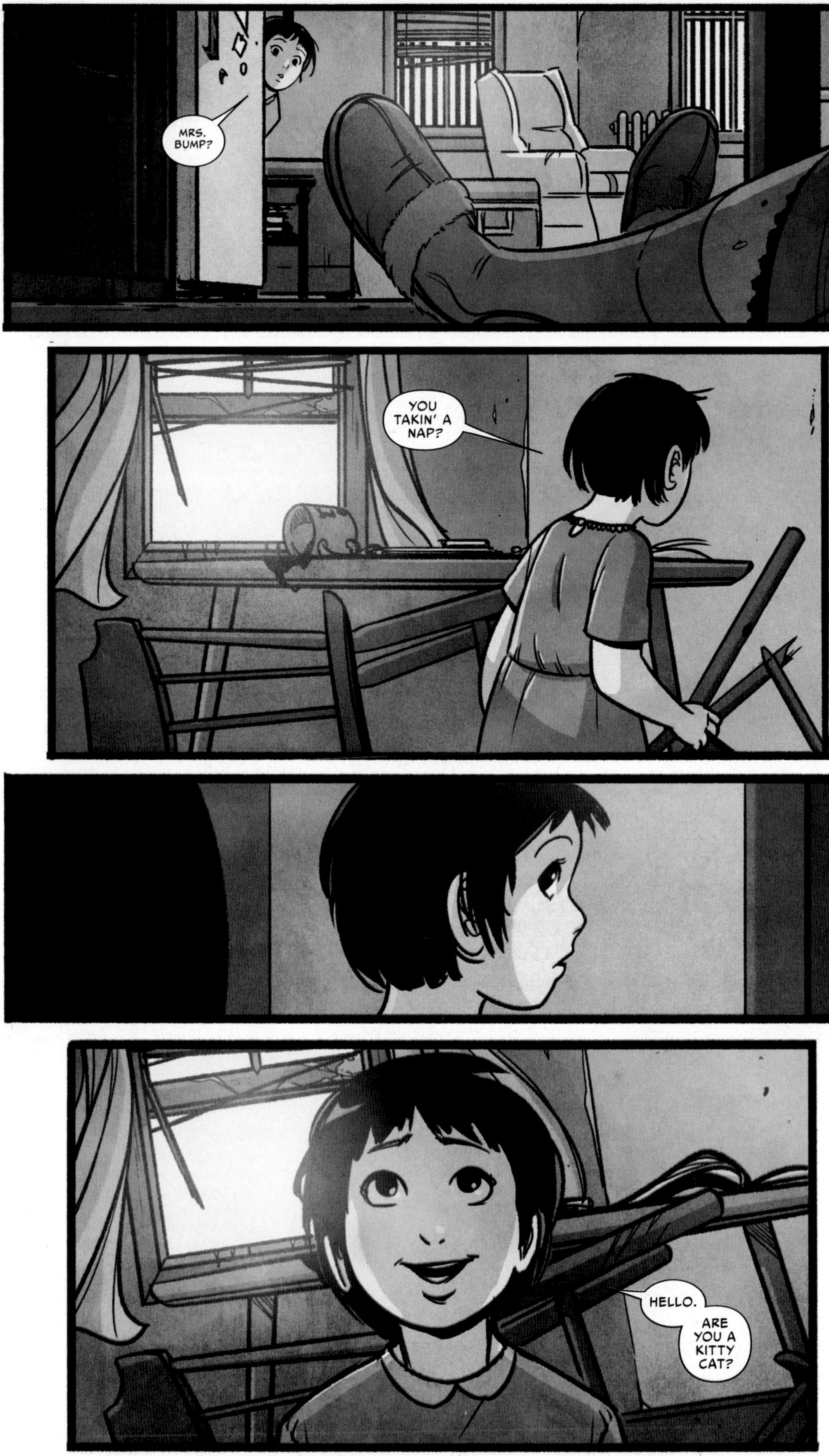
MRS. BUMP?
YOU TAKIN' A NAP?
HELLO.
ARE YOU A KITTY CAT?

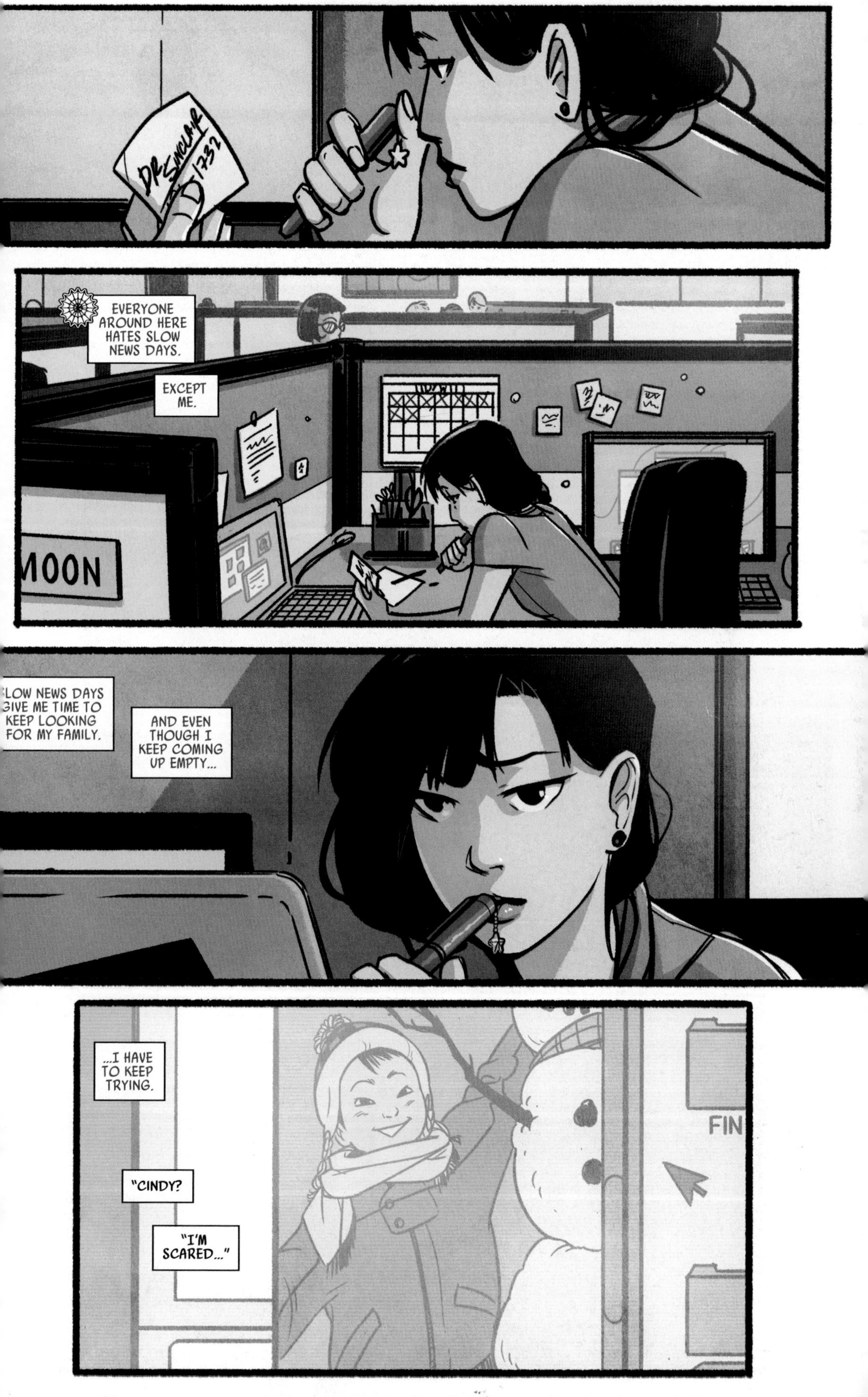
DR. SINCLAIR
EVERYONE AROUND HERE HATES SLOW NEWS DAYS.
EXCEPT ME.
MOON
SLOW NEWS DAYS GIVE ME TIME TO KEEP LOOKING FOR MY FAMILY.
AND EVEN THOUGH I KEEP COMING UP EMPTY...
...I HAVE TO KEEP TRYING.
"CINDY?
"I'M SCARED..."

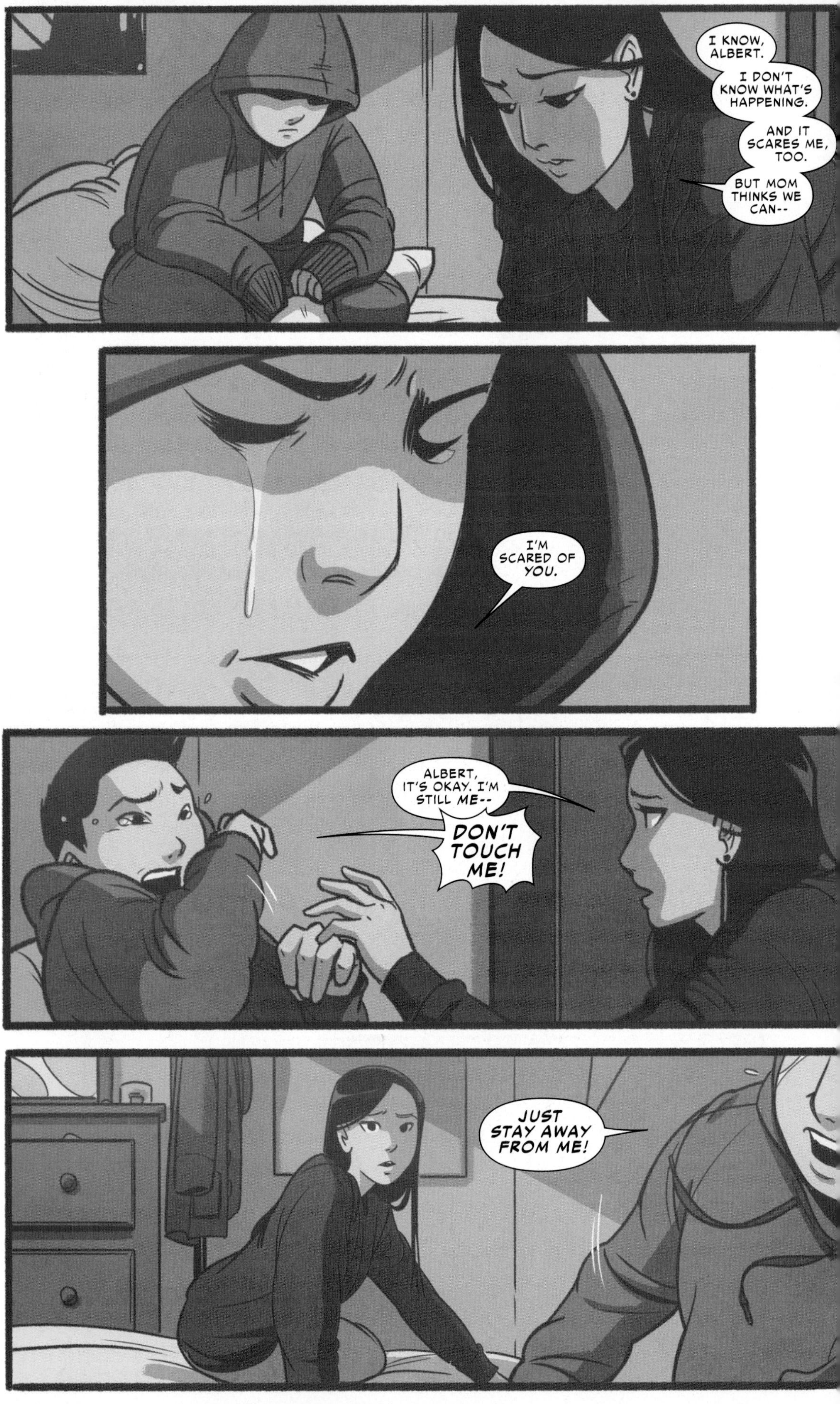
I KNOW, ALBERT.
I DON'T KNOW WHAT'S HAPPENING.
AND IT SCARES ME, TOO.
BUT MOM THINKS WE CAN--
I'M SCARED OF YOU.
ALBERT, IT'S OKAY. I'M STILL ME--
DON'T TOUCH ME!
JUST STAY AWAY FROM ME!

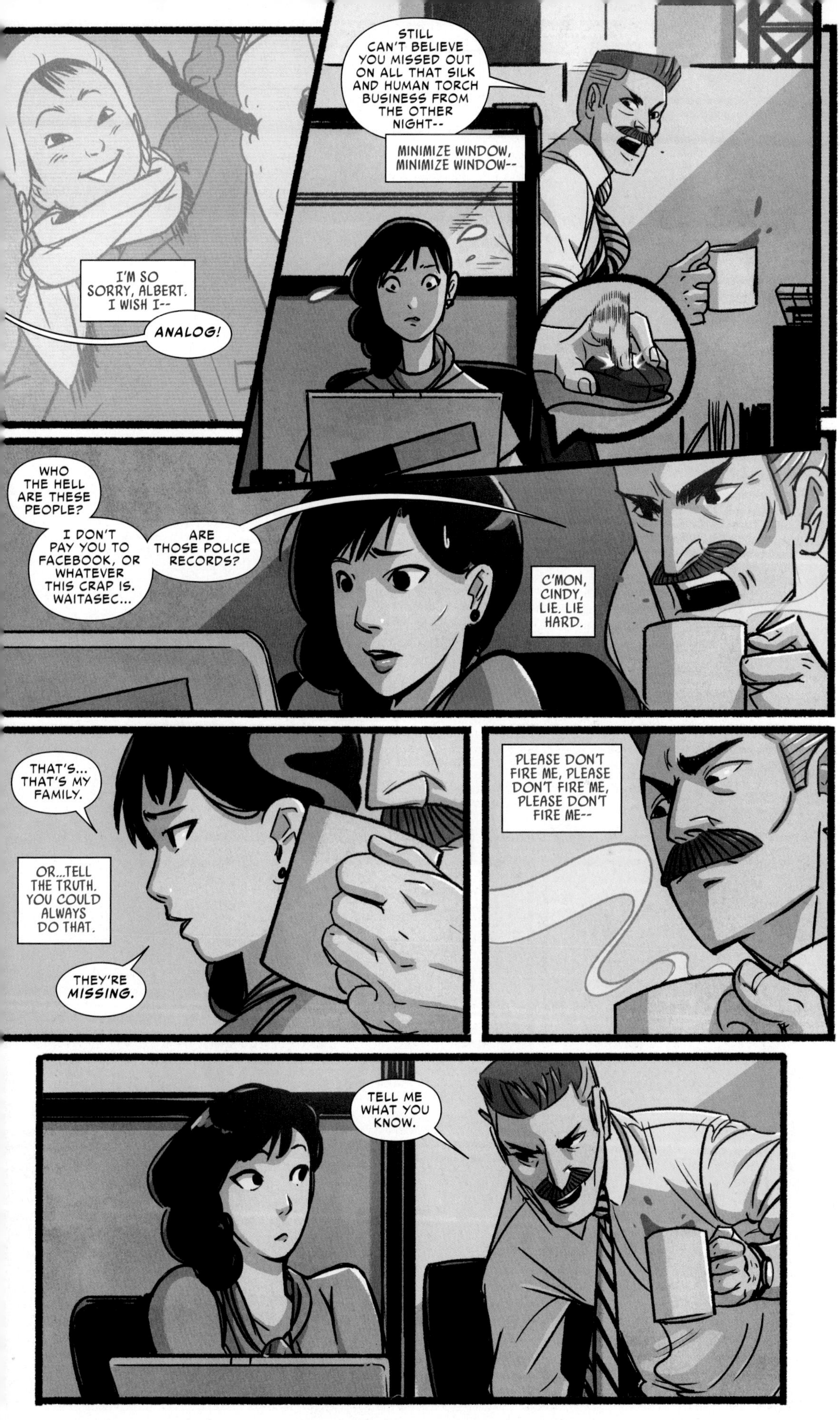
I'M SO SORRY, ALBERT. I WISH I--
ANALOG!
STILL CAN'T BELIEVE YOU MISSED OUT ON ALL THAT SILK AND HUMAN TORCH BUSINESS FROM THE OTHER NIGHT--
MINIMIZE WINDOW, MINIMIZE WINDOW--
WHO THE HELL ARE THESE PEOPLE?
I DON'T PAY YOU TO FACEBOOK, OR WHATEVER THIS CRAP IS. WAITASEC...
ARE THOSE POLICE RECORDS?
C'MON, CINDY, LIE. LIE HARD.
THAT'S... THAT'S MY FAMILY.
OR...TELL THE TRUTH. YOU COULD ALWAYS DO THAT.
THEY'RE MISSING.
PLEASE DON'T FIRE ME, PLEASE DON'T FIRE ME, PLEASE DON'T FIRE ME--
TELL ME WHAT YOU KNOW.

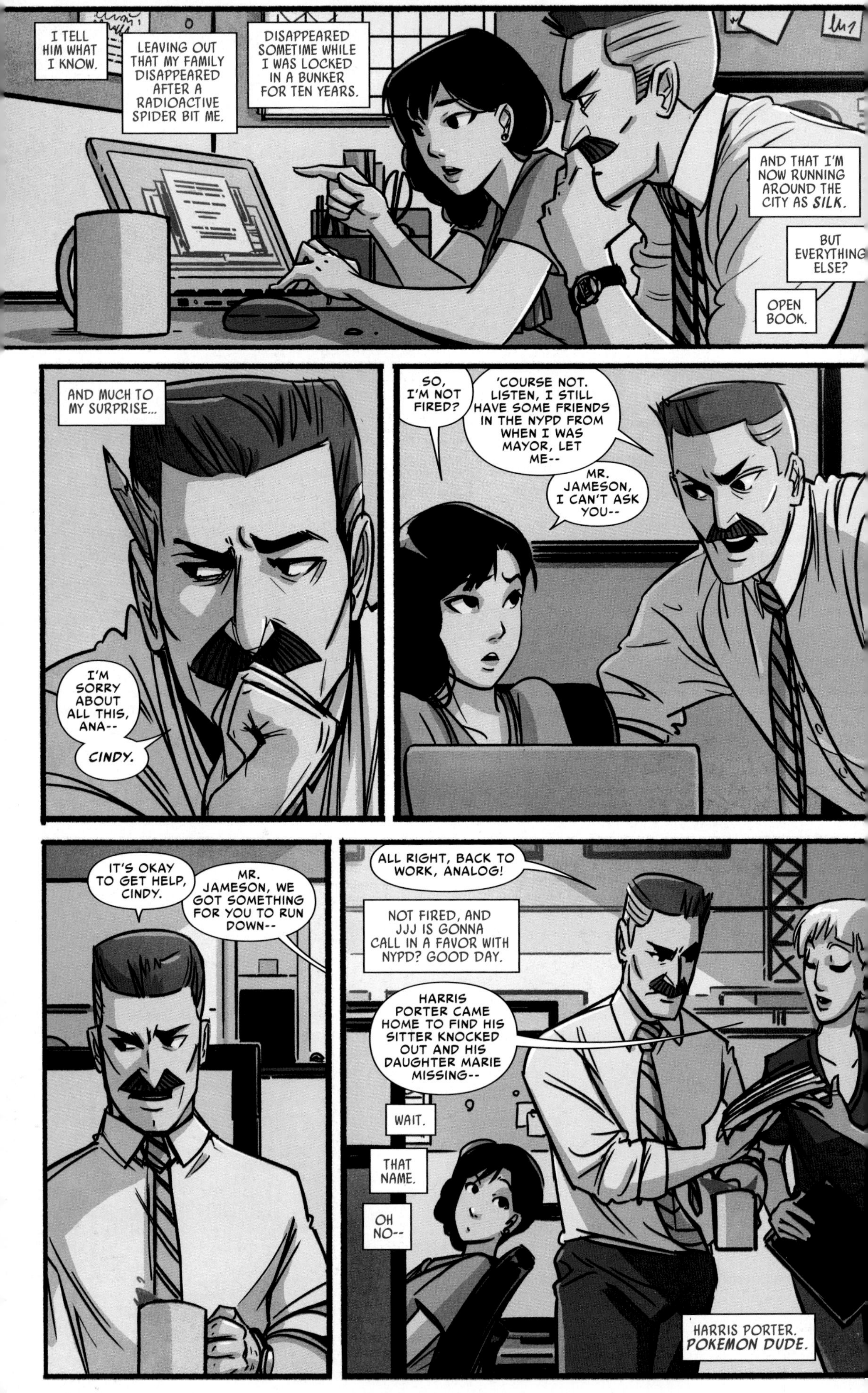
I TELL HIM WHAT I KNOW.
LEAVING OUT THAT MY FAMILY DISAPPEARED AFTER A RADIOACTIVE SPIDER BIT ME.
DISAPPEARED SOMETIME WHILE I WAS LOCKED IN A BUNKER FOR TEN YEARS.
AND THAT I'M NOW RUNNING AROUND THE CITY AS *SILK*.
BUT EVERYTHING ELSE?
OPEN BOOK.
AND MUCH TO MY SURPRISE...
I'M SORRY ABOUT ALL THIS, ANA--
CINDY.
SO, I'M NOT FIRED?
'COURSE NOT. LISTEN, I STILL HAVE SOME FRIENDS IN THE NYPD FROM WHEN I WAS MAYOR, LET ME--
MR. JAMESON, I CAN'T ASK YOU--
IT'S OKAY TO GET HELP, CINDY.
MR. JAMESON, WE GOT SOMETHING FOR YOU TO RUN DOWN--
ALL RIGHT, BACK TO WORK, ANALOG!
NOT FIRED, AND JJJ IS GONNA CALL IN A FAVOR WITH NYPD? GOOD DAY.
HARRIS PORTER CAME HOME TO FIND HIS SITTER KNOCKED OUT AND HIS DAUGHTER MARIE MISSING--
WAIT.
THAT NAME.
OH NO--
HARRIS PORTER. *POKEMON DUDE.*

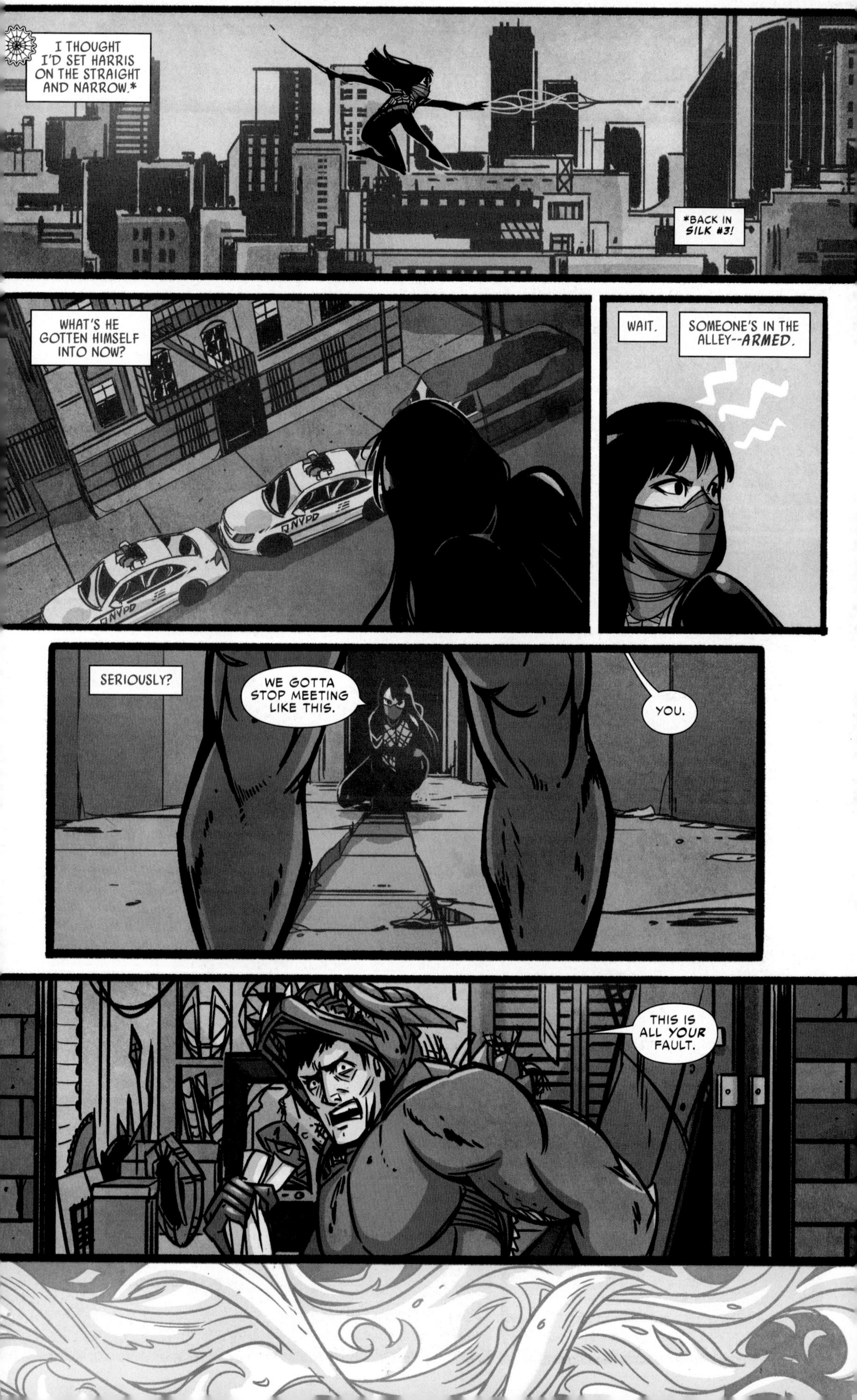
I THOUGHT I'D SET HARRIS ON THE STRAIGHT AND NARROW.*
*BACK IN SILK #3!
WHAT'S HE GOTTEN HIMSELF INTO NOW?
WAIT.
SOMEONE'S IN THE ALLEY--ARMED.
SERIOUSLY?
WE GOTTA STOP MEETING LIKE THIS.
YOU.
THIS IS ALL YOUR FAULT.

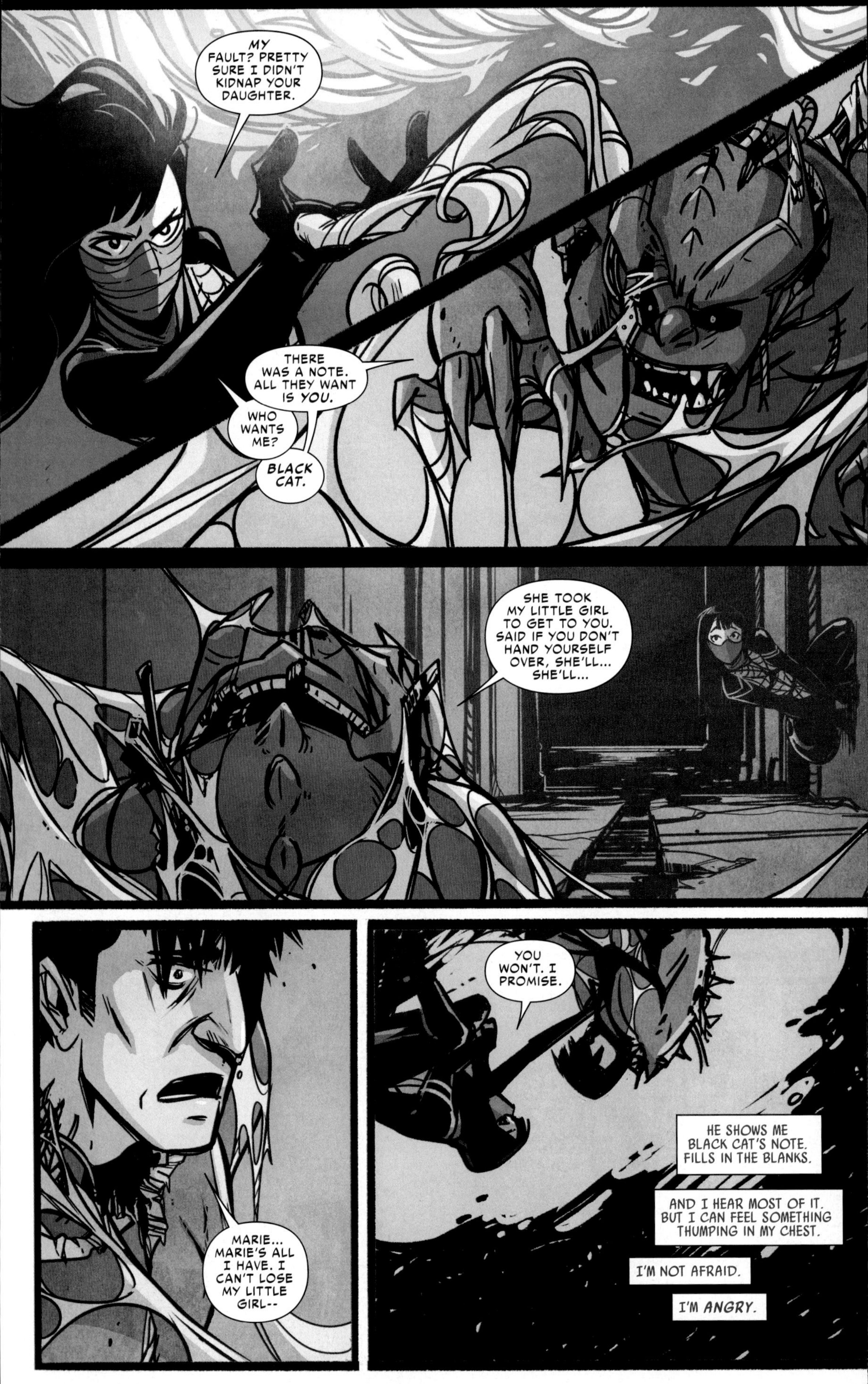
MY FAULT? PRETTY SURE I DIDN'T KIDNAP YOUR DAUGHTER.
THERE WAS A NOTE. ALL THEY WANT IS YOU.
WHO WANTS ME?
BLACK CAT.
SHE TOOK MY LITTLE GIRL TO GET TO YOU. SAID IF YOU DON'T HAND YOURSELF OVER, SHE'LL... SHE'LL...
MARIE... MARIE'S ALL I HAVE. I CAN'T LOSE MY LITTLE GIRL--
YOU WON'T. I PROMISE.
HE SHOWS ME BLACK CAT'S NOTE. FILLS IN THE BLANKS.
AND I HEAR MOST OF IT. BUT I CAN FEEL SOMETHING THUMPING IN MY CHEST.
I'M NOT AFRAID.
I'M ANGRY.

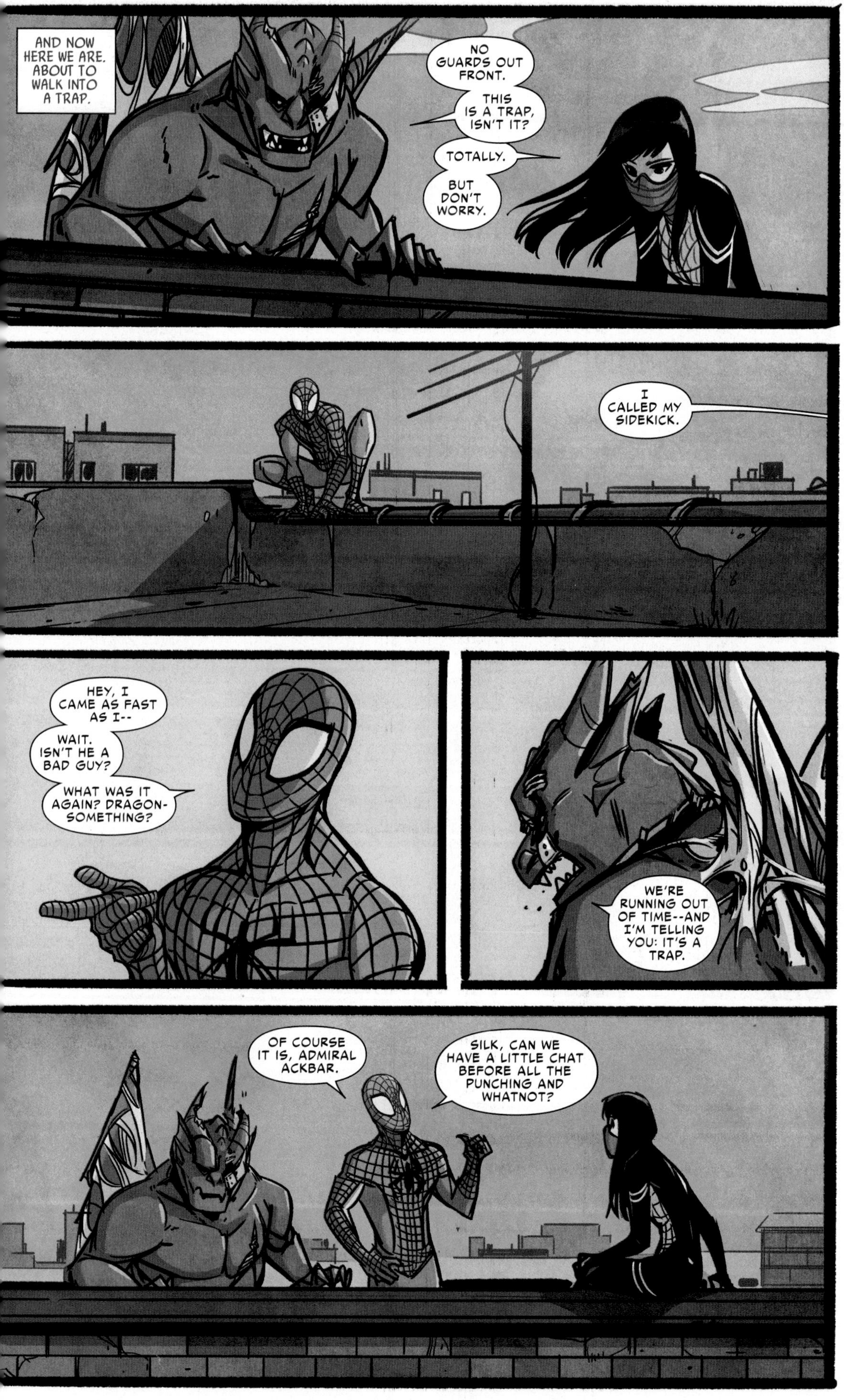

AND NOW HERE WE ARE. ABOUT TO WALK INTO A TRAP.
NO GUARDS OUT FRONT.
THIS IS A TRAP, ISN'T IT?
TOTALLY.
BUT DON'T WORRY.
I CALLED MY SIDEKICK.
HEY, I CAME AS FAST AS I--
WAIT. ISN'T HE A BAD GUY?
WHAT WAS IT AGAIN? DRAGON-SOMETHING?
WE'RE RUNNING OUT OF TIME--AND I'M TELLING YOU: IT'S A TRAP.
OF COURSE IT IS, ADMIRAL ACKBAR.
SILK, CAN WE HAVE A LITTLE CHAT BEFORE ALL THE PUNCHING AND WHATNOT?

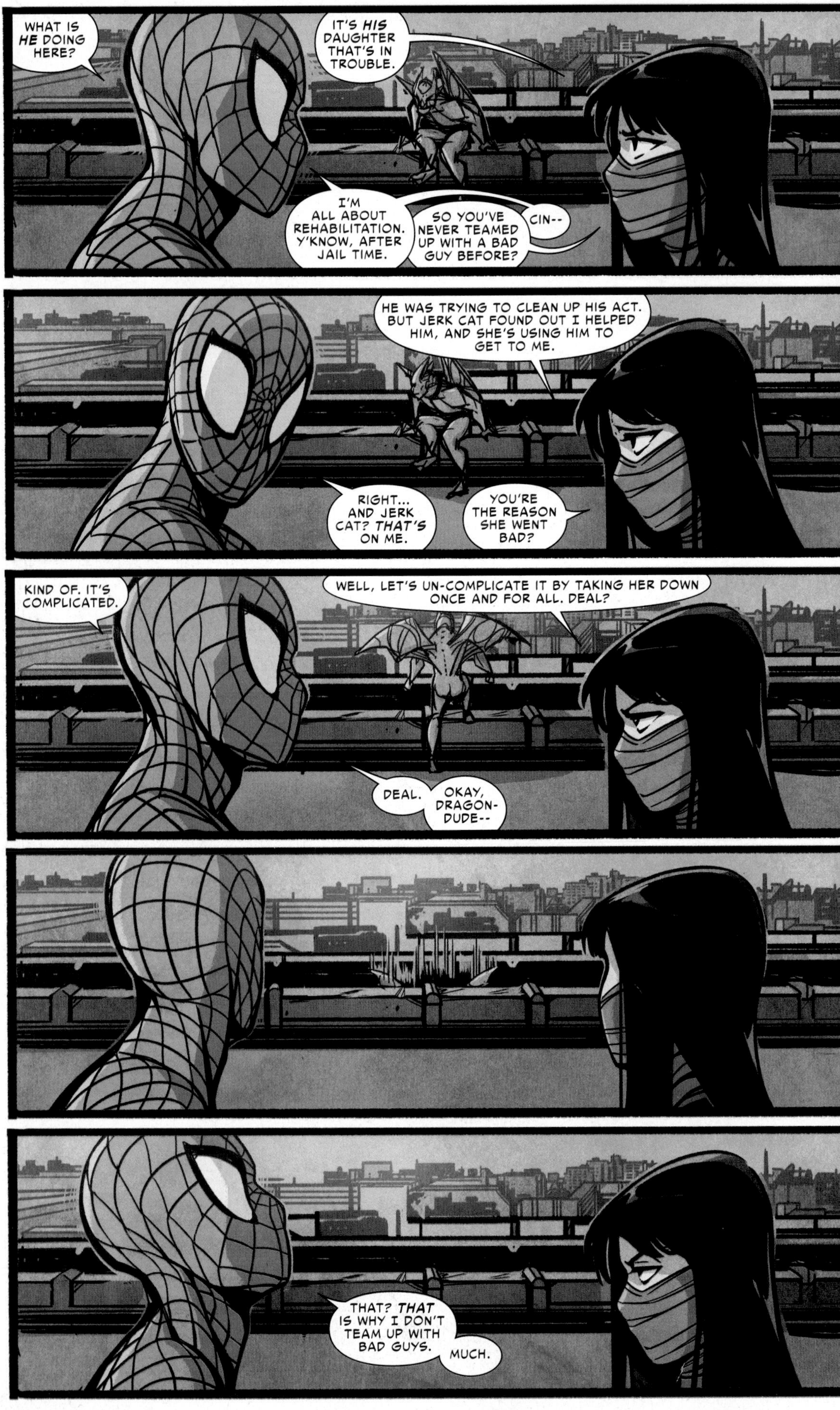
WHAT IS HE DOING HERE?
IT'S HIS DAUGHTER THAT'S IN TROUBLE.
I'M ALL ABOUT REHABILITATION. Y'KNOW, AFTER JAIL TIME.
SO YOU'VE NEVER TEAMED UP WITH A BAD GUY BEFORE?
CIN--
HE WAS TRYING TO CLEAN UP HIS ACT. BUT JERK CAT FOUND OUT I HELPED HIM, AND SHE'S USING HIM TO GET TO ME.
RIGHT... AND JERK CAT? THAT'S ON ME.
YOU'RE THE REASON SHE WENT BAD?
KIND OF. IT'S COMPLICATED.
WELL, LET'S UN-COMPLICATE IT BY TAKING HER DOWN ONCE AND FOR ALL. DEAL?
DEAL.
OKAY, DRAGON-DUDE--
THAT? THAT IS WHY I DON'T TEAM UP WITH BAD GUYS.
MUCH.

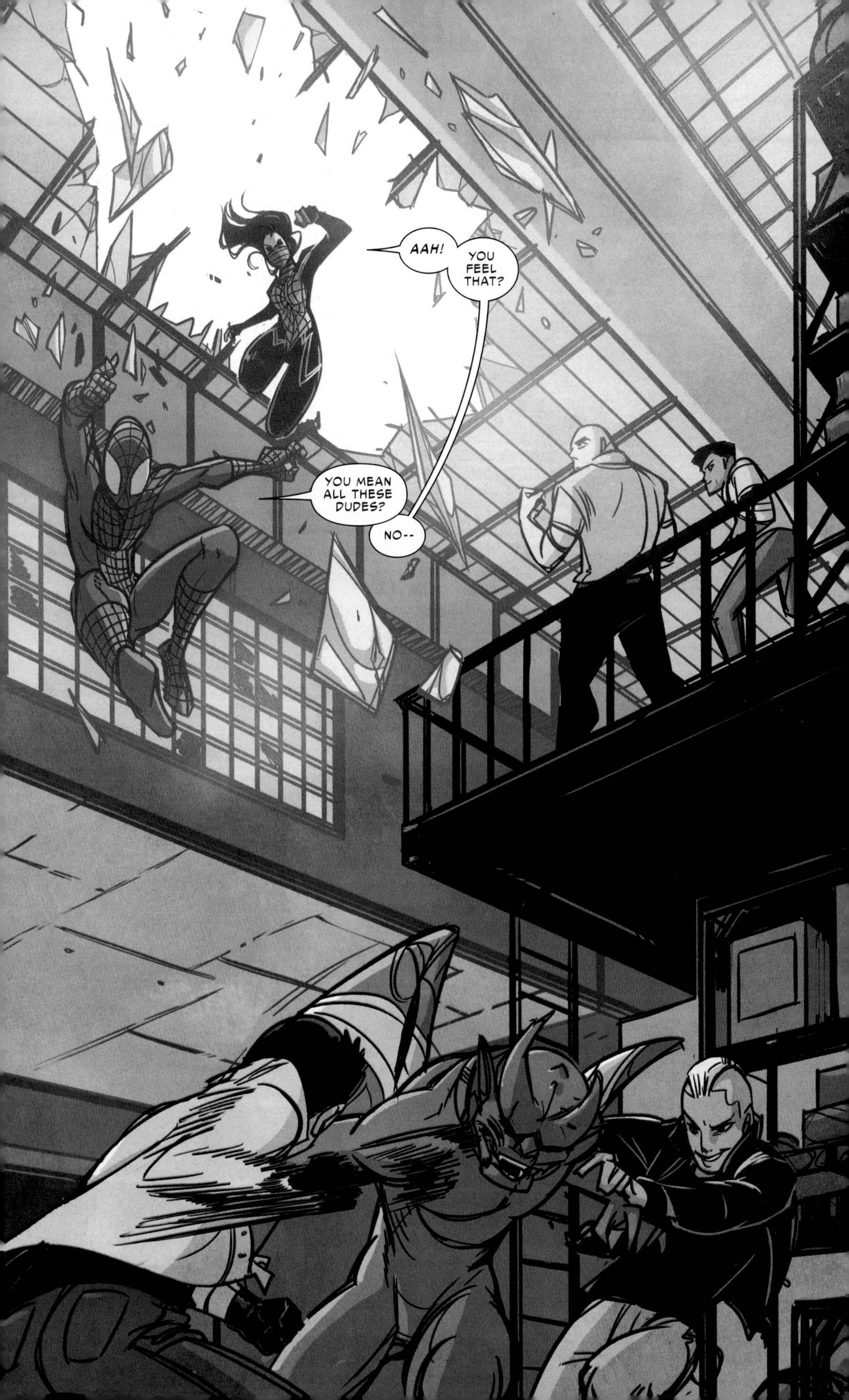
AAH!
YOU FEEL THAT?
YOU MEAN ALL THESE DUDES?
NO--

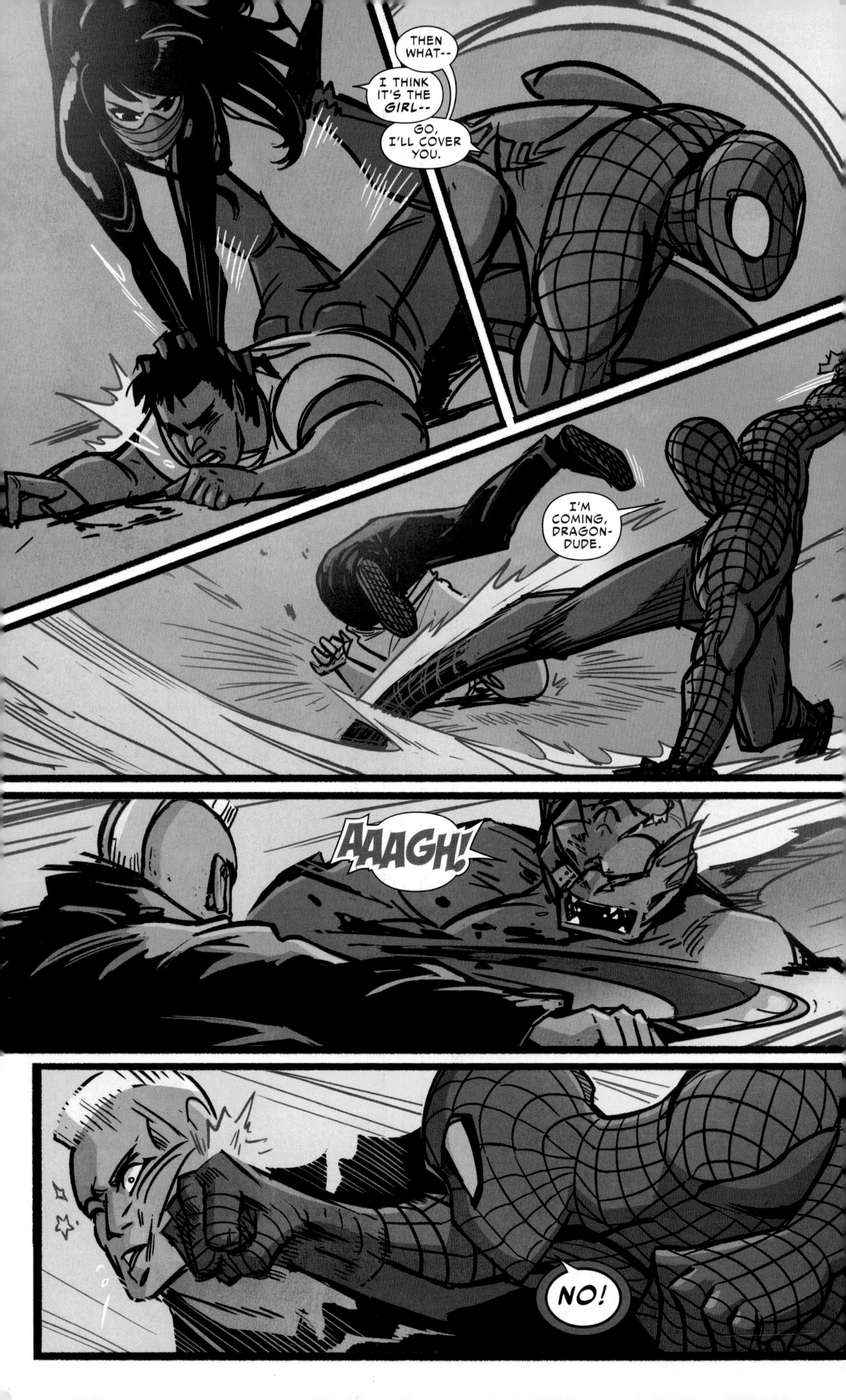
THEN WHAT--
I THINK IT'S THE GIRL--
GO, I'LL COVER YOU.
I'M COMING, DRAGON-DUDE.
AAAGH!
NO!

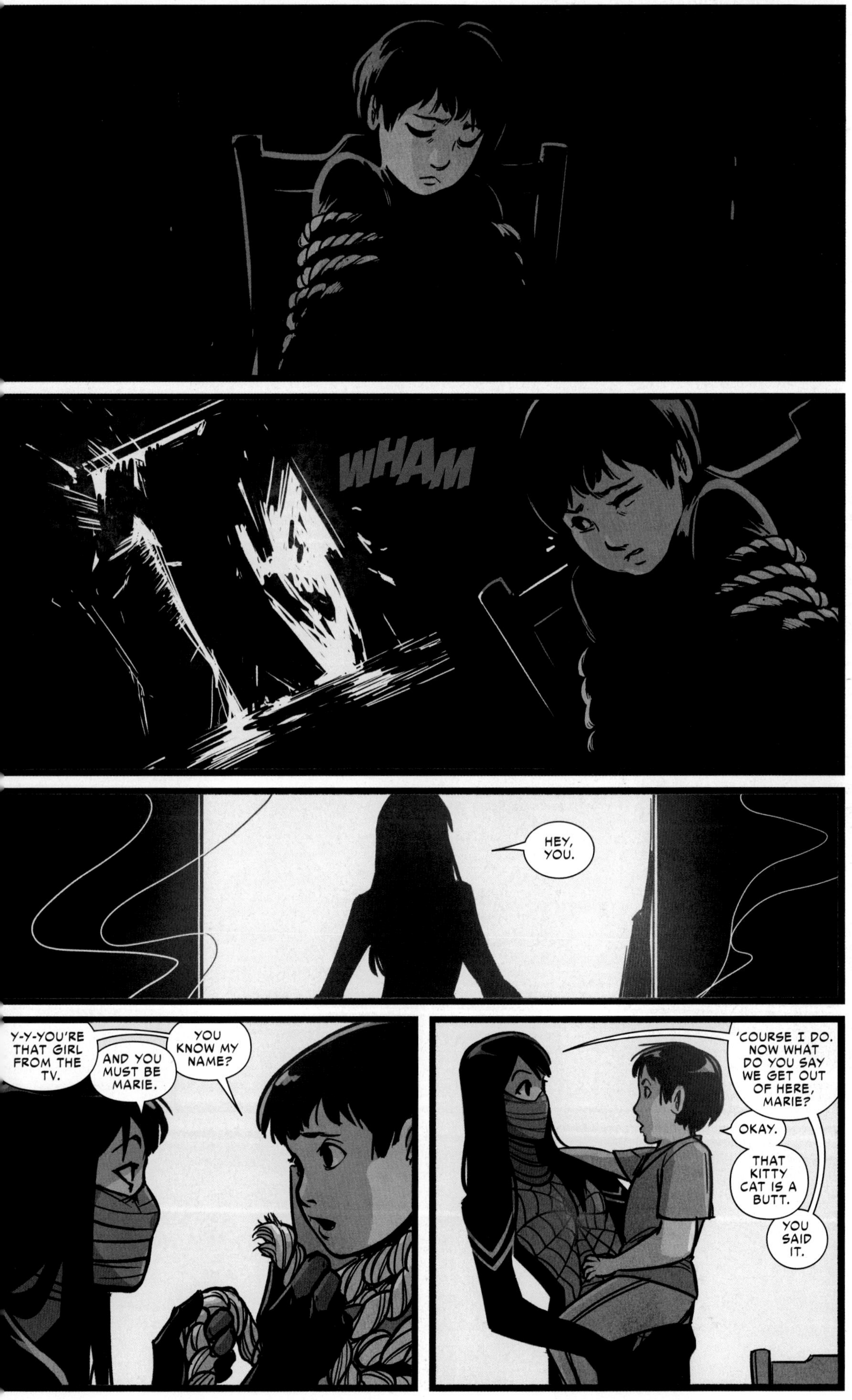
WHAM
HEY, YOU.
Y-Y-YOU'RE THAT GIRL FROM THE TV.
AND YOU MUST BE MARIE.
YOU KNOW MY NAME?
'COURSE I DO. NOW WHAT DO YOU SAY WE GET OUT OF HERE, MARIE?
OKAY.
THAT KITTY CAT IS A BUTT.
YOU SAID IT.

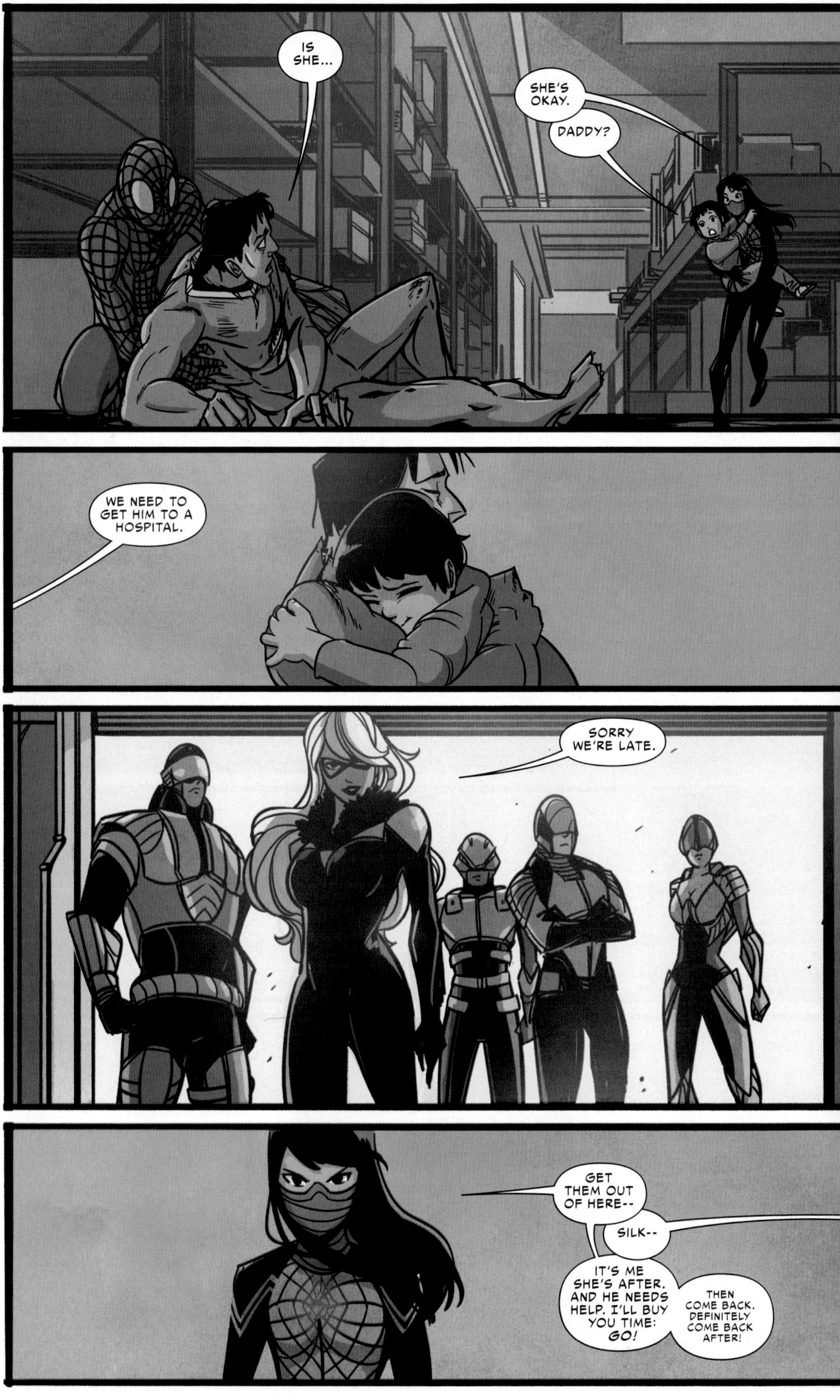
IS SHE...
SHE'S OKAY.
DADDY?
WE NEED TO GET HIM TO A HOSPITAL.
SORRY WE'RE LATE.
GET THEM OUT OF HERE--
SILK--
IT'S ME SHE'S AFTER. AND HE NEEDS HELP. I'LL BUY YOU TIME: GO!
THEN COME BACK. DEFINITELY COME BACK AFTER!

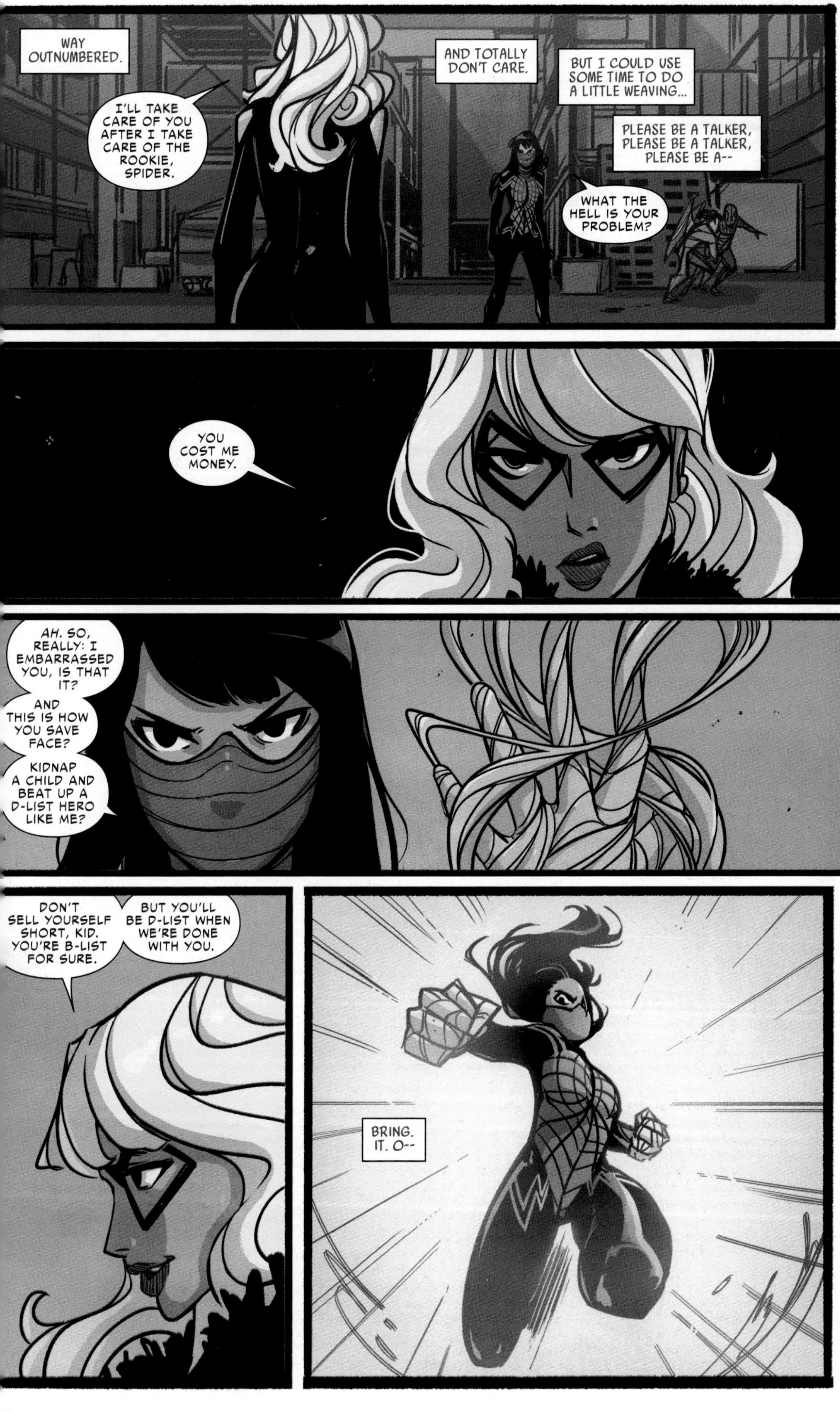
WAY OUTNUMBERED.
I'LL TAKE CARE OF YOU AFTER I TAKE CARE OF THE ROOKIE, SPIDER.
AND TOTALLY DON'T CARE.
BUT I COULD USE SOME TIME TO DO A LITTLE WEAVING...
PLEASE BE A TALKER, PLEASE BE A TALKER, PLEASE BE A--
WHAT THE HELL IS YOUR PROBLEM?
YOU COST ME MONEY.
AH. SO, REALLY: I EMBARRASSED YOU, IS THAT IT?
AND THIS IS HOW YOU SAVE FACE?
KIDNAP A CHILD AND BEAT UP A D-LIST HERO LIKE ME?
DON'T SELL YOURSELF SHORT, KID. YOU'RE B-LIST FOR SURE.
BUT YOU'LL BE D-LIST WHEN WE'RE DONE WITH YOU.
BRING. IT. O--

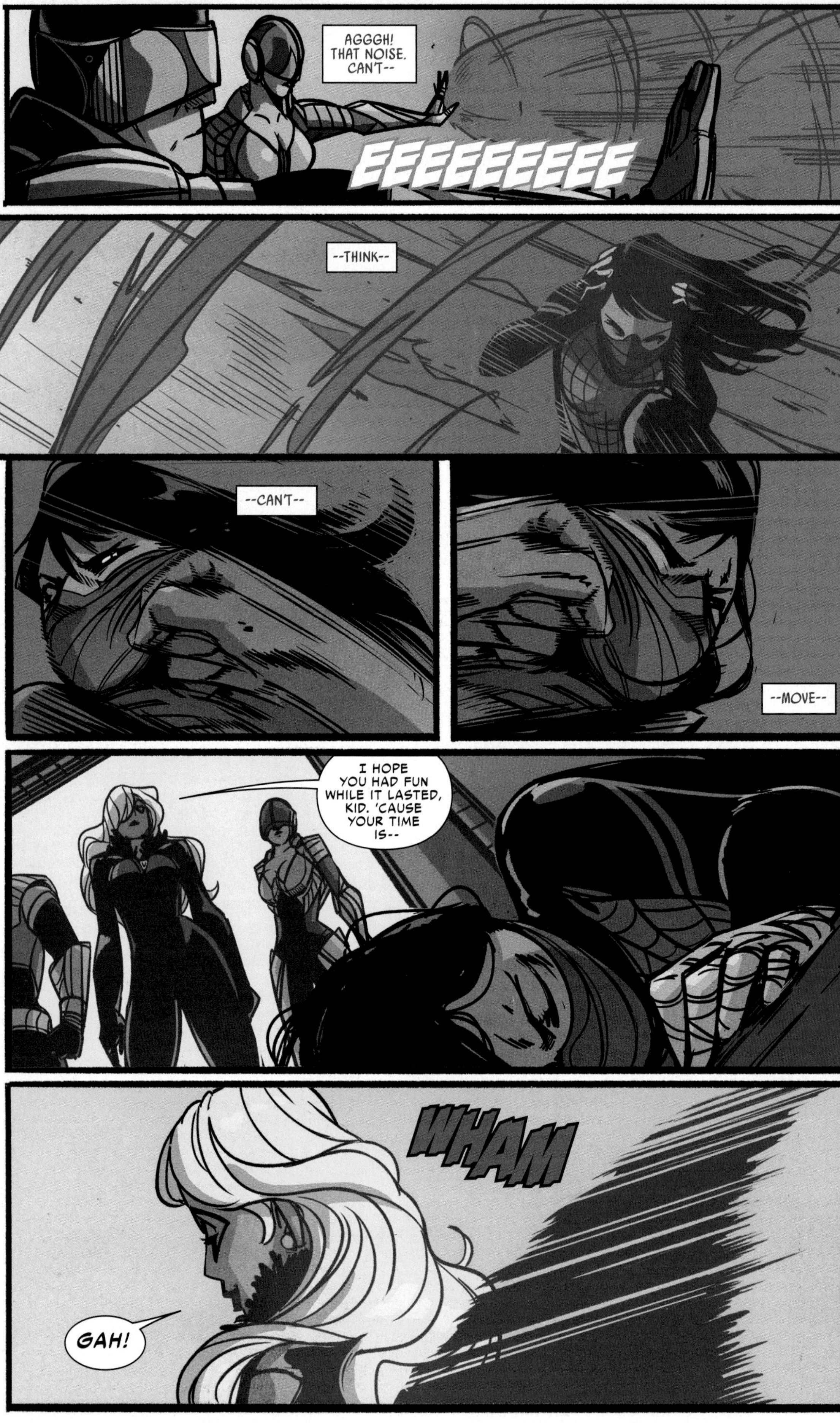
AGGGH! THAT NOISE. CAN'T--
EEEEEEEEE
--THINK--
--CAN'T--
--MOVE--
I HOPE YOU HAD FUN WHILE IT LASTED, KID. 'CAUSE YOUR TIME IS--
WHAM
GAH!

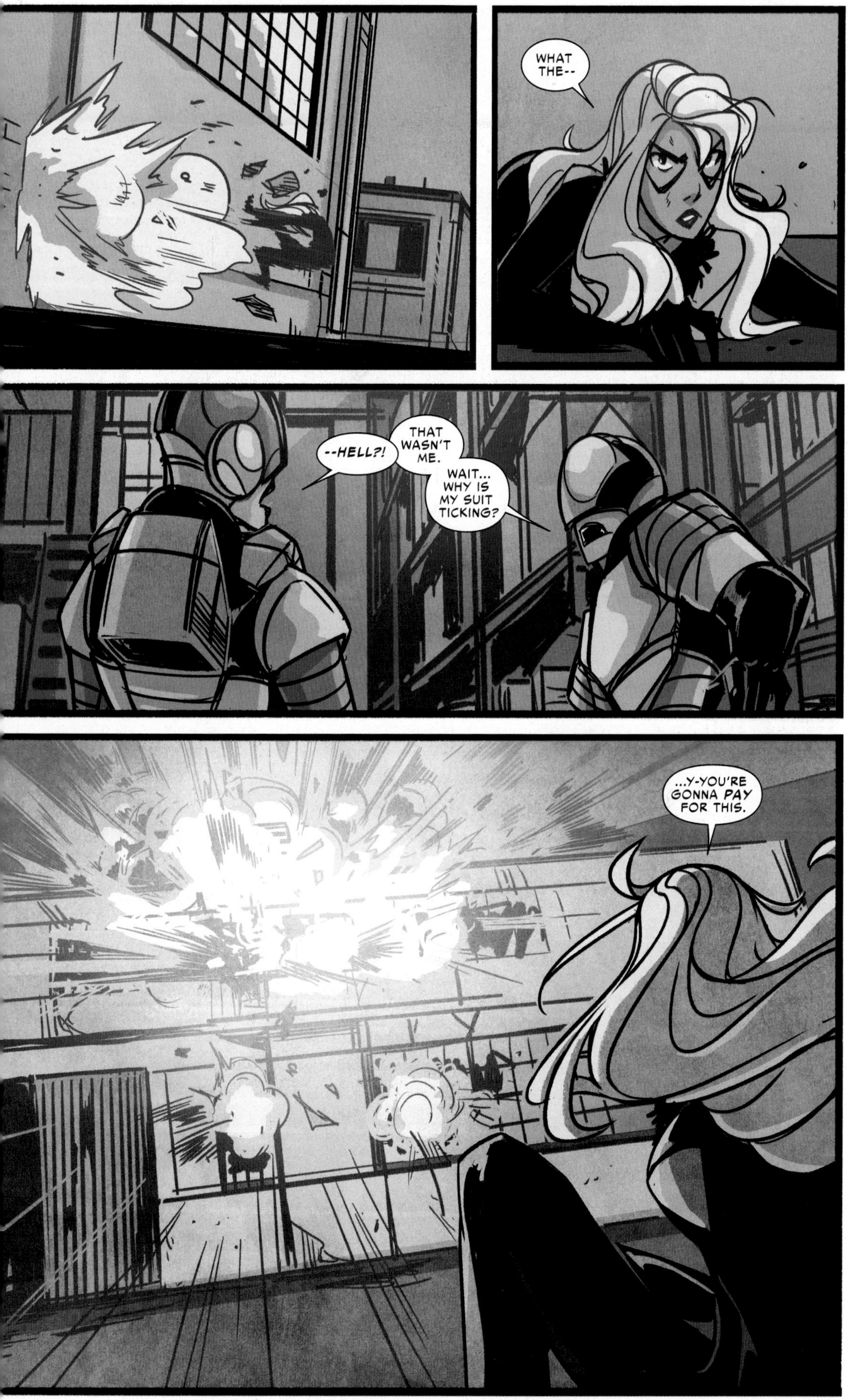
WHAT THE--
--HELL?!
THAT WASN'T ME.
WAIT... WHY IS MY SUIT TICKING?
...Y-YOU'RE GONNA PAY FOR THIS.

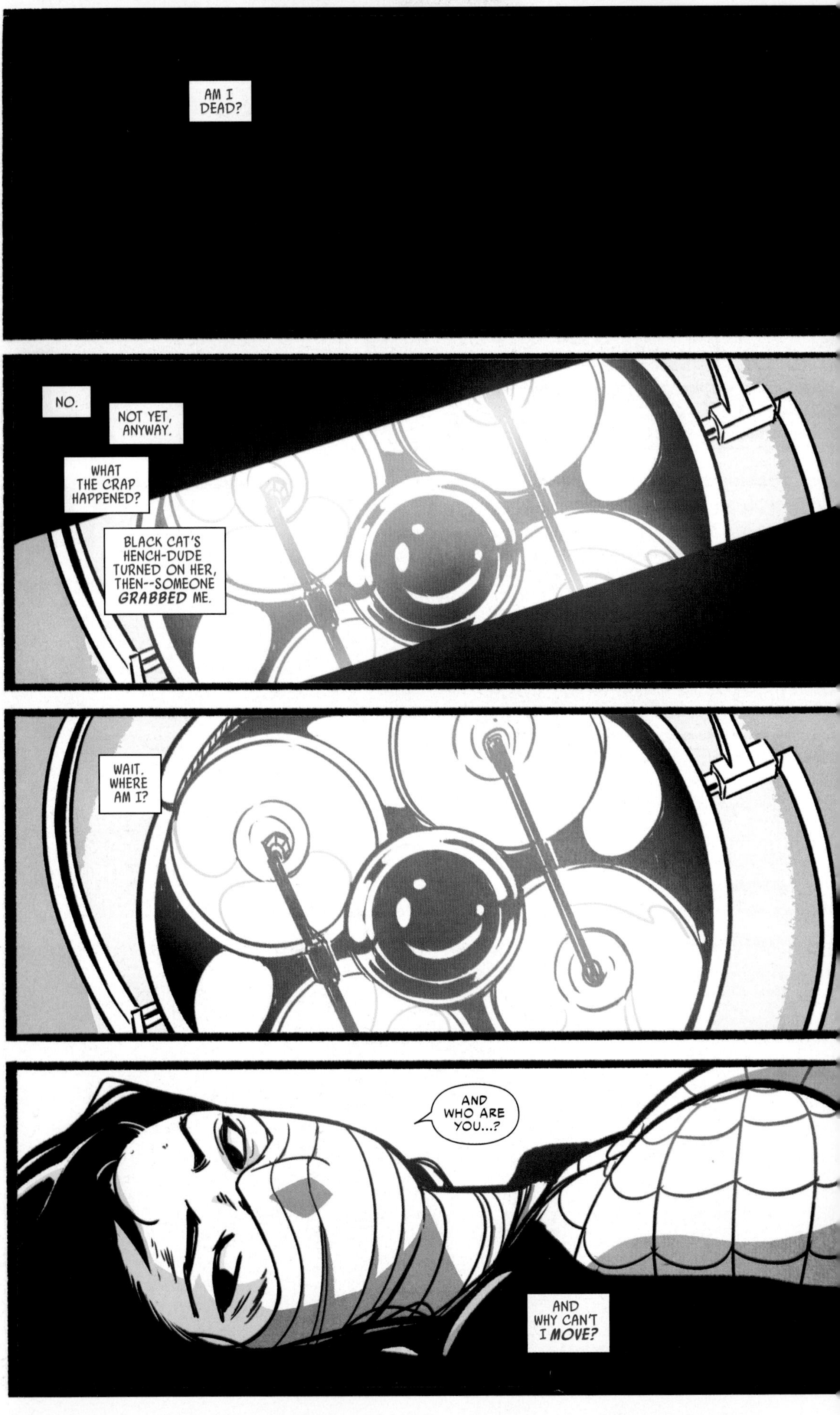
AM I DEAD?
NO.
NOT YET, ANYWAY.
WHAT THE CRAP HAPPENED?
BLACK CAT'S HENCH-DUDE TURNED ON HER, THEN--SOMEONE GRABBED ME.
WAIT. WHERE AM I?
AND WHO ARE YOU...?
AND WHY CAN'T I MOVE?

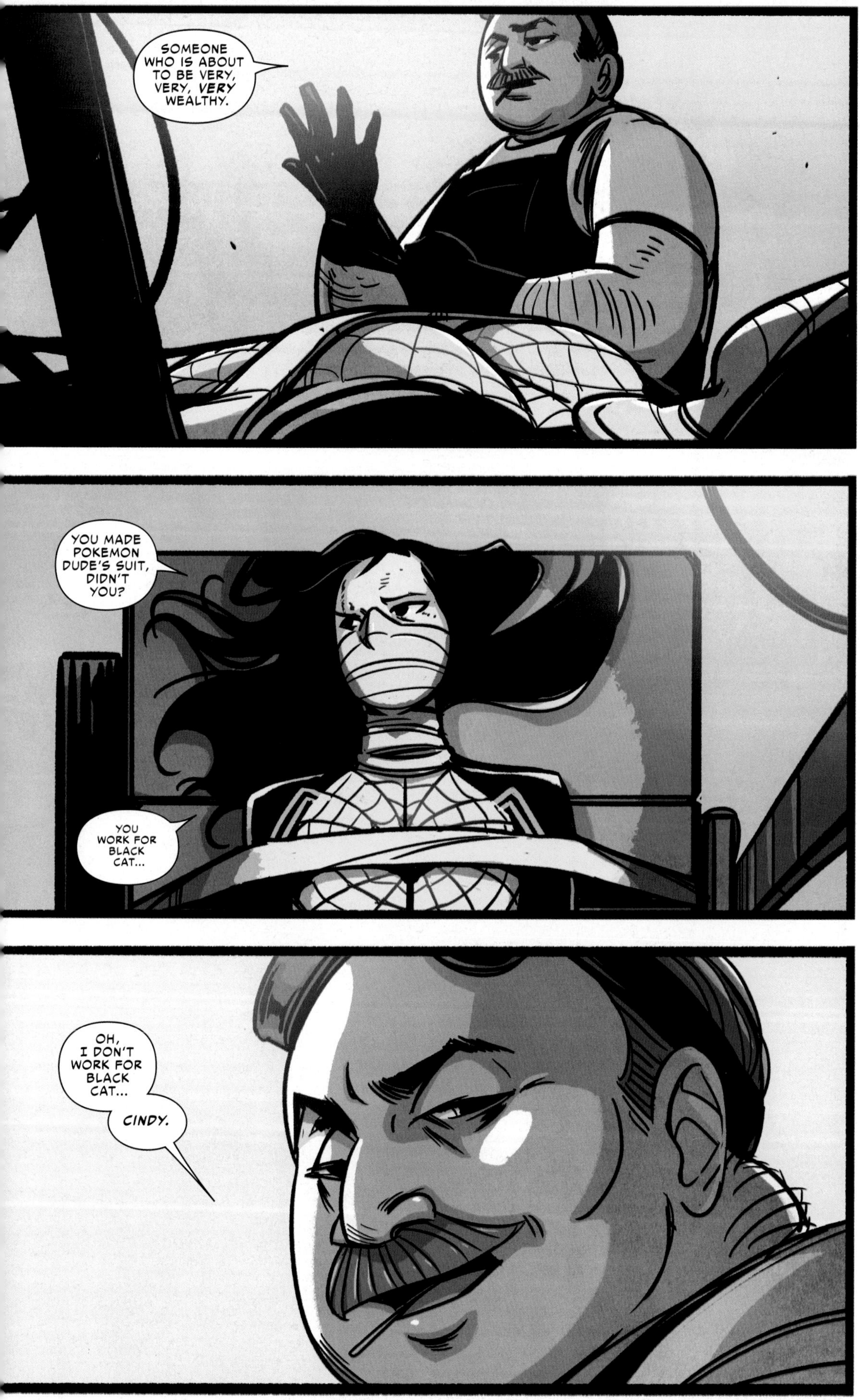
SOMEONE WHO IS ABOUT TO BE VERY, VERY, VERY WEALTHY.
YOU MADE POKEMON DUDE'S SUIT, DIDN'T YOU?
YOU WORK FOR BLACK CAT...
OH, I DON'T WORK FOR BLACK CAT...
CINDY.

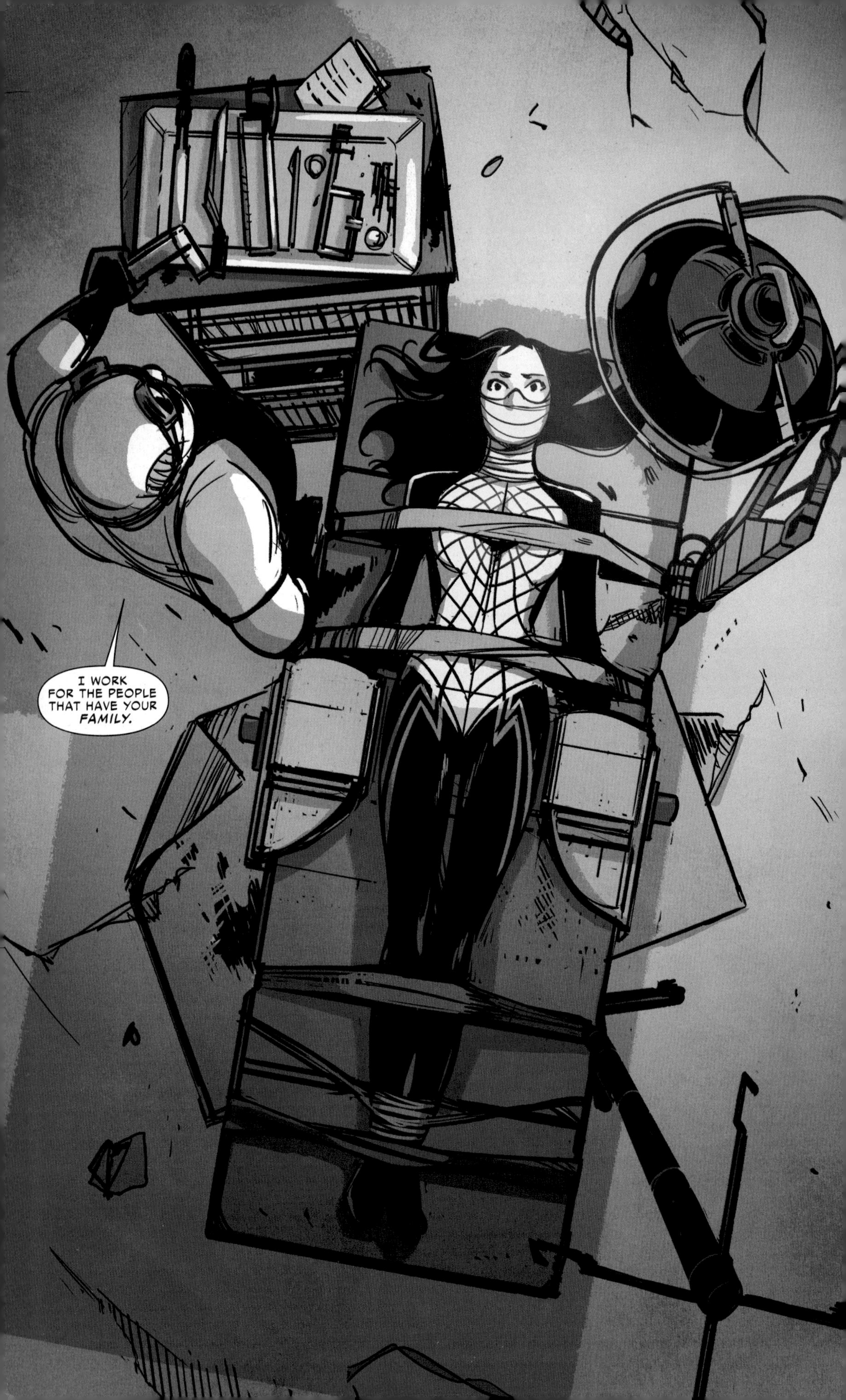
I WORK FOR THE PEOPLE THAT HAVE YOUR *FAMILY.*

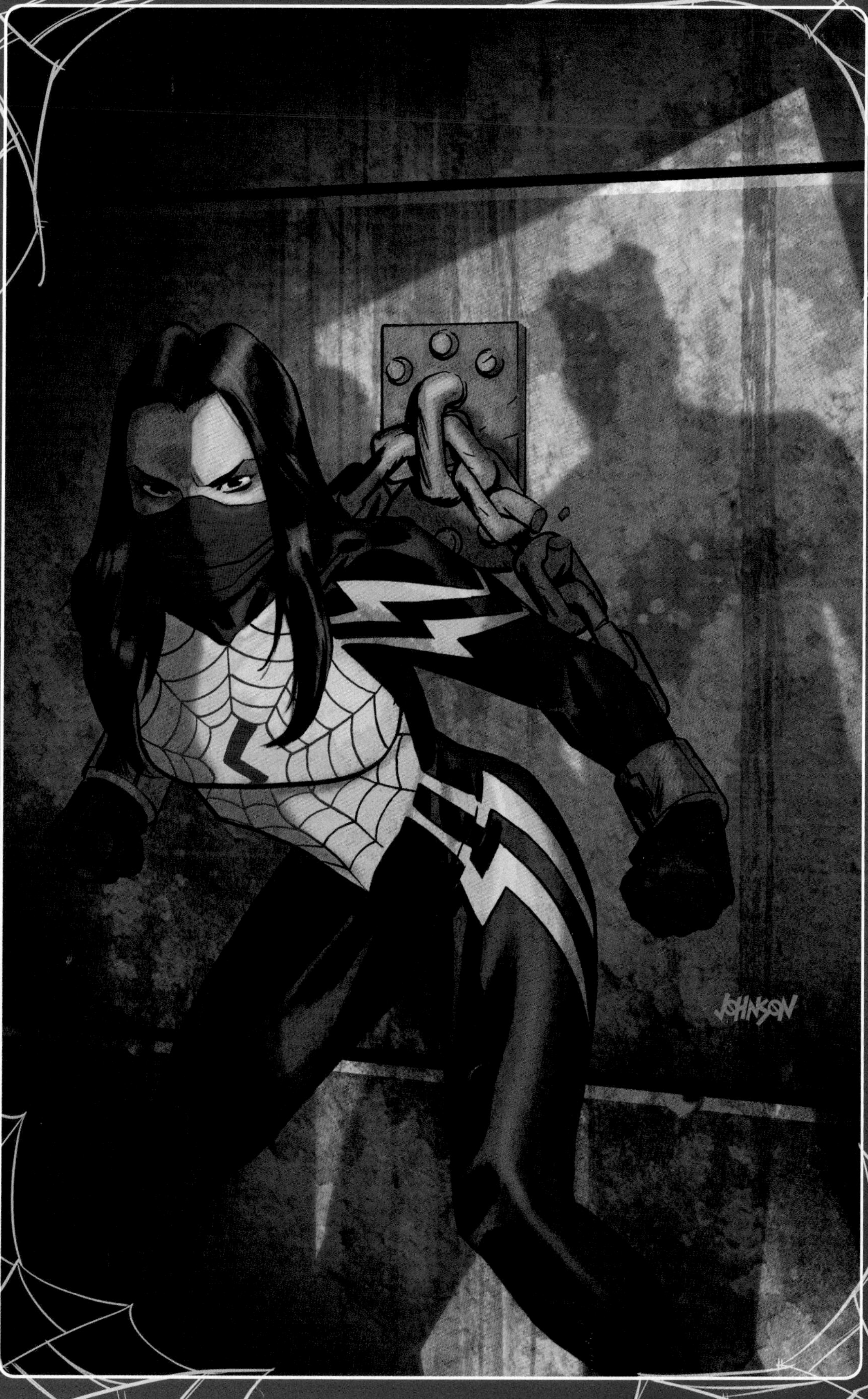
JOHNSON

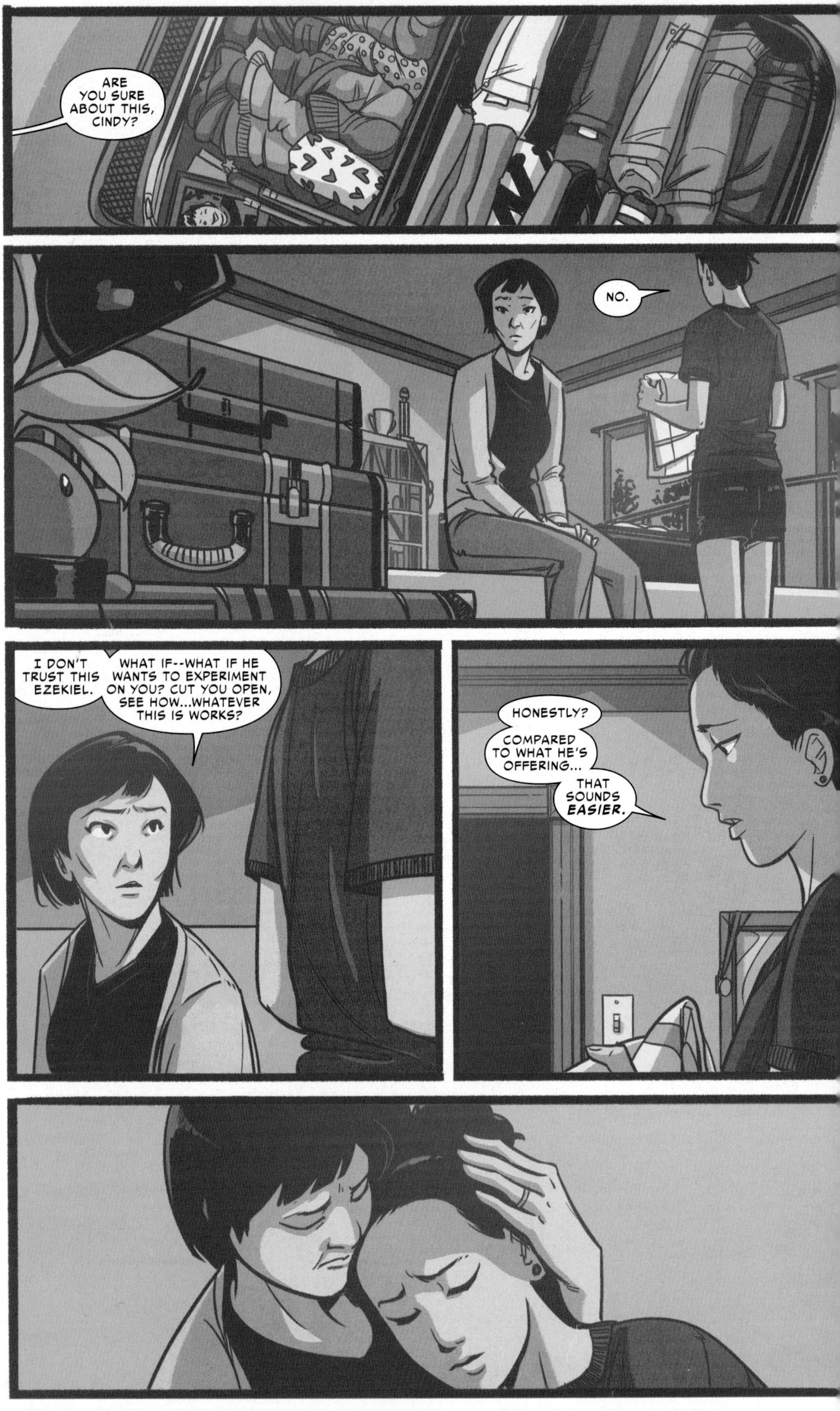
ARE YOU SURE ABOUT THIS, CINDY?
NO.
I DON'T TRUST THIS EZEKIEL.
WHAT IF--WHAT IF HE WANTS TO EXPERIMENT ON YOU? CUT YOU OPEN, SEE HOW...WHATEVER THIS IS WORKS?
HONESTLY?
COMPARED TO WHAT HE'S OFFERING...
THAT SOUNDS EASIER.

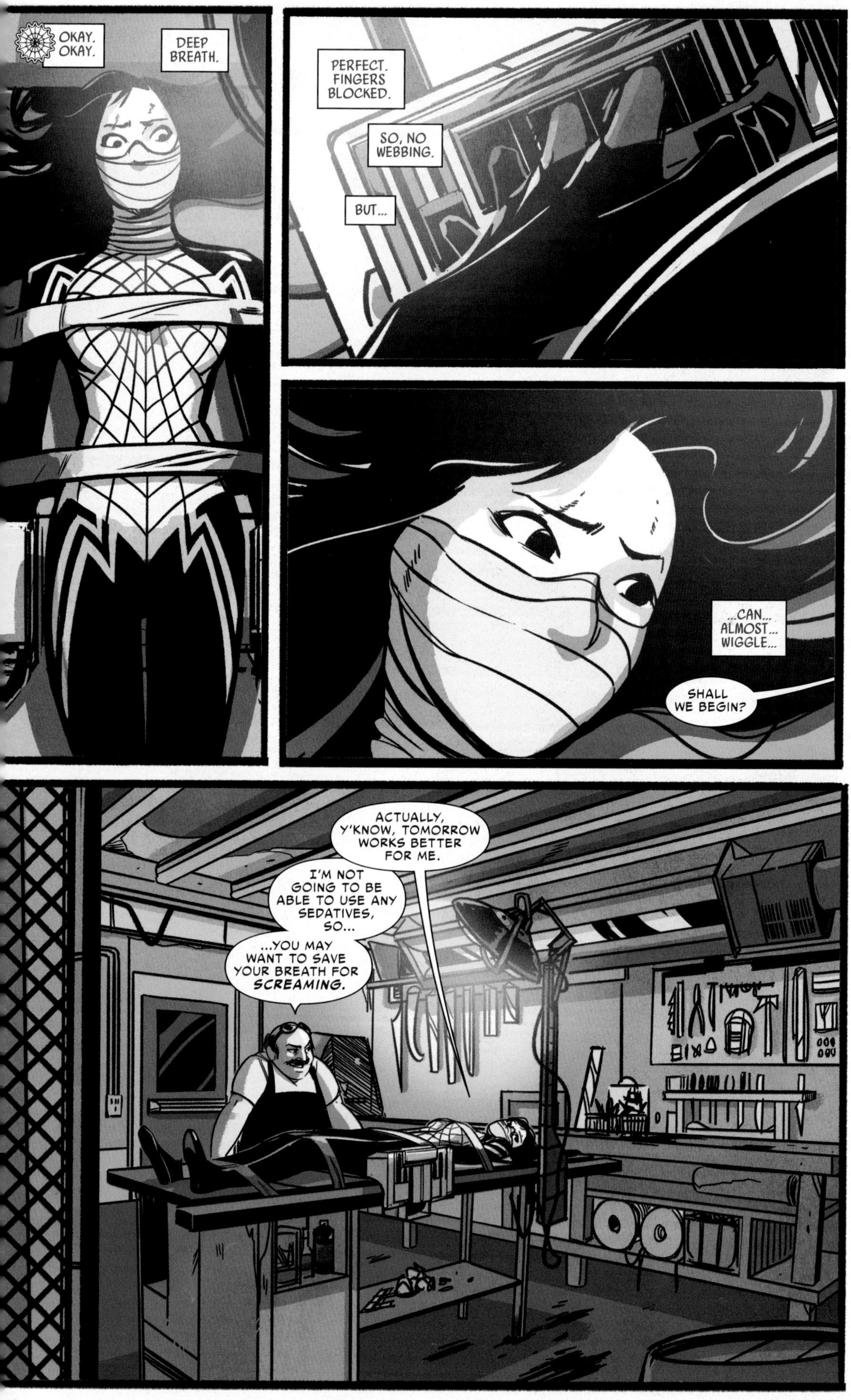
OKAY. OKAY.
DEEP BREATH.
PERFECT. FINGERS BLOCKED.
SO, NO WEBBING.
BUT...
...CAN... ALMOST... WIGGLE...
SHALL WE BEGIN?
ACTUALLY, Y'KNOW, TOMORROW WORKS BETTER FOR ME.
I'M NOT GOING TO BE ABLE TO USE ANY SEDATIVES, SO...
...YOU MAY WANT TO SAVE YOUR BREATH FOR SCREAMING.

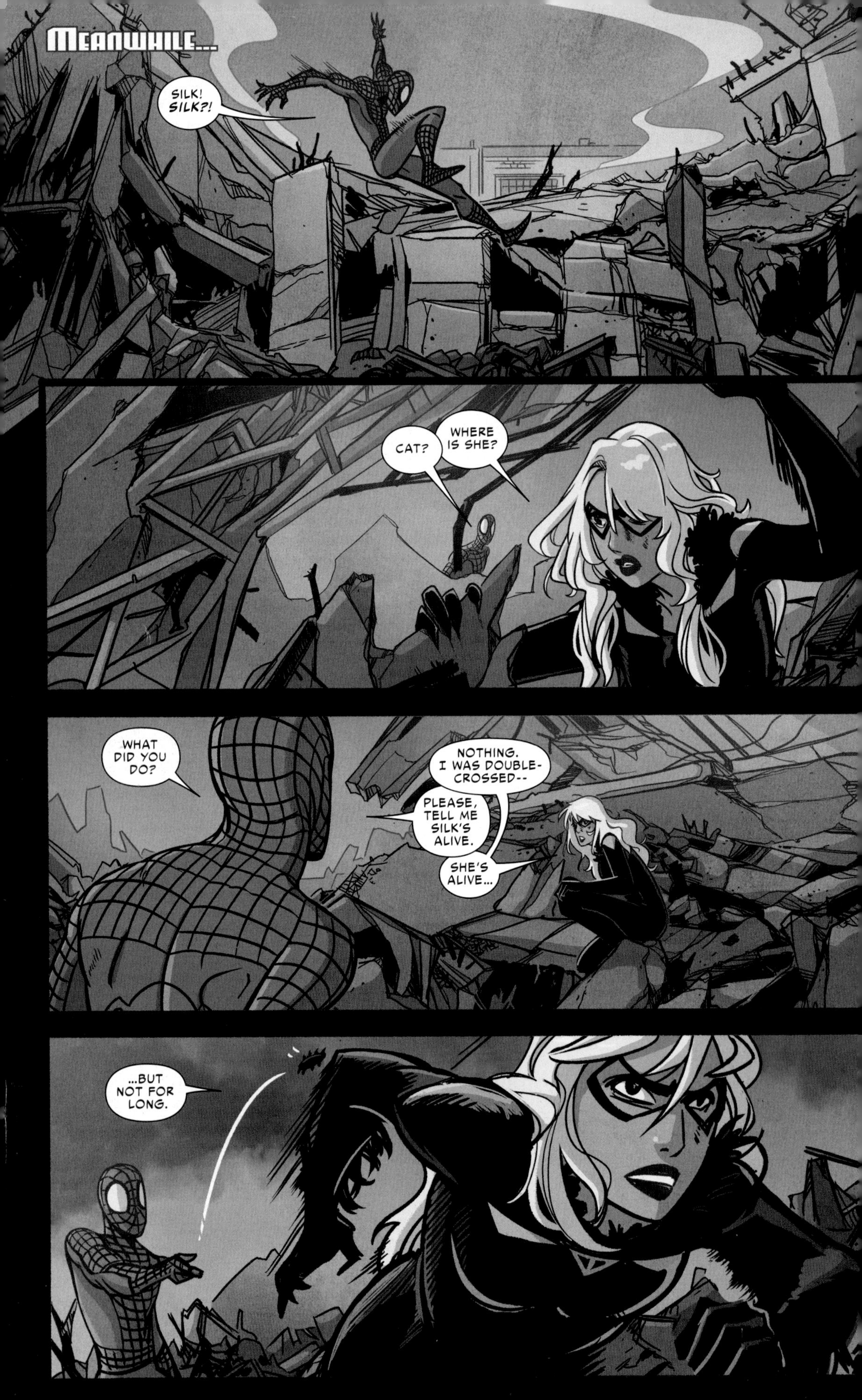
MEANWHILE...
SILK! SILK?!
CAT?
WHERE IS SHE?
WHAT DID YOU DO?
NOTHING. I WAS DOUBLE-CROSSED--
PLEASE, TELL ME SILK'S ALIVE.
SHE'S ALIVE...
...BUT NOT FOR LONG.

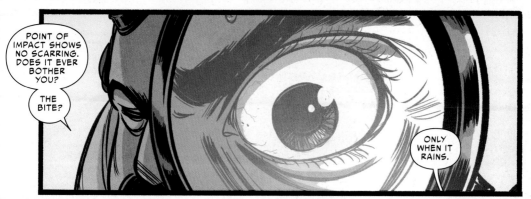

POINT OF IMPACT SHOWS NO SCARRING. DOES IT EVER BOTHER YOU?

THE BITE?

ONLY WHEN IT RAINS.

HOW DOES HE KNOW ABOUT THE BITE?

WHO THE HELL IS THIS GUY?

FOCUS. GET FREE. THEN GET ANSWERS.

KEEP HIM TALKING. DISTRACTED.

AND, Y'KNOW, NOT CUTTING INTO ME.

MY FAMILY.

YOU'VE SEEN THEM?

YOUR PARENTS? NO. BUT THE PEOPLE WHO HAVE THEM... MY GOODNESS, THEY'VE GOT THE DEEPEST POCKETS I'VE EVER SEEN.

BUT THEY PLAYED THEIR HAND...

C'MON...

THEY'VE GONE TO SUCH GREAT LENGTHS. WATCHED YOUR EVERY MOVE IN THAT BUNKER.

SO, I KNEW ANYONE WORTH THAT MUCH TO THEM...

...WOULD BE WORTH A WHOLE LOT MORE ON THE BLACK MARKET.

THEY'VE BEEN WATCHING ME? IN THE BUNKER? HOW?

AND THEY WHO?

WHO THE HELL ARE THEY?

I HAVE NO IDEA. AND I DON'T CARE.

BUT THE PEOPLE I'LL AUCTION YOU OFF TO? HYDRA. AIM. WHOEVER COUGHS UP THE MOST DOUGH--

CRACK

WHAT?!

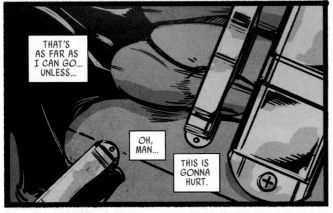

THAT'S AS FAR AS I CAN GO... UNLESS...

OH, MAN...

THIS IS GONNA HURT.

YEAH, WELL...

...I'M NOT FOR SALE!

WELL, WHATEVER *WASN'T* BROKEN IN MY HAND SURE IS BROKEN NOW...

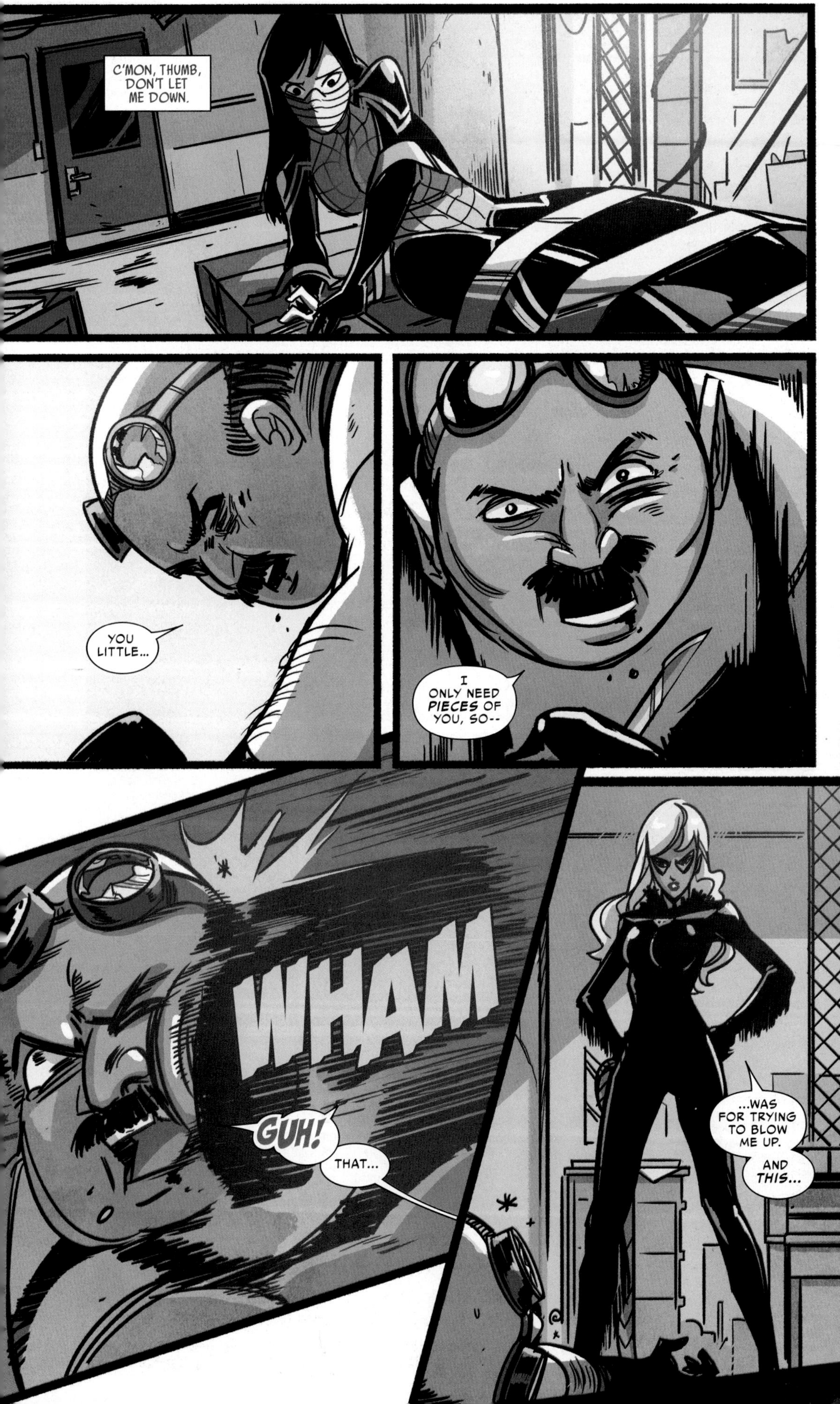
C'MON, THUMB, DON'T LET ME DOWN.
YOU LITTLE...
I ONLY NEED PIECES OF YOU, SO--
WHAM
GUH!
THAT...
...WAS FOR TRYING TO BLOW ME UP.
AND THIS...

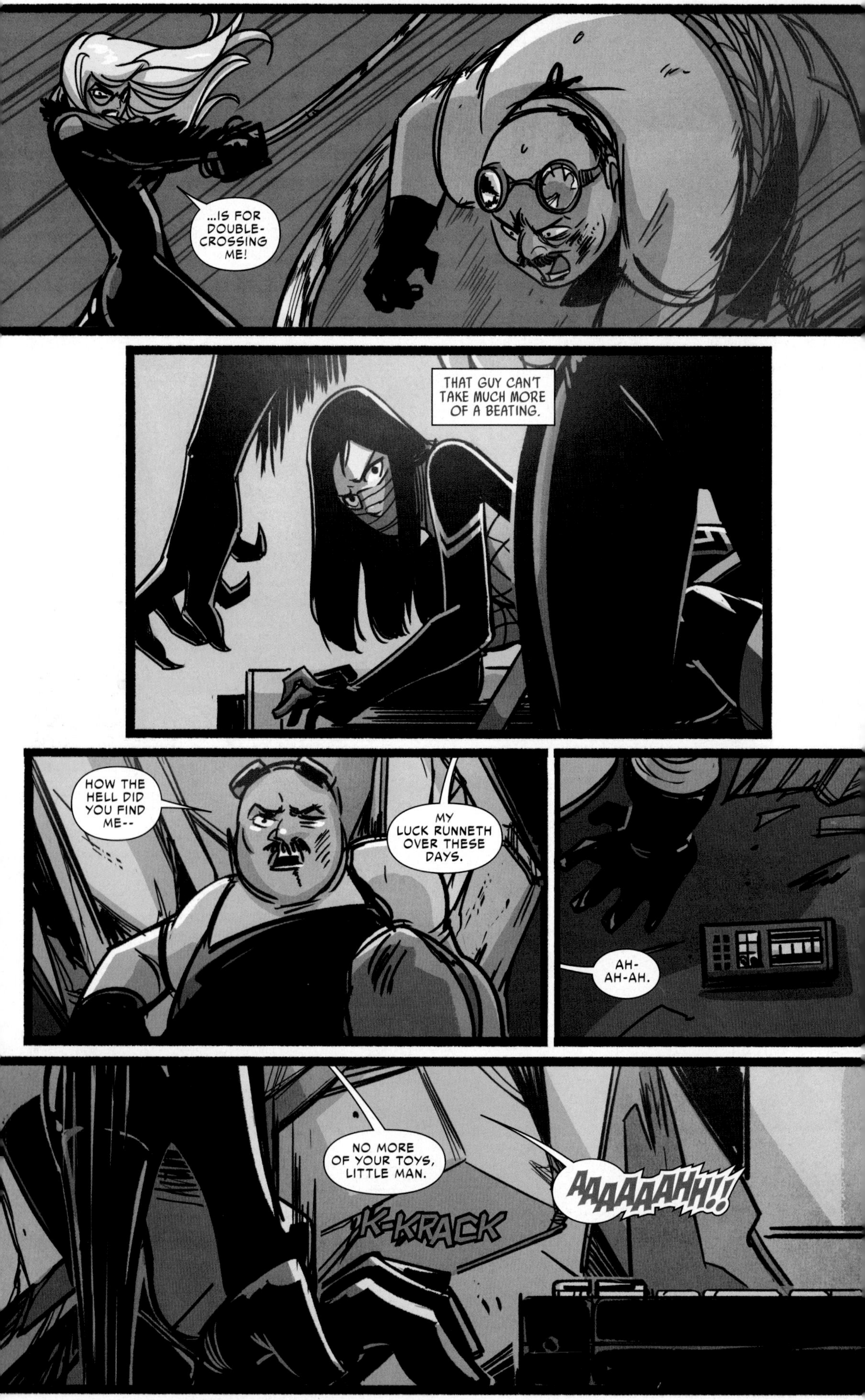

...IS FOR DOUBLE-CROSSING ME!
THAT GUY CAN'T TAKE MUCH MORE OF A BEATING.
HOW THE HELL DID YOU FIND ME--
MY LUCK RUNNETH OVER THESE DAYS.
AH-AH-AH.
NO MORE OF YOUR TOYS, LITTLE MAN.
K-KRACK
AAAAAAHH!!

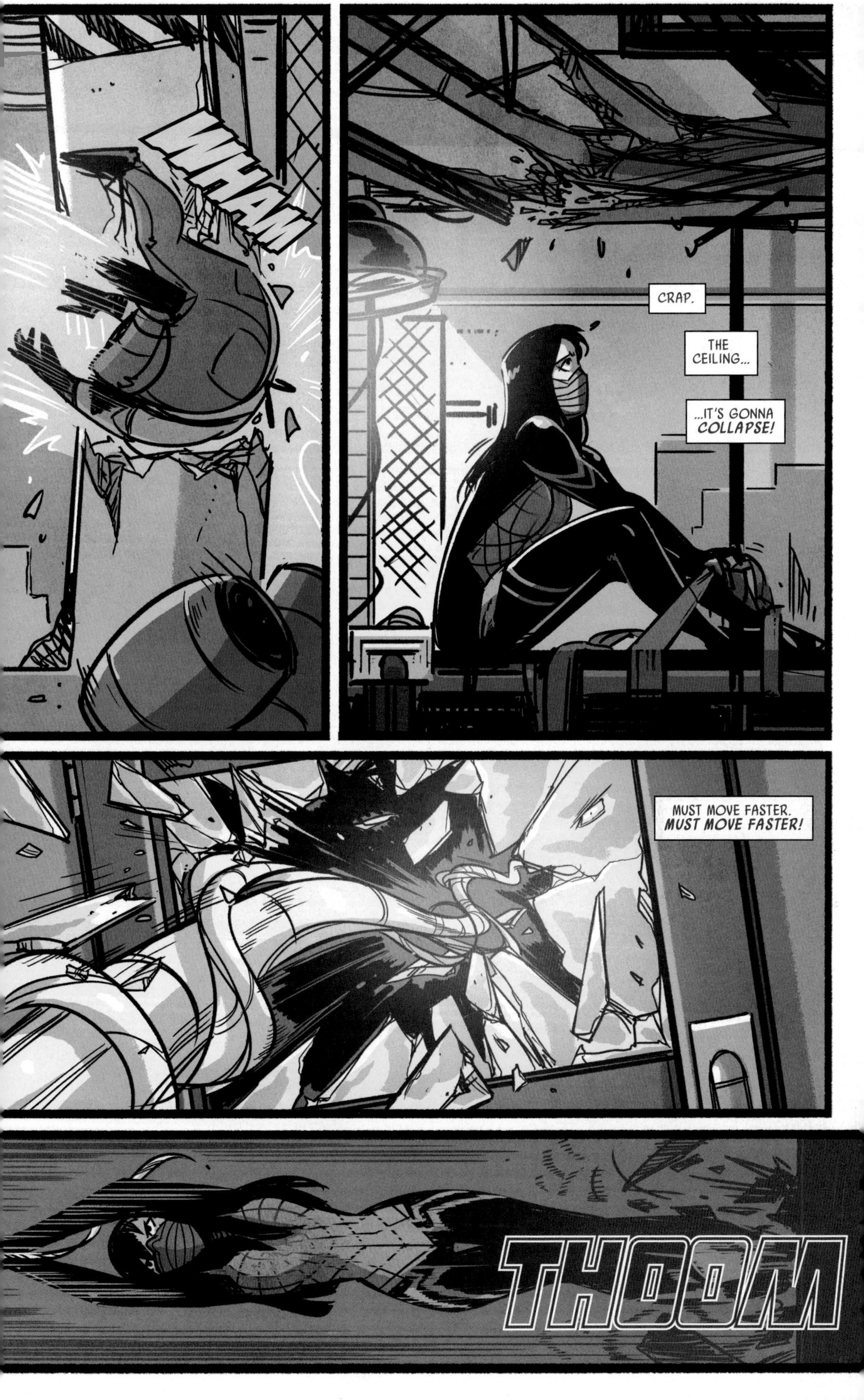
WHAM
CRAP.
THE CEILING...
...IT'S GONNA COLLAPSE!
MUST MOVE FASTER. MUST MOVE FASTER!
THOOM

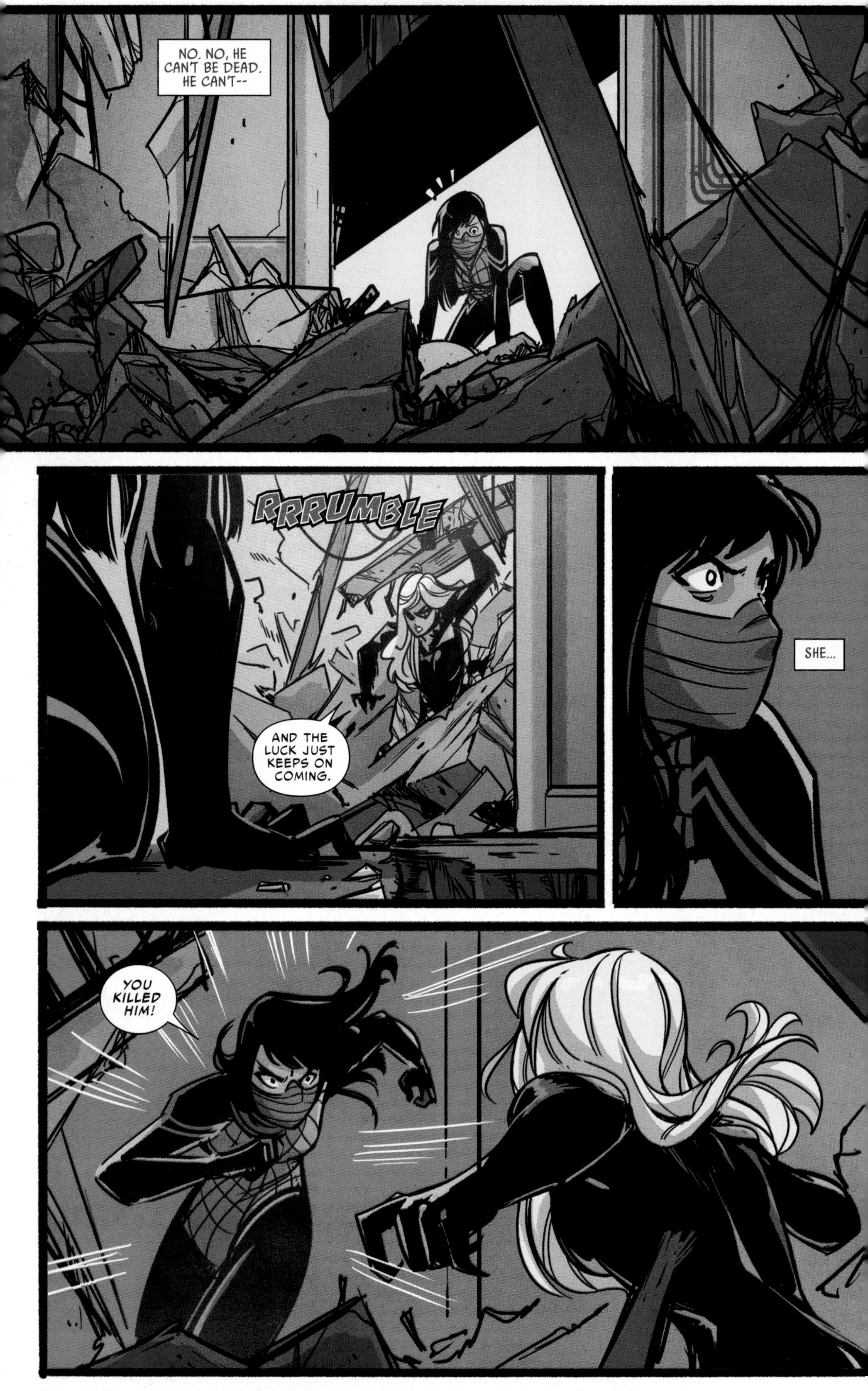
NO. NO, HE CAN'T BE DEAD. HE CAN'T--
RRRUMBLE
AND THE LUCK JUST KEEPS ON COMING.
SHE...
YOU KILLED HIM!

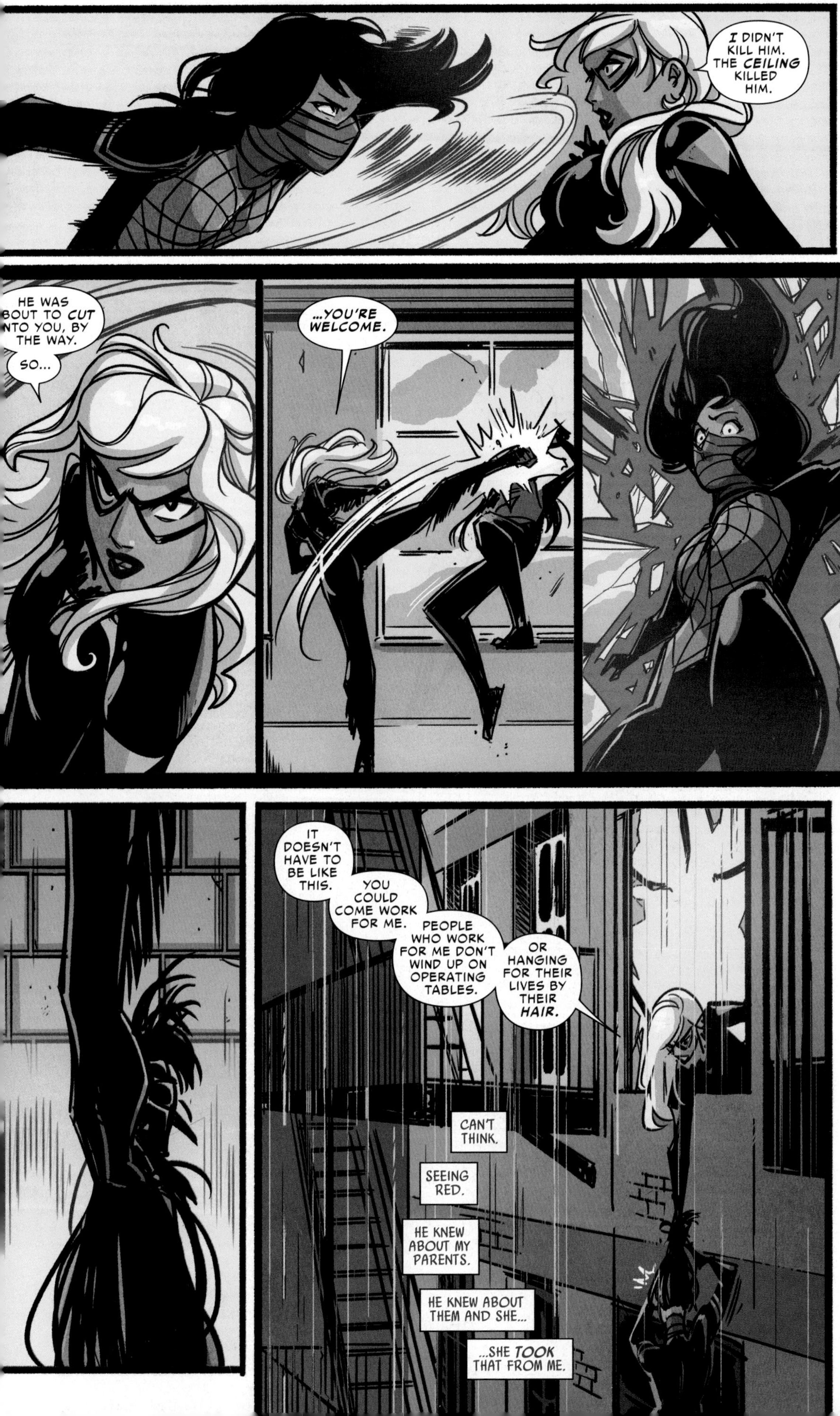

I DIDN'T KILL HIM. THE CEILING KILLED HIM.
HE WAS BOUT TO CUT NTO YOU, BY THE WAY.
SO...
...YOU'RE WELCOME.
IT DOESN'T HAVE TO BE LIKE THIS.
YOU COULD COME WORK FOR ME.
PEOPLE WHO WORK FOR ME DON'T WIND UP ON OPERATING TABLES.
OR HANGING FOR THEIR LIVES BY THEIR HAIR.
CAN'T THINK.
SEEING RED.
HE KNEW ABOUT MY PARENTS.
HE KNEW ABOUT THEM AND SHE...
...SHE TOOK THAT FROM ME.

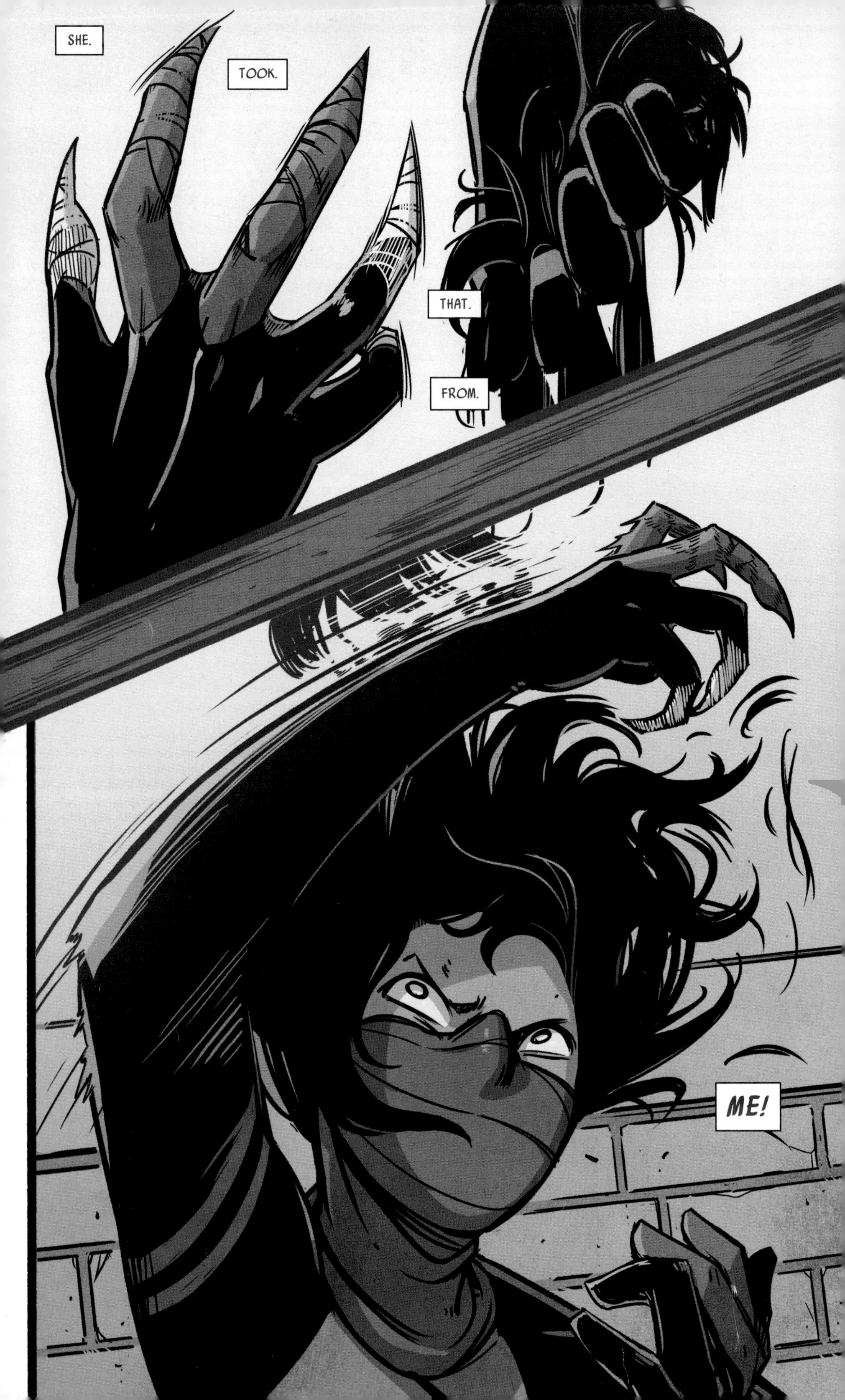
SHE.
TOOK.
THAT.
FROM.
ME!

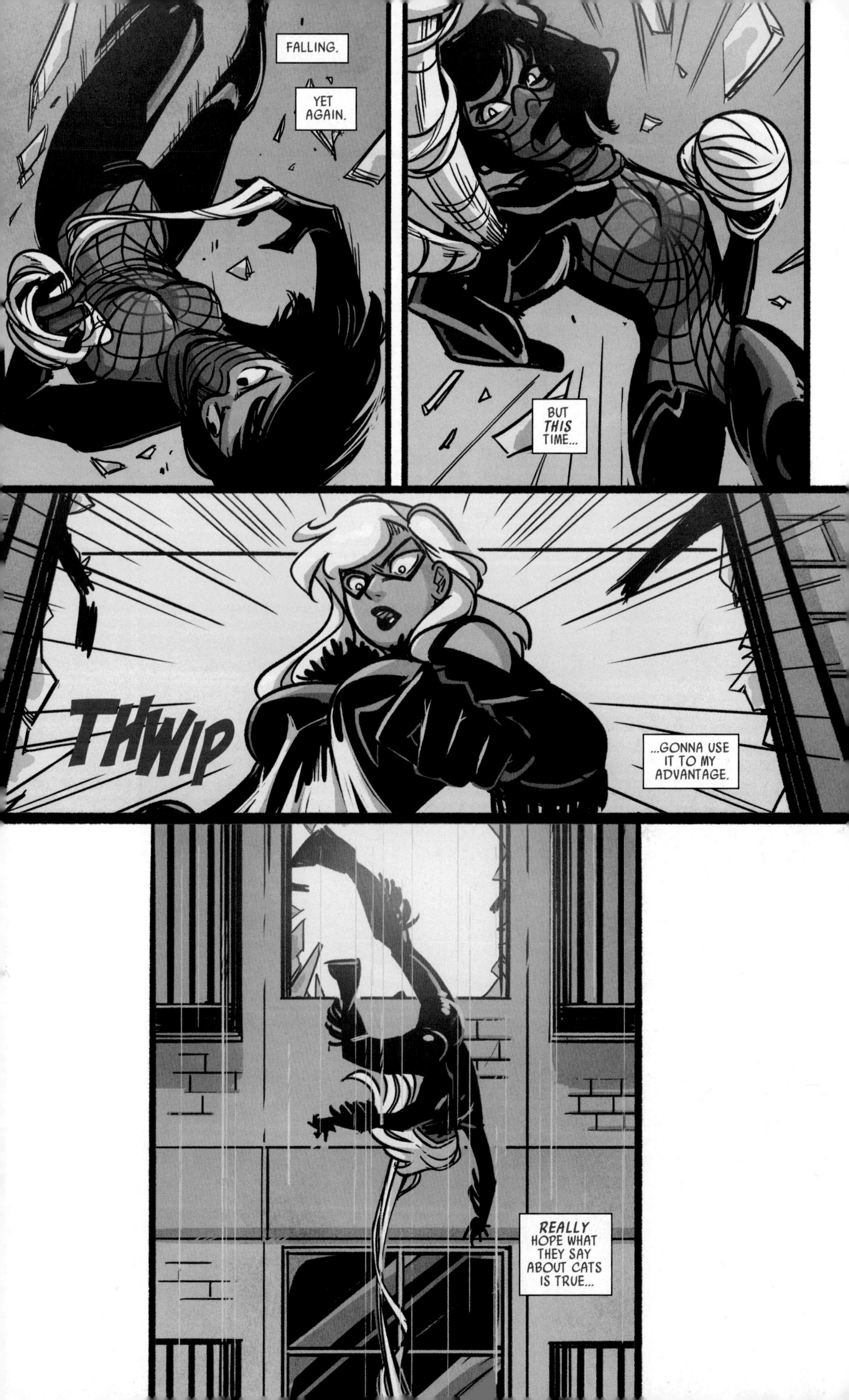
FALLING.
YET AGAIN.
BUT THIS TIME...
THWIP
...GONNA USE IT TO MY ADVANTAGE.
REALLY HOPE WHAT THEY SAY ABOUT CATS IS TRUE...

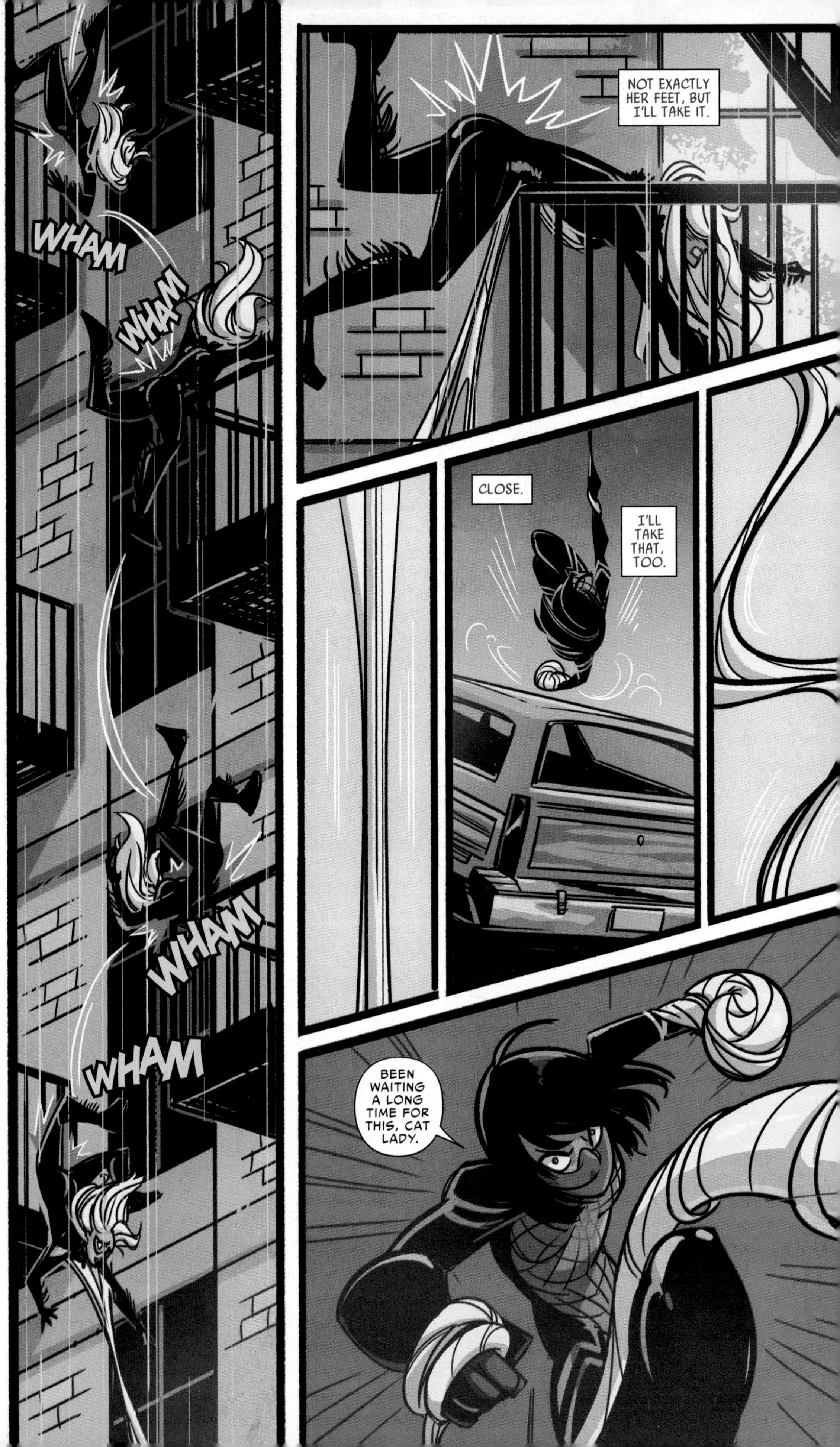

WHAM
WHAM
WHAM
WHAM
NOT EXACTLY HER FEET, BUT I'LL TAKE IT.
CLOSE.
I'LL TAKE THAT, TOO.
BEEN WAITING A LONG TIME FOR THIS, CAT LADY.

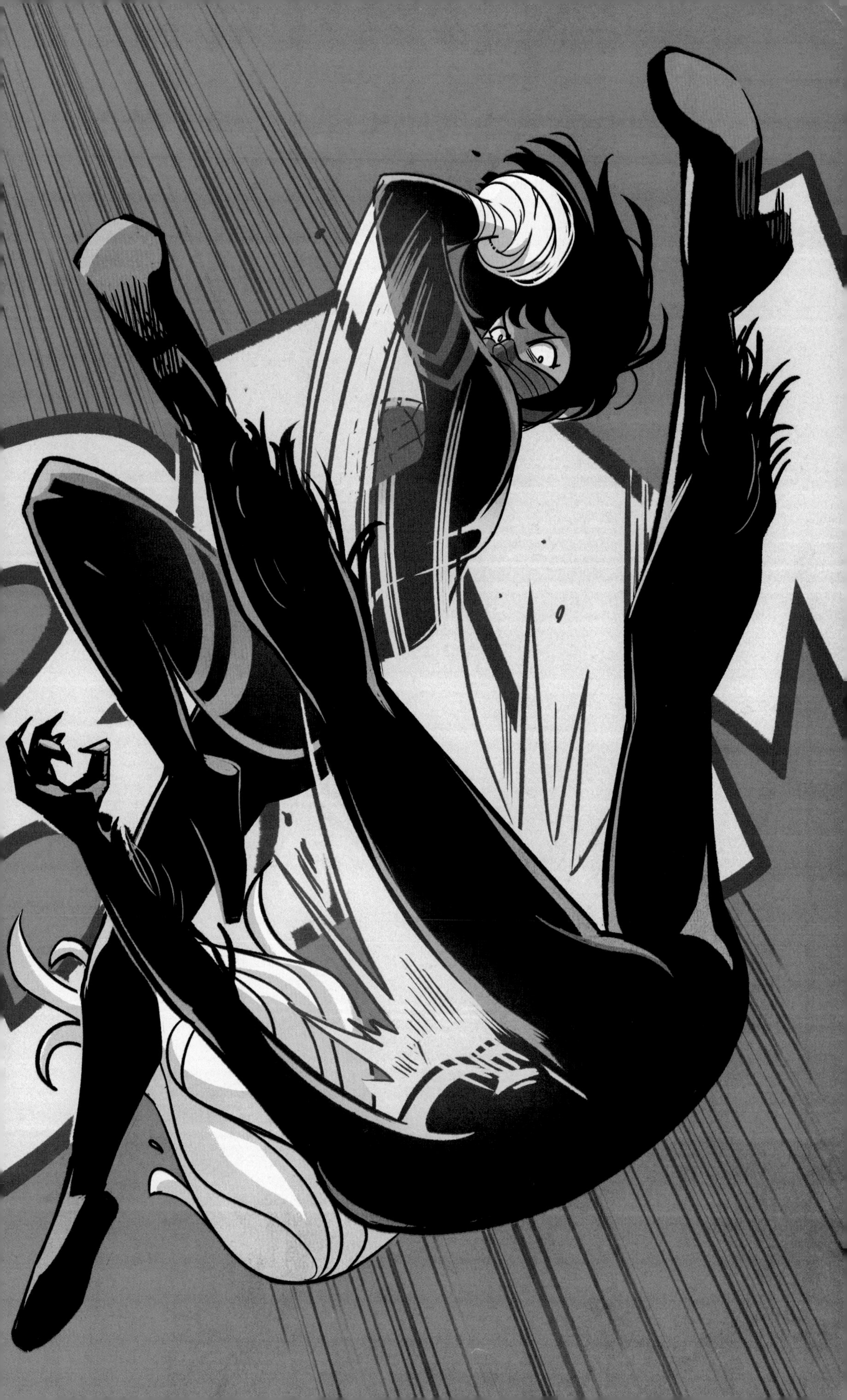

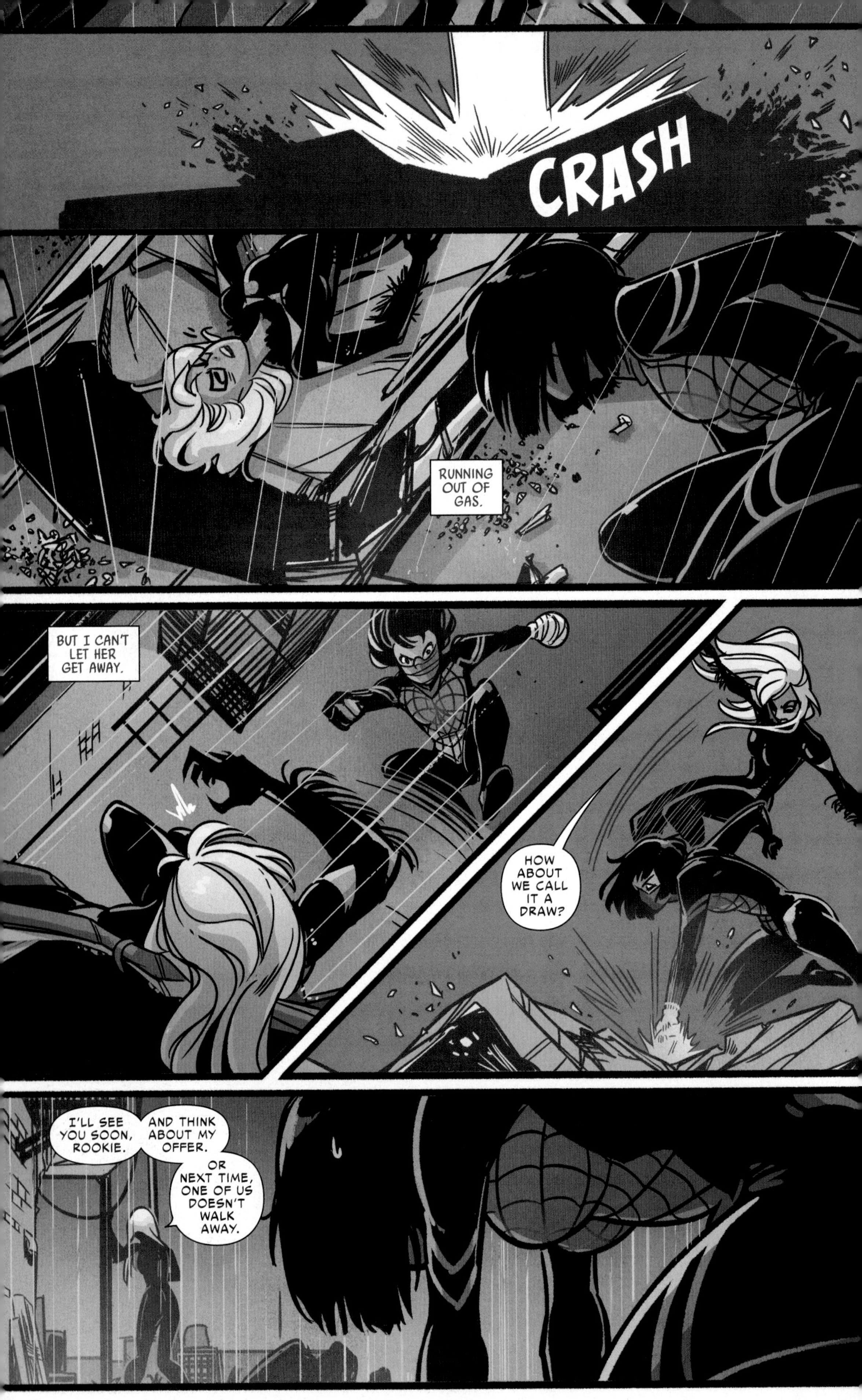
CRASH
RUNNING OUT OF GAS.
BUT I CAN'T LET HER GET AWAY.
HOW ABOUT WE CALL IT A DRAW?
I'LL SEE YOU SOON, ROOKIE.
AND THINK ABOUT MY OFFER.
OR NEXT TIME, ONE OF US DOESN'T WALK AWAY.

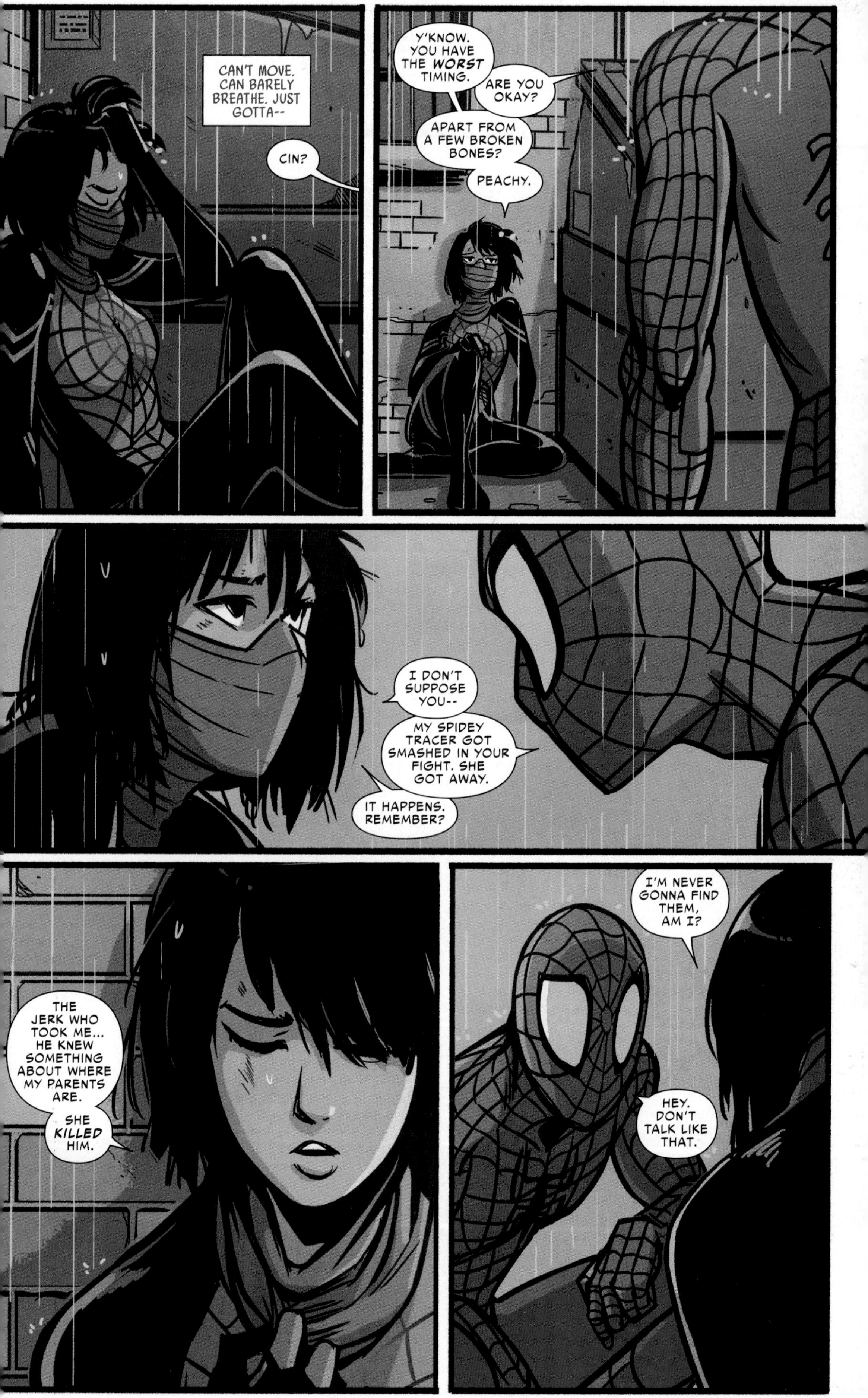
CAN'T MOVE. CAN BARELY BREATHE. JUST GOTTA--
CIN?
Y'KNOW. YOU HAVE THE WORST TIMING.
ARE YOU OKAY?
APART FROM A FEW BROKEN BONES?
PEACHY.
I DON'T SUPPOSE YOU--
MY SPIDEY TRACER GOT SMASHED IN YOUR FIGHT. SHE GOT AWAY.
IT HAPPENS. REMEMBER?
THE JERK WHO TOOK ME... HE KNEW SOMETHING ABOUT WHERE MY PARENTS ARE.
SHE KILLED HIM.
I'M NEVER GONNA FIND THEM, AM I?
HEY. DON'T TALK LIKE THAT.

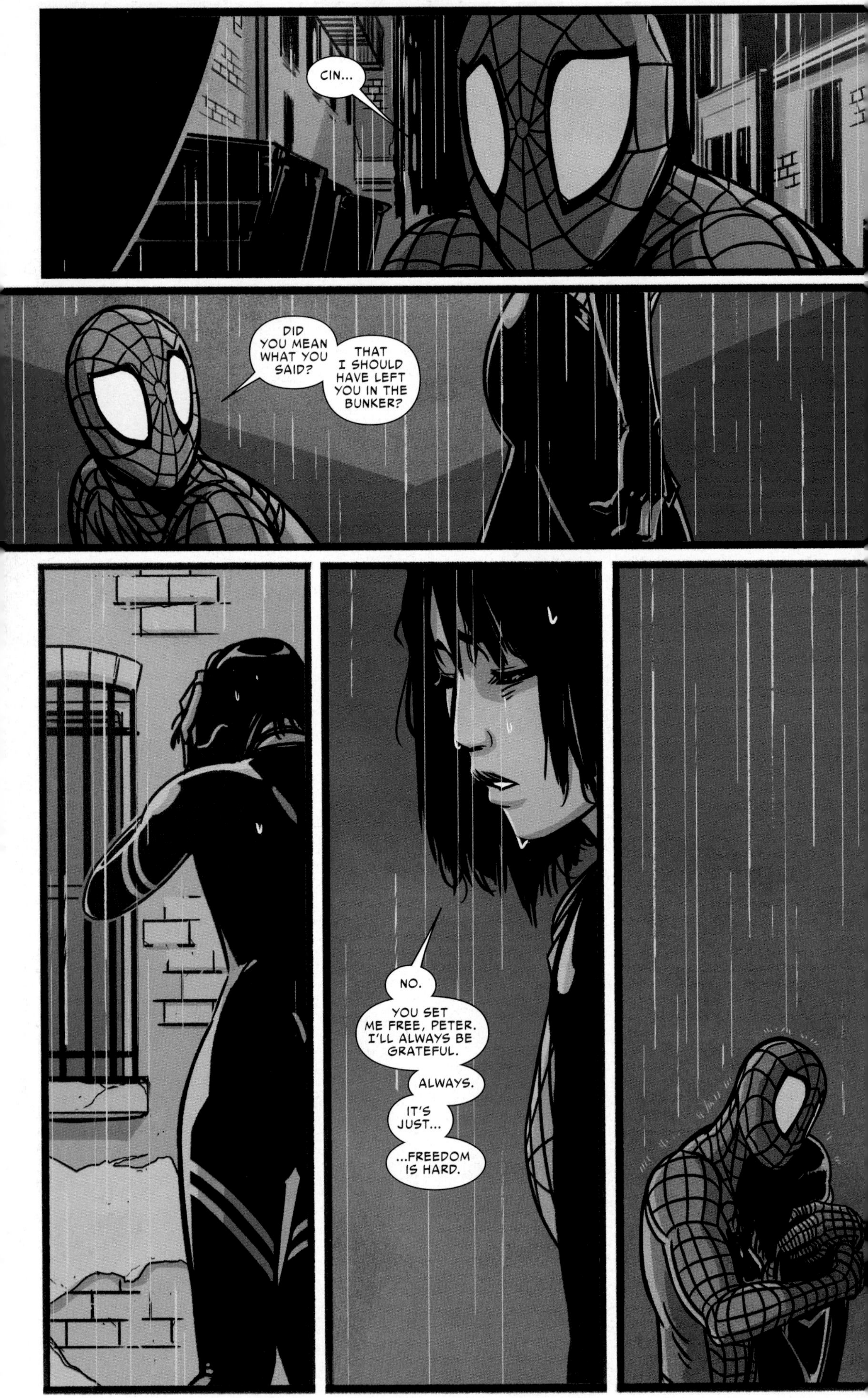
CIN...
DID YOU MEAN WHAT YOU SAID?
THAT I SHOULD HAVE LEFT YOU IN THE BUNKER?
NO.
YOU SET ME FREE, PETER. I'LL ALWAYS BE GRATEFUL.
ALWAYS.
IT'S JUST...
...FREEDOM IS HARD.

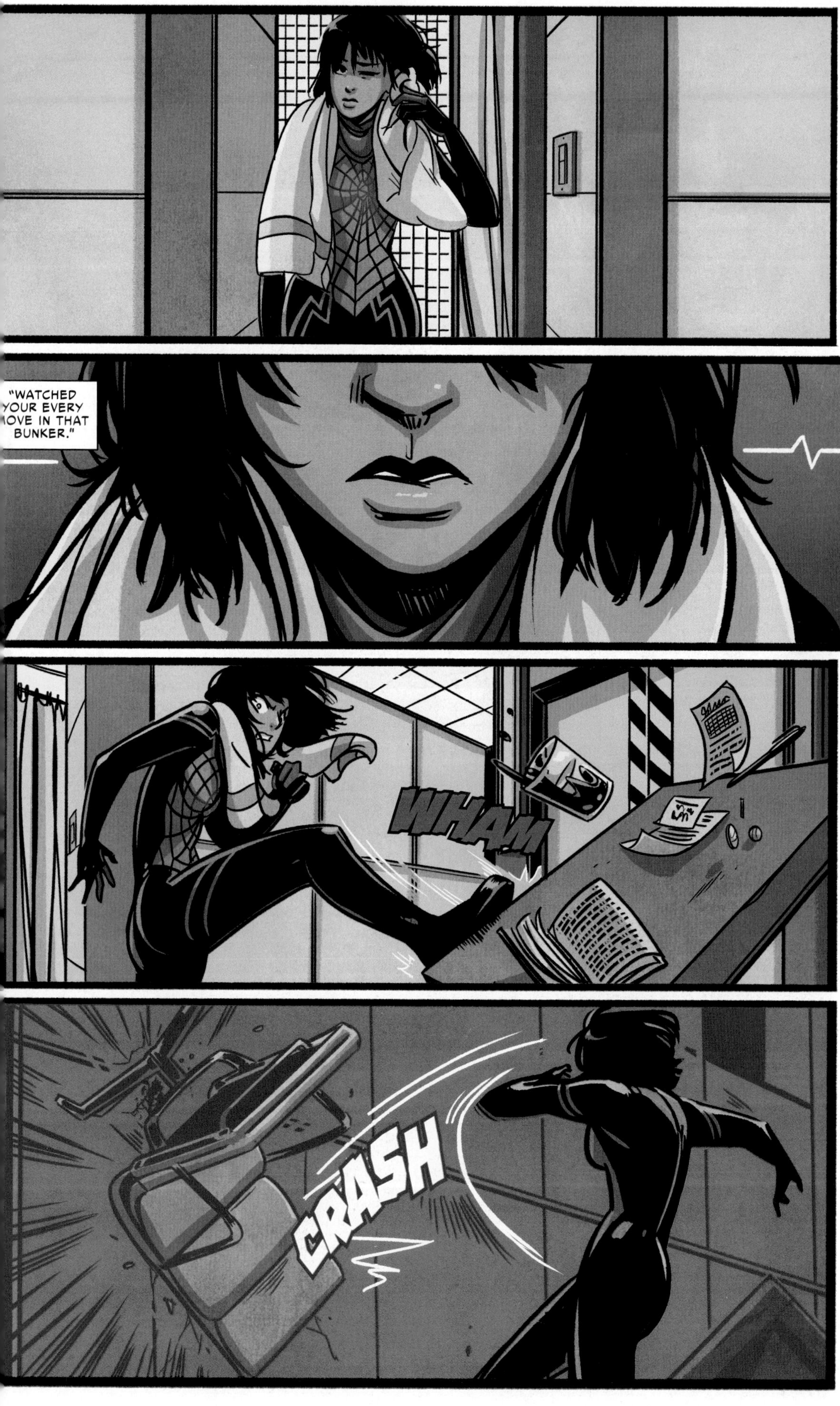
"WATCHED YOUR EVERY MOVE IN THAT BUNKER."
WHAM
CRASH

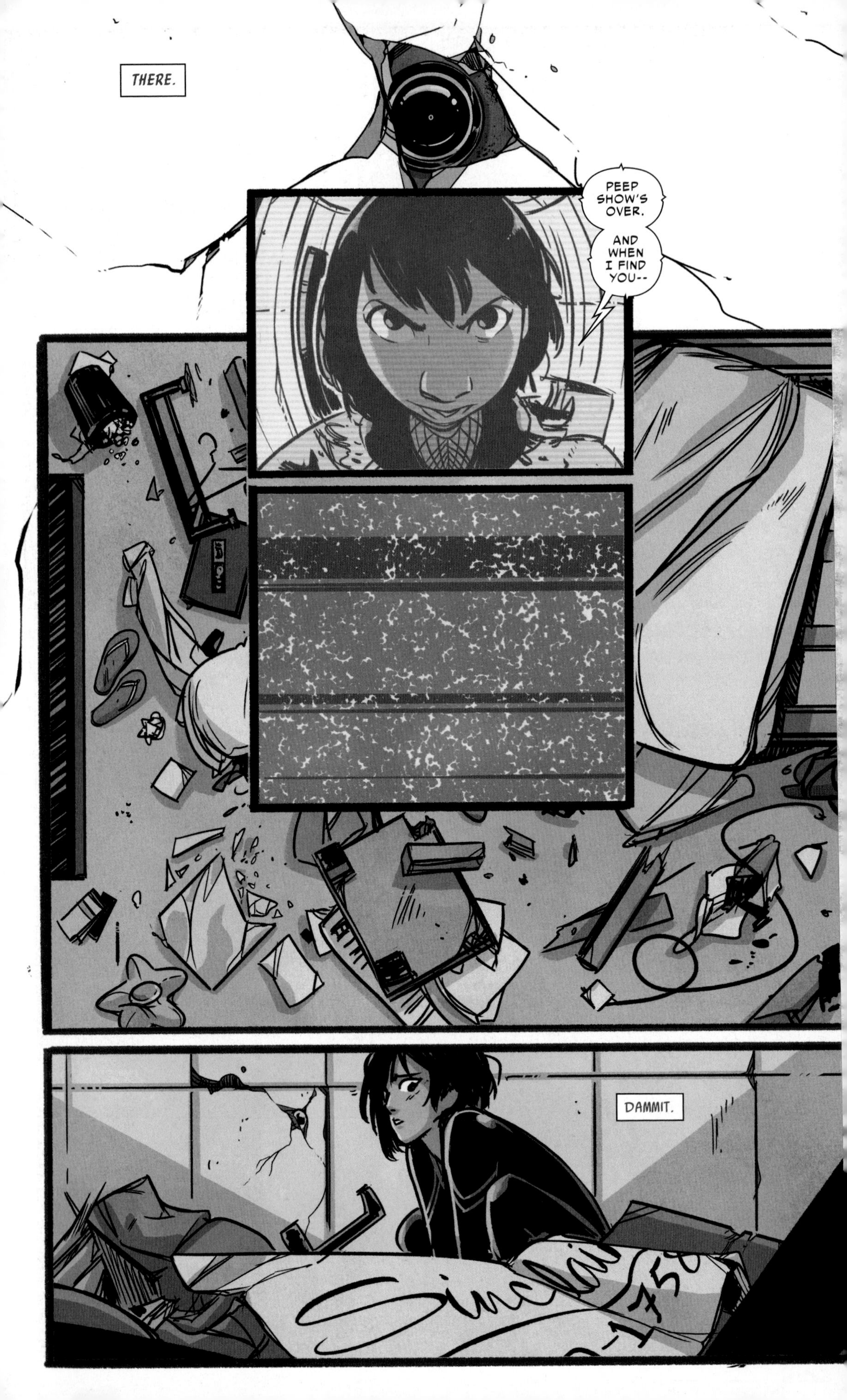
THERE.
PEEP SHOW'S OVER.
AND WHEN I FIND YOU--
DAMMIT.
Sinclair
1750

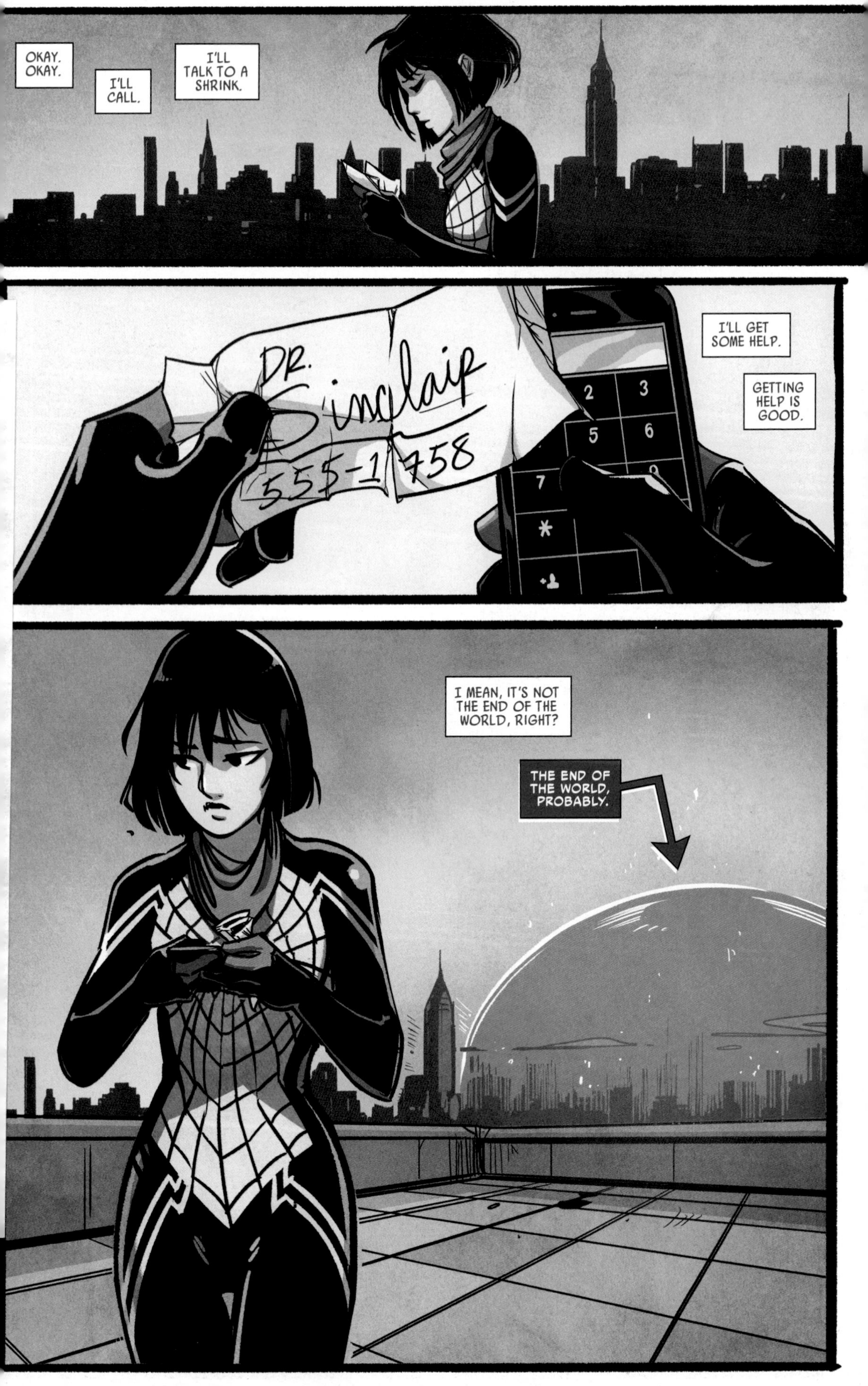
OKAY. OKAY.
I'LL CALL.
I'LL TALK TO A SHRINK.
DR. Sinclair
555-1758
I'LL GET SOME HELP.
GETTING HELP IS GOOD.
I MEAN, IT'S NOT THE END OF THE WORLD, RIGHT?
THE END OF THE WORLD, PROBABLY.

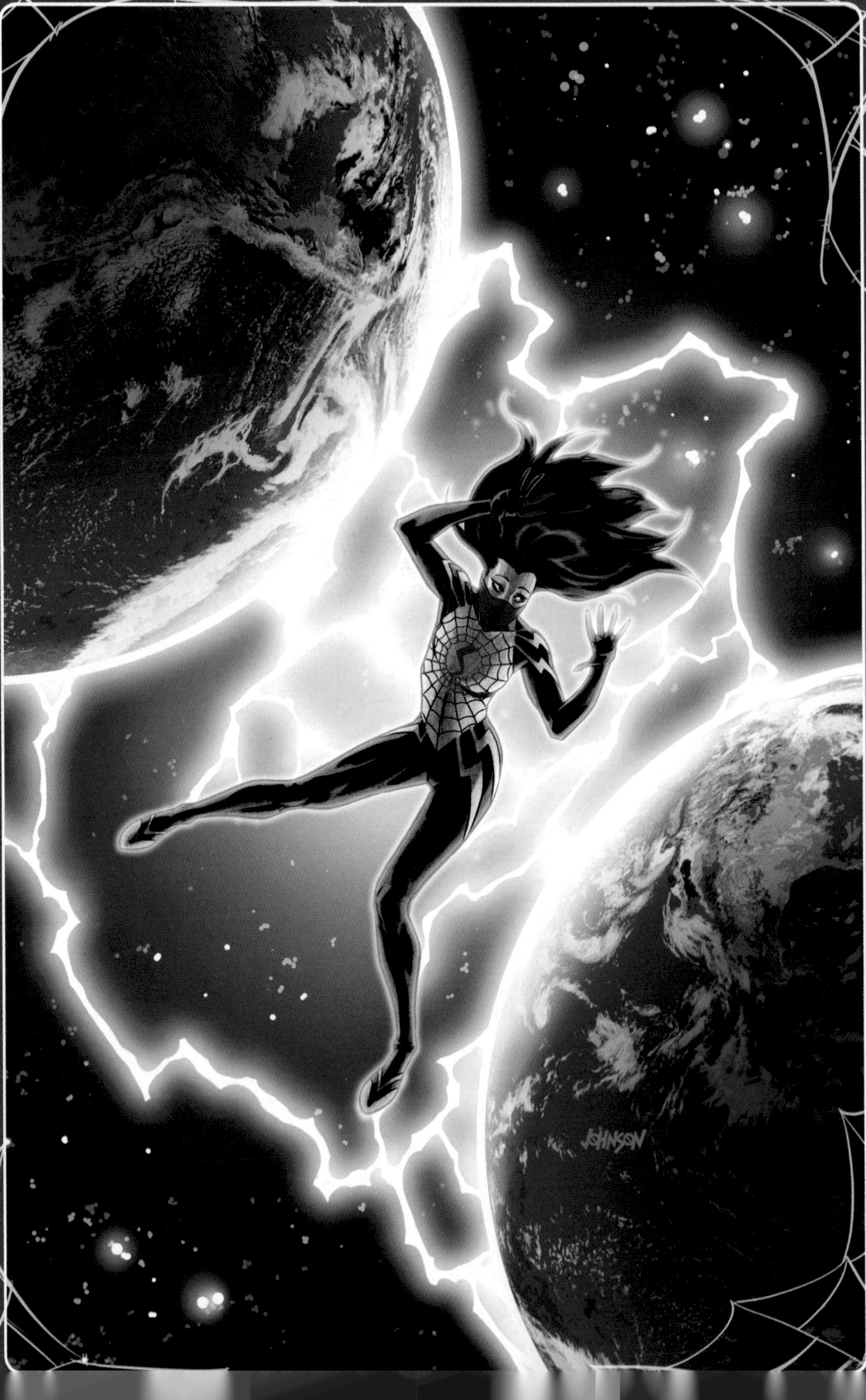
JOHNSON

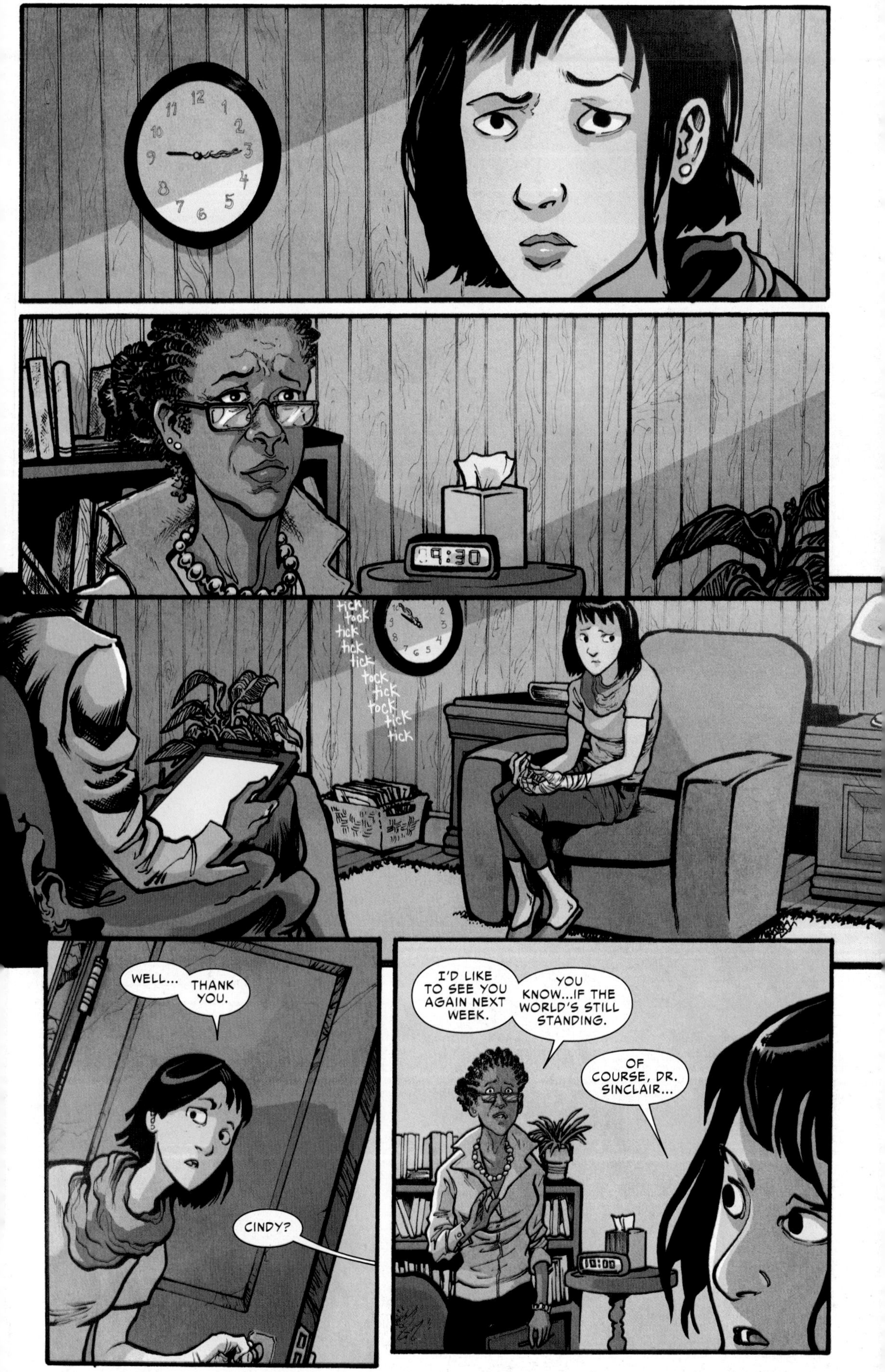
9:30
tick tock tick tick tick tock tick tock tick tick
WELL...
THANK YOU.
CINDY?
I'D LIKE TO SEE YOU AGAIN NEXT WEEK.
YOU KNOW...IF THE WORLD'S STILL STANDING.
OF COURSE, DR. SINCLAIR...
10:00

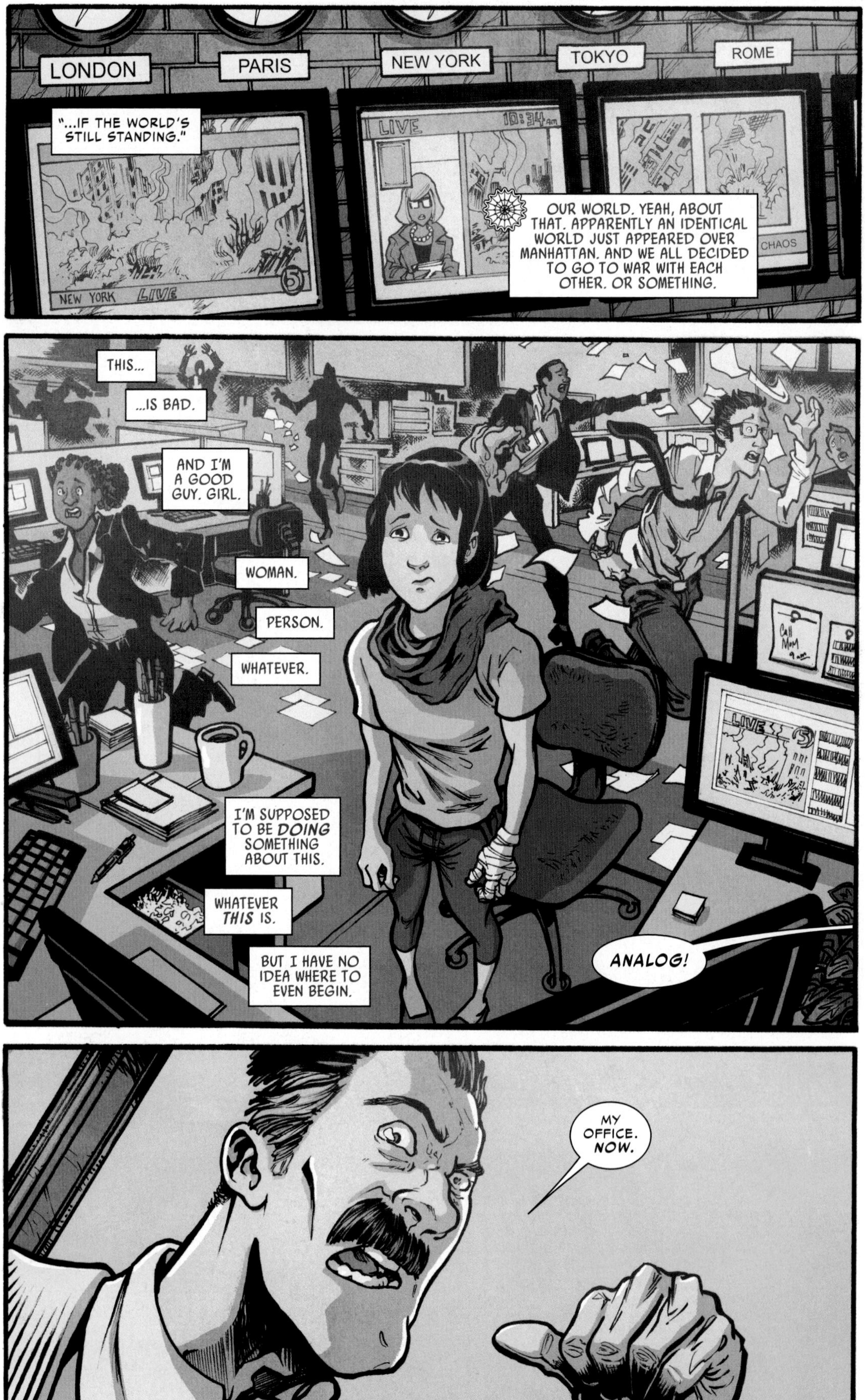
LONDON
PARIS
NEW YORK
TOKYO
ROME
"...IF THE WORLD'S STILL STANDING."
LIVE
10:34am
NEW YORK LIVE
OUR WORLD. YEAH, ABOUT THAT. APPARENTLY AN IDENTICAL WORLD JUST APPEARED OVER MANHATTAN. AND WE ALL DECIDED TO GO TO WAR WITH EACH OTHER. OR SOMETHING.
CHAOS
THIS...
...IS BAD.
AND I'M A GOOD GUY. GIRL.
WOMAN.
PERSON.
WHATEVER.
I'M SUPPOSED TO BE *DOING* SOMETHING ABOUT THIS.
WHATEVER *THIS* IS.
BUT I HAVE NO IDEA WHERE TO EVEN BEGIN.
ANALOG!
LIVE
MY OFFICE. *NOW.*

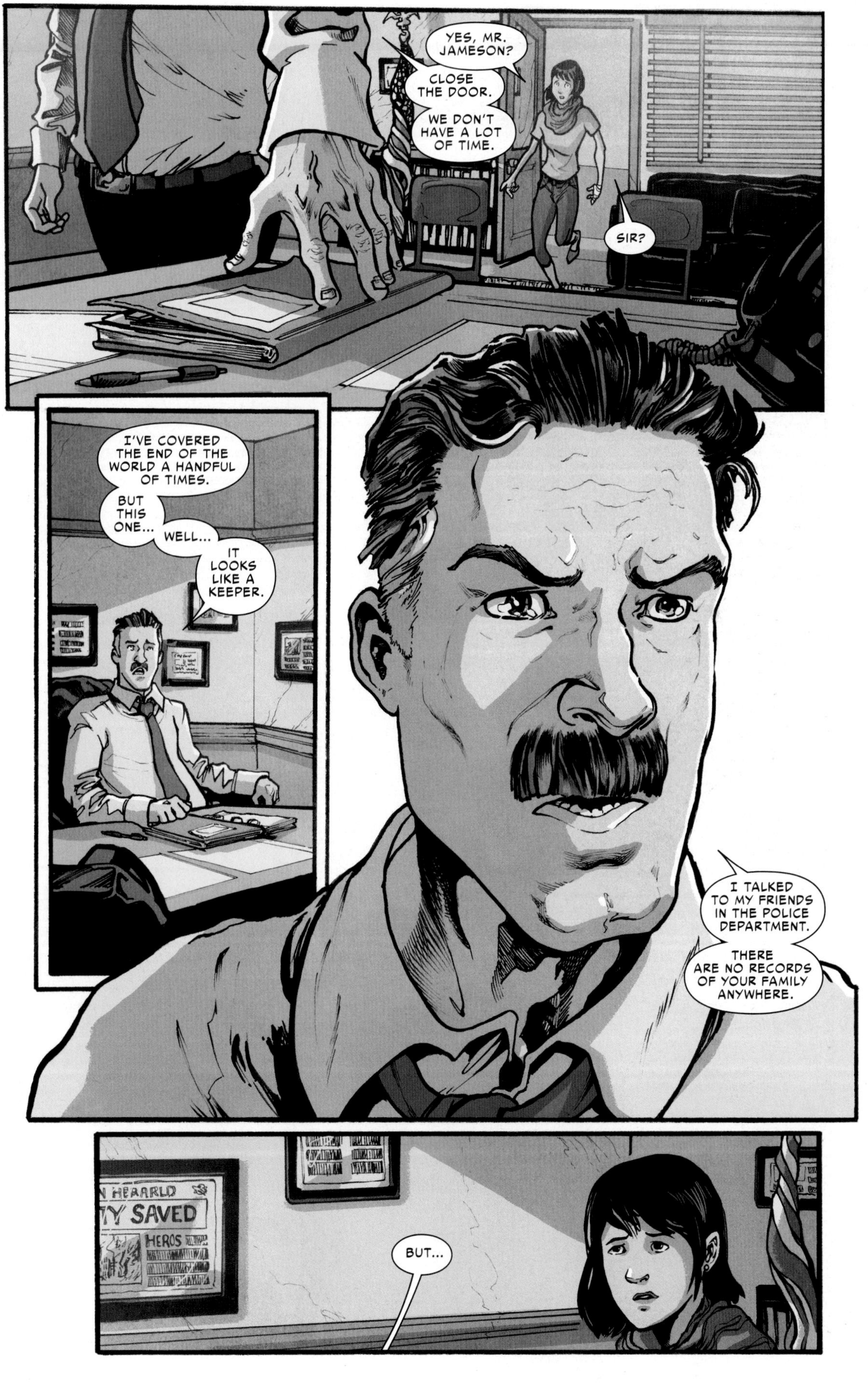
YES, MR. JAMESON?
CLOSE THE DOOR.
WE DON'T HAVE A LOT OF TIME.
SIR?
I'VE COVERED THE END OF THE WORLD A HANDFUL OF TIMES.
BUT THIS ONE...
WELL...
IT LOOKS LIKE A KEEPER.
I TALKED TO MY FRIENDS IN THE POLICE DEPARTMENT.
THERE ARE NO RECORDS OF YOUR FAMILY ANYWHERE.
HEARRLD
SAVED
HEROS
BUT...

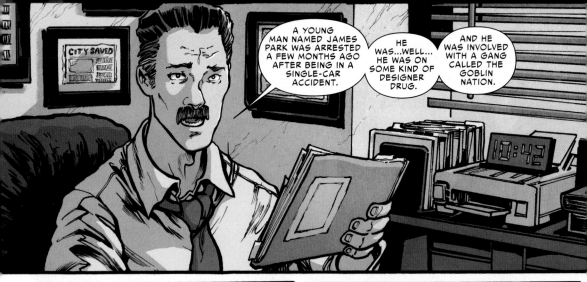

A YOUNG MAN NAMED JAMES PARK WAS ARRESTED A FEW MONTHS AGO AFTER BEING IN A SINGLE-CAR ACCIDENT.

HE WAS...WELL... HE WAS ON SOME KIND OF DESIGNER DRUG.

AND HE WAS INVOLVED WITH A GANG CALLED THE GOBLIN NATION.

WHAT DOES THAT HAVE TO DO WITH--

WHEN THE POLICE FIRST ASKED JAMES HIS NAME...HE SAID IT WAS *ALBERT MOON.*

THAT GOT LISTED AS AN ALIAS. AND THE RECORDS WERE SEALED, BECAUSE HE WAS A MINOR.

THAT CAN'T BE MY BROTHER. CAN'T BE. HE NEVER EVEN TOOK ADVIL. AND A *GANG?*

NO.

MR. JAMESON, I APPRECIATE YOUR HELP, BUT... THIS ISN'T MY BROTHER.

NOW, HOW CAN I HELP WITH--

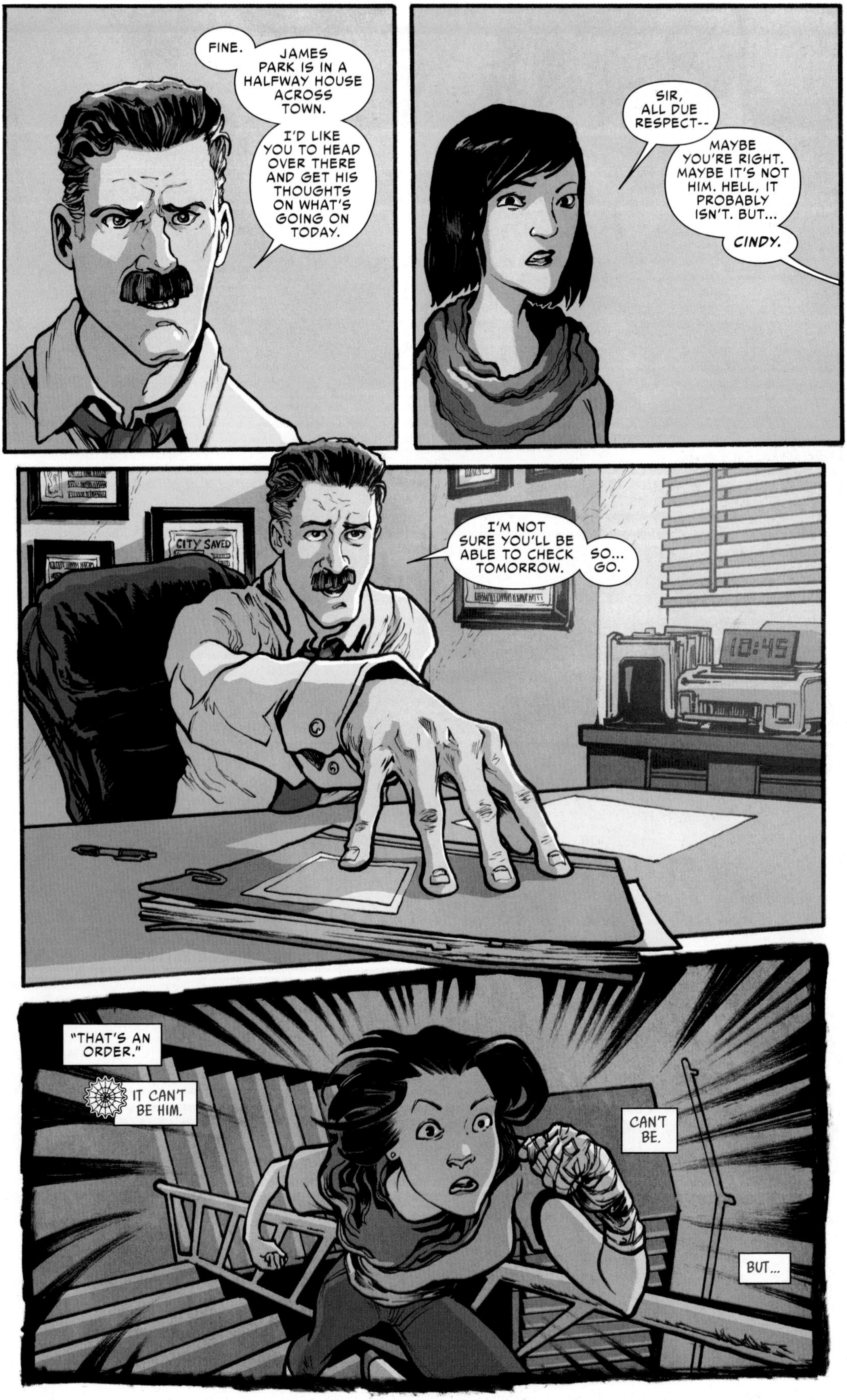
FINE.
JAMES PARK IS IN A HALFWAY HOUSE ACROSS TOWN.
I'D LIKE YOU TO HEAD OVER THERE AND GET HIS THOUGHTS ON WHAT'S GOING ON TODAY.
SIR, ALL DUE RESPECT--
MAYBE YOU'RE RIGHT. MAYBE IT'S NOT HIM. HELL, IT PROBABLY ISN'T. BUT...
CINDY.
CITY SAVED
I'M NOT SURE YOU'LL BE ABLE TO CHECK TOMORROW.
SO... GO.
10:45
"THAT'S AN ORDER."
IT CAN'T BE HIM.
CAN'T BE.
BUT...

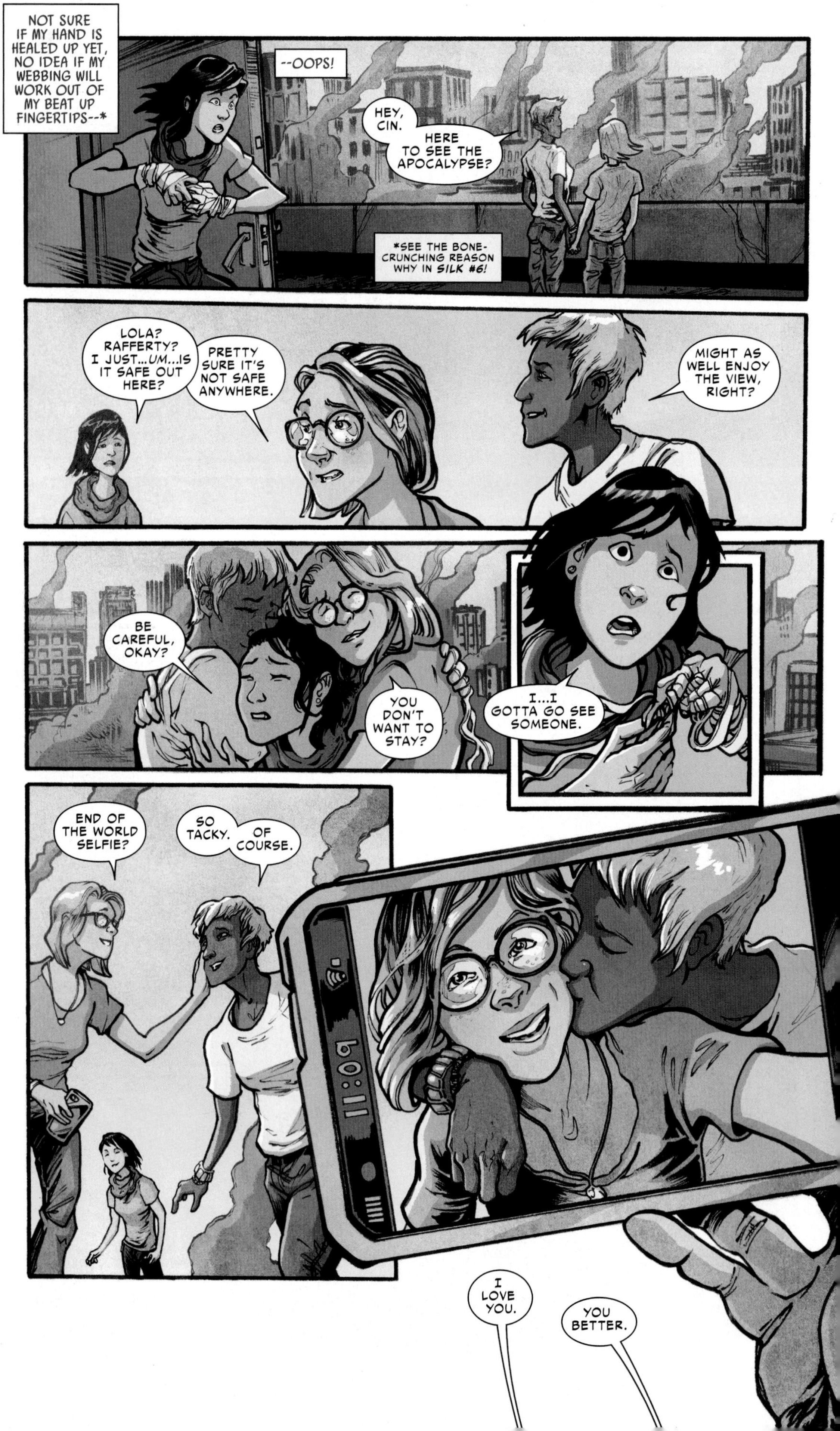
NOT SURE IF MY HAND IS HEALED UP YET, NO IDEA IF MY WEBBING WILL WORK OUT OF MY BEAT UP FINGERTIPS--*
--OOPS!
HEY, CIN.
HERE TO SEE THE APOCALYPSE?
*SEE THE BONE-CRUNCHING REASON WHY IN SILK #6!
LOLA? RAFFERTY? I JUST...UM...IS IT SAFE OUT HERE?
PRETTY SURE IT'S NOT SAFE ANYWHERE.
MIGHT AS WELL ENJOY THE VIEW, RIGHT?
BE CAREFUL, OKAY?
YOU DON'T WANT TO STAY?
I...I GOTTA GO SEE SOMEONE.
END OF THE WORLD SELFIE?
SO TACKY.
OF COURSE.
I LOVE YOU.
YOU BETTER.

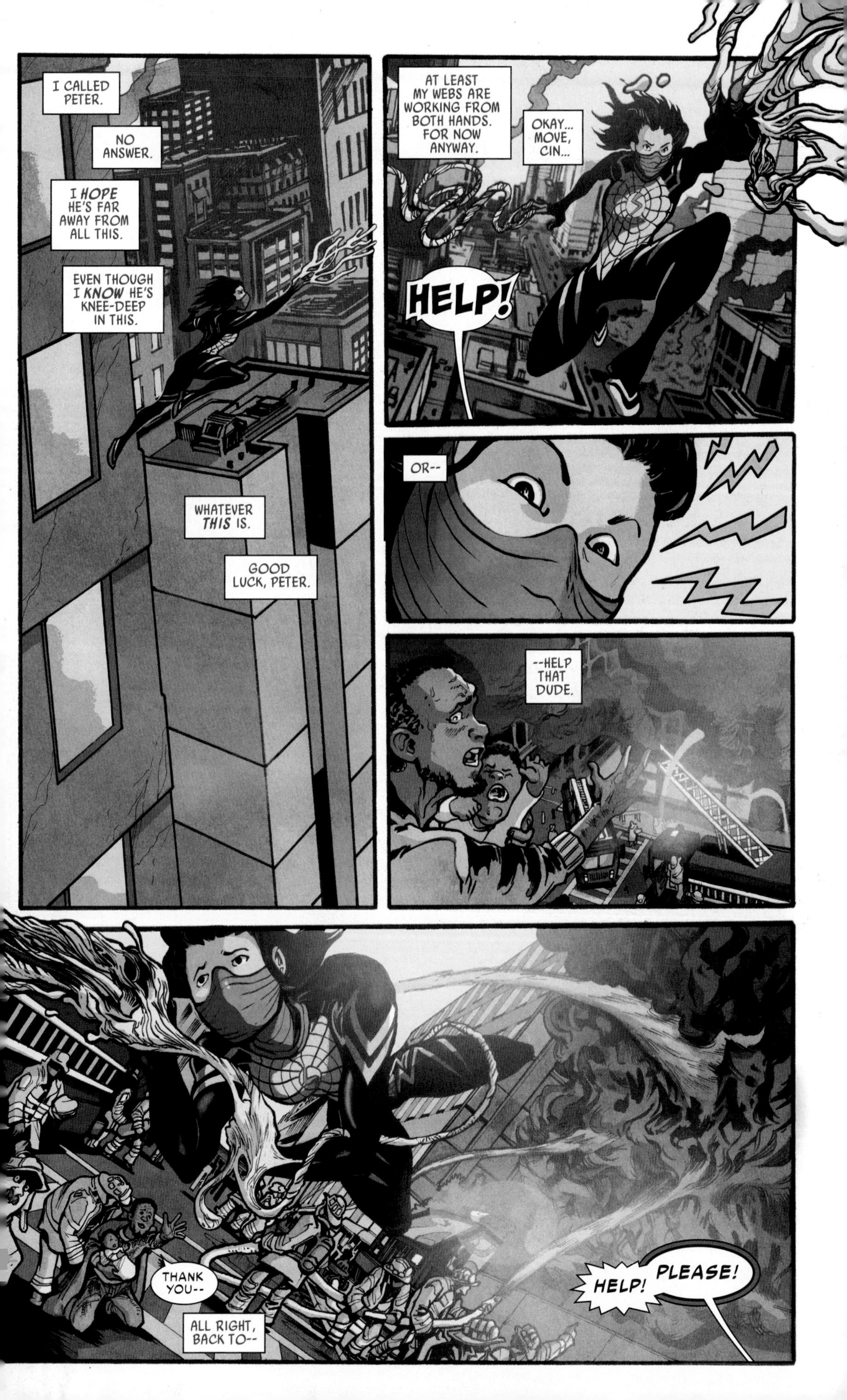
I CALLED PETER.
NO ANSWER.
I *HOPE* HE'S FAR AWAY FROM ALL THIS.
EVEN THOUGH I *KNOW* HE'S KNEE-DEEP IN THIS.
WHATEVER *THIS* IS.
GOOD LUCK, PETER.
AT LEAST MY WEBS ARE WORKING FROM BOTH HANDS. FOR NOW ANYWAY.
OKAY... MOVE, CIN...
HELP!
OR--
--HELP THAT DUDE.
THANK YOU--
ALL RIGHT, BACK TO--
HELP!
PLEASE!

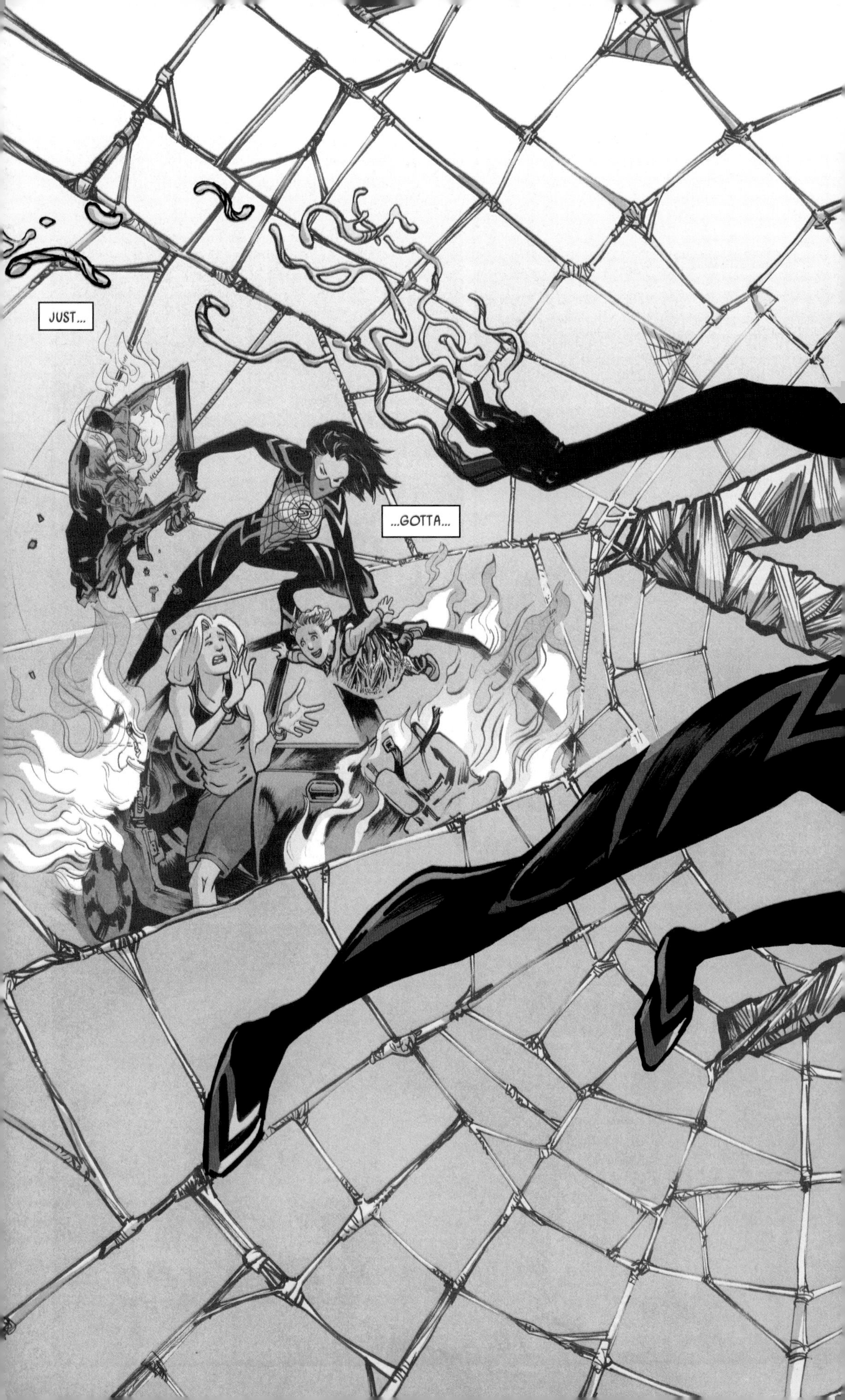
JUST...
...GOTTA...

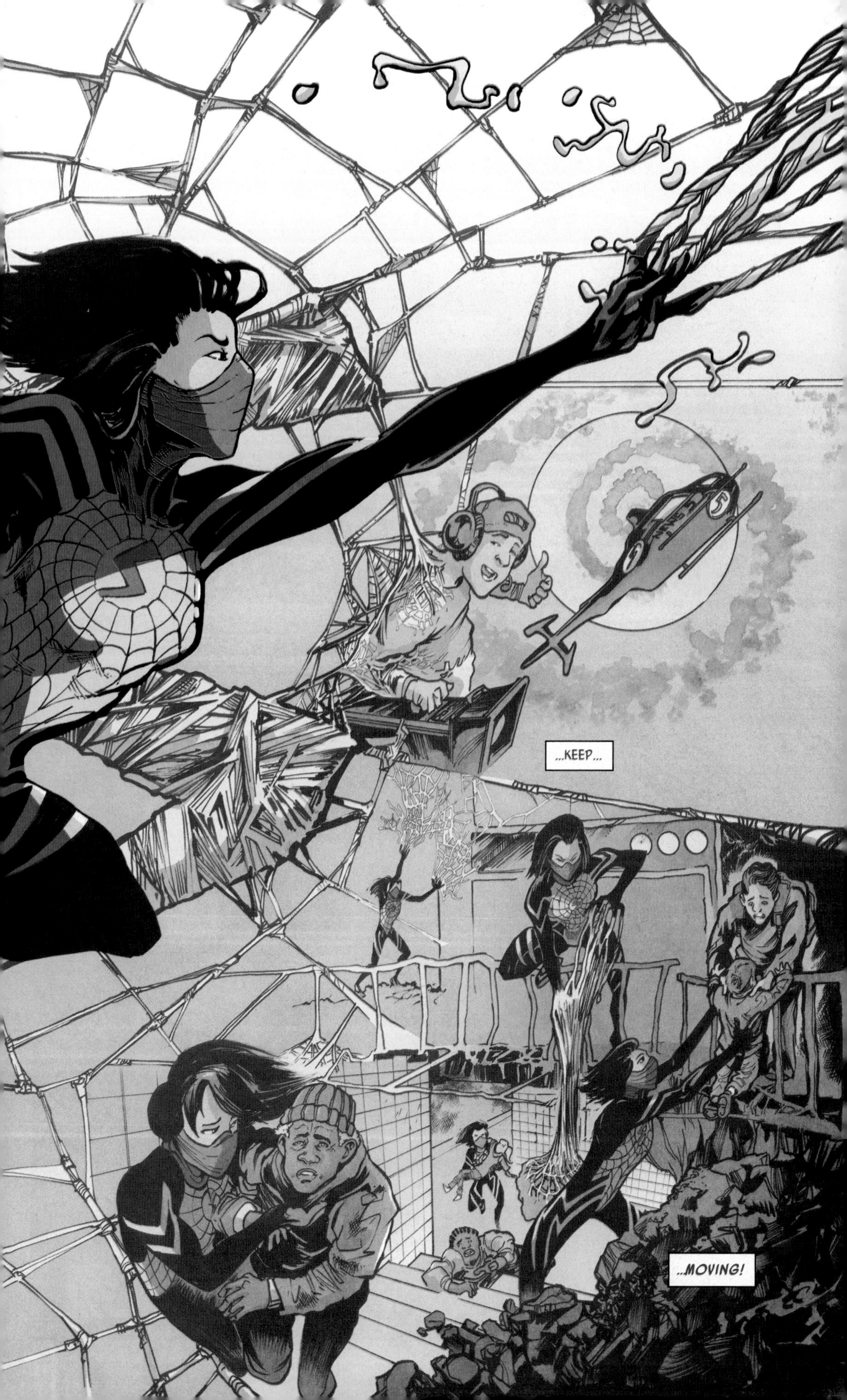
...KEEP...
...MOVING!

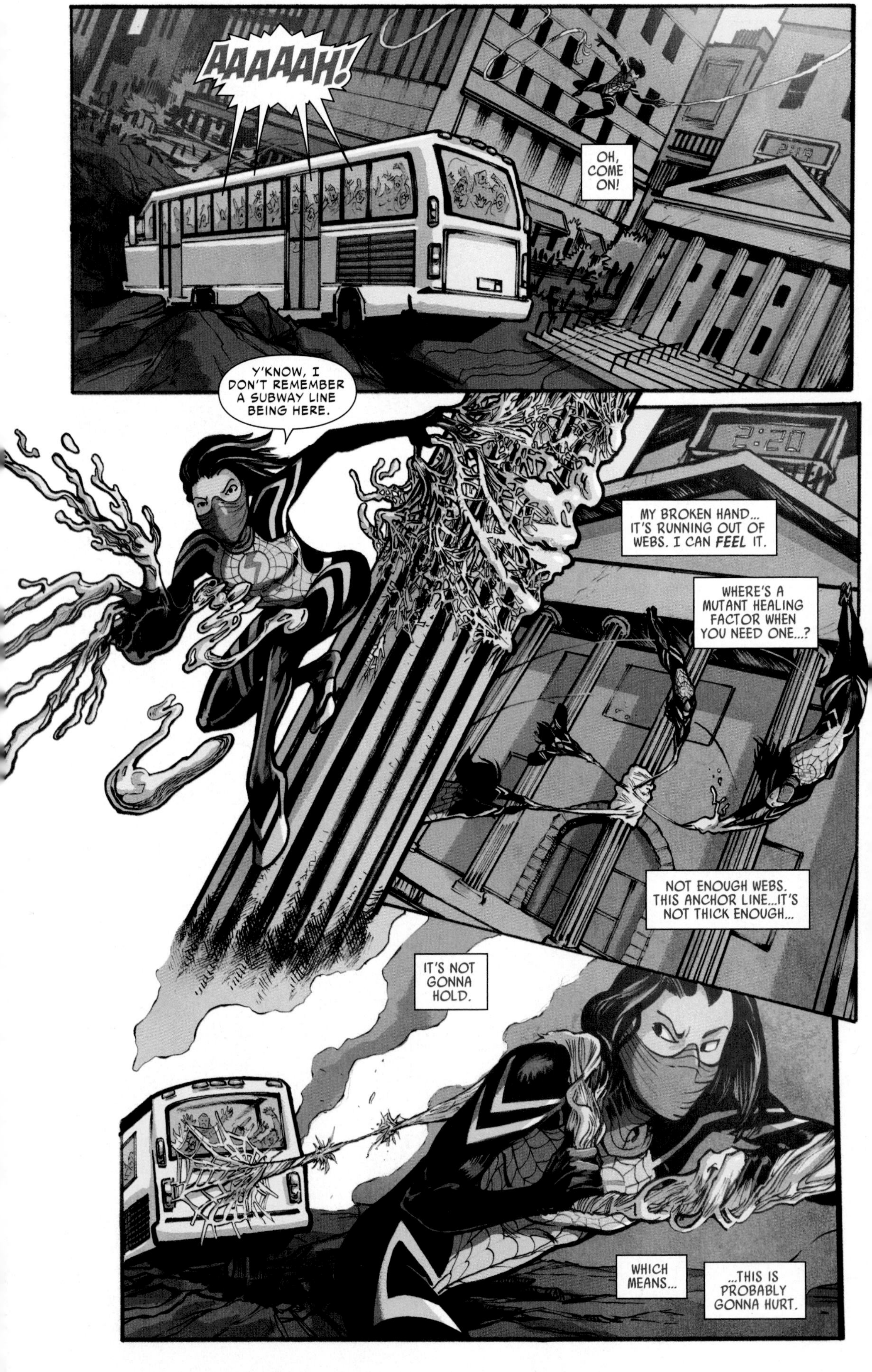
AAAAAH!
OH, COME ON!
Y'KNOW, I DON'T REMEMBER A SUBWAY LINE BEING HERE.
MY BROKEN HAND... IT'S RUNNING OUT OF WEBS. I CAN FEEL IT.
WHERE'S A MUTANT HEALING FACTOR WHEN YOU NEED ONE...?
NOT ENOUGH WEBS. THIS ANCHOR LINE...IT'S NOT THICK ENOUGH...
IT'S NOT GONNA HOLD.
WHICH MEANS...
...THIS IS PROBABLY GONNA HURT.

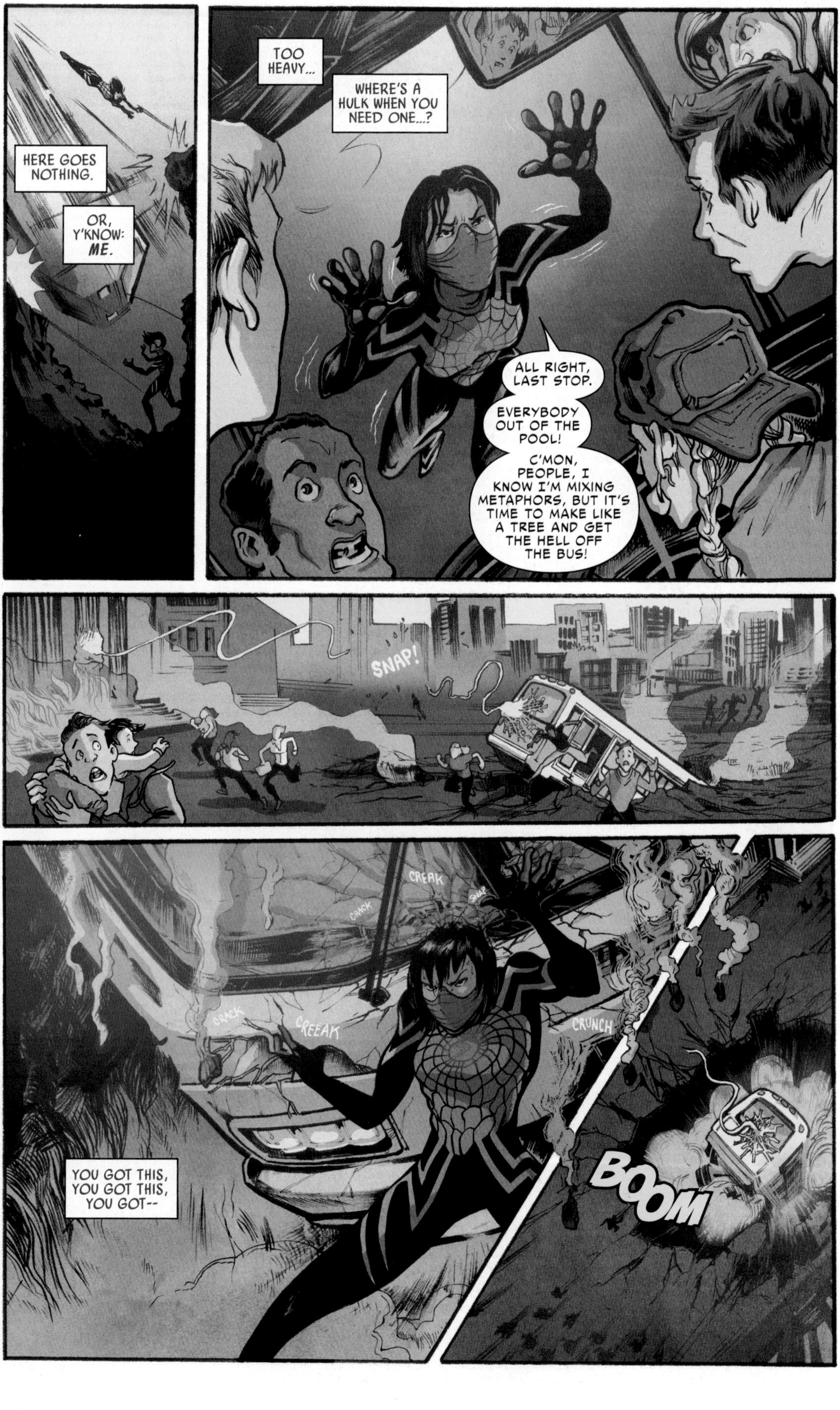
HERE GOES NOTHING.
OR, Y'KNOW: ME.
TOO HEAVY...
WHERE'S A HULK WHEN YOU NEED ONE...?
ALL RIGHT, LAST STOP.
EVERYBODY OUT OF THE POOL!
C'MON, PEOPLE, I KNOW I'M MIXING METAPHORS, BUT IT'S TIME TO MAKE LIKE A TREE AND GET THE HELL OFF THE BUS!
SNAP!
CREAK
CRACK
SNAP
CRACK
CREEAK
CRUNCH
YOU GOT THIS, YOU GOT THIS, YOU GOT--
BOOM

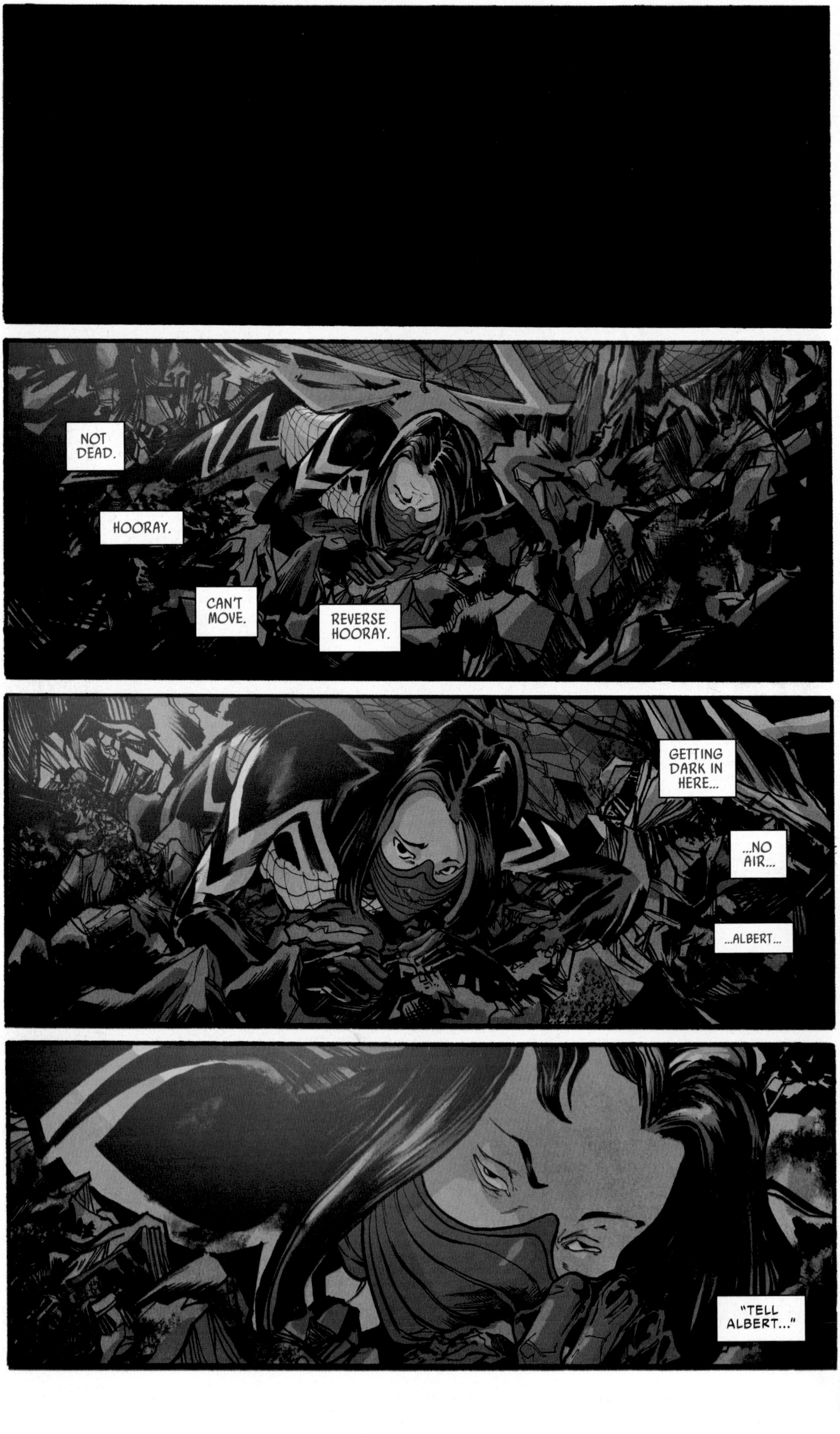
NOT DEAD.
HOORAY.
CAN'T MOVE.
REVERSE HOORAY.
GETTING DARK IN HERE...
...NO AIR...
...ALBERT...
"TELL ALBERT..."

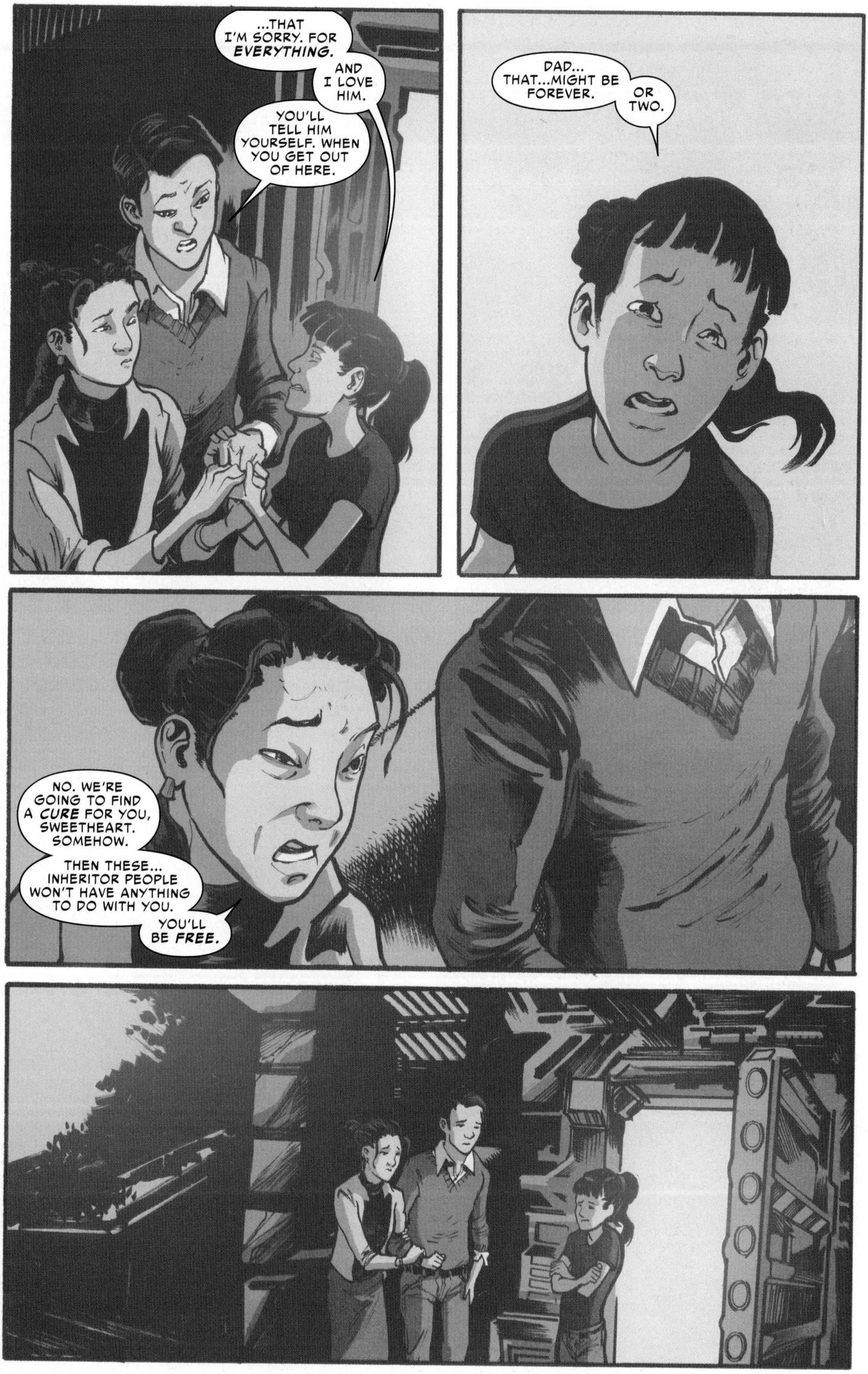
...THAT I'M SORRY. FOR *EVERYTHING.*
AND I LOVE HIM.
YOU'LL TELL HIM YOURSELF. WHEN YOU GET OUT OF HERE.
DAD... THAT...MIGHT BE FOREVER.
OR TWO.
NO. WE'RE GOING TO FIND A *CURE* FOR YOU, SWEETHEART. SOMEHOW.
THEN THESE... INHERITOR PEOPLE WON'T HAVE ANYTHING TO DO WITH YOU.
YOU'LL BE *FREE.*

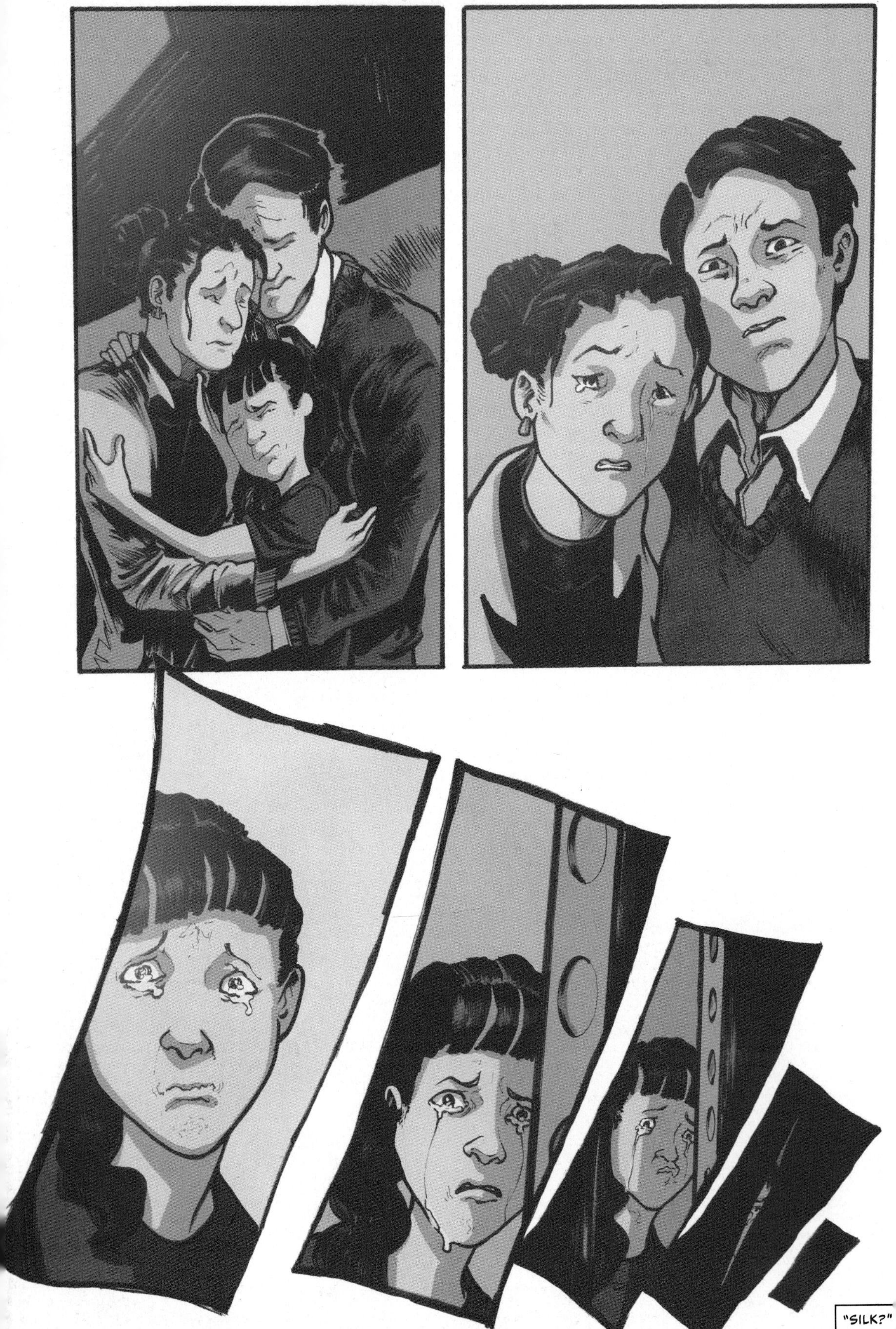
"SILK?"

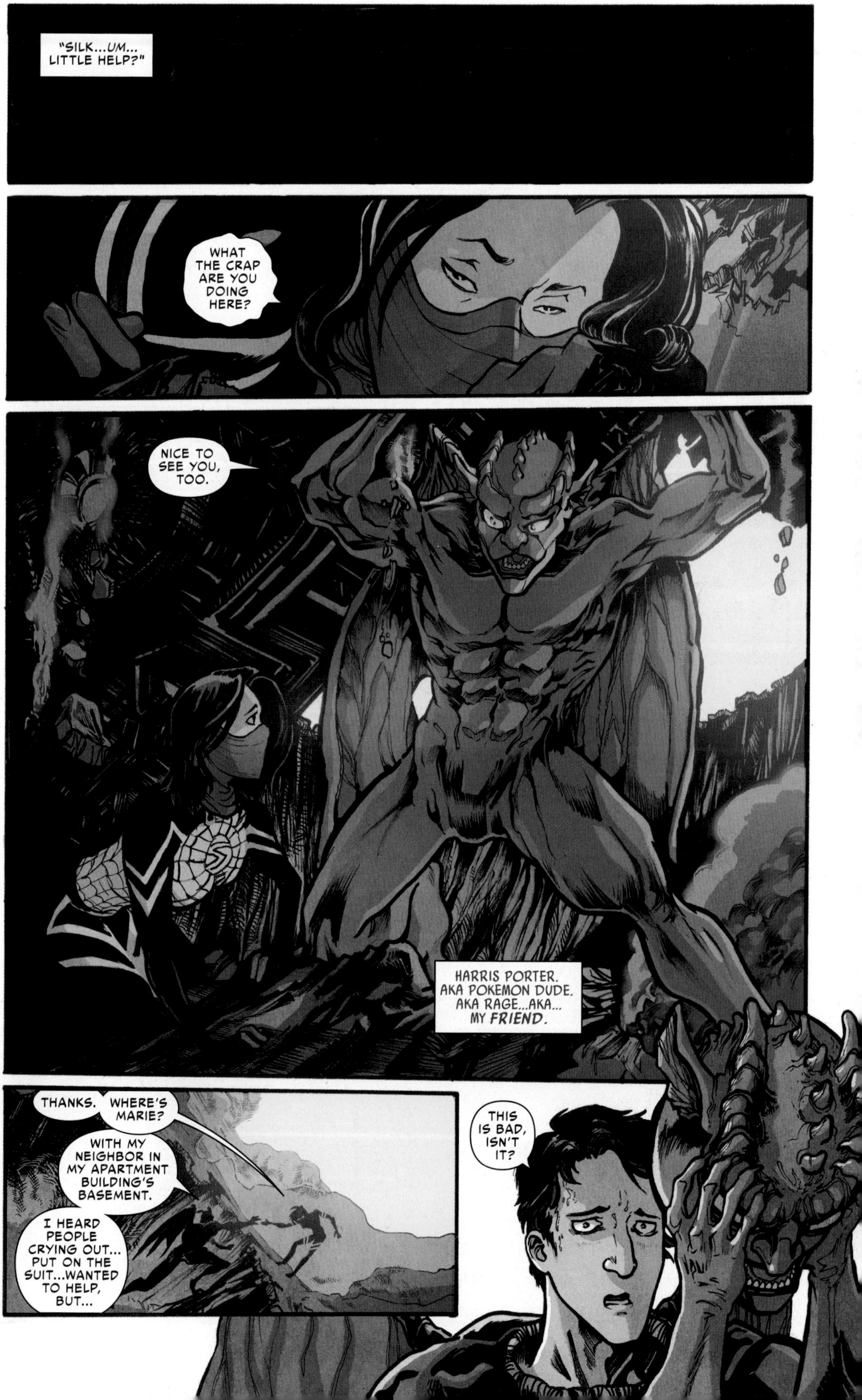
"SILK...UM... LITTLE HELP?"
WHAT THE CRAP ARE YOU DOING HERE?
NICE TO SEE YOU, TOO.
HARRIS PORTER. AKA POKEMON DUDE. AKA RAGE...AKA... MY FRIEND.
THANKS.
WHERE'S MARIE?
WITH MY NEIGHBOR IN MY APARTMENT BUILDING'S BASEMENT.
I HEARD PEOPLE CRYING OUT... PUT ON THE SUIT...WANTED TO HELP, BUT...
THIS IS BAD, ISN'T IT?

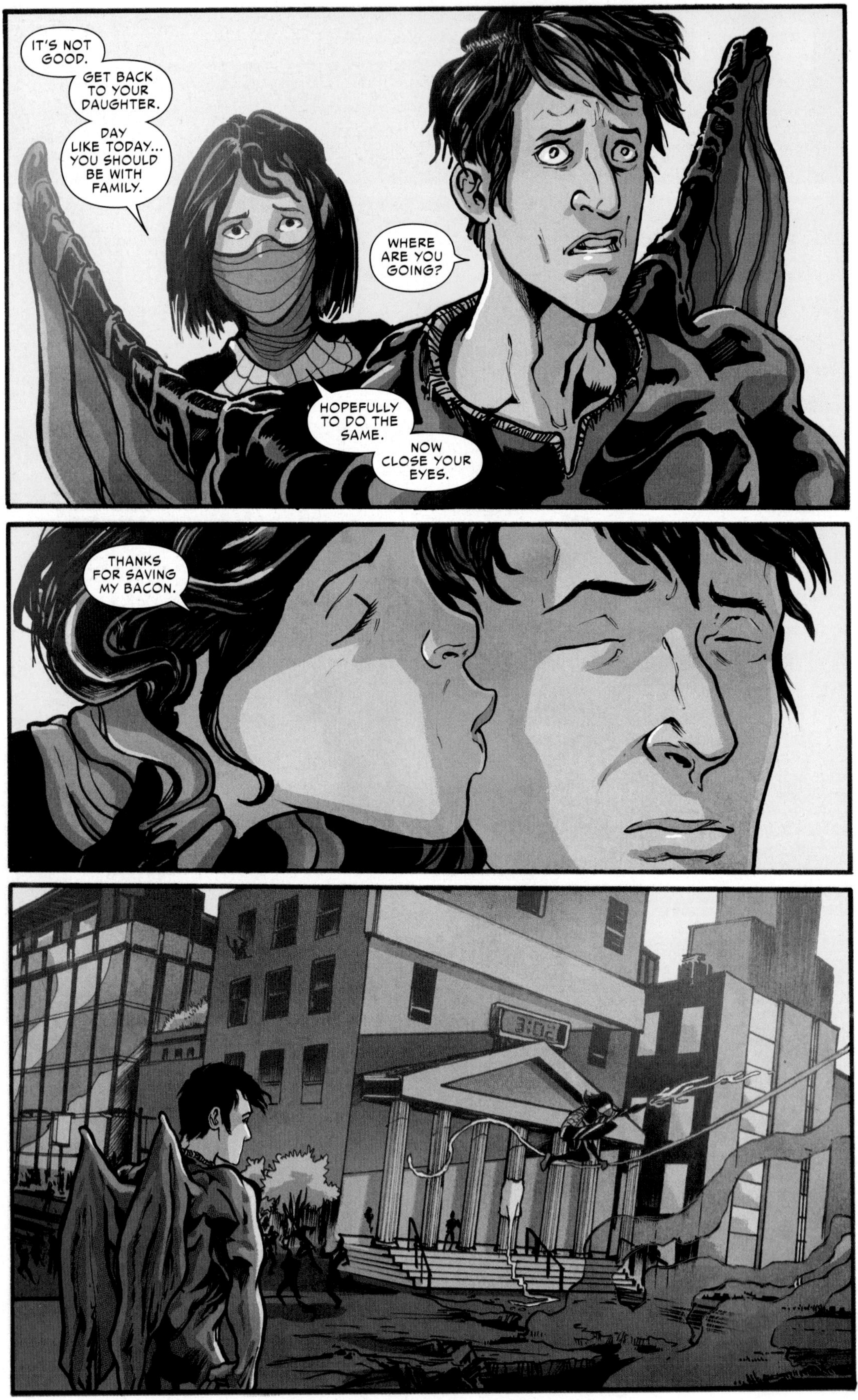
IT'S NOT GOOD.
GET BACK TO YOUR DAUGHTER.
DAY LIKE TODAY... YOU SHOULD BE WITH FAMILY.
WHERE ARE YOU GOING?
HOPEFULLY TO DO THE SAME.
NOW CLOSE YOUR EYES.
THANKS FOR SAVING MY BACON.
3:02

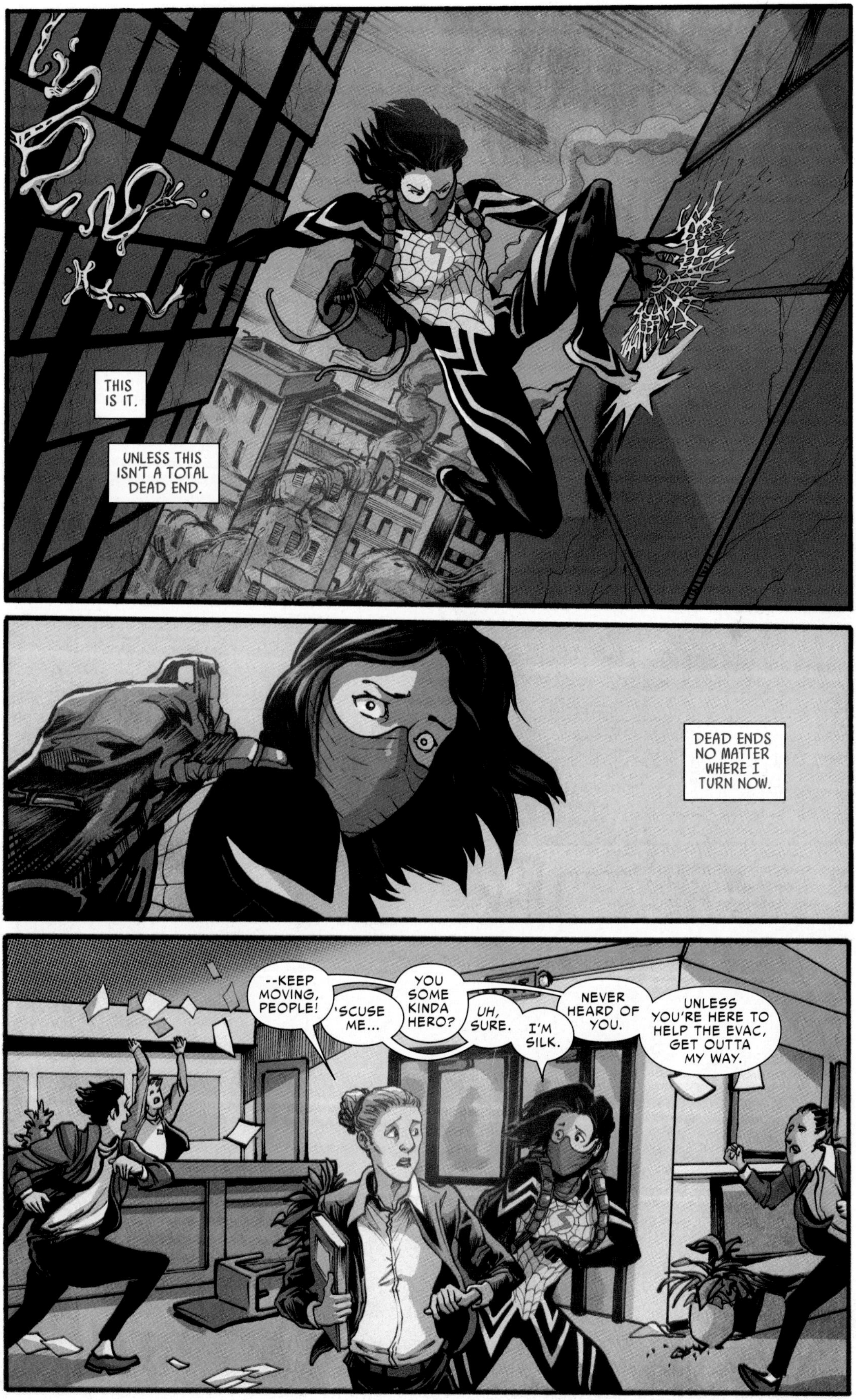
THIS IS IT.
UNLESS THIS ISN'T A TOTAL DEAD END.
DEAD ENDS NO MATTER WHERE I TURN NOW.
--KEEP MOVING, PEOPLE!
'SCUSE ME...
YOU SOME KINDA HERO?
UH, SURE.
I'M SILK.
NEVER HEARD OF YOU.
UNLESS YOU'RE HERE TO HELP THE EVAC, GET OUTTA MY WAY.

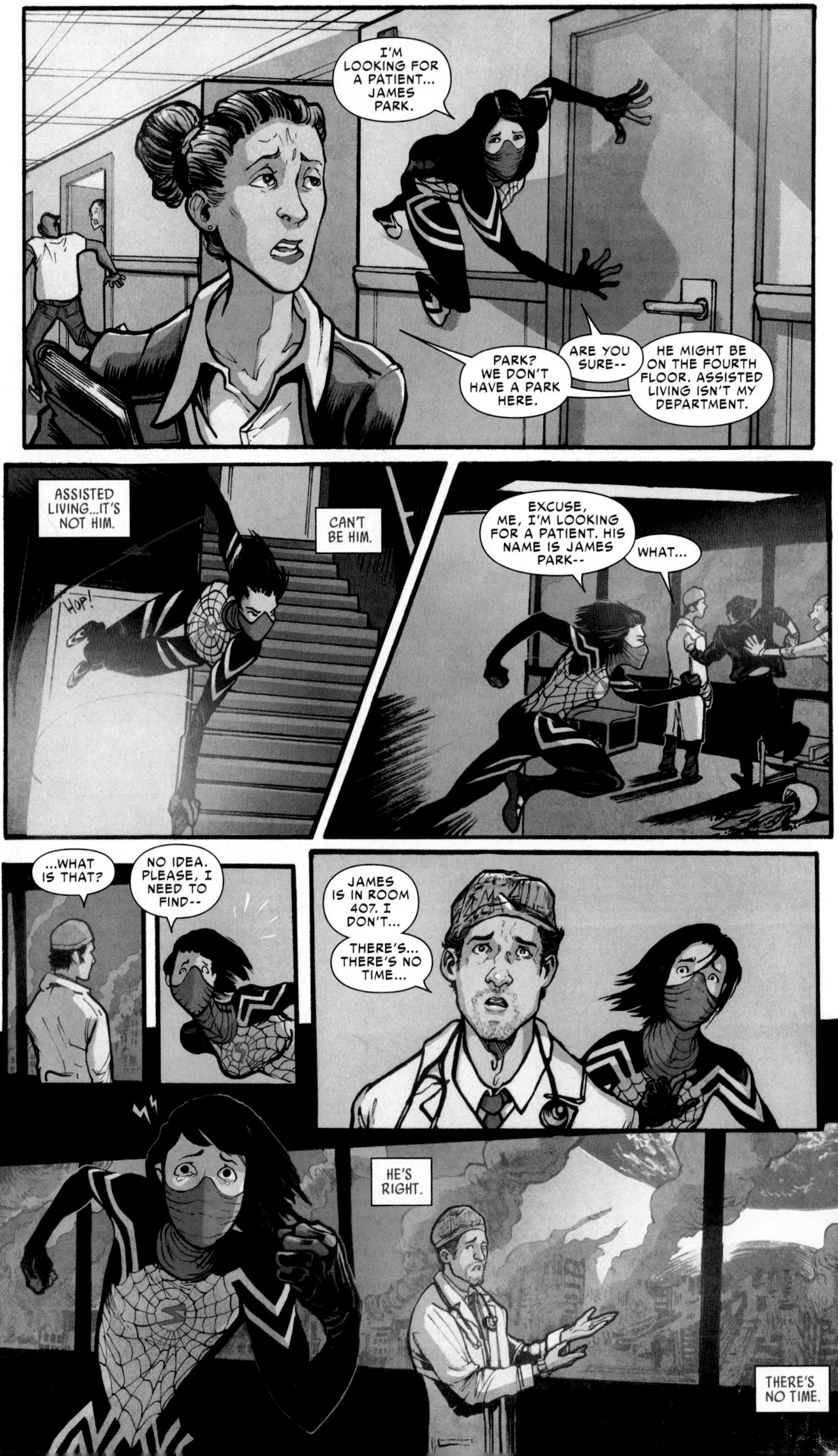
I'M LOOKING FOR A PATIENT... JAMES PARK.
PARK? WE DON'T HAVE A PARK HERE.
ARE YOU SURE--
HE MIGHT BE ON THE FOURTH FLOOR. ASSISTED LIVING ISN'T MY DEPARTMENT.
ASSISTED LIVING...IT'S NOT HIM.
CAN'T BE HIM.
HOP!
EXCUSE, ME, I'M LOOKING FOR A PATIENT. HIS NAME IS JAMES PARK--
WHAT...
...WHAT IS THAT?
NO IDEA. PLEASE, I NEED TO FIND--
JAMES IS IN ROOM 407. I DON'T...
THERE'S... THERE'S NO TIME...
HE'S RIGHT.
THERE'S NO TIME.

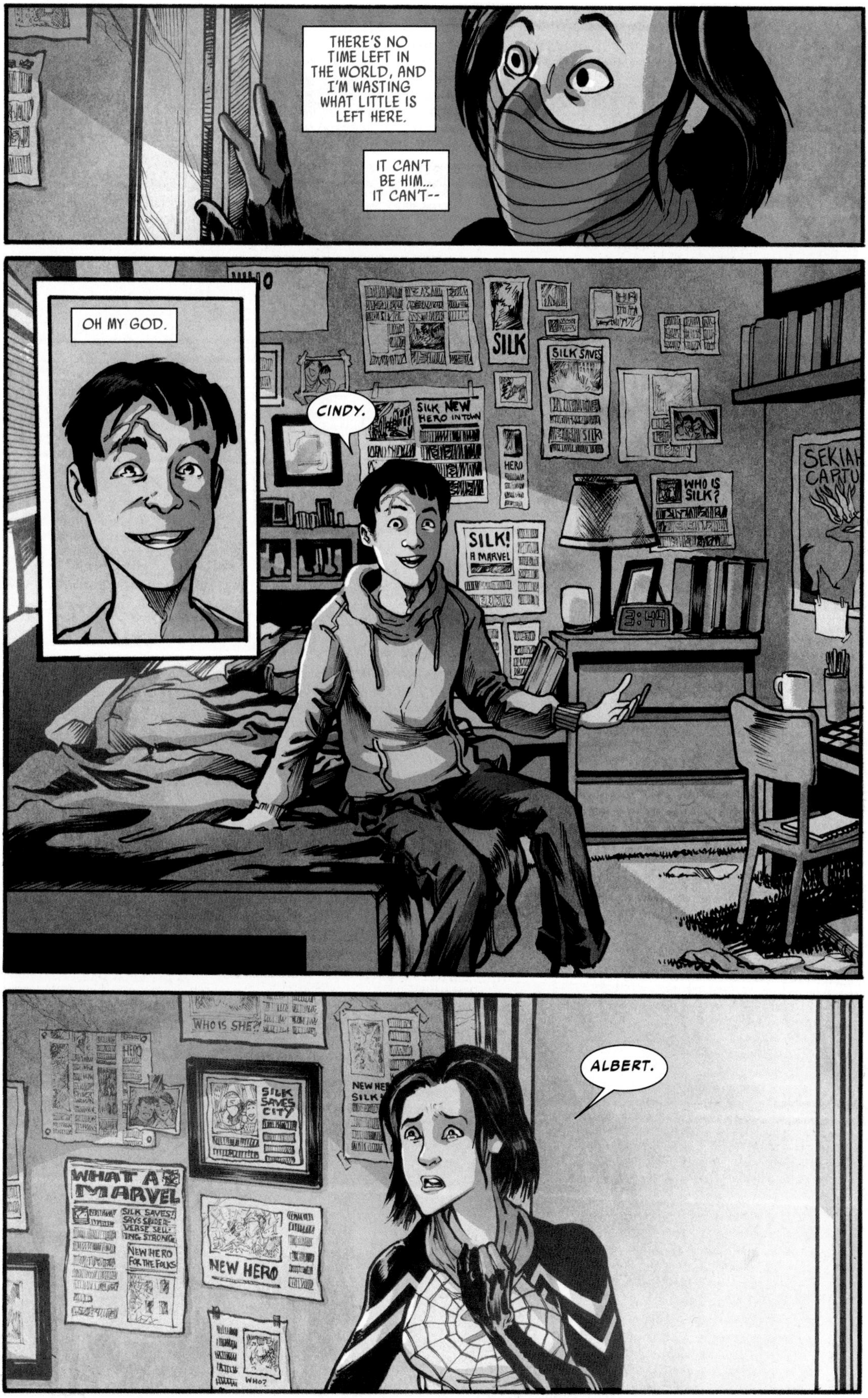
THERE'S NO TIME LEFT IN THE WORLD, AND I'M WASTING WHAT LITTLE IS LEFT HERE.
IT CAN'T BE HIM... IT CAN'T--
OH MY GOD.
CINDY.
ALBERT.

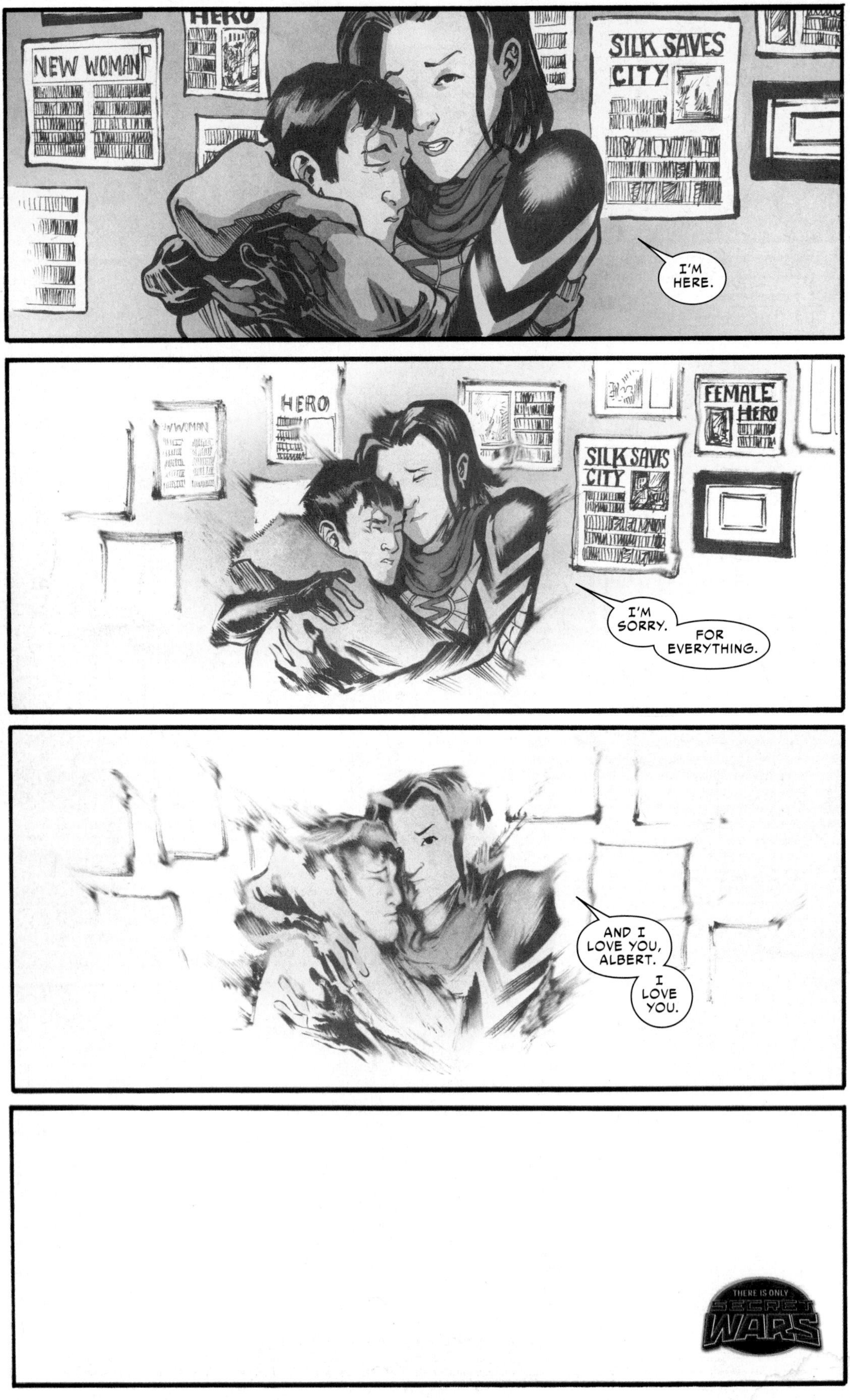
NEW WOMAN
HERO
SILK SAVES CITY
I'M HERE.
HERO
SILK SAVES CITY
FEMALE HERO
I'M SORRY.
FOR EVERYTHING.
AND I LOVE YOU, ALBERT.
I LOVE YOU.
THERE IS ONLY SECRET WARS

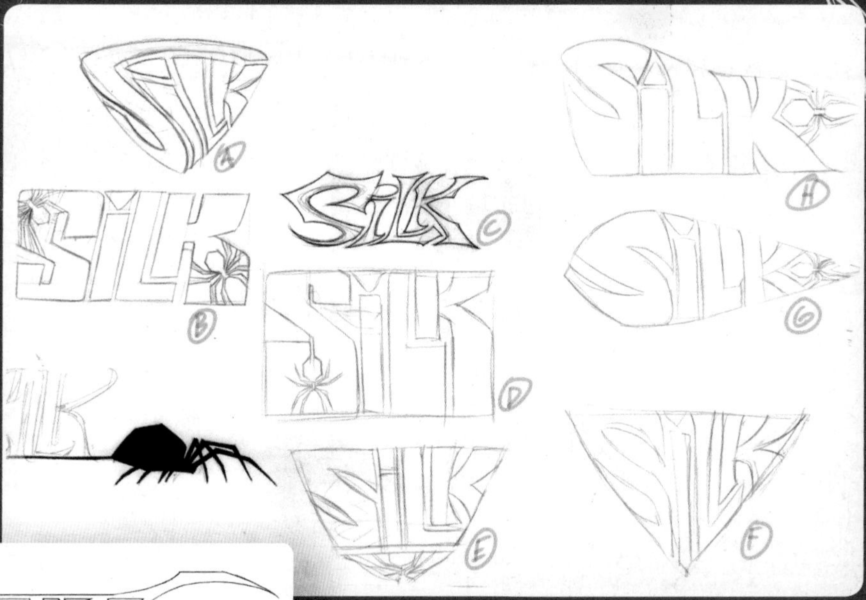

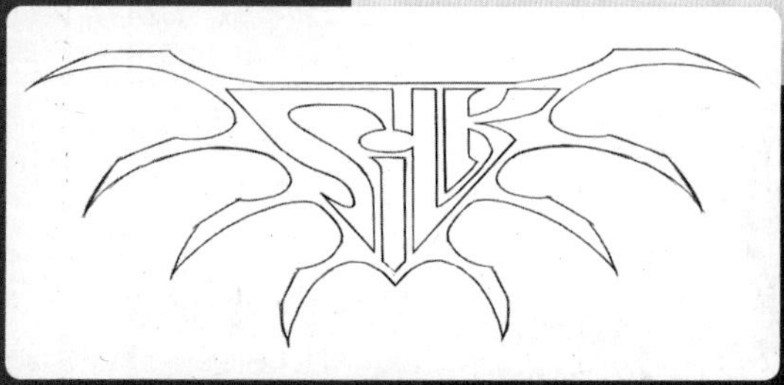

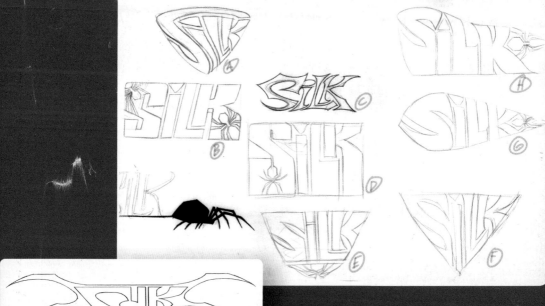

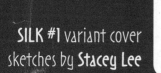

Original **SILK** logo sketches by **Dave Johnson**

SILK #1 variant cover sketches by **Stacey Lee**

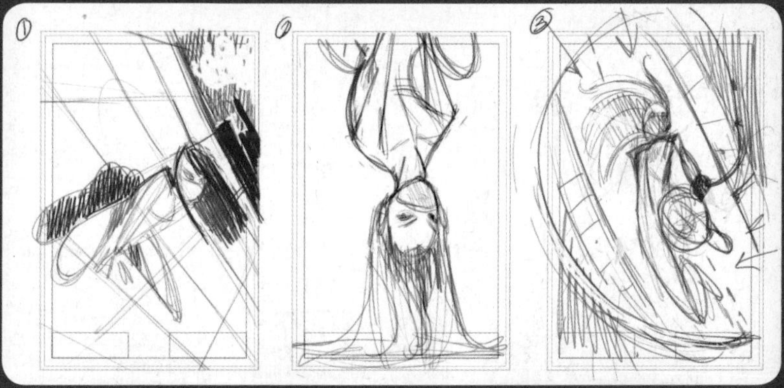

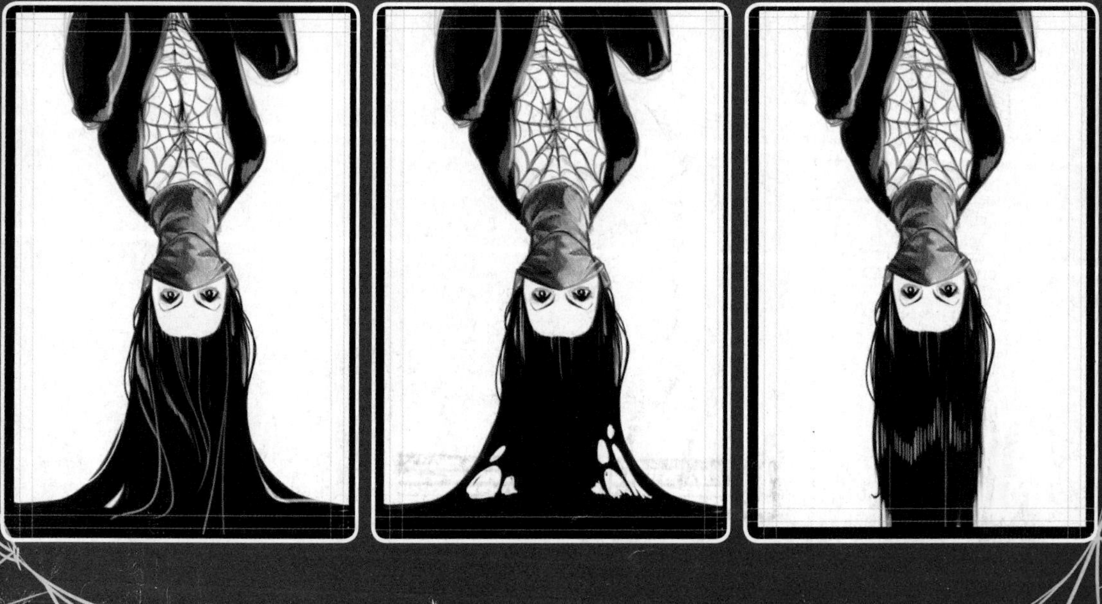

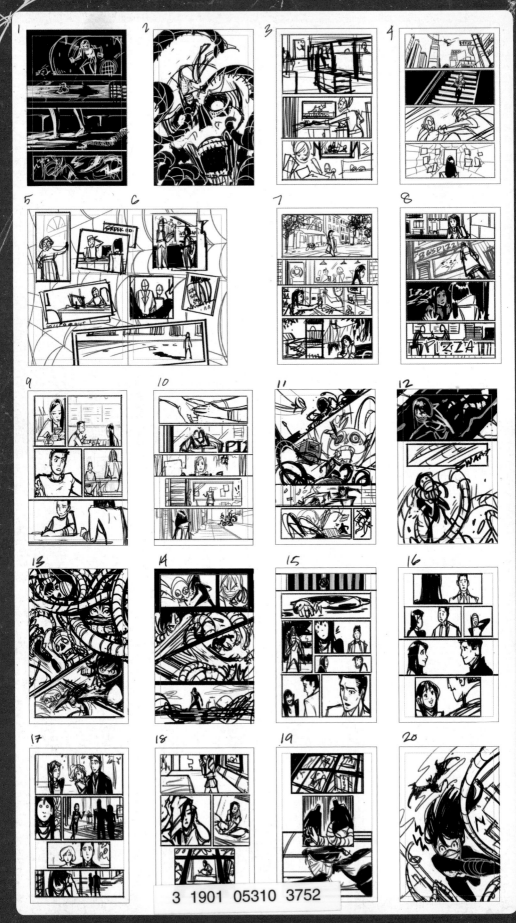

SILK #2 page layouts by Stacey Lee